Richard Andrews was born in 1953. He spent fifteen years in the Mediterranean and Middle East as a contract diver specialising in mine clearance and wreck salvage, and in 1975 assisted in the clearance of the Suez Canal Zone. His underwater training led to archaeological work in Israel, Italy and Sardinia. An expert on the Roman era, he lives in Oxfordshire with his daughter and divides his time between historical research and the restoration of firearms.

Paul Schellenberger was born in London in 1944, although his family originally come from Alsace in France. A Civil Engineer by profession, he has also worked as an architect and a furniture designer. His varied interests include art history and attempting to solve puzzles. He has a teenage son and a married daughter, and currently lives in Dorset.

THE TOMB OF GOD

*The Body of Jesus
and the Solution to a
2000-year-old Mystery*

RICHARD ANDREWS
&
PAUL SCHELLENBERGER

TIME WARNER
BOOKS

First published in Great Britain in 1996
by Little, Brown and Company
This edition published in 1997 by Warner Books
Reprinted 1999, 2000
Reprinted by Time Warner Paperbacks in 2002
Reprinted by Time Warner Books in 2005
Reprinted 2006

Copyright © 1996 by Pactolus

A CIP catalogue record for this book is
available from the British Library

ISBN-13: 978-0-7515-3839-7
ISBN-10: 0-7515-3839-6

Typeset in Bembo by M Rules
Printed and bound in Great Britain by
Clays Ltd, St Ives plc

Time Warner Books
An imprint of
Little, Brown Book Group
Brettenham House
Lancaster Place
London WC2E 7EN

A member of the Hachette Livre Group of Companies

www.littlebrown.co.uk

If a man will begin with certainties, he shall end in doubts,
but if he will be content to begin with doubts,
he shall end in certainties.

Francis Bacon (1561–1626),
The Advancement of Learning

CONTENTS

VIII

FOREWORD

I was curious. That was how it started.

Along with a very large audience in the 1970s, I had been fascinated by three television documentaries devoted to the 'mystery' of Rennes-le-Château in the south of France and the treasure alleged to be buried there. I was particularly intrigued by parchments that bore inscriptions which had never been understood. These reputedly eighteenth-century documents – so central to the story, yet so shrouded in hearsay – were tantalisingly cryptic. Could it really be that they had nothing meaningful to reveal?

Some years later, as other details emerged about the parchments, my love of puzzle-solving and geometry was activated. Realising that the parchments' geometric aspect had not been correctly pursued, and that there was therefore a remote possibility of finding a solution – if, indeed, one existed – I joined the game. A vague but discernible logic encouraged me to keep going. The sudden recognition of just what it was that the parchments represented was a mind-numbing revelation. The 'cipher' message, which for the twenty-five years since its first publication had defied analysis, was solved. A picture had begun to emerge.

It is hard to say whether it was my training as a civil engineer or my eclectic interests that had the greater bearing on the solving of the mystery. Probably it was the latter, but with a profession that relies on precision – not hunches – for the safety of uncounted masses of people, the instinct for *making sure* is deep-rooted. Along with this goes a philosophy of open-mindedness. I have long believed that it is as foolish to reject a phenomenon because it appears unlikely as it is to accept everything at face value.

But a little knowledge is a dangerous thing: it leads to a desire to know more, and many pathways opened up before me. There was no hope of tackling all the lines of investigation by myself within a reasonable time span. I needed a partner, one who would combine an interest in history and religion with the ability to suspend disbelief for long enough to absorb the details of my discovery. I found such a person in Richard Andrews.

Richard's life is redolent of a nineteenth-century soldier of fortune. A champion rifle shot, and a veteran of bomb and mine disposal in the Middle East, both above and below water, he was not about to be put off by any thought of risk. I knew that wherever possible in his travels he had pursued his true passion – Middle-Eastern history and archaeology. Richard's contribution was to be tremendous, pursuing the archive material that would flesh out the Secret, and playing an integral part in the process of unravelling. Had he known how much time he was going to have to spend in cemeteries, he would have been wise to have been called away on urgent business. Fortunately, he is not easily deterred.

Looking back, we undoubtedly passed more hours in graveyards than is probably healthy. We became fascinated by some distinctly premature deaths in the area of Rennes-le-Château. And it was death that led us back through time almost two thousand years. We became versed in the niceties of tombstone epitaphs and aesthetics – seeking the anomalous, the ambiguous, the departure from the norm. It would be true to say that this book is a post-mortem, not just of the dead but also of evidence long buried. As we dug, we found signs of some very strange burials indeed.

We started with the remnants of old 'excavations'. We found inaccuracies, things which simply did not add up, in the various published accounts of the goings-on in the area of Rennes-le-Château at the end of the last century. It soon became apparent that in order to produce a ripping yarn, our predecessors – fellow-authors – had leapt over obstacles, ignored information which disproved their argument, and galloped to the finishing-post brandishing 'evidence' of invisible temples, astral intervention, the guidance of exotic deities. In the interests of a fair trial, we have forced them into the dock along with the 'evidence'.

Marshalling the data was far from straightforward. There is a wealth of material, much of which has had a fairly unruly life of its own. We ploughed our way through 'documents' which existed only in the form of photographic copies or drawings of unknown provenance. At all times we questioned the validity of what we were looking at – did it ever exist? How much had it been meddled with? What was the intention of the originator? Thorny ground indeed.

As we accumulated evidence, there emerged a recurring system of symbolism that defied simple coincidence. It was not long before we realised that the trail was not false, that some of the dubious diagrams of others, when re-examined and corrected, actually had something very real to tell. Our subsequent researches took us into the heady world of fine art, but one piece of evidence – perhaps the most evocative of all – remained elusive.

In 1994 a famous oil painting was taken out of its frame in the restoration department of the Louvre and photographed. It was *Les Bergers d'Arcadie II*, painted by Nicolas Poussin between 1638 and 1640. We duly ordered a copy of the photograph in the expectation that it would have more to reveal than the framed version. The colours in the photograph were vivid and fresh, but the condition was not the revelation. Removal from the frame had uncovered a concealment. The original canvas extended beyond the confines of the framed image that had been presented to the world for three and a half centuries. Before transferring the copy to the drawing-board, we looked again at the subject of the picture – the familiar landscape, the shepherds with their staffs, and the centre of their combined attentions: an ancient tomb inscribed with a cryptic message. The key would finally turn.

At the start of our research we had no agenda, but embarked on the journey anyway. We did not know whether we would find anything, or what we would do if we did. In 1994 we realised that the body of evidence was substantial and compelling enough to warrant publication; 1995 saw the final pieces of the jigsaw fall into place. Our conclusions were startling, inherently dangerous, highly contentious, but ultimately the only logical deduction in the light of the evidence.

We had stumbled across perhaps the greatest secret ever, a secret which shed light on the Catholic Church's appalling over-reaction to criticism and rival dogmas over the centuries. That the Church had taken extreme measures to ensure the concealment of this, the ultimate heresy, is hardly surprising. Having based doctrine on an opposing belief, the Church could hardly admit that it had been wrong. What *was* surprising for us was the discovery of an alternative strand of Christianity, which had both co-existed covertly with mainstream Christianity and, more significantly, embraced the knowledge we now confronted and taken it to the heart of its teaching.

The more we investigated the traces of this 'unofficial' Christianity, the more we could visualise its potential for contemporary faith. For many people today mainstream Christianity, while promoting a valid code of conduct, requires a suspension of reason, a blind faith, that is unacceptable – causing them to drift away from the Church and reject formal worship. For others, the answer lies in fundamentalism and the solidity that unquestioning faith provides.

As the millennium approaches, and increasing numbers of people seek greater meaning in their lives, it seemed to us that the real answers may well have been there all along; answers which required neither the abandonment of reason nor the surrender of individual responsibility. The application of logic to dogma had revealed not the end of Western religion, but the beginning.

Paul Schellenberger
April 1996

THE TOMB
OF GOD

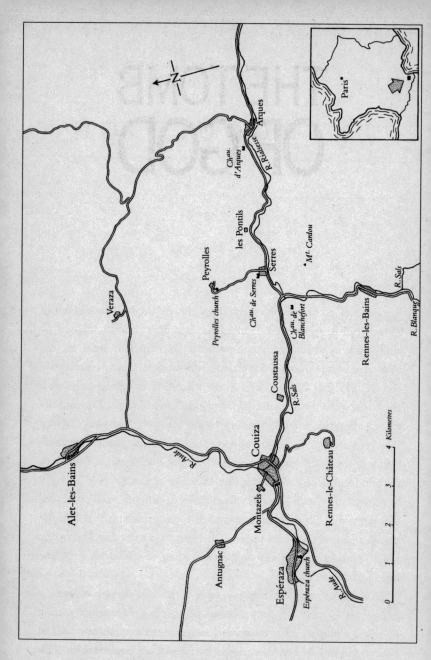

The principal locations in the mystery of Rennes-le-Château.

INTRODUCTION

Rennes-le-Château occupies an isolated site, perched on the summit of a steep hill in south-west France, sun-baked in summer, blasted by chill winds in winter. Although occupied since ancient times, its sole advantage is its position of dominance over the surrounding countryside (Figure 0.1). The Château de Rennes still exists, its fading grandeur a testament to the former strategic advantage of the village. The magnificent panoramic view extending to the snow-tipped peaks of the Pyrenees, a view much admired today, will have been small compensation for the rigours of dwelling in such an inaccessible place. Even with the modern road, dating from the turn of the century and recently improved, the winding journey from valley to summit is tedious. From a distance the village looks as though it is cut off from the rest of the world, a place which time forgot – an impression soon dispelled by the coach-loads of tourists weaving their way up the hill with only one object in mind.

Today, Rennes-le-Château is seen as a place of deepest mystery, a place which guards a secret yet to be uncovered, a place which during its many centuries of occupation has produced a confusing trail of bizarre and sinister events, enriched by tales of fabulous treasure. This legend of treasure has given birth to a tourist industry of a unique kind – an industry of speculation. Reports of 'new discoveries' are rife, and the books published in support of the various claims now number in their hundreds.

FIGURE 0.1 The village of Rennes-le-Château – a telephoto view from the Château de Blanchefort.

The history of Rennes and its environs can be traced back to the Stone Ages, but it was the Romans who established the first settlement of importance, and discovered the area's natural wealth in the form of precious metals.[1] The dark and gloomy entrances to their gold and silver mines can still be seen on the mountainsides. Roman coins and jewellery continue to be found today, but one major treasure has yet to be discovered: one of Roman provenance that might just have found its way this far west. The Temple of Jerusalem was looted and destroyed by the troops of Titus in AD 70. That the booty was taken to Rome may not be doubted, for the bas-reliefs illustrating Titus's triumph clearly depict the menorah – seven-branched candelabrum – and other items that could have come from nowhere else. There the stolen treasures remained for over three hundred years, until the Empire began to crumble.

In 410 the Visigoths, led by Alaric, sacked the city of Rome itself. However, their nomadic instincts were too strong for them to succumb to the pleasures of city life and they soon departed for pastures new, allegedly taking with them the treasure of the Temple. Two years later they arrived on the shores of southern Gaul. Their leader had died before they left Italy, and tradition has it that the treasure was buried with him in the bed of a river – temporarily diverted – to be lost for ever.[2] That his successor and followers, pillaging barbarians that they were, should abandon such wealth out of respect for their chief is so improbable that it has long been regarded with suspicion. The area of Rennes-le-Château appealed to the Visigoths and they settled there, establishing a permanent kingdom which spread over the Pyrenees into northern Spain.

If the Visigoths brought the treasure with them it has never since resurfaced, and its concealment somewhere in or around Rennes-le-Château cannot be discounted.[3] The Jewish historian Josephus, writing in the first century AD having witnessed the destruction of the Temple of Jerusalem, has left us this description:[4]

the other spoils . . . were carried in great plenty. But those that were taken in the Temple of Jerusalem, made the greatest figure of them all. That is the golden table of the weight of many talents. The candlestick . . . that was made of gold . . . And the last of all the spoils was carried the law of the Jews.

The 'law of the Jews' refers to the Pentateuch – the first five books of the Old Testament, attributed to Moses. The original stones on which the Ten Commandments had been inscribed had been housed in a purpose-made box of astonishing properties. This was the Ark of the Covenant, the design of which is given in precise detail in the book of

Exodus, and which would therefore be instantly recognisable. The fate of the Ark remains one of the great mysteries of the ancient world. It had disappeared from the recorded history of the Jews several centuries before the destruction of Jerusalem in AD 70, so in spite of the reference to the 'law' being among the spoils of Titus, one must presume – though one cannot be sure – that they did not include the Ark. There have been those who considered the Ark to be associated with Arques, not far from Rennes. As we show, there are other reasons to consider whether the Ark of the Covenant has a bearing on the mystery of Rennes-le-Château.

Two centuries of relative stability followed the arrival of the Visigoths at Rennes, until, in the sixth century, the Merovingians arrived from the north, imposing their dominance over the Visigoth kingdom. The Merovingians were invaders of high culture, and they buried their dead with gem-studded jewellery of extraordinary beauty. One of their kings, Dagobert II, is said to have married a Visigoth princess, Gizelle de Razès, at Rennes-le-Château, and much has been made of this claim despite the lack of supporting evidence. Needless to say, the legendary wealth of the Merovingians (actually, well supported by archaeology) gave rise to folkloric accounts of a fabulous treasure awaiting discovery in the region of Rennes.

Considering the ability of this locale to attract treasures, it should come as no surprise to learn that the ultimate prize of Christendom is also reputed to have gone to earth here. Unlikely as it might appear, the Holy Grail may well have arrived in much the way as related in the legend. It is reputed that some time in the first century AD Joseph of Arimathea, accompanied by Mary Magdalene, arrived here, bringing with him the cup called the Grail, said to have caught the blood of the crucified Christ. Southern Gaul had been used by the emperors of Rome as a convenient place of exile for illustrious undesirables or allies fallen from grace; both Herod Antipas and Pontius Pilate were banished to the region. It remains historically feasible that Mary and Joseph, two dedicated followers of Jesus, could have gone to Gaul in a self-imposed diaspora.[5] By the first century AD, merchant shipping routes were well established across the length and breadth of the Mediterranean, providing an easy means of passage for those not wishing to travel overland. Many Jewish families had settled in the region of Rennes-le-Château by this time, and according to one theory – to add to the stock of myths surrounding the area – Mary Magdalene was pregnant with Jesus' child when she arrived. A Messianic dynasty was thus established; in this picture the Holy Grail is identified with the bloodline of Christ.[6]

The identity of the Grail, however, remains as elusive as the origin of its legend. The earliest version of the story has the Grail as a magical stone; in later versions it has become the cup, or chalice. If these representations had been intentionally vicarious, the Grail could be almost anything. Knightly aspects of the legend were later incorporated in romantic medieval accounts of the court of King Arthur, but there was a connection with a factual knightly order: the Poor Knights of Christ and the Temple of Solomon, commonly known as the Knights Templar.

The Templars were a monastic, military order, sworn to chastity, poverty and obedience, who rose to prominence after the fall of Jerusalem to the First Crusade. Their headquarters was near the destroyed Temple of Solomon, a site they had been allocated by Baldwin II, ruler of the new Latin kingdom of Jerusalem, around the time of their formation in c. 1120.[7] There is some evidence that the original group of nine knights had formed an association some time before, and that only later was the title of the order adopted, and their existence revealed. For the first twenty years the membership scarcely expanded, and on more than one occasion the order came close to collapse. But in the 1130s, with the support of St Bernard and money coming in from all over the Christian world, their meteoric rise began. They were to become a major political and financial force, their vows of personal poverty not embracing the order as a whole. That their power extended even over kings was to be a principal factor in their sudden and appalling downfall, culminating in the dissolution of the order and the dispersal of their wealth and possessions. But the heyday of their existence, and the influences they experienced in the Near East, were to lend them a persistent aura of mystery. The Templars had conducted excavations under the Temple Mount, and their motives for tunnelling under such a sacred site are still a matter of conjecture. One theory is that they discovered a treasure which they brought back to France, concealing it in the area of Rennes-le-Château, and that this treasure was the one true, and most holy, Grail.

At first we were aware of this minefield of historical fact and romantic legend, but in no way fully conversant with the details. A desire to delve deeper was virtually forced upon us by the chance discovery of a remarkable meaning in some ancient parchments. Hitherto disregarded, misunderstood, or their authenticity disputed, they had – along with a host of associated paraphernalia – engendered much wishful thinking, but also wilful exploitation and even sheer lunacy.

Following this discovery, further research was carried out at various institutions of Oxford University: the Bodleian Library, the Taylor Institute, the Western Art Library of the Ashmolean Museum, and the libraries of the Schools of Geography and Science. The parchments had allegedly been uncovered by a Catholic priest in the church of Rennes-le-Château over one hundred years ago. The name of this priest was François Bérenger Saunière (Figure 0.2), and around his life-story the legend of Rennes as a place of mystery and hidden treasure was to reach new and dizzying heights. But we found other indications of preserved secrets – secrets which predated Saunière's discovery by well over two hundred years. We were greatly intrigued by the presence of the so-called 'Poussin Tomb' close to Rennes-le-Château. This tomb, it has been suggested, was the one depicted in 1647 by the famous French painter Nicolas Poussin in his most mysterious of works, *Les Bergers d'Arcadie II*, which shows a group of shepherds, observed by an enigmatic woman, gathered around a tomb, the side of which bears the inscription '*Et in Arcadia ego*'. This painting, the priest and the parchments were to combine in a way which we could not have foreseen.

FIGURE 0.2 Abbé Bérenger Saunière (1852–1917).

There comes a stage in all research when books can be of no more assistance, so, leaving libraries behind, we prepared to visit France to try to place our discoveries within the context of geographical reality. We arrived at Rennes-le-Château unprepared for the majesty and scale of the scenery. The photographs we had pored over in England did scant justice to the scene before us. The mountain-slopes which form the backdrop to this ancient hilltop village are wild and inhospitable, a succession of progressively higher and paler outlines stretching to the snow-capped Pyrenees in the distance. The area possesses a unique atmosphere, and it was easy to see why it fired the imagination of so many would-be detectives throughout the twentieth century.

The place we had come to in search of answers had been the source of a very different sort of problem to French authorities in the past, earning it a reputation as the country's Achilles' heel. Helped by its isolation, the region had become a hotbed of religious heresy, causing ongoing problems for the government in Paris. Bérenger Saunière was to continue this tradition of radicalism by voicing his anti-Republican views in the first sermon he gave at Rennes-le-Château. But it was ultimately his interest in uncovering the parish's past that would dispel the region's modern air of tranquillity and point to its most significant and astonishing place in history.

Born on 11 April 1852 in the neighbouring village of Montazels, which overlooks the valley of the Aude, Saunière was ordained into the priesthood of the Roman Catholic Church in 1879. In 1885, aged thirty-three, he became the incumbent of the parish of Rennes-le-Château. He was poor, supplementing his diet with fish and game taken during his long walks in the surrounding countryside. His personal account-books, which have survived to this day, attest to a meagre lifestyle and near-starvation diet. The parish church of St Mary Magdalene (the site of Dagobert II's reputed marriage to Gizelle de Razès), though restored by the ruling Voisins family in the fifteenth century, had fallen into a state of advanced disrepair by the end of the nineteenth century. But all that was to change when the new priest, with limited funds at his disposal, commenced a restoration of the altar. Various documents concealed in wooden tubes were discovered when the altar-stone was removed from its ancient supporting columns. And there were witnesses: Saunière was assisted in his restoration work by six individuals, two of whom were still alive in 1958 to confirm the discovery.[8]

Accounts vary as to the exact circumstances; but, whatever the events on that day, from that moment in time Saunière's fortunes changed. His discovery of four allegedly ancient documents set in train events the consequences of which would reach far beyond the spiritual welfare of his new flock. The new priest acquired great wealth and a luxurious existence, the material benefits of which came to be shared with companions and confederates during the course of his ministry. But, as ever in such rags-to-riches tales, events were to take a more sinister turn.

By the day of his own death in 1917, the broken bones of a friend and fellow-priest, Antoine Gélis, would lie in cold ground across the valley from Rennes-le-Château. Saunière's confidant, Henri Boudet, Abbé of the neighbouring town of Rennes-les-Bains, would lie – in accordance with his wishes – not with his mother and sister at Rennes-les-Bains, his home for over forty years, but with his brother's remains at Axat, some fifteen kilometres to the south. Dying from intestinal cancer (the official diagnosis), he made a painful journey to Rennes-le-Château to visit Saunière. It was by way of a reconciliation, for they had not spoken for six or seven years. But what did he have to impart that could not go by post? A few days later he died, with, it is said, Saunière at his side. The year was 1915. The three priests would take their secret to the grave, but two, Saunière and Boudet, would leave clues for posterity.

If the life of Saunière, his impact on the quiet village of Rennes-le-Château and his unexplained inheritance of fabulous wealth reinforced tales of treasure, to the residents of the area the answer appeared simple and required little decoding. The new priest had stumbled upon a source of material wealth hidden by their ancestors. However, throughout his life Saunière maintained a silence over the source of his funding, and persistently refused to reveal his 'secret'. This fuelled endless speculation which increased on his sudden death. His housekeeper, Marie Denarnaud (Figure 0.3), in whom he had apparently confided all, protected this confidentiality, talking in only the most general terms of the continuing existence of unlimited wealth in the area. Her refusal to discuss the matter any further added to a deepening mystery. What could this elusive treasure possibly be, and was it the source of Saunière's fantastic wealth?

Proximity to the Secret was dangerous: the list of those murdered or meeting a sudden or 'accidental' death is out of proportion to the

FIGURE 0.3 Marie Denarnaud (1868–1953), Saunière's housekeeper.

natural law of averages. As late as 1956, the bodies of three men were discovered by workmen digging within a stone's throw of Saunière's garden. Aged between twenty-five and thirty-five, they lay bundled together, buried in a shallow grave. One skull still retained the hair, part of the flesh and the moustache of its owner. The police who conducted the full exhumation came to no conclusion as to the year of death. All they would confirm was that remains of military clothing were found with the bodies, fragments which could as easily indicate the First World War as the Second. So the three men may have known Saunière, or they may not have. Either way, their proximity to his house added more strands to the web of mystery.[9]

We arrived at Rennes-le-Château to see for ourselves the sights that inspire so many speculations, and to ascertain whether certain reputed details had *any* basis in fact.

1
THE
PARCHMENTS

The 'official' version of Abbé Saunière's discovery of the parchments in 1887 (some accounts say 1886) is to be found at the Saunière museum at Rennes-le-Château, written up and displayed on the walls for all to see. Saunière's turbulent life-story is recounted through the use of large cartoons which, while a slightly eccentric medium of communication, are actually remarkably effective. The confusion surrounding the discovery of the parchments is compounded by this visual material, as two versions are shown of the auspicious event. Also on display are two columns.

Our attention was drawn first to the stone altar column. Set into the top of the pillar is a small mortice, compatible with the use of a lead or iron jointing-pin or tenon. This recess, no more than two and a half centimetres square, excludes any possibility of the parchments having been concealed in a cavity accessed from the top, leaving us somewhat surprised. Was the cavity opening in the base, or were we viewing a solid column? In either case, the riddle was impossible to solve for the moment – the column was large and did not invite upending.

This altar column had been reused by Saunière in 1891, the year of the diocesan celebration to commemorate Our Lady of Lourdes. He employed it as a support for the new commemorative statue erected in the church garden, inverting it for reasons known only to himself, and completing the construction with the carving of the statement 'mission 1891' on a plinth. So the column on display had passed from church to garden, and then to the museum.

The other column in the museum was of solid oak; more correctly called a baluster, it *did* contain a secret cavity. The corresponding cartoon shows Saunière accidentally knocking the wooden support to the ground. The dislodgement of a secret sliding panel in the top of the baluster exposed a cavity from which fell a glass phial. However, it is clear that the cavity is too small to have accommodated four large parchments. Perhaps the phial contained a small parchment which indicated the location of the main documents?

This dispute over the exact details of discovery was but a side-issue to us. The fact remained that the parchments had probably entered the hands of Saunière, and at a date prior to 1891. The whereabouts of the parchments during the immediate years after their discovery are uncertain. The story goes that the mayor of Rennes-le-Château demanded custody from Saunière, but the priest insisted they required translating from the Latin by experts, and promptly assumed the task of co-ordinating the operation. Faced with such an impasse, the mayor accepted Saunière's promise to provide him with copies, and there the affair rested for some years.

But what exactly was the nature of the parchments? This is a question not easily answered, for they may not be seen. They are not to be found in any museum or library accessible to the public; indeed, their current location is completely unknown. Some doubt that the parchments ever existed; others declare categorically that they never did; still others declare them to be (or to have been) fakes. Such positive declarations tell us more about the commentators than they do about the parchments, for it soon became apparent to us that vested interest has played a role. Exactly what that interest is, though, proves more difficult to resolve than the provenance of the parchments. However, it is clear from all the available literature on the subject that those who support the story essentially agree on what Saunière found and how he found it, but this concurrence carries far less weight than the evidence that slowly built up as our research progressed. The story may be pieced together as follows.

Abbé Saunière found four parchments sealed in wooden tubes. Two of these were genealogies (it matters not, but they are said to relate to the Merovingian dynasty), a third was the testament of one Henri d'Hautpoul of 1695. Two others had been 'composed' in the 1780s by Abbé Antoine Bigou. (That makes *five* parchments; this discrepancy over four or five would later prove to be of the utmost significance.)

Bigou had been the resident priest at Rennes-le-Château, and chaplain to the aristocratic Hautpoul-Blanchefort family, whose seat was the château at Rennes. When the Revolution's hostility to priests became evident, he went into exile in Spain, never to return. It is feasible that this was the occasion of the concealment of the parchments in the altar, or whatever secret place Bigou had devised; later to be discovered by Saunière.

At some time in the 1960s (1967 has been cited) the Prieuré de Sion (Priory of Sion) – an organisation to which we shall again refer – 'leaked' two of the parchments discovered by Saunière. We shall call these Parchments 1 and 2 ('Parchments', with a capital 'P', distinguishing these two from the other parchments found with them), and will take a close look at them shortly. Although illustrations of them have been published in books, no author has claimed to have held the original Parchments. An elaborate account (possibly true) of their ultimate fate has them now residing in the archives of the Knights of Malta.

A new perspective

The mystery of Saunière and the 'treasure' of Rennes-le-Château would have remained no more than a good story, to be believed or dismissed according to the scepticism of the individual, but for a decision that was made in the early 1960s. This was to result in the publication of a book and the depositing of various documents in the Bibliothèque Nationale in Paris.

French law requires that any written works intended for publication must be deposited at the national library, and thereby registered and made accessible to the general public. It does not matter that the document is badly typed on a few sheets of paper, or thrust into the reluctant hands of passers-by on the Rive Gauche – it must be deposited. In addition to legal control and the right of access, there are secondary effects of this law. Simply to be deposited endows a work with an air of authority, but more importantly its preservation is assured. Publication and the printing of thousands of copies need not occur for the document to survive.

And so it was that the Rennes story acquired a new perspective. Hitherto, the new wealth of the priest had been ascribed to the discovery of a tangible treasure, various origins for which had been proposed. The route to this treasure had been revealed by the discovery of some manuscripts. It was firmly believed by the inhabitants of the village that 'Monsieur le curé a trouvé un trésor!' But with the publication of *L'Or de Rennes* by Gérard de Sède in 1967, published in paperback as *Le Trésor maudit*, the treasure was revealed to be not merely monetary but 'spiritual', and the manuscripts themselves to be intrinsically valuable. Saunière had also been led to the decipherment of a strangely inept inscription in the graveyard of the church of St Mary Magdalene at Rennes, on the grave of Marie de Nègre d'Ablès, lady of Blanchefort, who died on 17 January 1781. The priest then ensured that no other person would be able to follow the trail: he destroyed the inscription on this too public and too revealing monument.

This version, the de Sède version, of the Saunière story is, no less than previous versions, open to accusations of fabrication. After all, so much of the 'evidence' has been lost or destroyed, or simply never came into the public domain. But for the moment we have chosen to ignore the question of authenticity and the motivation of interested parties, and concentrate only on the information provided by de Sède. Never before had any illustrations of the Parchments or the engraved stones been brought to the attention of the public. De Sède associated the two Parchments with a stone, or *dalle*, from the Rennes area, and so we shall compare the three pieces of evidence to ascertain whether or not a relationship exists. Significant details emerge in the course of our investigation; once the lock has been forced, the door will swing open at the lightest touch.

Parchment 1

The text of Parchment 1 (Figure 1.1) is a Latin version of the New Testament story of Jesus and his disciples walking in cornfields on the Sabbath. They had picked and eaten some ears of corn and are questioning whether or not in doing so they had transgressed, for the Sabbath was to be kept holy and no work was to be done. Some

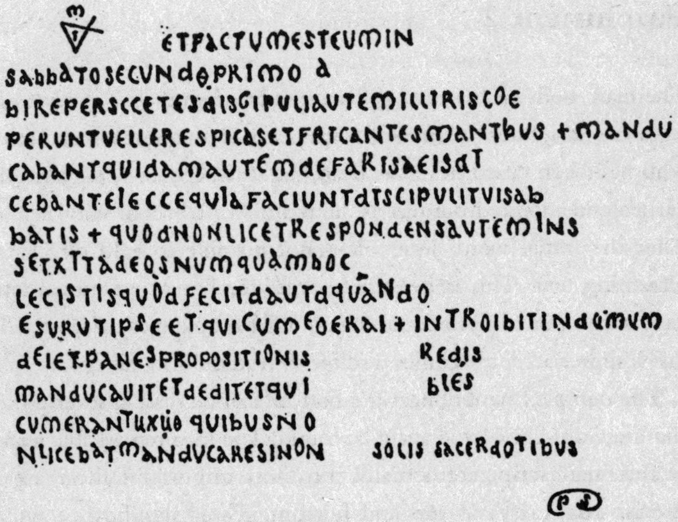
ETFACTUMESTEUMIN
SABBATOSECUNDOPRIMO A
BIREPERSCCETESDISCIPULIAUTEMILLIRISCOE
PERUNTUELLERESPICASETFRICANTESMANIBUS + MANDU
CABANTQUIDAMAUTEMDEFARISAEISAT
CEBANTELECCEQUIAFACIUNTDISCIPULITUISAB
BATIS + QUODNONLICETRESPONDENSAUTEMINS
SETXTTADEOSNUMQUAMHOC
LECISTISQUODFECITDAUIDQUANDO
ESURUTIPSEETQUICUMEOERAT + INTROIBITINDOMUM
DEIETPANESPROPOSITIONIS REDIS
MANDUCAUITETDEDITETQUI BLES
CUMERANTUXUO QUIBUSNO
NLICEBATMANDUCARESINON SOLIS SACERDOTIBUS

FIGURE 1.1 Parchment 1, from a photograph.

Pharisees who were present argue that the act was a transgression. But Jesus argues that it was not, and refers to the occasion when David and his companions were hungry and ate the shewbread in the House of God, which was lawful only for the priests – *solis sacerdotibus*.

The peculiarities of Parchment 1 are immediately apparent. Apart from the odd symbols at the beginning and end, the lines are of varying length and words are split over two lines. In particular, in the last line *solis sacerdotibus* is preceded by a large space and stands on its own. We are intended to read this in isolation, as 'Only for the priesthood' or, more probably, 'Only for the initiated'. One further detail should be noted. The letters falling at the ends of the last four lines (excluding the disconnected words) form the word

S
I
O
N

Parchment 2

The main body of the text of Parchment 2 (Figure 1.2) is once again from the Scriptures. It tells of the supper in Bethany at which Lazarus, who had been raised from the dead, sat at table with Jesus, and Mary Magdalene anointed the feet of Jesus and wiped them with her hair. After the initial word 'Jesus', it is not possible to read directly the remaining text. This is because a large number of additional letters have been inserted, for reasons which will become evident later. When this is appreciated it becomes possible to read the text, albeit falteringly.

The complex symbol near the bottom can be read in reverse order, and the word SION will again be found. The least remarkable features of this manuscript are actually the most important: these are the asterisk-like marks at top and bottom. Their significance will be returned to later.

JESVSEVRGOaNTCESEXATPESPaSCShaEVENJTThETh9aNIaMVKaT
FVEKaOTIaZa=VVSMOKTYVVS9VEMMSVSCTYTaVITIYESVSFEaCEKVNT
laVIEM=TTCaENaPMThTETOMaRThahMINISTRKabaTlhaSaRVSO
VCROVNXVSEKaTTE=dISCOVMlENTaTlVSCVJMMaRTaLERGOaChCEP
TILKThKaMYNNGENTTJNaKaTPFTJTICT9PRETTOVSTETVNEXTTPE
dPESTERVaETEXTEJKSTTCaYPIIRTSNSVISPEPdESEKTPTETdOMbESTM
PLFTIaESTEEXVNGETNTTOdaEKEdIXaLTEKGOVRNVMEXdGTSCTPVhL
TSETVTXTVddXSCaRJORTIS9VIYEKaTCVhMTKadTTTVRVS9TVaREhO(CVN
hEN VIVMNONXVENVTTGKECENPaTSdENaaKVSETddaTVMESGTE
GENTES? dTXTNVFEMhOECNON9VSTadEEGaENTSPERRTINEbEaT
adCVTMSEd9VhaFVKELKTETlOVCVIOShCahENSECa9VaEMVTTIEba
NMTVKPOTKabETEdTXTTEJKGOTEShVSSINEPTLLaMVNTTXdIEKMS
EPVlGTVKaEMSEaESEKVNETILL9VdPaVPJEKESENhTMSEMPGEKha
hEMTTSNObLTISCVMFMEaVTETMNONSESMPERhaVbEISCJOGNO
VILIEKOTZVKbaMV9LTaEXTMVdaCTST9VTaTlOLTCESTXETVENE
aKVNTNONNPROTEPRTESV=ETaNTvMMSEdVTLVZaKVMPUTdEK
Eh=T9VEMKSVSCTaOVTTaMORRTVTSCPOGTTaVKEKVNTahVTEMP
KVTNCTPEJSSaCEKCaOTVMVMTETLaZaKaRVMTNaT(RFTCTKENTY
LVTaMVLVTTPROPYTEKTLhXVMahThGNTCXVGTaZETSNETCKCa
dEbaNTINTESVM

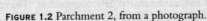

JÉSV. MEdÈLa. VVLNÉKVM + SPES.VNa. PŒNITENTIVM.
PER.MaGdaLaNÆ. LaCHYMaS + PECCaTa.NOSTKa. dILVaS.

FIGURE 1.2 Parchment 2, from a photograph.

The Dalle de Coume Sourde

This slab (*dalle*) of stone survives only in the drawing of its inscription (Figure 1.3), though it is possible to assume that it originates from the location not far from Rennes-le-Château called Coume Sourde. There is good reason to doubt it ever existed, but for now we ignore this

possibility and see what we can learn from the drawing. The illustration
shown here is taken from the version first provided by de Sède. Other
commentators have reproduced this drawing, and at first sight their versions appear to be the same. However, they differ in small details,
implying that the draughtsman did not know the significance of what
he was copying. Another view is that the differences result from deliberate changes made in order to render the diagram useless. This
'conspiracy theory' may appear to gain credibility as the investigation
unfolds.

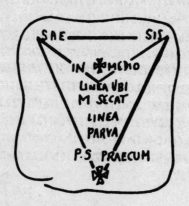

FIGURE 1.3 Inscription on the Dalle de Coume Sourde, from a drawing.

The design is not complex: one triangle within another, and some
words, clearly Latin and clearly ungrammatical. There are also what
appear to be abbreviations of other Latin words. Some commentators
have declared the Latin to be so ambiguous as to be unintelligible,
because the nouns have not been declined (that is, their endings have
not been adjusted to indicate their roles). So we do not know who does
what and to whom. We shall have cause to reconsider this; for the
moment, it is enough to say that there is a significant difference
between unintentionally bad Latin and intentionally bad Latin.

Hidden messages

It is now time to look at another player in this drama: Henry Lincoln. In the 1960s, Lincoln was a writer for television. According to a book of his on the subject, *The Holy Place*, he became embroiled in the mystery of Rennes-le-Château by virtue of his occupation and by the chance purchase of Gérard de Sède's *Le Trésor maudit* while he was on holiday in France. The year was 1969.

He relates how, having finished reading the book, it happened to fall open at the page on which Parchment 1 is reproduced, and that individual letters from the text began to assume a kind of pattern. These are the letters that stand slightly above the lines, and which at first sight would seem to have been displaced as the result of careless drafting. What Lincoln discovered was that these letters spell out a message in French: *A Dagobert II roi et a Sion est ce tresor et il est la mort*. The letters may be picked out thus:

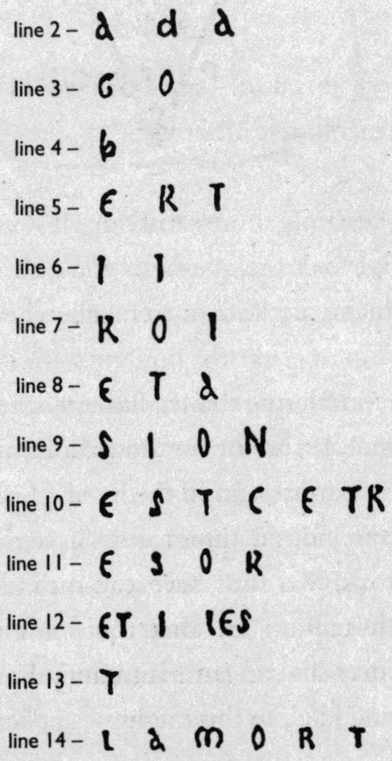

line 2 – **a d a**

line 3 – **G O**

line 4 – **b**

line 5 – **E R T**

line 6 – **I I**

line 7 – **R O I**

line 8 – **E T a**

line 9 – **S I O N**

line 10 – **E S T C E TR**

line 11 – **E S O R**

line 12 – **ET I IES**

line 13 – **T**

line 14 – **L a M O R T**

Interpreting the meaning of the phrase from Parchment 1 is not quite as simple as it might first appear, because there are no accents present. This provides scope for alternative interpretations. For example:

> THIS TREASURE BELONGS TO DAGOBERT II KING AND TO SION
> AND HE IS THERE DEAD

With accents, this reads:

> À DAGOBERT II ROI ET À SION EST CE TRÉSOR
> ET IL EST LÀ MORT

The alternatives of *là* ('there') and *la*, the definite article for the noun *mort*, have to be considered. The latter would give:

> THIS TREASURE BELONGS TO DAGOBERT II KING AND TO SION
> AND IT IS DEATH

But one may reject 'it is death' since this would be more correct as *c'est la mort*. Henry Lincoln felt otherwise:[1]

> 'It is death' is certainly more satisfying. It is vague enough to lead nowhere and it avoids the question: *who is the 'he' that is there dead?* Dagobert's remains are known to be elsewhere. (our italics)

However, when considering the Parchments one has to be on guard for *double entendres* and obscure or outmoded meanings, in the first case as these are often intentional, and in the second because language changes with time. Some previous commentators have not appreciated this. It is also necessary to consider the alternative meanings of *à* ('to' and 'at').

If a nineteenth-century dictionary is consulted one discovers that *mort* (adjective) may also mean 'dormant'. For example, *argent mort* meant 'money lying idle', so this might be applicable to hidden treasure.

Mort also means 'lifeless', 'insensible', 'still' or 'inanimate'. Therefore, without attempting to arrange the words into any idiom other than that of the original French, the various possibilities include:

> TO DAGOBERT II KING AND TO SION IS THIS TREASURE
> AND HE IS THERE DEAD

> TO DAGOBERT II KING AND AT SION IS THIS TREASURE
> AND IT IS THERE DORMANT

> TO DAGOBERT II KING AND TO SION IS THIS TREASURE
> AND HE IS THERE LIFELESS

> TO DAGOBERT II KING AND AT SION IS THIS TREASURE
> AND HE IS THERE DORMANT

There are obviously other combinations of meanings, but as our investigation proceeds, a particular concept will become pre-eminent. There are also hidden letters to be found in Parchment 2, but these make no contribution to the solution and so are discussed in Appendix A.

Hidden geometry

In addition to the concealed message in Parchment 1, Lincoln subsequently noticed that certain features suggest a geometric interpretation. Why should this be a possibility? To see why, we must first take a brief look at this particular branch of mathematics and its application.

From very early times, geometry held a fascination which is hard to appreciate today, as enthusiasm for the subject has cooled somewhat over the last two centuries. A deep-seated need to understand a world whose arrangement and events are mainly chaotic – unpredictable – has driven humankind in a quest (first with superstitions as a guide, later with science) to identify any point of stability from which to view the world. If we wish to locate ourselves in our environment, we first need a means of delineating the space we occupy. A system of basic assumptions and rules that are found to be universal and extendable may then be imposed on the imponderable three-dimensional space around us – it provides a secure foothold from which we can reach out towards dizzier heights. But such a system may become abstract – divorced from the physical world which it was originally set up to describe. Geometry developed into a complex and sophisticated toolbox, useful in building and surveying, for example, but it also took on an independent life as a subject of mathematical enquiry. In its heyday, geometry occupied a lofty place at the cutting-edge of man's intellectual pursuits.

The origins of geometry in the West may be traced back through the ancient Greeks, and names like Euclid and Pythagoras, to Egypt and the other ancient civilisations of the Middle East. Even prehistoric cultures display a non-technical appreciation of geometry in their depictions of natural forms and decorative patterns. Once geometry had acquired an intellectual status, it was natural that its application should extend to embrace other exclusive activities, such as architecture and fine art, but also to the conveyance of esoteric knowledge. Plato used geometric examples to explain philosophical concepts. The cathedral-builders of the Middle Ages devised their plans and details, such as rose windows, to conform to obscure geometric relationships. Men of the Renaissance, including Leonardo da Vinci, studied geometry for its own sake as well as for its application to practicalities and perspective in paintings. But it is in the esoteric – occult – context that we find it appearing in the mysterious Parchments.

That geometry should have been used in times past to convey a secret is not that unexpected; that Henry Lincoln should have deduced that geometry is to be found in the Parchments is more surprising, because it is far from obvious. The sequence described below is explained in some detail as we felt it important to convey the methods that led us to our final extraordinary conclusion. Nothing is superflu-ous; we have not described all the mental processes, U-turns, blind alleys and red herrings. There are references to appendices containing supplementary arguments. Ultimately, the logic and independent con-firmation of what follows should leave the reader in no doubt.

Lincoln's analysis led to the diagrams shown in Figures 1.4 and 1.5, in which he arrived at the arrangement of two triangles. He went on to draw two circles and further lines, which, though not necessarily wrong, took him down an intellectual cul-de-sac. We shall not follow him this far, but shall look more closely at his initial constructions.

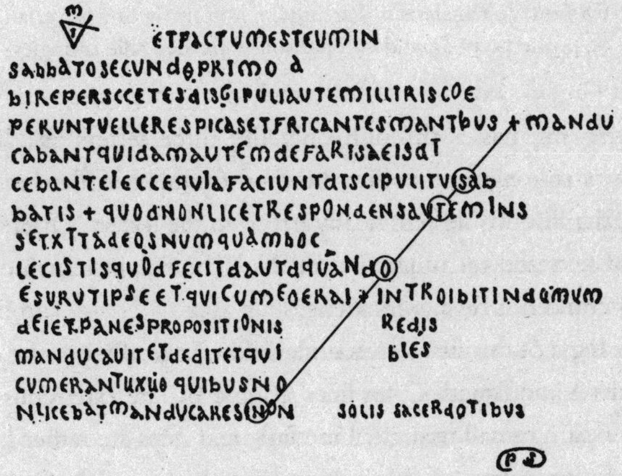

FIGURE 1.4 Lincoln's analysis of Parchment 1.

Associating the triangular arrangement of the Dalle de Coume Sourde with the small triangular device at the top of Parchment 1, and having questioned the purpose of the three crosses that are within the text (they are clearly not punctuation, and appear to serve no other function), Lincoln was inspired to connect the crosses by straight lines. But which to which? Experimenting, he joined the two crosses in lines 4 and 10, since this line would pass through the least amount of

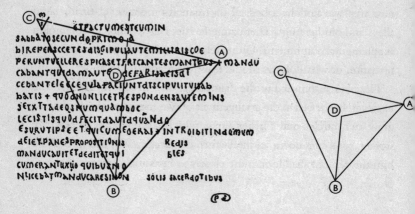

FIGURE 1.5 Lincoln's analysis of Parchment 1: constructing the triangle ABC and the point D, and comparison with the Dalle triangles.

text: the line passes through only the three letters 'S', 'I' and 'O'. Placing a rule along this line, he then found that if extended downwards, the line would pass neatly between the letters 'O' of the last two lines of text and terminate on an 'N'. The reappearance of the word SION could not be a coincidence.

The logic of this first step is undeniable. Logical too is the connection of points A and B with C, for lines AC and BC are extensions of the sides of the existing small triangle. Lincoln's next steps are rather less obvious. The remaining cross on line 7 is joined to the cross at A. On the assumption that the construction is, in fact, leading to replication of the Dalle diagram, he then drew a line from B to the mid-point of line AC, the isolation of the last letter 'a' on line 2 perhaps supporting this step.

There are three possibilities: the deductions are fallacious; they were a lucky guess and are correct; Henry Lincoln was told what to do. This was not to be the last time that we found ourselves asking similar questions. However, it does appear that Lincoln's result might have some significance: the internal triangle thus completed is isosceles, with sides AD and BD equal, and the angles at A and B equal. Lincoln then considered that the diagram obtained is the one on the Dalle. His next step was to draw a circle with its centre near the 'a' on line 2, at the mid-point of AC, and of diameter AC. But we shall leave his path at this point to consider his conclusion that the diagram obtained has replicated the Dalle pattern. It has not.

Apart from minor quibbles about the precise equivalence of the angles, there is clearly a significant difference between the Dalle diagram and the one that Lincoln generated from the Parchment. On the stone, the arrangement of the two triangles is clearly intended to be symmetrical, with the axis of symmetry passing through the two crosses. This is not true of the two triangles in Lincoln's diagram.

Regaining the trail

Before we go any further, we should draw attention to a small correction we have made to Lincoln's own diagram. There, the point B was not quite correctly located: the line AB, instead of arriving at the right-hand lower point of the 'N' on the bottom line, should come to the bottom of the left-hand upright of the letter 'N'. When this correction is made the line drawn from the newly located point B to point C will be found to align more closely with the side of the small triangle (Figure 1.6). In addition, the line from A to B will be found to pass neatly between the letters 'O' in the last two lines, rather than cutting the 'O' on the bottom line as in Lincoln's diagram. From the description in his text, this is clearly what he had intended; the error being introduced in later drafting.

One of Lincoln's circles may now be drawn. This passes through the cross on line 10 of the text. It does *not* pass through the cross on line 7, as stated by Lincoln.[2]

We are not content, however, with the correspondence between the diagrams of the Dalle and the Parchment. Also, the Parchment's strange triangular device has an untidy line pointing upwards and to the right.

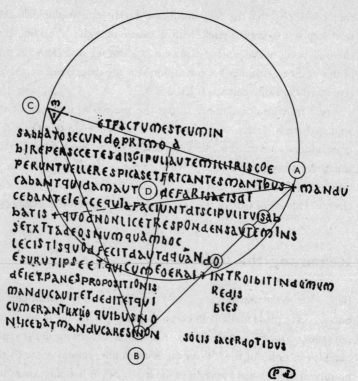

FIGURE 1.6 Lincoln's analysis corrected, and a circle added.

This suggests that the diagram has to be completed in some way, and if we consider at the same time that the two triangles are not symmetrically arranged, perhaps we are intended to correct this fault. There is indeed a logical way forward, which Lincoln had not detected, but which leads to a completion of the diagram that arguably makes it equivalent to that on the Dalle de Coume Sourde. The process of completing this stage in the decipherment of Parchment 1 provides an insight into the way in which the puzzle was set; it is described in Appendix B. It is sufficient here to see the result and to recognise that there is now an apparent correspondence between the diagram on the stone and that on the Parchment. The two may be compared in Figure 1.7.

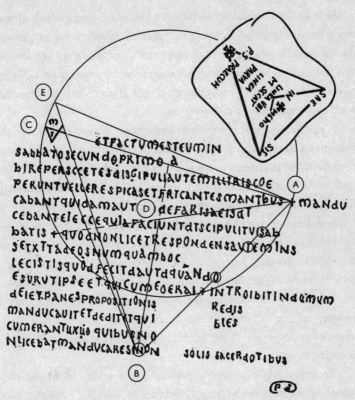

FIGURE 1.7 Construction of the new triangle ABE, which resembles more closely the Dalle figure.

So far, then, we have corrected an error of Lincoln's and reinforced (but not confirmed beyond doubt) his identification of the Dalle diagram in the Parchment. We do not support the further constructions he made, which led nowhere. The correspondence between these two diagrams is not, however, an end in itself, merely a first step on a long and arduous road. Although we shall have further occasion to refer to Henry Lincoln and his writings in the general context of the story, it is necessary to make clear that, while acknowledging his contribution so far, from this point on our path diverges dramatically from his. He had selected a false trail, marked by ambiguous, misleading signs.

We have been careful not to pursue a line of reasoning which unwittingly invokes speculation to support speculation. When we are groping for the next handhold, we shall make this clear; when we are dissatisfied, we shall say so. Sometimes we were required to maintain a dogged pursuit when the trail had gone cold, but always we were rewarded with a new sign and further progress.

A search for other possible geometric constructions in the Parchment, inspired mainly by the confirmation that Lincoln's completion of the geometry was not satisfactory, led to a variety of other lines being drawn. One of these is shown as a dashed line in Figure 1.8. Initially visualised as joining the new point E to the lower apex of the triangular device, but then noted also to pass rather neatly through the 'm' shape and the 'I' shape, this line when extended was found to pass through 'I', the third letter of the bottom line, and above it an 'm', the third letter on the penultimate line. This seems unlikely to be accidental, particularly since this line is also seen to pass through the letters 'I' and the left leg of letters 'N' in other lines. Perhaps this line is also intended to be parallel to the line BD (which, to a reasonable degree of accuracy, it is).

The many other geometric possibilities that we considered were ruled out one at a time to leave a hard core of justifiable examples, indicated by dashed and solid lines in Figure 1.9. Careful observation of the way these lines relate to the text of the Parchment will indicate why they have been drawn. However, it is worth taking a closer look at certain features.

The texts of both Parchments are written in a script known as uncial, the earliest recorded forms of which are found on Greek and Roman manuscripts from around the fourth century AD. Some of the letterforms resemble modern roman capitals, but others, including 'a' and, in particular, 'm', are more rounded and often look more like lower-case roman letters. As we shall see, the forms of the letters take on a special significance. (We denote them here by the character that most resembles the uncial form, for example 'm' but 'N'.)

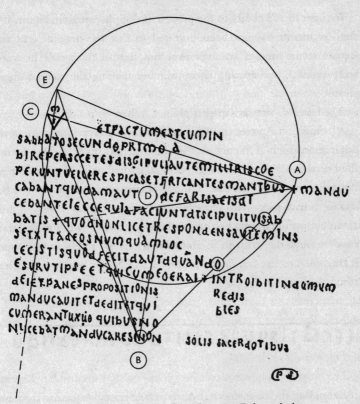

FIGURE 1.8 A line drawn from the point E through the
'm over I' combinations.

The roman 'N' is often carelessly written, though there are important exceptions. The 'N' at the beginning of line 14 is meticulously rendered, and gives the impression that each of the three lines forming it has been drawn with a straight-edge. We have drawn two lines through this letter, as shown, and the vertical line appears to be emphasised by the layout of the text, since lines 5 to 10 are indented to align with it. Another vertical line has been drawn passing through the left legs of the letters 'N' in lines 4 and 9, passing also through the 'I' of line 10 and skimming the side of the letter 'O' in line 14. These two vertical lines are parallel.

In order to add clarity to the process of decipherment, in Figure 1.9 the Parchment has not been oriented so that the lines of text are 'square' to the page, as would be expected. Instead, the parallel lines are truly vertical, anticipating their role and making the various steps clearer.

The letter 'O' acts as a marker of lines. Wherever possible, within the restrictions of the prose, the 'O's, and in many cases the circular part of other letters such as 'd', are used in this way. Examples of three lie on the line that is also tangential to the oval flourish enclosing the letters PS at the very end of the text. This use of circular or oval shapes will be shown to have precedents of surprising antiquity.

An almost horizontal line drawn between lines 8 and 9 of the text passes through the 'arrowhead' above the letters 'U' and 'a' in line 9 and is tangential to the top of the letters 'S I O N' on line 9, which are raised above the line:

LECISTISQUOdFECITdAUTdQUANdO

Extending the base-line AB of the Dalle triangles passing through 'S I O N' shows it to be perpendicular to the line drawn through the 'N' on the last line; this may be taken as confirmation of this alignment. Finally, the sloping line joining the crosses on lines 4 and 7 – part of the Dalle diagram – has been extended to the left. The reason is evident: it is one of four lines that meet at a common point.

An apparently minor detail that would later prove to be of major significance is the angle between the line AB and the vertical line. From a superficial examination this appears to be 45°, but on measurement it is found to be 46½°, to the nearest half-degree. It should be noted as 45° + 1½°.

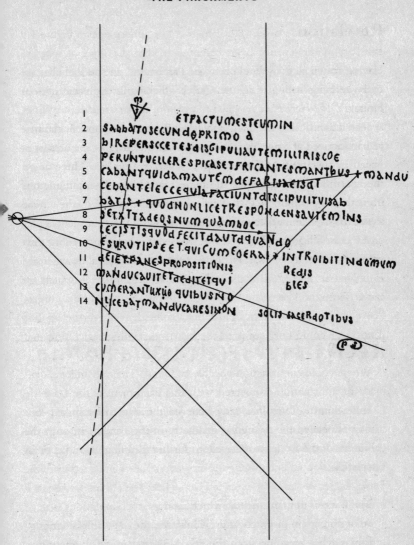

1 ETPACTUMESTEUMIN
2 SABBATOSECUNDOPRIMOA
3 BIREPERSCCETESDISCIPULIAUTEMILLIRISCOE
4 PERUNTUELLERESPICASETFRICANTESMANTbUS + MANDU
5 CABANTQUIDAMAUTEMDEFARISAEISAT
6 CEBANTELECCEQUIAFACIUNTDISCIPULITUISAb
7 bATIS + QUODNONLICETRESPONDENSAUTEMINS
8 SETXTTADEQSNUMQUAMboC
9 LECISTISQUODFECITDAUTDQUANDO
10 ESURUTIPSEET.QUICUMEOERAI + INTROIbITINdomum
11 dEIETPANESPROPOSITIONIS   REdIS
12 MANDUCAUITETdEdITETQUI   blES
13 CUMERANTUXUObQUIBUSNO
14 NLICEbATMANDUCARESINON   SOLISSACERDOTIBUS

FIGURE 1.9 Various other lines suggested by letters in the text.

Revelation

Having drawn all these lines on to the Parchment, we suddenly had an overwhelming feeling of *déjà vu*. Quickly flicking through the pages of Lincoln's *The Holy Place* revealed the reason: the arrangement of lines appeared identical to the geographical alignments that Lincoln claimed to have arrived at from his investigations of the maps of the area produced by the Institut Géographique Nationale (I.G.N.). This was no superficial similarity, for when the angles made by the lines fanning out from the single point to the vertical line were checked, they were found to have a remarkable correspondence with the equivalent angles on Lincoln's diagram (Figure 1.10). An extraordinary possibility thus presented itself. *The vertical line to the right of the Parchment represents the Paris Meridian and, if this is so, the point of convergence of the lines to the left of the Parchment is the village of Antugnac.* Now this could be a coincidence – a remarkable coincidence, but a coincidence nevertheless. But if not, one could only come to the heart-quickening conclusion that *Parchment 1 is a map.*

Where could confirmation possibly be found? The only independent piece of information connected with this Parchment is the Dalle de Coume Sourde. Lincoln clearly believed the two to be linked, but having associated the triangular geometry of the Parchment with the geometry of the Dalle, he derived no further meaning from this or its inscription:[3]

> The Latin is ungrammatical, which renders it so ambiguous as to be of no certain or practical use. However, the inevitable attempt to wrench a meaning from the text is again a useful distraction from the extremely simple geometric design which surrounds it.

Ungrammatical it may be, but it is not ambiguous. When describing this slab, we have referred to a distinction between Latin that is bad through ignorance and Latin that is bad by design. The point is that if

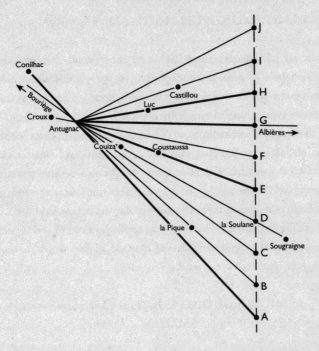

FIGURE 1.10 Lincoln's 'fan' diagram, showing geographical alignments on the town of Antugnac. Compare the lines passing through points A, E, G and H with Figure 1.9.

this were the best effort by someone virtually unversed in Latin, they may well have been unaware of the ambiguities in the composition. This is not very likely. If both Parchment and slab date from the eighteenth century, as has been proposed, and the author, as also proposed, was a priest, such a degree of ignorance is inconceivable. The declension of nouns is almost the first aspect of Latin to be taught. On the other hand, if the Parchment and slab inscription are modern forgeries, we have good reason to suspect who is responsible and the same comment would apply. But what if the poor grammar is deliberate, intended to deter the less perceptive observer – what then? The inscription on the slab reads:

IN MEDIO LINEA UBI M SECAT LINEA PARVA

Is it really so ambiguous? Since 'M' is an abbreviation (or, perhaps, merely a shape), it cannot be declined, so we cannot determine whether it is the object or the subject of the sentence. The same is true of the other two nouns in the text, but these are the same word – LINEA. This simplifies the problem. There are only two options: either 'M' cuts the line, or the line cuts 'M'. Also, since we suspect the ungrammatical form to be deliberate, we might also deduce that the sequence of words (the placing of the verb does not follow the rule of classical Latin – it should be at the end) is also deliberate, and follows the form of the vernacular. This would be similar in English and French in this instance. If a direct translation is made of the words as they appear, a very clear statement emerges:

IN MIDDLE OF LINE WHERE M CUTS LINE
SMALL

It is possible to present this more eloquently and make the small alterations required to put this into idiomatic English, so that it reads:

IN THE MIDDLE OF THE LINE WHERE M
CUTS THE SMALL LINE

So the poor Latin is, one might say, a form of code intended to deter the intelligentsia!

Is there still any doubt that it is 'M' that is doing the cutting? Let us see whether the Dalle itself or the Parchment can resolve the problem. The text of the Parchment, as we have seen, is written in uncial script, so there are only 'm's, and no 'M's. On the Dalle there are three 'M's, but only one cuts a line. It is the 'M' of MEDIO, and the line it cuts is a small line – in fact, one of the two smallest lines in the diagram. But our attention is being drawn to the middle of the line cut by 'M', and on the Dalle there is nothing there of note. So what of the Parchment geometry?

We suspect that Parchment 1 is a map, and that the vertical line is the Paris Meridian. The possibility that 'M' represents 'Meridian'

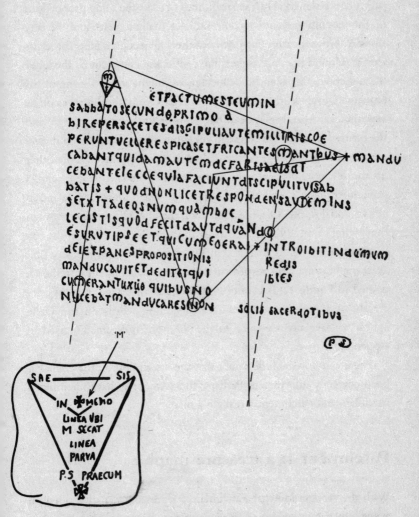

FIGURE 1.11 Parallel lines suggested by 'm over I' combinations, and below the 'M' on the Dalle.

naturally springs to mind, and in the Parchment diagram the vertical line does cut a small line (Figure 1.11). (It should be noted that the small line cut by the 'M' on the Dalle is, in fact, the mirror image of the Parchment – a fact of great significance, as we were to find much later.) More remarkably, the small line is cut in the same proportions on the Parchment as it is on the Dalle; actually a quarter of the way along it. Now, locating the centre of this line using dividers for accuracy, it is found that, precisely at the centre, the line is cut by the letter 'I', and above this is an 'm'. Once again the 'm above I' symbol has been used, and clearly we should relate this in some way to its other appearances. Also, the symbol has been drawn such that the 'I' and the centre leg of the 'm' slope in the same direction, a direction that compares with the slope of the dashed line passing through the other 'm above I' symbols at the top and bottom of the text. A line parallel to the first one is clearly the intention, and when drawn it is found to be tangential to the 'O' of 'S I O N' on the line AB, running through the left leg of the 'N' below, passing through the small gap in the top loop of the 'R' below that, and finally running through the very slim 'S' at the bottom. The purpose of these two parallel lines (both shown dashed in Figure 1.11) cannot be guessed at this stage, but they are clearly of some importance. The remaining words on the Dalle appear to have no relevance to the solution; they are discussed in Appendix C.

There can now be little doubt that the inscription on the Dalle has been correctly interpreted. Perhaps, then, we really have identified a meridian, and Parchment 1 really is a map.

Parchment 1: a treasure map?

With the recognition that Parchment 1 represents a map, a question arises: what is its purpose? In view of the allegations that Bérenger Saunière discovered the Parchments and almost immediately became mysteriously wealthy, the answer would have to be a 'treasure' map. But with the 'map' as we have it at this stage there is little to indicate where any treasure might be. Various possibilities could be considered: the apex of either triangle, for example, but this seems too facile. But Parchment 1 was soon to reveal more secrets, and also a feature which would prove to be the *leitmotif* and key to the mystery.

Referring back to Figure 1.6, lines AB and AC can be seen to intersect at 60°, the internal angle of an equilateral triangle. Such a triangle has all its sides equal – hence its name. If an equilateral triangle is intended to be found in the Parchment and we were to know the length of one of its sides, it would be possible to complete it.

The triangular device at the top left-hand corner of the Parchment has been cut by the line joining the 'm above I' symbols. This might somehow indicate a point on the line AC. So let us see if a triangle constructed with sides of length equal to the distance from the centre of the top side of the small triangle to the cross on line 4 will produce an interesting result. Extending the line AB, and drawing a new line to form the left-hand side of the triangle set at the correct angle of 60° to both AB and AC, produces the result shown in Figure 1.12.

Immediate confirmation is provided. The new line is tangential to four 'O's, in lines 2, 7, 8 and 9, emphasised by shading. Other letters also acknowledge the line's passing. Although intuition set us on the path to this result, it could have been quickly achieved by trial and error. A set-square adjusted to the appropriate angle and moved across the diagram would soon have highlighted the sequence of 'O's.

If we locate the centre of the triangle by constructing lines that bisect its internal angles (and which are, consequently, perpendicular to the sides), we discover two things. Firstly, the centre lies on a line that is tangential to the tops of the letters of line 7, and is at the 'R' which stands above that line. Secondly, the bisector of the top left-hand angle bisects the lower right-hand side of the triangle precisely at the cross on line 10. All the confirmation one could wish for is provided. This bisecting line also runs down the sloping tail of the raised 'R' on line 7.

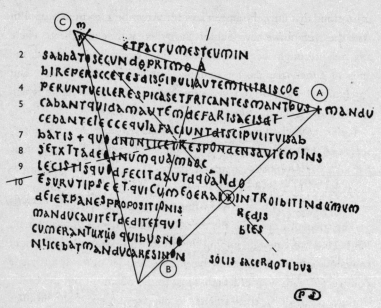

FIGURE 1.12 Construction of the equilateral triangle.

Concealed in this way, does the 'R' now look something like a 'P'? We shall have cause to return to this.

A further development of this diagram will not seem to be that relevant at this stage – this is one of those moments when we are obliged to anticipate later discoveries. Two equilateral triangles combined form the familiar 'Seal of Solomon' or 'Star of David', the geometric term for which is a hexagram. A second triangle is added to the first as shown in Figure 1.13. The left side of this triangle passes through the cross on line 7 – the second line to do so – and is tangential to the curved elements of several letters of the text (the 'e' of line 10, the 'C' of line 9 and the 'd's of lines 5 and 3).

The most significant elements of geometric information so far discovered are summarised in Figure 1.14. If the foregoing geometric derivations appear in any way unreliable, or superficial, it is worth remarking that further independent confirmation presented later in the book will eliminate any doubts.

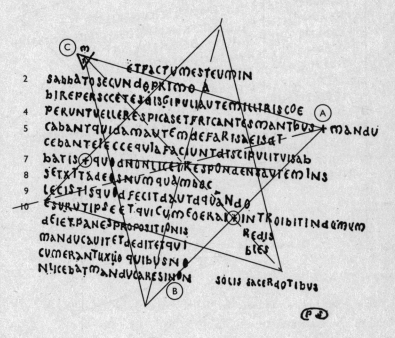

FIGURE 1.13 A second triangle is constructed, giving a hexagram.

Meridians and the map

Figure 1.15 shows the 'map' as it stands at this stage with the various components combined. The supposed Paris Meridian is the solid vertical line to the right of the diagram. This, and the line parallel to it on the left of the diagram, may both be regarded as meridians, with a small 'm'. It should be explained that a meridian is any great circle – one of diameter equal to that of the Earth – that passes through the Earth's poles. These lines, otherwise known as lines of longitude, converge at

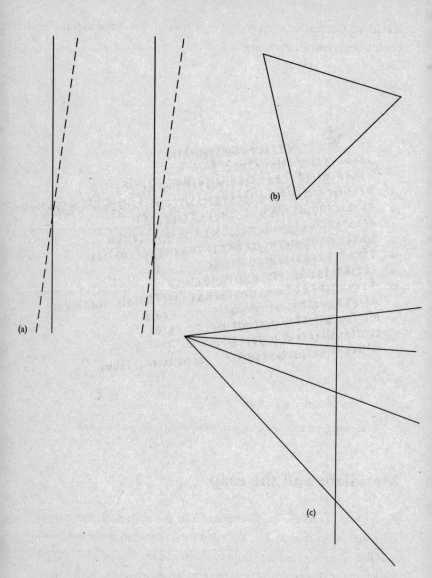

FIGURE 1.14 The main geometric elements identified in Parchment 1:
(a) two pairs of parallel lines, (b) a tilted equilateral triangle and (c) lines
radiating from a point.

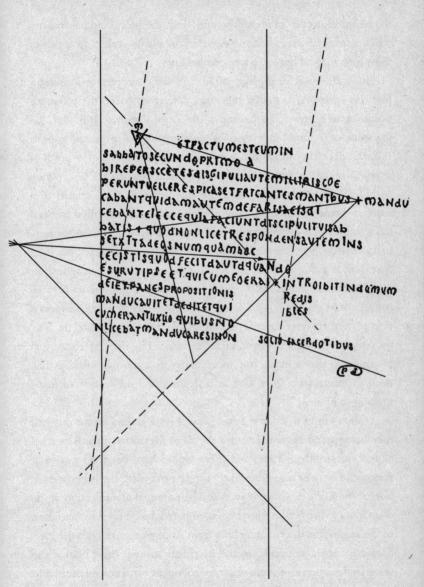

FIGURE 1.15 The 'map' inferred from Parchment 1.

the poles. However, in regions remote from the poles, and particularly when a small land area is being depicted on a large-scale map, a pair of meridians may be drawn as two parallel lines.

This is the basis for the vertical lines of the coordinate grid systems used on maps. A particular meridian is selected to be the reference point for all others and is known as the Zero Meridian. It is allocated the value of $0°$, and other 'degrees' of longitude are measured from it. A Zero Meridian is traditionally referred to by the name of its point of origin, the current internationally accepted zero being the Greenwich Meridian. Formerly there had been many in use, each related to a national point of reference. The French one quite naturally had been based on a point located within the capital city, and for reasons normally regarded by others as national pride and Gallic obstinacy, the Paris Meridian is still reserved as the zero for maps produced by the Institut Géographique National. Of course, it makes very good sense to have the Zero Meridian related to the country's principal observatory. Fortunately, for international navigation, air traffic control and the like, the French also use the Greenwich Meridian. The Paris Meridian will be found to play a major role in our story as it unfolds, and we shall need to return to it for a look at its history and the history of map-making in France.

It follows from this that the two parallel vertical lines on the diagram may be regarded as candidates for the Zero Meridian, since Rennes is almost due south of Paris, and there would have been no particular reason to consider one more likely for that role than the other were it not for the Dalle de Coume Sourde. The potential identification of the diagram as a map was, it must be remembered, based on the correlation of the angles that the radiating lines from Antugnac make with the Paris Meridian: any line parallel to the Meridian will cut these lines at the same angles, therefore some other independent evidence is required to determine where the Paris Meridian should lie. This is clearly the purpose of the Dalle, which has resolved the matter in favour of the right-hand line.

In time we were to test this construction on the I.G.N. map of the area, and take a close look at what lies to the east of Antugnac in the hope that topographical confirmation could be found. But while working on Parchment 1, we had simultaneously succeeded in wresting some meaning from a second, 'hidden' message of Parchment 2, and it is to that we now turn.

2
THE CIPHER
CODE

At first glance, Parchment 2 (Figure 1.2) contains nothing more than a meaningless jumble of letters. The presence of 'jesus' at the beginning of the first line suggests that this is going to be a legible text, but no further progress is possible. The letters that follow, unspaced and without punctuation, cannot be formed into words.

It is just possible that a Latinist would notice that the letters constitute a Latin text with the addition of a large number of superfluous letters interspersed throughout. An indication that this may be so is the high incidence of doubled letters. The readable text is, however, of no consequence: it is the additional letters that are of interest, as they are the substance of a coded message. The manner in which these letters are to be gleaned from the text, tabulated, subjected to letter substitutions and read off in a sequence deriving from the game of chess (all of this revealed via Gérard de Sède)[1] ensures that decipherment is impossible without full knowledge of the procedure. Computers are of no help, since the letter substitutions are made from an independent text chosen by the code-maker. The most experienced code-breaker could not deduce the steps required.

The decipherment sequence itself is of little relevance to the main thread of our story. We do not need to repeat here the tortuous route

of deduction; the solution, ready-made, had also been provided by de
Sède as:

BERGÈRE PAS DE TENTATION QUE POUSSIN
TENIERS GARDENT LA CLEF PAX DCLXXXI
PAR LA CROIX ET CE CHEVAL DE DIEU
J'ACHÈVE CE DAEMON DE GARDIEN À MIDI
POMMES BLEUES

and can be translated from French in the following, rather literal way:

SHEPHERDESS NO TEMPTATION THAT
POUSSIN TENIERS HOLD THE KEY PEACE 681
BY THE CROSS AND THIS HORSE OF GOD I
COMPLETE [or I DESTROY] THIS DEMON
GUARDIAN AT MIDDAY BLUE APPLES

Before exploring the possibility of interpreting this enigmatic message,
it should be noted that whoever supplied de Sède with the deciphering
sequence and solution had either to be the originator, or to have discovered the sequence written out and concealed by the code-maker.
And there lies a clue to the date of the Parchment. For the sequence
provided by de Sède involves the use of the normal, 'modern', 26-letter
alphabet, and, as pointed out by several viewers following Henry
Lincoln's television appearance on the subject, the letter W was not
incorporated into the French alphabet until after the eighteenth
century. Even the 1914 revision of Cassell's *New French and English
Dictionary* lists the letter Z as 25th in the French alphabet.

Curiously, instead of drawing the logical conclusion that the cipher
code must have been added more recently, Lincoln chose to acknowledge the viewers' comments, revise the sequence to take account of the
25-letter alphabet, and then modify another step to make it all work
properly. Did he imagine that de Sède or his informant had made an

error in repeating the sequence when to do so necessitates *another* modification to the sequence? It is sufficient to say that a one-letter shift down the alphabet is required instead of the two-letter shift for the 26-letter alphabet. This glaringly false move gave us real hope that not only the true date of the Parchments would be revealed, but also those responsible. We shall need to return to these matters later, but for now the important thing is not to be deluded by the assumption of an eighteenth-century date for the Parchments, or, to be more cautious, for the cipher.

So what is to be made of the solution to the cipher – a solution that is apparently meaningless? The first part of it, 'shepherdess no temptation that Poussin Teniers hold the key', appears to hold some trace of meaning, but any hope one might have of finding the full meaning of the text is soon overwhelmed by the nonsense which follows. The complete phrase is so puzzling that one must consider the possibility of a further code substitution being required. This is a depressing prospect, since there is no indication of how to proceed. Lincoln's further ruminations on the subject were found to lead nowhere, and we were now deeply wary of his methods. So we decided to start again – this time with a clean slate.

The devil and the railway

Perhaps *bergère* does not only mean 'shepherdess'. Is there another meaning which might be intended? Indeed there is, for a *bergère* is a type of armchair, and in this context it is a term that will be familiar to anybody with an interest in furniture, particularly antique furniture. We wished to know the earliest date for this usage, and so consulted Pierre Larousse's *Grand Dictionnaire universel du XIXe siècle*. Using the nineteenth-century edition of this authoritative dictionary has the advantage that words and senses current in that period but which may since have dropped out of use will not be missed. We were hopeful that other, more relevant meanings of *bergère* were there to be discovered. The given definition for this piece of furniture is 'fauteuil large et profond, garni d'un coussin'. The earliest quoted use of *bergère* is from Pierre de Beaumarchais (1732–99); so it was certainly in use at an early enough date. Other meanings have included the name of a bird, a tree of India and an ancient female hairstyle, none of which appeared to be relevant. We also consulted Albert Barrère's *Argot and Slang* of 1889, which gives 'sweetheart' and 'last card in a pack' as popular uses of *bergère*.

Overall, we preferred the armchair, and – if we return to the starting-point of this story – the reason is plain to see. Just inside the doorway of the church at Rennes-le-Château is a sculpture which formed part of Bérenger Saunière's redecoration of the church. This sculpture, which supports the holy water stoup, or *bénitier*, is of an unpleasant-looking devil. His posture is curious: sitting, but without a chair (Plate 1). And on the side of a hill to the east of Rennes-le-Château is a rock carved into the shape of a throne, known locally as the Devil's Armchair – le Fauteuil du Diable.

Confirmation that Saunière's devil is connected to this vacant throne is provided by the devil's right hand. The thumb and forefinger form a circle. Close by the Devil's Armchair rock is la Source du Cercle – 'the Spring of the Circle'. The high iron content of this water gives it a rust-coloured appearance which stains the nearby rocks and ground, giving it supposedly the colour of the devil's skin. But does this statue relate to the cipher? It would appear so, for the Devil's Armchair has no occupant – the devil is not there, but in the church without his armchair. And an armchair without the devil is an armchair without temptation – the *bergère pas de tentation*. Perhaps we should seize the opportunity to sit in his armchair while the devil is at church, and gaze eastwards, for that is undoubtedly the direction in which we would be looking.

So far so good, but we could not expect that alternative meanings for the rest of the message were going to complete the solution as easily as that. Many alternatives, including pre-1900 slang, were traced, but, fascinating as they were, they took us nowhere. However, in addition to the *double entendre* we were now aware that a word, or words, could convey the sense of a geographical location. Failing to make progress with the remaining words, we turned our attention to the Roman numerals: DCLXXXI.

The Roman form of the number yielded nothing, but 681 had a familiar connotation. I.G.N. maps are simply covered with three-digit numbers; these are spot heights. Could 681 be a spot height? The range of heights found on the map of the area, from around 200 in the valley of the Aude to 1230, the high point of the Pech de Bugarach, certainly spans 681. However, if the cipher were of any great age, the answer would have to be no, since the spot heights on I.G.N. maps are given in *metres* above sea level at Marseille. The use of the metric system in France became compulsory in 1799, but it was not until the new map of France produced by the État-Major (military staff office) was commenced in 1817 that metric elevations were incorporated. But we do not want to hinder progress here by worrying about exactly when the coded message was introduced into Parchment 2. Let us ignore the date, and check the theory.

Somewhere on the I.G.N. map of the area there had to be one spot height labelled 681 which would have a meaningful relationship to other features identified by the cipher. A methodical and somewhat agonising search of the map identifies 681 at a remote location – Col de l'Espinas – on the road heading east from Véraza and Terroles (Figure 2.1). There is little doubt that this is a correct identification, as we shall see.

Now, suspecting that 681 represents a location on the map – as does *bergère*, one should clearly search for further locations suggested by the remaining pieces of the code. *La croix* could very well refer to one of the many *calvaires* or wayside crosses to be found dotted around rural France. But which one? Help was at hand, for in drawing the Parchment geometry on to the map (as we shall show) our attention had focused on a symbol adjacent to a railway line. This is a cross, the standard symbol for a *calvaire*, but it is labelled 'Cr^x.' (Figure 2.2). We shall call this *La Croix*.

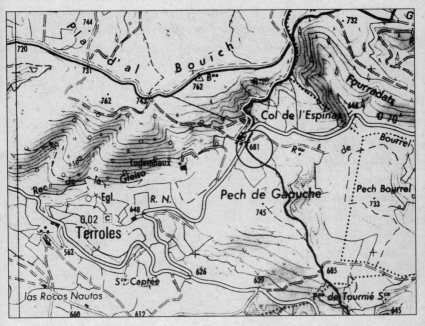

FIGURE 2.1 The identification of *681* as a spot height at Col de l'Espinas.

By this time we had become so familiar with the shapes and angles of the Parchment geometry that we recognised almost immediately that a straight line from *681* to Cr^x. would have a similar alignment to the upper side of the equilateral triangle. By joining the dot at the base of the cross, which marks the precise site, with the dot adjacent to *681*, which performs the same function, the line is indeed found to be at that angle – actually at 75° to a meridian. And when thus drawn on to the map, an extraordinary fact becomes apparent. The railway line follows the valley of the Aude and is therefore seldom straight, but when it emerges from a tunnel just to the north of *La Croix* it straightens to approach the bridge crossing the Aude, and in so doing forms a line at right angles to the *La Croix–681* line. An extraordinary coincidence

FIGURE 2.2 The identification of *La Croix* with the cross (marked 'Cr.ˣ') by the railway line north of Alet-les-Bains.

certainly, but one not to be ignored since the cipher message says 'by the cross and this horse of God' – could the 'horse of God' be the railway?

Fanciful perhaps, but the line of the railway, when extended southwards, is seen to head directly towards the town of Espéraza. If this were to be the second side of a square, what of the right-hand side extending southwards from *681*? Drawing this in and completing the square by making the other sides equal to the *La Croix–681* distance (see Figure 5.9 on p. 125) produces an inconclusive result, since the bottom left-hand corner, although in Espéraza, does not fall at a well-defined point (we shall have cause to review this), and the bottom right-hand corner coincides with no marked feature of any sort. However, immediately adjacent to this corner is marked Col Doux (Figure 2.3). *Col* means the same in English and French – a low point along a mountain ridge – and *doux* means, depending on its context, either 'soft' or 'peaceful'. We therefore have either 'peaceful col' or 'col of peace', and we have found the PAX, or peace, of the cipher. So, we are required to sit in the Devil's Armchair and gaze eastwards towards *Col Doux*!

For the time being, we cannot be absolutely certain of this interpretation of the message as a geographical square; this is to come later in a positive and conclusive manner. But, as the concept could have been derived only from the map (rather than from the ground), let us check the geometry. The orientation of the railway line as shown on the map can be nothing other than a happy coincidence, and thus not precise. So rather than extending that line, let us draw an accurate line through *La Croix* at 15° to a meridian, or 75° to a line of latitude, also known as a parallel. This line passes through the small circle indicating the church in Espéraza (Figure 2.4). Is this intended to be the fourth corner of the square? We do not need to draw the whole square to check this, and indeed it may be done more directly and accurately. From the simple geometry of the square and its angle of tilt we know the angles, or bearings, of its diagonals. The diagonal from *681* to Espéraza church would have to follow a bearing of S 60° W. Placing a

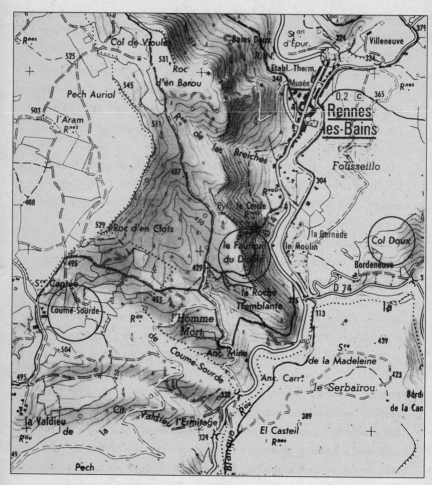

FIGURE 2.3 The identification of *PAX* with Col Doux ('col of peace').

straight-edge on these two points and measuring the angle made with a convenient N–S grid-line confirms this to be 60°, as accurately as it is possible to measure.

Our interpretation of the cipher message so far is therefore probably

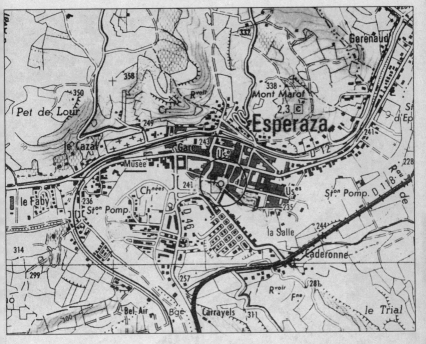

FIGURE 2.4 The south-west corner of the square – the church at Espéraza.

correct. But how could these apparently random geographical features have come to be in the required locations? We shall concern ourselves with that later.

What of the 'horse of God', though – could this really refer to the railway? Our thoughts turned to the possibility of slang words or nicknames. Once again, the *Grand Larousse* came to our aid. In the nineteenth century 'cheval du bon Dieu' could refer to an insect. It was, according to the dictionary, a 'nom vulgaire d'un grillon des champs' – 'a common name for a field cricket'. Well, CHEVAL DE DIEU would be a reasonable contraction of 'cheval du bon Dieu', but what on earth could a cricket have to do with this?

We were on our guard now for the use of *double entendres*, so we now

FIGURE 2.5 The railway bridge near *La Croix* – the 'cheval de Dieu'?

looked up *grillon* in the *Grand Larousse*. It does indeed have more than one meaning: in addition to 'cricket', it is 'nom que l'on donne à des piles carrées servant d'arcs-boutants pour soutenir les bûches que l'on empile en travers dans les chantiers'. That is, 'the name given to square piers acting as buttresses supporting cross-timbers which are placed in construction sites'. This has to be a reference to the railway bridge across the River Aude, just south of *La Croix*. The cross-timbers would be the sleepers that support the rails. If the bridge has square-section piers supporting its spans, the description would fit. (Our visit to the bridge itself is pre-empted at this point by presenting Figure 2.5, which shows that the bridge is indeed supported by *grillons*.) The logic of the *double entendre* is more readily appreciated in the French language, as no translation is required to get from one step to the next. But it is still obscure!

The *bergère* and 681 had suggested a date for the cipher later than 1800, the railway brings the date forward to probably post-1860, and the 'W' in the alphabet suggests later still. Tackling the cipher is proving to be rather like an archaeological dig, the finds at various levels indicating the dating.

When we turned to that inherently strange phrase in the encoded message 'J'ACHÈVE CE DAEMON DE GARDIEN', we were to achieve a significant breakthrough. DAEMON DE GARDIEN has been rather literally translated by some as 'demon guardian', presumably with reference to the demon or devil inside Saunière's church. However, although in French 'demon' is not spelt with the 'ae' diphthong, the word spelt *démon* has two meanings. The less obvious is 'genius', or 'spirit', so a more idiomatic and meaningful translation, which does no injustice to the French, would be 'guardian spirit'. We would suggest that the 'guardian spirit' is the geographical square we have just drawn, and that J'ACHÈVE should be translated as 'I complete' rather than the alternative 'I destroy'.

In Saunière's redecorated church, immediately above the devil without his armchair, are four angels standing before a cross and beneath them the inscription PAR CE SIGNE TU LE VAINCRAS – 'by this sign thou shalt conquer him' (Figure 2.6). This phrase is commonly found in Catholic churches but does not normally include the article *le*. Its inclusion is a subtle alteration which nevertheless completely changes the meaning. Normally it would read 'By this sign thou shalt conquer'. Now, *vaincre* does not only mean 'to conquer'; it can also mean 'to overcome, master, get the better of, outdo, surpass or excel'. And *le* does not only mean 'him'; it also means 'it'. Also, the verb *achever* can mean 'to finish, close, end, conclude, terminate, perfect, crown, consummate, despatch or kill'.

When all the possible senses of *vaincre* and *achever* are considered together, a meaning emerges. The sign referred to is the 'sign of the cross', which is being demonstrated for us by Saunière's angels in such a way as to make perfectly clear the geometric configuration traced by the hand, which, on returning to the forehead to complete the sign of the cross, completes the diagonals and two opposite sides of a square (Figure 2.7). And, labouring the point somewhat, the cross behind the angels in the church is equal-armed, in the Celtic style – in other words, it is a 'crossed-square'. It would now seem reasonable to deduce that the square is the 'guardian spirit'.

Still unaccounted for in the original cipher message are QUE POUSSIN TENIERS GARDE LA CLEF and À MIDI POMMES BLEUES. Translating À MIDI as 'at midday' seems inevitable because, although *midi* has meanings other than 'midday' – including 'south' and 'meridian' – they are invariably prefaced by the article; thus 'to the south' would be translated as *au midi*. Whether the compiler of the code would have been prepared to take liberties with the language to the extent of writing À MIDI when meaning 'to the south' seems unlikely. So for the moment we are at a loss to know what this might mean.

In contrast, there are many possible meanings of POMMES BLEUES. In French, almost anything which is spherical and has a prominent colour can be referred to as a *pomme*, with the appropriate colour tacked on at the end. Thus *pommes d'or* are oranges or tomatoes,

FIGURE 2.6 The angels in the church at Rennes. The inscription translates as 'By this sign thou shalt conquer him.'

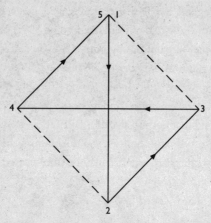

FIGURE 2.7 The sign of the cross as traced out by the angels –
the 'guardian spirit'.

while *pommes de pins* are fir cones. If the particular species of fir cone
referred to as *pommes bleues* can be found in the area (though it is not
typical of the surrounding flora), this may be what we are looking for.
But is there anything else both spherical and blue which occurs in the
locality? The answer is grapes: red wines are produced in the area, and
dark grapes with the bloom of ripeness are distinctly blue in appearance.
There are, unfortunately, quite enough vineyards in the area to make
this identification less than specific. More interesting is the unexpected
discussion of grapevines by a known collaborator of Gérard de Sède,
Pierre Plantard, in an article in the socio-political magazine *Circuit*.[2]
Vine references were to assume a considerable importance as our investigation continued. The vine and its fruit have had important
associations in the history of Christianity, which was constantly at the
back of our minds in view of the legend of Joseph of Arimathea and
Mary Magdalene.

This leaves only the statement QUE POUSSIN TENIERS GARDE
LA CLEF, which proved to be the least ambiguous of all. It unequivo-
cally refers to two famous painters – Nicolas Poussin and David

Teniers – and legend has it that Saunière had more than a passing acquaintance with the work of both. According to de Sède, the Abbé had obtained copies of paintings by both artists on a visit to Paris. The Poussin was his famous *Les Bergers d'Arcadie II* (The Shepherds of Arcadia), also known as *Et in Arcadia ego*. Presumably the two painters jointly hold the key to the understanding of the geometric confirmation.

Bearing in mind that both POMMES BLEUES and À MIDI are still somewhat unresolved, the geometric information contained in the coded message within Parchment 2 may be summarised as follows:

Sitting in the chair vacated by the Devil
look eastwards towards Col Doux
From there proceed in an approximately northerly direction to
    reach *681* and turn left.
Head towards *La Croix*
and on reaching that spot, turn left again to proceed along the
    railway line
But do not follow this when it starts to curve. Keep heading on
    the bearing which it has given and continue to Espéraza
    church
You will have completed a square, the guardian spirit

But what is one supposed to do after completing the square?

A reasonable deduction, bearing in mind Saunière's angels and the diagonals, would be to assume that something lies at the centre of the square. The site indicated at the centre of the cipher-square is east of Luc-sur-Aude, and south of a tiny village with a chapel called Castillou, but it is not impressive. It lacks all the requirements that would make a suitable location for an important cache. But any doubts that we had as to its suitability were overridden by an amazing chance discovery.

Early in the eighteenth century, work on an accurate survey of the whole of France was commenced by Jacques Cassini and his son César-François Cassini de Thury. They proceeded by triangulation, working out from the Zero Meridian through Paris which Jacques's father, Jean-Dominique Cassini, had helped to establish in 1669. The project, known as the 'Cassini map', was finally completed in 1818. We had obtained from the Bodleian Library a photograph of the section of the 1780 Cassini map for this area (Figure 2.8) – and what a surprise it held. We had not been looking for this place-name as we had no idea it existed, but there it was: '*La Mort*'. A hamlet or farm was indicated as a small building. Needless to say, a hamlet called Death no longer exists; it was probably not a popular address. But how curious to find La Mort, when this had appeared in the Parchment. Perhaps this was the meaning of the concealed message about Dagobert and his treasure?

Cassini had shown La Mort due east of Luc-sur-Aude, and today there is no building in that location, but further to the south lies a farm called Métairie de Luc. Could Cassini have placed this too far north? This would appear to be the view of the I.G.N., whose latest map at 1 : 50,000 scale shows the name of this farm as Métairie *de la Mort*.

Now, the nineteenth-century État-Major map marks this farm as a *bergerie* – and shows many others in the vicinity – but it is not named. Why the I.G.N. should revert to this name is a mystery; what source did they use? Clearly not the État-Major, and why consult the Cassini after two hundred and fifty years? Only a necromancer would wish to reinstate a name like Death. Or was it necessary for La Mort to become once again identifiable? If so, the reason could be sinister. Such an opinion would undoubtedly reinforce the identification of La Mort as the location of the treasure, but at this early stage of our investigation these ideas were simply theories, and would remain so until we visited the hamlet itself. Indeed, the time had come to test all our theories and see if there were further clues to the 'treasure' in the landscape of southern France.

FIGURE 2.8 La Mort on the 1780 Cassini map, marked between Montazels and 'Peyroles'.

3
THE GUARDIAN
SPIRIT

Our groundwork in England had raised numerous questions but provided few answers. Armed with maps old and new – contemporary
Michelin and I.G.N., copies of the first État-Major series of 1866 and
the earlier Cassini version – we returned to southern France. We
needed to find out whether the precise geographical directions we had
extracted from the Parchments could shed any light on the mystery of
Rennes-le-Château. We needed visible evidence to reassure us that
we had not gone down a cul-de-sac, as so many had before.

Alet-les-Bains, like Rennes-les-Bains, is a spa town of ancient origin,
known to the Romans as Electum. It lies approximately five kilometres
north of Montazels, the village where Saunière was born. The River
Sals joins the larger Aude just below Montazels before meandering
northwards to pass through the constricted gorge at the northern limits of Alet. Here lay our first objective – a point marked on the I.G.N.
map by a cross. Our decoding of the message in Parchment 2 had pinpointed *La Croix* as one of the corners of the square. We were hopeful
that this site would shed more light on the elusive geometric information we were currently toying with – and we were not disappointed.

La Croix

On the I.G.N. map, *La Croix* is on the north-western side of the rail-way line. To the south, the railway crosses the gorge of the Aude and the river and road below, before disappearing into the mountainside opposite and re-emerging to head towards the station at Alet-les-Bains. Crossing to the northern bank of the river by a small footbridge, we searched for the cross along a well-trodden path. As the path descended, so the railway line rose, creating the need for an increasingly high embankment between the two. We were on the verge of abandoning our search when a shape suddenly caught our eye. High on the railway embankment, and barely noticeable from the acute angle, was our first goal of the day – *La Croix* (Figure 3.1).

Craning our necks, we saw that the monument was bizarrely placed on top of an older engraved stone, which looked to be of seventeenth-century origin. Reading the inscription was not difficult apart from two areas where the stone had crumbled, confusing the identity of the letters. The inscription reads:

IMPVLSVS EVERSVS SVM

VT CADEREM

ET D$\overline{\text{X}}$S SVSCEPI TME

The L of IMPULSUS is damaged, but that is what it has to be. The strange, incorrect spacing of the last words has been retained above. The other area to cause some doubt is D$\overline{\text{X}}$S. This is clearly an abbreviation – indicated as is usual in Latin inscriptions by the line above the X – but one unfamiliar to us. It was not until our return to England that we were able to make any progress with this inscription. In Oxford, Professor Michael Winterbottom of Corpus Christi College was kind enough to translate. While agreeing that the abbreviation did appear to be D$\overline{\text{X}}$S, it was, he deduced, intended to be the abbreviation for

FIGURE 3.1 *La Croix* – the monument by the railway line.

Dominus – 'the Lord' – DN̄S. He recognised the phrase as a verse from one of the Psalms in the Vulgate (the Latin translation of the Bible), and with a little detective work he tracked it down. It is verse 13 from Psalm 117, numbered 118 in the King James Authorised Version.

This English translation of the Bible takes some liberties with grammar, so Professor Winterbottom re-translated from the Latin, and checked it also against the original Greek. His translation reads:

> I was thrust and overthrown
> so as to fall
> and the Lord took me up

Verse 22 of the same psalm, which refers to 'the stone which the builders refused', would later take on a significance as yet unforeseen, as would other details of this inscription.

We turned our attention to the cross which sat on top of the stone, and after which we had named the location. This was of noticeably more recent origin than the inscription on the tablet below. Cut from local material, the cross was of octagonal section and rose from a stepped base bearing an inscription that was clear and unmistakable:

> RESURRE-
> XIT
> 1801 – 1876

RESURREXIT means 'raised again', and would be expected to refer to the Resurrection of Jesus, which this inscription may well do, but in view of the dates it is more likely that it refers to the cross itself. The railway had been completed in 1876, and so the dismantling of a previous cross – old and possibly in poor condition – in the path of the track, followed by its replacement with a new replica, is highly likely. The old tablet, still in good condition, would simply have been re-erected. But it is the year 1801 that poses the question: what happened in 1801, and what could have spanned the period 1801–76? The railway was not even a dream in 1801, and no relevant events seem to have occurred that year. Furthermore, the span of seventy-five years is considerable.

The answer is that the year 1801 has no significance other than being 75 less than 1876. The railway was completed in 1876, so that had to appear on the cross; the other number just had to be 75 less. If the railway had been completed in 1875, the other year would have been 1800. Why? Because 75 is the numerical partner of the *leitmotif* of the Secret: 75° is the angle of the left side of the tilted triangle; it had already appeared when the cipher square was being finalised, and it was to recur time and again during our study of the mystery.

Among the personal papers of Bérenger Saunière found after his death was a cryptic note. This was decoded by a M. Alain Chatillon to read:[1]

> MLL SALUT LES RENNES D'ARQUES – RAPT
> LE GOUFFRE EN NID – PLAN – TE – SERT –
> DANGER LXXV – FTT

Although various possibilities suggest themselves, we have been unable to derive any comprehensible meaning from these words. It is also difficult to ascertain whether or not Chatillon's decipherment is correct, but the appearance of LXXV – 75 – gives us good cause to believe that it is at least correct in parts. The reference to Arques further supports this view, as will be seen; and the number 75 does, indeed, represent 'dangerous' knowledge.

Whoever had been responsible for the monument at *La Croix* possessed an understanding of the basic geometric principles within the Parchments. Was it Henri Boudet, priest of the parish of Alet-les-Bains at the time, who was responsible for this cross, set high up on a railway embankment, virtually out of sight to all who might pass on the path below?

Forcing aside thoughts of likely candidates, we attempted to photograph the monument, finally succeeding by one of us holding aloft the camera on its tripod, while the other climbed the embankment to determine the camera angle. From the top, it was possible to scrutinise the cross more closely, and it had more to reveal. At the top of the cross is the usual IN RI, and below this a circle containing a strange figure with eight points.

While this unusual emblem could have been a highly stylised crown of thorns, it is very similar to a symbol used by the Society of the Rose Cross, otherwise known as the Rosicrucians. This most secretive of secret societies, much discussed but little understood, goes back at least to the early seventeenth century, a period which saw a great resurgence of interest in the sciences and arts. The pursuit of such interests sometimes led to the study of ancient or secret knowledge and philosophies, activities regarded as heretical and therefore persecuted by the Catholic Church. The Rosicrucian declaration of a new era of intellectual freedom and condemnation of the Catholic Church showed that the Society was engaged in such activities. The presence of the eight-pointed star on a Christian cross might therefore be indicative of some heretical or secret association.

In the Middle Ages, some seekers after occult knowledge adopted the sign of the Rose and the Cross,[2] and we were to become aware from our own research that the Knights Templar were implicated in the symbolism of the Rosy Cross (as the cross decorated with roses came to be called). The eight-pointed symbol at which we were looking – derived from two squares superimposed – had been employed by the Rosicrucians from the seventeenth century onwards to symbolise the eight points of a geometric universe guarded by eight angels.[3] For the first time, we wondered whether the activities of the priests involved in the story had taken them beyond the accepted bounds of Catholic doctrine, a thought which was to gain more credence as our investigations proceeded.

From the top of the embankment we stepped on to the railway

track itself, and looked down the track towards the bridge. The line ran straight as an arrow, under the footbridge, over the river, then over the road before disappearing into the dark recesses of the tunnel; a compass reading confirmed that it ran exactly as shown on the map. We remembered that Abbé Gélis, who was to be brutally murdered, had purchased shares in the railway. A coincidence – perhaps?

We retraced our earlier steps to the footbridge and looked at the railway bridge across the Aude. Of lattice-girder construction, supported by masonry piers rising from the bed of the river far below, this was the *grillon* of the *double entendre*, the 'cheval de Dieu' in the coded message.

As we gradually descended into the outskirts of Alet-les-Bains, we noticed some rather curious fragments embedded in the hillside where the path had recently been widened. Here and there in the packed soil were tiny pieces of pottery. These were pieces of amphorae, and, judging by the location and size of the remains, the area contained a Roman dump of some kind. The amphora was the standard form of terracotta jar used by the Romans for the preservation and transportation of foodstuffs, both solid and liquid. Their style varied from one period to another and this, coupled with the type of clay used, enables the twentieth-century archaeologist to determine the period and place of their origin.[4] We gently turned the fragments over, searching for the initials or thumbprints frequently impressed in the unfired clay by the potter – to no avail, but at least here was tangible evidence of Roman remains.

The amphora fragments had brought home to us the reality of Roman occupation in the area. It made the legendary presence of Joseph of Arimathea seem somehow more feasible. The arrival here of Jesus Christ, and even the burial of his body hereabouts – two aspects of an enduring legend – could not be completely discounted. But the need to press on brought our thoughts back to the present and to our next goal – Col de l'Espinas, and the spot height of 681.

681

Two kilometres south of Alet-les-Bains, along the valley of the Aude, is the road heading east to Véraza and Terroles. One kilometre further on the road divides, on the right winding southwards to Arques, and on the left – after a hairpin bend – rising to the col at l'Espinas. We had come here to stand on another corner of the cipher square, and hopefully to resolve an intriguing discrepancy. The coded message had contained one number – 681. We now knew this referred to the spot height at the Col de l'Espinas, and therefore to the top right-hand corner of the cipher square. This, combined with the monument at *La Croix*, provided the second corner of the square, determining the orientation and length of the side.

One question bothered us as we climbed the final few metres – the apparent confusion over the height of the pass. The detailed survey maps issued by the I.G.N. before 1994 bore the number clearly given in the coded message. The recent Michelin map, by contrast, fell one metre short, marking the spot height as 680 metres.

The matter was easily resolved, for a sign by a tree named the pass, and gave its spot height as 680 metres (Figure 3.2). No confusion there. But it was unusual to see a sign at all – not all minor passes are marked. Could it be that someone was trying to make a point?

The two principal corners of the square had been visited with rewarding results; and these points, combined with the bearing indicated by the railway line, were actually all that was required to define the whole square. The remaining two points were unlikely to hold any mysteries, as they had quite clearly been outside the control of the code-maker. The relationship of *681* to *La Croix* had required only that the cross be sited at the correct point along the straight section of railway line; the location of the church at Espéraza being a clear case of serendipity. Nevertheless, the church had to be visited.

The high altar is the church's most remarkable feature. Extra-ordinarily elaborate in various costly marbles of different colours, the

FIGURE 3.2 The sign at Col de l'Espinas – clearly indicating a height of 680 m above sea-level.

centrepiece in white is a representation of the Trinity: an equilateral triangle within a swirling cloud (Figure 3.3). Although not unknown in this context, finding such a triangle here nevertheless gave us a *frisson* of excitement.

Col Doux, the PAX of the cipher, is located in mature forest, and as it was only a general indication of the south-east corner of the square, no marker was expected. Nor indeed did we find one; although that is not to say that others will have no more luck searching there. It is, perhaps, for this reason that another starting-point had been indicated in the cipher message – an existing feature which, though not part of the geometry, would provide an indication of the path to be pursued. This is the Devil's Armchair, just across the valley of the River Sals – our next destination.

Our interpretation of the Parchments and their coded messages had hinted at the reason why the devil in Saunière's church was stooping so uncomfortably: his means of support lay over four kilometres away

FIGURE 3.3 The triangle of the Trinity in the church at Espéraza.

in the woods above Henri Boudet's house at Rennes-les-Bains.

It took questions to a local family to find the Devil's Armchair. The hills rising above Rennes-les-Bains are crisscrossed with ancient tracks, and it is difficult to keep one's bearings. When we finally found it we were in for a pleasant surprise. The chair (Figure 3.4) – more of a throne – had been laboriously carved from a boulder, and was about a metre and a half across. We realised that our interpretation of the cipher code and subsequent identification of this stone had been correct, for the armchair looked directly to the PAX of the message – towards Col

FIGURE 3.4 The Devil's Armchair, situated in the woods above
Rennes-les-Bains.

Doux, just visible through a curtain of trees. Closer inspection of the chair revealed, scarcely visible due to wear and lichen, a device carved into each arm. The left arm bore a tilted triangle, and the right arm a combination of a cross and a circle, or parts of a circle. Geometry again!

We sat looking out over Col Doux. We had established the basic geometry necessary to identify the square, the DAEMON GUARDIEN of the treasure, which we believed to hold the secret location at its centre. The intricate nature of this trail of clues had left us without words. The Devil's Armchair was empty for a reason: the Devil was busy in the church at Rennes-le-Château, and was likely to be detained there for some time.

One final practical exercise remained: to visit the centre of the square, where the diagonals of the cipher square intersect on the map – the farmstead called Death.

La Mort

When viewed on the I.G.N. map, the spot appeared remote and lacking any salient feature that might distinguish it from the surrounding countryside. Instead, we used the Cassini map (Figure 2.8 on p. 63) to follow the course of the old King's Highway, now made redundant by modern roads. The old route ran from Luc-sur-Aude eastwards towards Peyrolles, before swinging south to the village of Serres. We set out for the centre of the square armed with an invaluable high-tech aid. The Global Positioning System (G.P.S.) handset, called 'Magellan', is a box of electronic wizardry. Powered by four pen-light batteries and smaller than a standard paperback, it could read out our position to an accuracy of ten metres by receiving signals from satellites orbiting the Earth.

It became clearer with each step that this gadget was about to come into its own. Our surroundings were monotonous: the old King's Highway – a simple dirt road – ran through rolling countryside of low scrub and boulders, and from it we looked southwards over the area in which lay the centre of the cipher square. There was nothing of note to be seen: no cross, or indeed any artificial structure. La Mort, true to its name, seemed devoid of life. We read off the coordinates – northings and eastings – from the map, and switched on Magellan; within seconds the display gave us our present position. The centre of the square lay to the south as predicted, but we were standing too far to the west. We walked on, checking the G.P.S. reading as we went.

Finally, with the grid reference confirmed, we realised we had arrived at the centre of the cipher square. Relief at having got there was tinged by a sense of anticlimax. We were standing on gently sloping, shale-covered ground, the only vegetation the occasional small tree or hardy shrub. Some piles of flat stones, commonly seen in the area, attested to early attempts at land clearance. We had determined the centre of the square with an accuracy undreamt of even ten years ago, but if the treasure were to be found here, one would still be faced with excavating an area with a diameter of ten metres – the accuracy of the G.P.S. Moreover, the lack of confirmatory features on the ground would have made the location impossible to find in times past. On every front the area failed to exhibit the requirements of a good hiding-place for a major treasure, a matter to which we shall return.

Surveyors for the Cassini map had travelled through the area in the mid-eighteenth century, recording the chilling name for the attention of future investigators such as ourselves. According to a local tale, three counterfeiters had been hung from a gibbet in the area, forever leaving their mark on the pages of the first complete and comprehensive atlas of France.

The name La Mort which appeared on the eighteenth-century Cassini map was not used on the next new map of France, the 'État-Major' of the nineteenth century (indeed, no place-name appeared here at all). Nor had it been used on the I.G.N. maps up to 1994, on which the name had become Métairie de Luc. It is quite feasible that the hamlet or farmstead of the eighteenth century had been abandoned in hard times, and the name forgotten. When later reoccupied, it is natural that the name of the nearby town should have been adopted, so it became the Métairie de Luc. There is no reason to see anything sinister in the disappearance of the old name.

But the name's reappearance is another matter. Why should the I.G.N., on the issue of a new 1:50,000 scale map in 1995, reintroduce La Mort? We decided to see if the present owner could shed some light on the matter. When she was asked, it became obvious that the I.G.N. had not consulted her. So would they have referred to the Cassini map for place-names rather than their own previous map? Such a scenario is unlikely. It would appear that someone wishes La Mort to be once more identifiable. And as this association of the now well-publicised 'Dagobert' treasure with La Mort is rather too obvious, perhaps this indicates that someone wishes to draw attention *to* La Mort and thus *away* from the real location of the treasure.

If La Mort were not the end of the treasure-trail, one had to consider the alternative meanings of IL EST LA MORT: perhaps even 'he is there dead or lifeless'. Moreover, we had another line of investigation to pursue which promised greater rewards. However, several questions remained over La Mort's suitability as a site. If the centre of the square marked the site of the 'treasure', the treasure could be anywhere in an area some ten metres across, similar, if not identical, to where we were standing. If the compilers of the coded message had known the exact site, they had left no visible marker or clue to aid us in its uncovering. By virtue of the local landscape, it would also be a difficult site for those 'in the know' to protect. We left the site, empty-handed and still perplexed by what we had seen. If the 'treasure' had been buried at 'La Mort', was it still there? If it was not, who had removed it, what had it consisted of, and where had it been taken?

We descended from the high ground, deep in thought, barely noticing the change from the uncultivated and desolate plateau of La Mort to the rich and fertile lower valley. Hard at work at the hottest time of the day was an elderly woman, back bent as she picked grapes from the vine. She turned, lifting the heavy basket of fruit, and in doing so she saw us. Reaching into the basket she chose two bunches and approached. Her soft words of welcome as she held out this friendly gift thundered in our ears: 'Voilà, messieurs. Pommes bleues?'

Realising she was somewhat puzzled by our reaction to her offer of some grapes, we attempted to relax and enquired about her harvest. She had been left alone to tend the family vineyards, and lamented the absence of her son and daughter seduced by more lucrative employment in the city. This kind and generous soul remained unaware of the true nature of the gift she had given. *Pommes blues*, she confirmed, was the local dialect term for grapes. So could the final part of the cipher message refer to grapes? In which case, what would *à midi* mean? Once again there was a potential Christian connection – the vine and its fruit.

4
ANCIENT SIGNS
AND SECRETS

Squares and pyramids

The '681–*La Croix*' square we had found in the Parchment cipher and spent many hours examining on the ground had confirmed our theory, and in many respects enhanced it. We had found a bizarre cross which cryptically displayed the number seventy-five, a spot height which had inexplicably changed, and some revealing symbols on the empty armchair of the cloven-hoofed character employed by Saunière. But we had considerable doubts about the suitability of La Mort as the ultimate hiding-place. Drawn as we were to the many implications of the name, honesty forced us to admit it had provided few clues. Perhaps the centre of the square was not the answer – perhaps we had overlooked another point on the Parchments where lines converged.

We decided to look again at Parchment 2 to see if there was a hidden geometry, as there had been on Parchment 1. At first sight it is hard to see where to begin, and, indeed, the solving of this part of the puzzle is the hardest to explain. Unlike the first Parchment, where identifying the steps was mainly a matter of logic, here the solution requires a knowledge of some rather esoteric aspects of geometry. The solution was to prove complicated, but was ultimately to show us the way forward. It is worth reinforcing at this point that, had the process of deduction been straightforward, this grandest of secrets would not have stayed secret for so long.

There are many small features to be seen on Parchment 2: dots, small letters, raised letters. Ignore them. Most striking is the arrangement towards the bottom right-hand corner of the Parchment, which separates the main body of the text from the two lowest lines. It is immediately clear that when turned upside-down the letters NOIS will read SION. This text, having yielded the encoded message so laboriously concealed, must now remain inverted for the next phase of decipherment.

Also prominent, but not apparently of great significance, are the asterisk-like symbols above and below the body of the text. Closer examination shows these to consist of small circles with superimposed radial lines: the longer, horizontal and vertical ones dividing the circles into quadrants; the shorter diagonals giving a subdivision into octants. Once again, a geographic intention may be implied if this arrangement represents a compass rose, with the longer lines indicating the cardinal points N, S, E and W, and the shorter ones the intermediate bearings NE, NW, SE and SW. But this is not all that one may infer from these symbols. The geometry of the square, and especially of two squares in a particular configuration, has a significance here.

Two squares and centre-lines are drawn as in Figure 4.1. The smaller square, standing on its corner, is drawn first, then the vertical and horizontal lines joining its corners. We now have a symbol which strongly resembles the 'crossed square' of Saunière's angels. The horizontal line is found to be tangential to the bottoms of the letters on the line with the dropped 'S' (when viewed the right way up), and the vertical line is acknowledged by most of the letters it passes. The larger square, whose vertical sides are defined by the corners of the smaller square and which is justified by the 'quadrant' division of the small circles, is added next. No great claims can be made for the construction at this stage, but it is a start. And we do have our reasons.

The arrangement of a small square diagonally placed within a larger

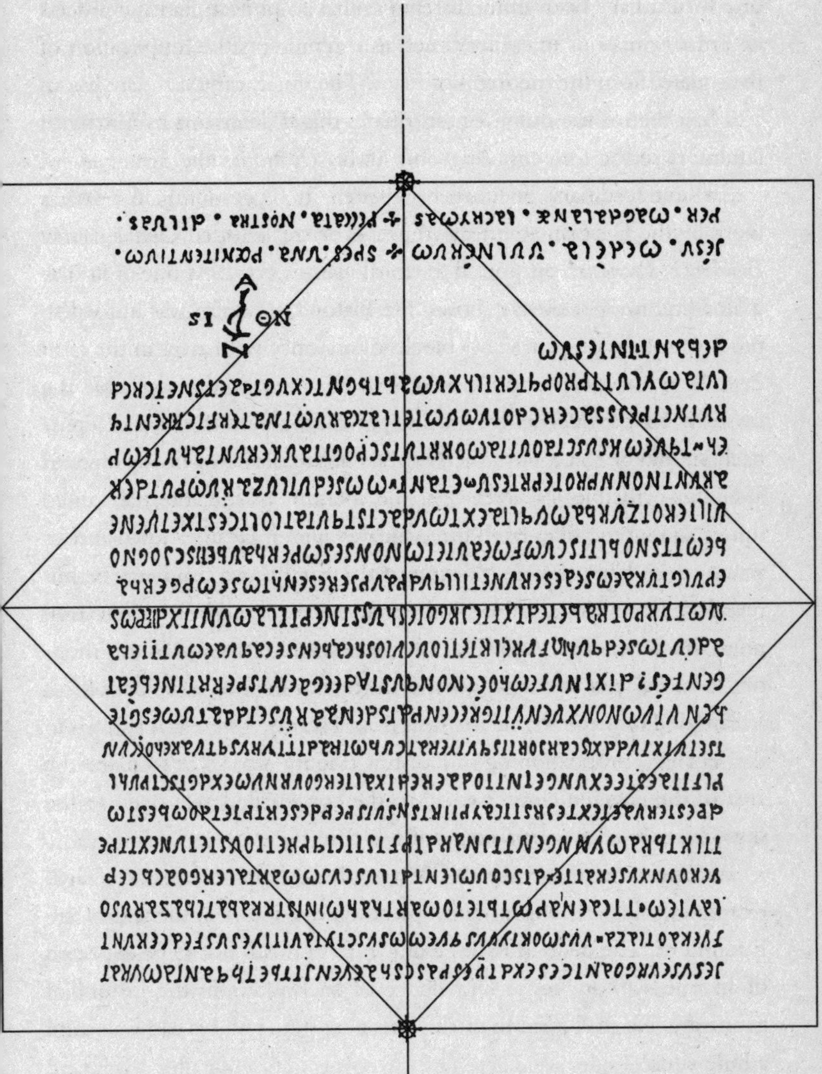

FIGURE 4.1 Construction of two squares and centre-lines on Parchment 2.

one would have been immediately familiar to philosophers, architects and master masons in earlier times, as it represents the 'duplication of the square' from the theorems of Plato. The inner, canted square has an area half that of the outer, larger square; this is described by Vitruvius (architect to the Emperor Augustus) in his *De architectura*.

An 'extraordinary document'[1] printed in Regensburg in 1486, a work by the German architect Wenzel Roritzer entitled *On the Correct Building of Pinnacles*, purported to reveal *masonic secrets*. As one of its diagrams (Figure 4.2) clearly shows, the Platonic theorem was utilised to produce square (in plan view) blocks of masonry with areas in the ratio 2 : 1. Why this proportion should have been regarded as desirable is a mystery. That the decorative features protruding from the sides of a pinnacle should be so proportioned appears not to derive from any obvious aesthetic principle. Nevertheless, the rotation of the internal canted square so that the sides of all three squares align is clearly shown and, as will be seen later, the *occult* origin of the Parchment geometry is thus revealed. Knowledge of Plato's theorem is not enough: its application must also be known. Another early illustration of the use of this theorem is to be seen in the wonderful thirteenth-century sketchbook[2] of Villard de Honnecourt, an architect from Picardy, where it is applied to the 'correct' proportioning of cloisters (Figure 4.3) so as to make the area of the covered cloister equal to the colonnaded area open to the sky. This may seem surprising, but it is true.

Turning now to the 'SION' device, the 'A' attracts attention. It is extremely wide and drawn with a precision that is rare in the text of this Parchment. The deduction to be drawn from this is not to be expected of anyone without some knowledge of backwaters in the history of geometry. We shall need to qualify this next step, but this can wait until a little later.

The 'A' may be identified as the apex of a triangle – but not just any triangle. It is the apex of the Great Pyramid. We are all too aware that mention of the Great Pyramid will send many running from what they expect to be yet another exercise in fanciful, pseudo-archaeological

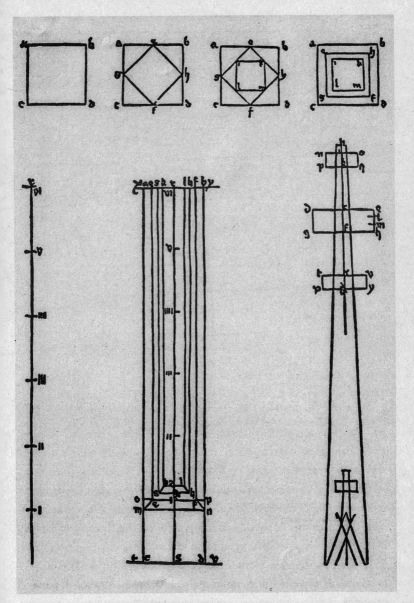

FIGURE 4.2 Diagram from Wenzel Roritzer's *On the Correct Building of Pinnacles* (1486), showing the role of Plato's canted squares.

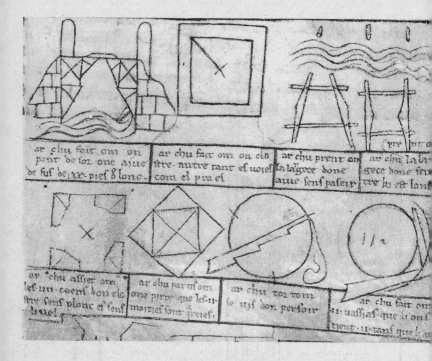

FIGURE 4.3 A page from the sketchbook of Villard de Honnecourt (thirteenth century), showing how Plato's canted squares are used to determine the proportions of cloisters.

number-juggling. We can but crave indulgence, with the promise that it will not be regretted.

As may be seen, the left-hand side of the 'A' extended downwards meets the side of the large square at its centre (Figure 4.4a). Our geometric background allowed us to recognise immediately the association of the *plan* view of the pyramid with its *elevation* (Figure 4.4b). Extending the left-hand side upwards to meet the centre-line of the large square, and then drawing in the right-hand side of the pyramid, provides highly satisfactory confirmation: the line is found to pass through the large 'N' and the small 'n' ringed in Figure 4.4a. The

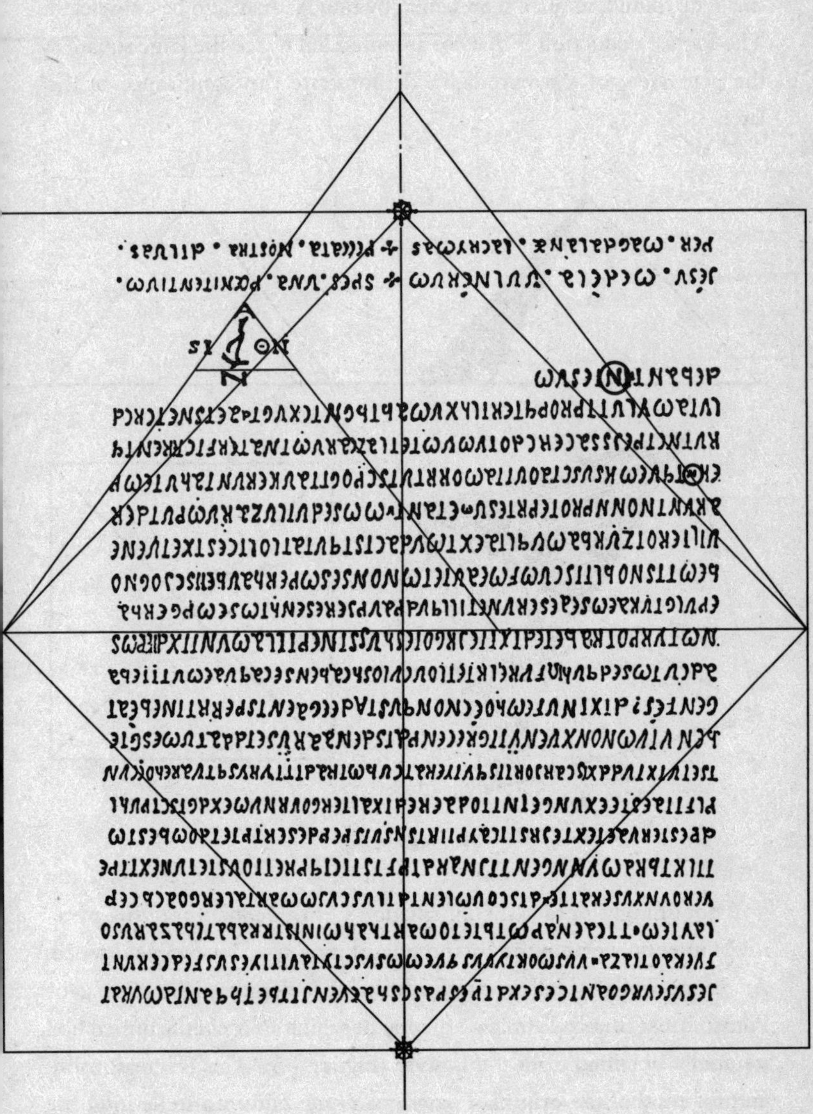

FIGURE 4.4 (a) Parchment 2 geometry derived from (b) elevation and plan views of the Great Pyramid.

smaller pyramid, its apex represented by the 'A', may also be completed. The logical deduction is that we are intended to see the large square as the plan view of a pyramid; we demonstrate the significance of this later.

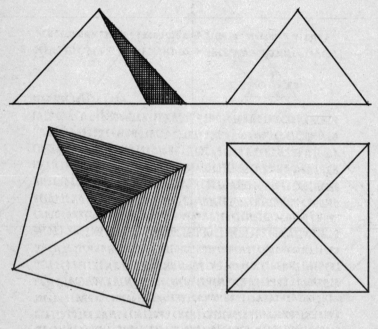

FIGURE 4.4 (b)

Astonishingly, potential confirmation of this deduction of the pyramidal intention within the Parchment solution was already in existence. At Shugborough Hall in Staffordshire is a depiction in marble of Poussin's *Les Bergers d'Arcadie* – a copy of which Bérenger Saunière had reputedly obtained from the Louvre (Figure 4.5). This is a reasonably faithful copy of the original Poussin painting, but with some interesting amendments. Most obvious of these is the mirror-reversal of the image. This should not be regarded as implying an occult significance. Engravings are more often than not reversals of the original, since the

FIGURE 4.5 The marble 'Shepherds' monument at Shugborough Hall, in Staffordshire.

process of taking the print from the block reverses it. When the intention is to make prints that are not reversed, the engraver must engrave the block as a mirror-reversal of the original. Clearly, the sculptor of the Shugborough bas-relief had to work from an engraving; the original Poussin has always been in the national collection of the Louvre since leaving the French royal collection.

But some details of the original painting have been altered. To the top of Poussin's tomb has been added another ogee-sided sarcophagus, surmounted by a pyramid! Subtle alterations to the figures may also be noted. Particularly revealing is the alteration to the hand of the kneeling shepherd. In reversing the image one thing that could not be reversed was, of course, the inscription, so the kneeling shepherd still points to the first line of the inscription with his forefinger (which has actually been broken off), but the angle of his thumb has been changed slightly. Why should this be? So that he may still point to the same part of the phrase – ET IN ARCADIA EGO – as in the painting; namely, to the letters ARCA, but now with his thumb. Collectively, these alterations focus on the idea of a tomb: ARCA is to be read as an independent word, and ARCA is Latin for 'tomb'.

The inscription below the tableau has never been deciphered.[3] Many more questions would be raised by the works of Poussin, and are dealt with in subsequent chapters, but for now we had some support for the pyramidal intention in the Parchments.

If the centre of the 'pyramid square' marks the location of the treasure, or, in the words of the cliché, 'X marks the spot', then we had been right to head for 'La Mort' – the centre of the '681–La Croix' square. But La Mort had seemed an unlikely site for the ultimate hiding-place, so perhaps the Parchments held further clues as to the correct way to proceed.

A key to the mystery: a 1½° deliberate error

At this time we had no reason to be sure that the two Parchments were truly related. Certainly there is their simultaneous public appearance and a certain similarity of style, but it has been stated that they are copies of the originals, and if so the similarity might stem from the common hand of the copyist. If Parchment 2 is to relate in a meaningful, geometric, way to Parchment 1, they have to have at least one feature in common.

Searching Parchment 2 for such a feature was a painstaking process, but eventually it yielded the line shown dashed on the right-hand side of Figure 4.6, defined by the features ringed and the shaded 'O's. Once again, 'O's are prominent. In addition, the letters on every line of the text reflect the passing of this line in some way, often having one feature tangential to the line; in many cases this applies to adjacent letters on either side of the line. Another feature which drew our attention to this line was the similar inclinations of the lines passing through the 'm over I' symbols in Parchment 1. Careful measurement of this angle revealed that it is almost identical to the angle on the first Parchment, and is 7½°.

Provision has been made for a small angular correction in Parchment 2. There are two '+' symbols approximately at the centres of the last two lines of the manuscript, between the words *lacrymas* and *peccata*, and between *vulnerum* and *spes*. A line drawn through the centre-point of the large square and through these symbols produces an angle to the centre-line of the square of 1½°. This recognition of an angular discrepancy is of the utmost importance, as will be seen later, but in order to make the process clearer we shall pre-empt the revelation and reveal the role of the 1½°.

As we saw, in Parchment 1 the side of the triangle is at 45° + 1½° to the Meridian and the dashed line is at 7½° to the Meridian. In Parchment 2 the dashed line is at 7½° to the square's centre-line, but has

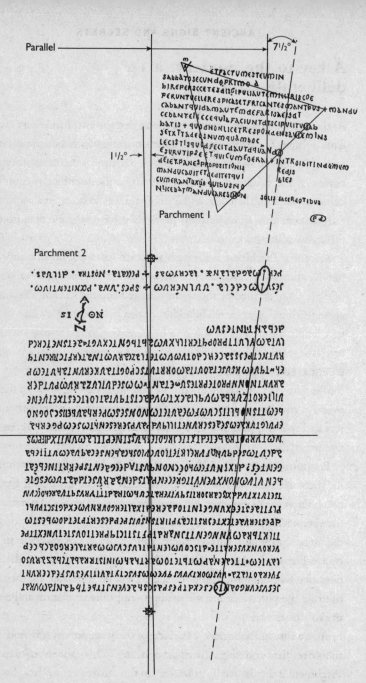

FIGURE 4.6 Angles on Parchments 1 and 2 compared: angles of 7½° and 1½° emerge.

the 1½° indicated by the line through the '+'s. The triangular geometry on the one and the square geometry on the other are to be rotated through an angle of 1½°. (As we shall see, further indications that this is the correct assumption are to be found in the most surprising places.) This is to be the final key – or, if misunderstood, the stumbling-block – to the correct completion of the puzzle. It also proves to be a test of honesty, for if one were to deliberately ignore it and subtly adjust the geometry to suit, there would be no final revelation.

Although a clear relationship between the two Parchments is indicated, it has to be appreciated that this relationship is one of *orientation*, and not of scale or position. In other words, we now suspect how the two Parchments are meant to be aligned one with the other, but not in any way how linear measurements may be correlated. For this, some other feature would be required.

Exploratory geometry

What other correspondence could there be between Parchment 1 and Parchment 2? In Parchment 1 we have identified an equilateral triangle, tilted such that one of its sides makes an angle of 45° with the Meridian (when corrected). In Parchment 2, we have the smaller of the two squares orientated such that its sides are at an angle of 45° to the vertical and horizontal. So let us see whether the two diagrams are intended to be superimposed.

We have no knowledge of the relative scales of the diagrams in the two Parchments, so let us therefore make the simplest possible assumption: that the smaller square (and for that matter the large one too) and the equilateral triangle are to have the same centre; also, that the side of the square and the side of the triangle, which are at 45°, are to be brought into coincidence. This apparently vague assumption was found to yield a clear and surprising result. This can be followed in Figure 4.7.

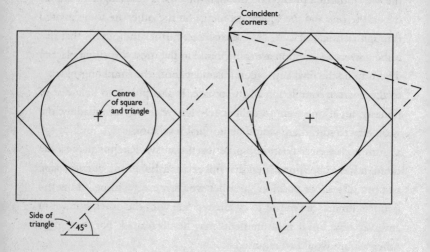

FIGURE 4.7 Plato's canted squares and the equilateral triangle.

The first step in constructing the equilateral triangle is to draw a circle such that the sides of the smaller square, and also the sides of the equilateral triangle, are tangential to it. When the triangle is completed one corner is found to fall on the corner of the large square. This is neither coincidental nor forced, and may be rigorously proved using the theorems of Euclidian geometry (the logical deduction of the relationships of geometric figures, lines and angles, as studied at school until quite recently by most people). Once seen, it is obvious – like many an obscure fact – but it did come as a surprise.

This provides a potential insight into the philosophy of the code-maker. An obscure geometric construction may have been used as the key to further comprehension. We have had to wrench this from the Parchments; others who were, and are, initiated – *sacerdotal* – would not have this difficulty. Parchment 1 had been quite clear on this point. It is only for the initiated – *solis sacerdotibus*.

The hexagram or 'Seal of Solomon'

It is, naturally, possible to draw the complementary equilateral triangle using the same construction, but based on the opposite side of the square, and so produce the figure called a hexagram. There are two reasons for illustrating this. The symbol appears in one of the Priory Documents – those mysterious documents, alluded to earlier, which were deposited in the Bibliothèque Nationale around the time of the appearance of de Sède's book. This particular document refers to the shepherds in *Les Bergers d'Arcadie* by Nicolas Poussin as gazing upon a hexagram (see Appendix D). It is a curious reference since the hexagram does not appear in the actual painting, but here at least is a second, more specific reference to Poussin.

More importantly, the hexagram appears in the identical association with the square in Giordano Bruno's book *De triplici minimo et mensura* of 1591 (Figure 4.8). (We had been quite unaware of the existence of this geometry in Bruno's work when we derived this figure from Parchment 2.) The treatment of Bruno at the hands of the Holy Inquisition and his ultimate fate followed the pattern meted out to other free-thinkers of his time. Condemned as a heretic because of his unconventional philosophy, he was burnt at the stake in Rome in 1600. Bruno, during his many travels, had come into contact with other like-minded individuals of his time, including several eminent figures later involved in the Rosicrucian revival.[4] Even more of a surprise was the discovery of an isolated equilateral triangle used by Bruno as the endplate to *De triplici* (Figure 4.9). The surprise comes from the angle at which this triangle is presented to the reader – it has sides inclined at 45° and 75° to the bottom edge of the page. This was to be our first indication that the tilted triangle is to be found elsewhere than in the Parchments, and that it has an occult significance in its own right. Emerging from each side of the triangle in Bruno's endplate is a serpentine form. Frances Yates thought that these might represent spirits.[5] To us, they looked like the tendrils of a vine.

FIGURE 4.8 The hexagram and Plato's canted squares, as
depicted in Giordano Bruno's *De triplici minimo et mensura*
(1591). The smaller square is almost hidden by the hexagon,
but two of its corners are just visible.

Having had our interest stimulated by the symbolism of Giordano
Bruno, we decided to investigate other sources. According to one of
the Priory Documents, the Priory of Sion had been an organisation at
one time associated with the Templars.[6] In the purported list of Grand
Masters of the Priory, compiled in the twentieth century by a 'Henri
Lobineau', one name stands out: Leonardo da Vinci. So we took a
look – with new eyes, we hoped – at all of his published work in the
hope of finding something revealing. Among the considerable number of his drawings in the collection of Her Majesty the Queen at
Windsor is a page of doodles including a geometric construction
(Figure 4.10). Starting with three circles of equal diameter, Leonardo

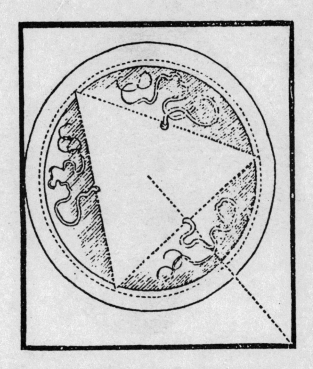

FIGURE 4.9 The tilted equilateral triangle, drawn by Giordano Bruno as the endplate to *De triplici minimo et mensura*.

has proceeded to execute a construction culminating with an equilateral triangle tilted at 45°. In fact, the great man made an error and joined the wrong points right at the end, producing a triangle which just fails to be equilateral. (In Figure 4.10 the equilateral triangle is highlighted; the original is feint.) His apparent interest in the tilted triangle was intriguing, but not informative. The significance eluded us at the time, and we could not know that the three circles were to appear again, but next time with an intimate connection with Rennes-le-Château.

Before leaving this relationship of square and triangle for the moment, we should note that the hexagram or 'Seal of Solomon' is not

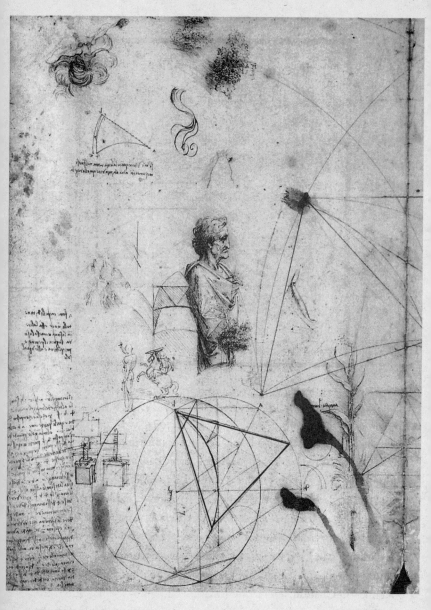

FIGURE 4.10 The tilted equilateral triangle, as it appears in a page from the sketchbooks of Leonardo da Vinci.

the end-point of this sequence of geometric construction. Triangles have been drawn based on two opposite sides of the smaller square. As there are four sides to a square, two further triangles may be drawn, giving a twelve-pointed star called a dodecagram.

Interesting though this discovery of occult symbols may be, it has not apparently advanced our knowledge of the purpose of the map. The large and small squares and the equilateral triangle all have the same centre-point. This would represent overkill if intended only to reinforce the identity of this point.

The reference to 'Sion' in the concealed message A DAGOBERT II ROI ET A SION EST CE TRESOR ET IL EST LA MORT could, as previously discussed, mean 'at Sion', and the 'SION' below the apex of the small pyramid triangle could be suggesting that the treasure is below the apex of a pyramid. Seen in plan-view, this would, of course, also be at the centre of the squares and triangle, shown previously in Figure 4.7. Clearly something is still missing, and no amount of further study of the Parchment diagrams will reveal it. Further progress is achieved with help from two further quarters: from the coded message contained within Parchment 2, as explained earlier, and from the works of the artist David Teniers the Younger. According to the cipher message, the square (perhaps we should say *a* square) is to be rotated through 15° so that its upper side makes an angle of 15° with the horizontal – with the east–west axis, or line of latitude. Intuitively it is probable that the rotation is to take place about the top-left, north-western corner since this is a point of coincidence of the original triangle and square. But it might equally have to be done about the centre – or, for that matter, an apparently arbitrary point.

It will be necessary here to pre-empt our explanation of the mapwork in order to avoid excessive complication and confusion, and say that the composer of Parchment 2 did have in mind a rotation about the north-west corner. Independent confirmation of this is forthcoming. So, we could say that the square has been rotated about its top left-hand corner to lie with its upper side superimposed on that of the equilateral triangle (Figure 4.11). Presumably, it must also be possible to deduce this transposition by means other than reference to the coded message, and if 'Poussin Teniers hold the key', this must have been possible prior to the existence of the features utilised in the code. It was to the work of these artists that we now turned, and once again the Abbé Saunière was to enter the picture.

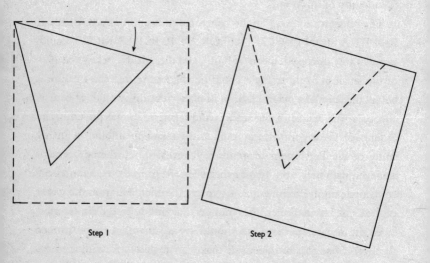

Step 1   Step 2

FIGURE 4.11 Triangle and square – the square gets its tilt from a rotation through 15° about its north-west corner.

5

THE PRIEST
AND THE
PAINTINGS

If Bérenger Saunière *did* first discover the parchments in 1886, then several years were to pass before they left the area of Rennes-le-Château. Legend has it that Saunière approached his bishop, Billard, with his findings (whether prompted by others or his own conscience is a matter for conjecture), and found himself directed north to the spiritual head-office of St Sulpice in Paris, where the parchments were handed over to church scholars. These mysterious documents thus elevated the priest into Parisian circles far removed from the rural atmosphere of the Languedoc. Much has been made of the various affiliations he made at this time – both business and romantic – but suffice it to say that he ended up in some surprising company for a man of the cloth.

Saunière's visit to Paris is but one of the priest's many disputed actions at this time. While it is impossible to trace every movement of a single priest visiting the capital city of France over a century ago, evidence does exist of his trip to the city during March 1892, and the register of masses at the church of St Sulpice confirms his presence.[1] When we visited the church itself, its sombre air certainly made it appear an eminently appropriate destination for a country priest.

Not so the company of one Joseph (Joséphin) Péladan, whom Saunière is also alleged to have visited. Péladan had created his own order of the 'Rose-Cross of the Temple and the Grail' in Paris in the spring of 1890. We had studied the original publications issued by Péladan and had been unimpressed by the propaganda they promoted. Péladan had strayed from the path of logic and created a society which clutched at every esoteric straw in the wind. The more we read, the more unlikely it seemed to us that Saunière would have had anything to do with such a shady organisation. That said, it is perhaps through Péladan's circle of friends that Saunière met the famous singer Emma Calvé, a story which does have a basis in reality. If so, Saunière had certainly stepped into a different and altogether new society, remote from his priestly origins. Calvé was to visit Saunière at Rennes, recipient no doubt of the lavish hospitality that accompanied his programme of construction, evidence of which can be seen in the receipts for fine goods preserved today in the museum of Rennes-le-Château.

However, it is his visit to the city's most famous art gallery that appeared to us the most curious of his reputed Parisian activities. For he is alleged to have gone to the Louvre with a purpose. He had apparently been instructed to obtain copies of the following paintings: *Les Bergers d'Arcadie* by Nicolas Poussin; *St Antony Hermit* by David Teniers; and a portrait of Pope Celestine V, artist unspecified.

If this information is correct, why did Saunière go to the trouble of purchasing copies of three paintings, only one of which was popularly known, the second obscure, and the third positively unknown? What did he intend to do with them? The paintings, we suspected, must have a common denominator, related in some way to the knowledge gleaned from the Parchments. If Saunière had supplied St Sulpice with a solution to the Parchments, had someone known that there was a mystery contained in certain paintings held in the Louvre, and informed him of the fact? If Saunière did return to Rennes with the copies, they have not since re-surfaced. Despite the many questions raised by the story, the presence of Poussin on Saunière's list – an artist who had already provided important clues to the pyramidal intention within the Parchments – indicated that this line of enquiry might well be worth pursuing.

As we delved deeper into the paintings in question, a very familiar set of geometric features emerged. Before we explain the exact nature of those discoveries, it is worth putting the use of subliminal ingredients in art into a wider context. More specifically, should we be surprised to see a painting with a geometric composition? In general terms the answer to this is no; in the singular manner we found, most certainly yes. But let us start with the general scenario.

From the moment our ancestors progressed from painting on the walls of caves to scratching images on fragments of bone, it was inevitable that portable, two-dimensional art would be here to stay. Later, having developed a taste for two-dimensional, or plane geometry – found to induce in the human psyche a great sense of order, of being in control – it was inevitable that paintings should be delineated and 'framed' by geometric forms. Thus paintings became rectangular, or occasionally circular. When paintings started to be executed on canvas stretched over a wooden frame, shapes other than rectangular would have become problematic. As a result, the rectangle became the most popular format.

If the outline of a picture were to be dominated by geometry, why not the subject? It seems that a subconscious acknowledgement of this must have preceded any conscious, intellectual response. It will have become evident to the early painters that, for example, the subject of a portrait should not be situated to the left of the canvas if looking to the left. More significantly, it became conventional for artists to seek a harmonious arrangement by balancing the elements of a composition. This was initially achieved by trial and error, but it came to be appreciated that rules could be devised to govern such matters, and that plane geometry would be the means to that end. Paramount in such matters would be the Golden Mean (for an explanation of which see Appendix E). The universal efforts to geometrise the natural world are epitomised in Leonardo da Vinci's diagram of a man within a square and a circle. Such efforts are legitimate, because, within the extraordinary variations to be observed in the human form, a norm may be devised and subtly adjusted to ensure conformity with the *geometric* ideal.

Just as geometry progressed into extremes of cerebral activity, as discussed earlier, the composition of paintings would also come to exploit greater geometric complexity. There have been many studies of this, one of the most detailed being by Charles Funck-Hellet.[2] (A selection of his analytical diagrams are shown in Appendix F; the predominance of polygrams and polygons, both singly and in combination, is immediately evident.) After the sixteenth century the obsession with complex geometry in works of art would wane, but, as we were beginning to discover, it would not be forgotten in the twilight world of one esoteric group.

If the influence of geometry on the composition of paintings is for the most part discreet, only the harmony of composition proclaiming its presence, the opposite may be said of symbolism in art. Visible symbolic elements in a painting communicate directly with the viewer. They may be overt, or subtle; they act as a kind of shorthand, conveying a wealth of meaning with the minimum of fuss.

Arising out of clear associations, such symbols may stand alone to represent the item, or person, or concept from which they derive. For example, because of the legend that St Jerome plucked a thorn from a lion's paw, one may always identify that particular saint by the lion that follows him everywhere. One may even deduce an allusion to St Jerome if a lion is present without him – presumably pining for his saint. It is in this manner that such symbols as the lily for purity, or the shell for a pilgrim, have become established. But symbols may not always be within the public domain. A carnation held between finger and thumb, the arrangement of the sitter's fingers in a portrait – such motifs may convey nothing to us, but may carry great meaning for the *cognoscenti*.

We shall see how superficially innocent elements in a painting may conceal an occult symbolism, and indeed an occult geometry. But let us return to the subject which prompted this – Abbé Saunière's acquisition of three paintings.

Poussin and Teniers

The two painters, Nicolas Poussin (1593–1665) and David Teniers (whether father or son was not clear), had been implicated in the decoded cipher message of Parchment 2: we were told that 'Poussin Teniers hold the key'. Without the assistance of the aforementioned 'Priory of Sion', via its mouthpiece, Gérard de Sède, it would not have been clear how these artists were involved, or which of their paintings were relevant. However, de Sède's book *L'Or de Rennes* made it clear that the relevant paintings are those referred to above.

As there are several paintings of St Antony, including many depictions of the Temptation of St Antony, by David Teniers the Younger, it had not been possible to discover which of them might be the relevant painting. We could find no reference to *any* Temptation of St Antony by David Teniers Senior, so we concentrated on the work of his son, whose life spanned the years 1610–94.

De Sède had apparently insisted, in discussion with Lincoln, that the relevant painting was *The Temptation of St Antony*, rather than the vague *St Antony Hermit*. But *St Antony and St Paul in the Desert* is the only painting by Teniers to show St Antony *not* being tempted, so it might be relevant in view of the 'no temptation' reference in the cipher message. However, this would appear to be an irrelevant speculation, since de Sède was insisting that the painting was called *The Temptation of St Antony*, and he was getting his information from the Priory of Sion (in fact, as it transpires, from Pierre Plantard and Philippe de Cherisey, the two principal players in the twentieth-century revival of the Priory of Sion). Either the informant knew the truth, or he knew nothing, one would have thought. In any case, the painting *St Antony and St Paul* was said to have been lost, and did not appear in catalogues until the 1990s.

It is possibly significant that the vague title to which de Sède originally referred was *St Antony Hermit*, which could have referred to any painting of St Antony. That he subsequently said that it is a Temptation of St Antony suggests very strongly that he, and probably his collaborators also, were ignorant of the painting's true identity. No one had succeeded in identifying and illustrating this painting, and no one had tracked down the portrait of Pope Celestine. However, our initial studies of the Poussin were to lead us to hope for greater success with the other two.

The Poussin painting of the Arcadian shepherds, or, as we shall refer to it henceforth, *Les Bergers d'Arcadie II*, to be found in the Louvre (Plate 2), was painted between 1638 and 1640 but was not the artist's first on the theme. An earlier painting completed around 1630, sometimes referred to as *Et in Arcadia ego*, but which we shall call *Les Bergers d'Arcadie I* (Plate 4), is significantly different in composition from the second. It incorporates in the foreground the river-god Alpheus representing the source of Arcadia's underground stream, which is to be seen cascading from the vessel he holds in his left hand. The later painting has three shepherds accompanied by an enigmatic woman. The river-god is omitted; at the base of the rock on which one shepherd rests his foot is a shallow dry channel, as if the spring had dried up.

The role played by the woman in the two paintings is quite different. The earlier painting has her more involved in the shepherds' discovery of an inscription. With a breast exposed and her dress raised to show her thigh, she is much more the classical nymph. In the later painting her dress is modest and she has an air of serenity, resignation – knowledge, perhaps; her only gesture of intimate involvement with the shepherds is to rest her right hand on the shoulder of one of them. In the later painting the shepherds are seeing for the first time the inscription, if not the whole tomb; but the woman is apparently already aware not only of the inscription's existence but also of its meaning. There has been a change in emphasis between the two versions. One is inclined to deduce that Poussin was inspired to paint the new version in order to convey a depth of meaning not present in the previous one. Our later discoveries would lead us to consider that it was the artist himself who had undergone further enlightenment during the intervening period, and oblige us to present an analysis of these two paintings which conflicts dramatically with the many that have gone before.

In *Les Bergers d'Arcadie I* an ogee-sided monument bears the inscription. Tombs were represented in this way according to a convention, widely used in esoteric paintings of the sixteenth and seventeenth centuries.[3] Furthermore, this may be a very *specific* tomb, but we shall investigate that later. The tomb, projecting from the rugged face of a natural outcrop of rock, has apparently not been seen before by the shepherds and their female companion, who appear to be in the act of deciphering the inscription. The group look on as their bearded colleague traces the time-worn letters with his index finger. This logical image is, however, undermined by the curious position of the inscription. One would expect a degree of symmetry on such a formal edifice. But no, the words are so bunched up at the right of the tomb that EGO is forced on to a second line. Arguably, this arrangement suits the composition of the painting, and ensures that the inscription is legible. But it is hard to imagine that a painter as meticulous as Poussin would have found no alternative had he wished. The arrangement is intentional and ensures the viewer's recognition of an esoteric concept. Indeed, we may go so far as to say that, to the *cognoscenti*, the entire symbolism of the painting would have been, and still is, instantly recognisable.

Les Bergers d'Arcadie II discards the formal tomb for a rather plain block of masonry. The location of the inscription is, in this painting, somewhat improved.

The famous inscription ET IN ARCADIA EGO is enigmatic since it does not contain a verb. Some commentators add a line of dashes after the phrase, implying an unknown completion of the sentence. However, no such dashes appear in either of the Poussin paintings; and in a painting by Il Guercino, *Et in Arcadia ego* (*c.* 1618) – the first painting in which the phrase is known to occur – there is no room for any dashes, since the phrase is abruptly cut off by the right-hand margin of the painting, with the 'O' of EGO just visible (Plate 3). A continuation of the sentence, *out of view*, is thus perfectly feasible.

Some would have it that the phrase stands perfectly well as it is, citing other Latin phrases that omit the verb – 'Et tu, Brute!' for example. But there is clearly a world of difference between the two. Julius Caesar's exclamation stands equally well in direct translation without a verb – 'And you, Brutus!' Indeed, it is hard to imagine a suitable alternative phrase *with* a verb. The proof of this is to be seen in every translation of 'Et in Arcadia ego'. A verb is always introduced: 'I *am* also in Arcadia', 'I too *was* in Arcadia'; not 'And in Arcadia I', 'And I in Arcadia'.

Without the dashes, the phrase suggests that it may be an anagram. An interesting suggestion was made by a viewer of the television series made by Henry Lincoln. This viewer, who is quoted but not named in *The Holy Blood and the Holy Grail*, suggested:

I TEGO ARCANA DEI

This may be translated as: 'Begone! I conceal the secrets of God' (the 'I' of the anagram being the imperative singular of the verb EO, and therefore meaning 'go' or, more elegantly, 'begone').

This ingenious anagram is interesting in that it suggests that the inscription indicates the contents of the tomb. This is, of course, what one would expect of such an inscription. However, when the arrangements of the words ET IN ARCADIA EGO are examined in the three paintings, it is clear that this is not the intention. In any case, it seems illogical for a monument to bear an inscription that instructs the observer to go away. Monuments, including tombstones, are intended to be observed, even to attract attention.

In the Guercino, the inscription faces away from the shepherds, and the stonework on which it is to be found is not obviously a tomb; indeed, it is simply the end of a stone wall, the higher part of the wall on the right confirming this. The presence of the skull, which is turned towards the viewer, provides the association with death, and it is the skull that appears to address the viewer with the words of the inscription.[4] The earlier Poussin also incorporates a skull, but this time placed on top of a monument which is clearly a tomb. If Poussin based this painting on the Guercino (and he certainly had opportunity to see it), it is clear that Poussin understood the symbolism. It seems probable also that he understood the esoteric meaning of the phrase, in view of his strange placing of the inscription.

If the phrase's meaning is to be found in the words as they stand and not from any implied continuation to form an intelligible sentence, then the most likely means of concealing this message would be in the form of a code. The simplest form of code is, of course, the anagram.

It may be that the anagram is suggested by the *sound* of the words; this is frequently the origin – the core idea of the anagram is a *homophone*. It is not too difficult to imagine how Arca-*dia* (*arcar-deear* – the contemporary pronunciation, not the modern one) could be identified with the sound of Arca *Dei* (*arcar-dayee*), thus suggesting an anagram. Arca Dei would mean 'Ark of God' or, as it is more commonly referred to, the Ark of the Covenant. Could this have any connection with the town of Arques, which lies not far from Rennes-le-Château? We have already commented on the adjustment in the Shugborough Hall monument to ensure that the bearded shepherd still points to ARCA (DIA), in spite of the reversal of the image compared with the painting. This, combined with the quite excessive emphasis of the idea of 'tomb' by superimposing the pyramid and ogee sarcophagus, convinces us that we are to interpret ARCA as 'tomb'; this would be another legitimate translation of the word. So, two possibilities.

Could the mystery, the treasure, be the Ark of the Covenant? A wild idea perhaps, but Pierre Plantard (who will be seen to have played a significant role) had claimed that the treasure of the Temple of Jerusalem – including the menorah, the seven-branched candelabrum – is in the keeping of the Priory of Sion, to be returned to Israel at the appropriate moment![5] The Roman legions under the command of Titus had looted the Temple of Jerusalem. Bas-reliefs depicting the 'triumph' clearly show objects which could have come only from the Temple; perhaps the Ark was among them. Not very likely, perhaps – it would undoubtedly have elicited some comment, particularly if it had performed for the Romans as it was said to have done for the Jews. But in fact the Ark had disappeared without trace long before this, at some time after the tenth century BC. The Old Testament becomes strangely silent on the subject, the Ark having figured constantly as the talisman of the Israelites, ensuring them victory over all their enemies. The deduction can only be that it was no longer in their possession,[6] so it was certainly not in the Temple when looted by Titus.

As for the 'Temple' treasure, we think that Plantard was having a joke – rather a meaningful one, as it happens – at the expense of everyone. But it would appear that another comment made by Plantard was in earnest. When his family coat of arms had been illustrated in *The Holy Blood and the Holy Grail*, he was to complain that the motto had not been correctly reproduced; that after 'Et in Arcadia ego' – for that he claims is his motto – there should have been a series of dashes. This clearly implies a continuation of the enigmatic phrase. He was, apparently, quite agitated about this.[7]

The Arcadian rebus

But what could one make of the alternative translation? That is 'Arca Dei', meaning 'the tomb of God'. We had already come across the legend that Jesus lies buried in the locality of Rennes-le-Château – not that we had given any credence to it. But if that is what some people believe, then, in the context of interpreting the inscription, it should not be dismissed out of hand. With that in mind, it was an amusing exercise to try to make anagrams out of the letters, but with ARCA DEI as the core; but we found it impossible to form grammatically correct Latin phrases. ARCA is inevitably the direct object of the verb, and should thus be in the accusative case, which is ARCAM. However, the process stimulated a thought process which led to another possibility.

If the phrase ET IN ARCADIA EGO is to be continued to make it meaningful, and several more words are required, there would be no possibility of deducing what these might be. But what if the trick is to complete it in the shortest possible way to make it grammatical, not only with the smallest number of words, but also with the smallest number of letters? And what was it that Pierre Plantard actually had to say about dashes after his family motto? He was specific – there are three dashes!

The solution is quite clear now. There is only one word missing, and this word has only three letters. The word is SUM. Panofsky, in his analysis of the grammar of the phrase 'Et in Arcadia ego', has no doubts that the missing verb is SUM – the present tense, not the past.[8]

Prefixing SUM, which on its own means 'I am', with EGO emphasises the 'I'. So, the phrase may now be read as something along these lines: 'I am also in Arcadia', 'I am even in Arcadia' or 'I am, moreover, in Arcadia'. Death is also to be found in Paradise; or, in the midst of earthly delights, the transience of life cannot be disregarded. Some commentators have been more adventurous with the grammar in the absence of a verb; for example, Christopher Wright has it as: 'And I too was in Paradise',[9] but this just misses the mark on both grammatical and philosophical grounds.

So the phrase is:

ET IN ARCADIA EGO SUM

Now, this may not appear to add much to our knowledge, but if an anagram is still the intention, we now have an M for ARCAM. The outcome of this deductive process will cause a shock of recognition, a leap of the imagination; for it will underline a concept that gradually evolves in parallel with our investigation of all the evidence – the route to the great Secret – and will suggest the nature of the Secret itself.

But we are in danger of running before we can walk, and there are signposts on our route that must be noted along the way.

Shepherds obscured

Poussin had provided some tantalising glimpses, but these had all been viewed on a small scale, from pictures in books. Having solved the Parchments (as far as we could judge), it was imperative to examine the other paintings referred to by de Sède, to see what further light they might shed on the mystery. No one, so far, had traced the portrait of Pope Celestine V. No one had decided which painting by Teniers was correct, or, if it was a Temptation of St Antony, which of the many. If Saunière had obtained this from the Louvre and it was one of those in the Louvre, the number of possibilities would be reduced to two. As for *Les Bergers d'Arcadie II*, there were no doubts or ambiguities: the painting hung in the Louvre, from where a copy was readily obtainable.

Lincoln had asked Professor Christopher Cornford of the Royal College of Art to analyse the geometry underlying the painting's composition; the result is shown in Figure 5.1. Cornford derived a pentagonal layout in which the Golden Mean is inherent. The layout echoes the overall proportions of the rectangular painting (a matter to which we shall have occasion to return). Unnoticed by Lincoln or Cornford (or not commented upon) is the apparent relationship between the lower left side of Cornford's pentagon and the staff held by the second shepherd from the left: they are parallel. This might have sparked some interest, one would have thought, since the implication is that the staff is itself part of the pentagonal layout. There is always the problem in working from photographs in books that they have invariably been cropped, removing some of the painting; we have checked this on a complete illustration. The proportions do not exactly fit Cornford's diagram: the angle of the diagonal is nearer 35° than 36°, as it should be, but this may be considered satisfactory as there may have been some distortion of the canvas and frame over three hundred years. However, the pentagon does require to be distorted somewhat in order to make all the lines meet at the corners.

Our discovery on first examining *Les Bergers d'Arcadie II* was far

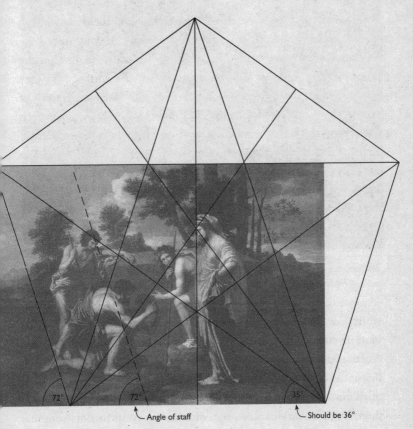

FIGURE 5.1 Poussin's *Les Bergers d'Arcadie II* – geometric analysis by Professor Christopher Cornford.

more exciting. It is quite clear that the staff on the far left of the painting is at 75° to the horizontal, and therefore, potentially, the left-hand side of a tilted triangle (Figure 5.2). The staff on the right also looked at first sight to be equivalent to the dashed lines on the Parchments, those at 7½° to the vertical, but this is not so. It is actually at 5° to the

FIGURE 5.2 *Les Bergers d'Arcadie II* – the 75° angle of the staff on the left of the painting suggests the presence of the tilted equilateral triangle.

vertical, an angle that could prove to be interesting, perhaps, by virtue of its 'fiveness', as discussed later in connection with the Pythagoreans. As far as the secret geometry was concerned, this was all the progress that could be made. Attempts to find other traces of the geometry identified from the Parchments met with no success. Yes, one could draw in the triangle in various ways, but without any confirmation from features in the painting. Reluctantly – and somewhat deflated – we had to give up. The correlation with the left-hand staff was certainly exciting, but not enough to confirm the Parchment geometry. But then fate took a hand and revealed the unexpected.

Before giving up on the geometry, we decided to obtain a better, larger, copy (if such existed) of *Les Bergers d'Arcadie II*. Our initial telephone call to the Louvre's shop to enquire whether a reproduction of this well-known painting is available elicited a polite *non*. We felt, though, that our knowledge of the language might not have been up to the task, so a second attempt was made by a friend whose very good French is in daily use. This time there was a positive response: the reproduction would be posted direct from the R.M.N. (Réunion des Musées Nationaux, the organisation responsible for all matters of this sort). We received, not the modern colour reproduction we expected, but a lithograph – an early engraving of the painting. Embossed with the R.M.N. seal of authenticity, this was clearly a modern copy but taken off the original block. Our initial disappointment that this was not what we had expected soon gave way to pleasure at what this version had to reveal.

The engraver had done a reasonable job, clearly working by eye alone rather than from a tracing, and, despite an overall heaviness of the figures, the attention to detail was good. In fact, it was good bordering on obsessive. So it came as a surprise to find that the range of mountains on the right is subtly different to the original painting and the colour photograph of it. Elsewhere, details had been reproduced leaf by leaf, twig by twig – but *not* the mountains (Figure 5.3a). This discrepancy was noted and put mentally to one side, until one day, when looking through a book containing black-and-white illustrations of Poussin's work, we found a photograph of the painting in which the mountains *were* the same as in the engraving (Figure 5.3b). So the painting had obviously changed between the taking of the black-and-white and the colour photographs (Figure 5.3c). This was astonishing. We had to obtain a good-sized copy of the former to make quite sure that the mountains were as they appeared, and we had to do so as soon as possible while the negative still existed. The ever-helpful staff at the R.M.N. duly sent a print of the negative they currently held, in the hope that it was the one we wanted. And it was. There, quite clearly, are the mountains shown exactly as in the engraving.

Clearly the painting had not changed itself, so there are two possibilities: either a cleaning of the painting between photos had removed old overpainting, or – hard to believe – an employee of the Louvre had added more sky. Either way, the change indicated a desire at some stage in the painting's life to disguise the mountains as painted

FIGURE 5.3 *Les Bergers d'Arcadie II* – the mountains compared in (a) the lithograph of the painting, (b) the black-and-white photograph of the painting, (c) the colour photograph of the painting in its present state and (d) the scene as it appears today. The principal differences are on the skyline to the right of the crags. In (c) the ground dips slightly, then rises to a slight summit. This is identifiable as Rennes-le-Château, visible in (d). In (b) the dip has been painted out, and 'Rennes' has disappeared.

Rennes

by Poussin. This raised a further question: had the cleaning (or twentieth-century repainting) been carried out as a matter of course at the Louvre – perhaps all paintings of a certain age are overhauled on a rota? – or, giving rein to a conspiracy theory, had the moment been carefully timed? Gérard de Sède claimed to have located the real tomb depicted in *Les Bergers d'Arcadie II* as that at les Pontils, near Arques.[10] But with the painting in its pre-cleaned state, de Sède would not have been able, with any justification, to have revealed this, since without the mountainous backdrop to identify its location, the tomb could really be *anywhere*. Subsequent, careful examination of the painting at the Royal Academy in London, using a magnifying glass, showed quite clearly that the present paintwork is, in that top area of the painting, contemporaneous – that is, the paint of the sky and the paint of the mountains are of the same date and obviously placed there by Poussin. There is no trace of new cloud obscuring parts of the mountain ridge. This is, after all, the most likely case – a recent cleaning having removed an old alteration.

We can conclude, then, that at some time in the past – and this has to be before the engraved copy was made – there was a deliberate alteration to the painting, possibly with a view to eliminating details that would make it possible to identify the real location. Unfortunately this engraving is not dated, but there is another engraving of the painting by Poussin, held in the Bibliothèque Nationale in Paris. This copy is normally attributed to Bernard Picart, who engraved it as a mirror image. The R.M.N. exhibition catalogue of 1994 does manage to provide an estimate of its date: 'without doubt . . . during the seventeenth century and before its acquisition by the King [Louis XIV]'. If the catalogue is correct, it means that the alteration was made before King Louis acquired it, because the mountains are shown as in the other engraving. An examination of the provenance of the painting might give clues as to who was responsible for the alteration.

The 'Poussin tomb'

We had to visit the site of the tomb at les Pontils to decide for ourselves whether the mountains that form the backdrop to this famous tomb actually correspond to those in the painting (Figure 5.3d).

The location of the tomb is a rocky knoll overlooking a bend of the River Rialsesse, one kilometre east of Serres, on the south side of the road near the hamlet of les Pontils. There is no tomb to be seen these days, for it was demolished in April 1988 by the owner of the land, disconcerted at the attempts of treasure-seekers to open the tomb – one final attempt employing explosives. Only the base-slab remains to confirm that the correct site has been found. The present and former appearances of the site are shown in Figures 5.4 and 5.5. Sightseers are not welcome and access has been blocked, but all there is to be seen may be viewed from the road anyway. The tomb demolished in 1988

FIGURE 5.4 Les Pontils – the site of the 'Poussin tomb' as it appears today.

FIGURE 5.5 Les Pontils – the 'Poussin tomb' as it appeared before
its demolition in 1988.

was not even the original. A plausible but unsubstantiated story relates
that Colbert, minister to Louis XIV, had supervised its destruction on
the king's orders. Why we consider this story to be credible will later
become clear.

The identification of the site rests not only on the tomb itself, but
also on the species of tree surrounding it, and the mountains that rise to
the south – and it was these features we had come to see. The trees at
the site are evergreen oaks, *Quercus ilex*, somewhat stunted due to the
poor ground in which they grow. These trees are distinctive and could
well be the same species as painted by Poussin. The mountains do bear
a strong resemblance to those in the painting – in particular those to the
right in the painting, west and south of the Site, may be readily identified. To the far right the distant prominence of Rennes-le-Château

may be seen. But behind the tomb, the crag should emerge from the densely wooded slopes of a massive mountain rising to the left (east), whereas the painting shows the crest of this mountain descending quite sharply from the crag. Above, where there is blue sky, there should be woods. This discrepancy should be enough evidence on which to reject the identification – unless, that is, Poussin had made the alteration on aesthetic grounds, or someone had later changed that part of the painting, as they had the mountains on the right. The latter possibility was to gain ground when our study of the painting progressed from illustrations in books to much larger reproductions, and to special-technique photographs held at the research department at the Louvre.

The mystery surrounding Poussin's undocumented period (for which no details of his life are known), his connections and patrons, the rumour that King Louis XIV had ordered the destruction of the tomb – all combined to intrigue us. That Poussin had an important role to play in the preservation and conservation of a message for a future generation was now a distinct possibility; and Abbé Saunière, whether by dint of his own endeavours or prompted by others as yet unknown, had apparently availed himself of a copy of *Les Bergers d'Arcadie II* during his trip to Paris in 1892. With this thought in mind we left the tomb at les Pontils. The mystery of Rennes-le-Château was proving to be one of astonishing complexity, but we could not complain of a lack of clues.

Back in England we decided to track down and examine the other named paintings to see whether they could throw further light on the problem. Of the two, only one had been attributed to a particular artist. So we now turned to the catalogues of David Teniers.

Temptations and hermits

David Teniers the Younger was a very prolific artist. Over one thousand paintings by him are catalogued, and his total production is believed to have been around twice that number. Such productivity was achieved over a long career: he started to paint at a very early age, continued into his eighties, and frequently completed a painting in a single day.

There seems to have been a surprising demand for paintings depicting *The Temptation of St Antony*, for Teniers was to produce a large number of them. Five major art galleries have examples, while the number in private collections is not known. The Louvre has two; they are similar, and are referred to as the *grande* and *petite* versions.

It is hard to appreciate the attraction that Teniers's vision of Antony's temptation must have excited for so many versions of it to have been painted. The old saint, not only being tempted by the sins of the flesh (at his age, the Devil was surely being optimistic), is seen patiently enduring the company of a multitude of Brueghelesque demons and monstrous hybrid creatures. The Devil, having failed to seduce Antony with wine, women and whatever else was hard to get in the desert, had resorted to irritating the poor man to distraction.

Other investigators of this story have been dismayed by the large number of candidates for the Teniers which Saunière is said to have acquired, though the field is surely narrowed by the stated source of his copy. We had reasoned that, if Saunière had purchased reproductions of paintings *from* the Louvre, these would be of paintings *in* the Louvre – which the Poussin is, of course. The alternative Teniers, *St Antony and St Paul*, had never been in the Louvre, so on this basis is unlikely to be the painting in question. However, having also seen the Hermitage version of *The Temptation of St Antony* (not dissimilar to the Louvre versions), we had to concede that the problem was not so much to decide which of the many was the appropriate version, but that they appeared to shed no light on the Saunière mystery. They are quite clearly devoid of occult geometry. If some other relevant clue was to be found there, it continued to elude us.

Only slightly deterred, we set about examining all catalogues of Teniers's works on which we could lay our hands. Quite what we were looking for, it is hard to recall; perhaps a small miracle. And it was in the Western Art Library of the Ashmolean Museum in Oxford that our

small miracle happened: there we came upon the 'lost' *St Antony and St
Paul* (Plate 5). It had been in the collection of the second Lord
Palmerston at the family seat at Broadlands (appearing in the Broadlands
inventory for 1791) and had remained there until acquired by Edwina
Ashley, Countess Mountbatten, in 1942. Stupefaction best describes
our reaction on recognising, prominently displayed in the painting, the
occult geometry. The two saints had obligingly arranged their staffs so
as to cross each other at an angle of 60° and, furthermore, had oriented
them to produce angles of 75° and 45° to the horizontal. Such an
overt exposition of the geometry left us in no doubt that this painting
is the relevant 'Antony'.

Curious, is it not, that Saunière should have been able to procure a
copy at the Louvre? And more curious that he should have been aware
of which painting to request, a painting not on display in that museum?
Of course, it is possible that there is yet another occult St Antony
painting in the Louvre that we have not found, but if this is so, it is not
catalogued as a Teniers. Today it is possible to obtain copies of some
paintings not in French collections from photographs held by the
R.M.N., but these are principally of works by French artists. It is feasible that Teniers, though Flemish, had been considered to be closely
enough related to the French 'greater family' to warrant inclusion. But
this begs the question. Saunière must have been told which paintings to
acquire. Even if the entire story of Saunière's visit to the Louvre is a fabrication, as some would have it, someone in the 1960s and '70s, when
this information became public, knew of the painting's significance.
Apart from the somewhat tenuous connection noted between the
Parchment geometry and the shepherd's staff in Poussin's *Les Bergers
d'Arcadie II*, this fact is the first reliable anchorage for a drifting hulk of
a tall story.

St Antony and St Paul examined

This delightful painting depicts St Paul the Hermit (not the much earlier, letter-writing St Paul), receiving St Antony the Hermit. Some interpretations reverse the host and guest roles, but for the purposes of our analysis who is receiving whom is irrelevant. St Antony is identified here by the capital T on his right shoulder – a symbol commonly used to indicate his presence. The raven that used to bring him half a loaf each day can be seen arriving just off centre. On this occasion the bird arrives with, miraculously, a whole loaf.

The carefully placed staffs of the two saints show the way to proceed and there are four fairly straightforward diagrams to be drawn:

The four steps

1. If the staff-lines are continued, they intersect the top and bottom edges of the painting at equal distances from the left edge (Figure 5.6). The vertical line joining these points passes through the rim of Antony's bowl, where Teniers has thoughtfully painted a crack (Plate 7a).

2. The staff-line extended upwards to the right meets the top of the painting above the tower of the church on the rocky hill (Plate 7b). If a vertical line is drawn down through the apex of the tower's roof, the area of the painting contained between the two vertical lines and the top and bottom of the painting will be seen to have sides of equal length: it is a square (Figure 5.6). (While a square is inevitable from a line crossing the painting at 45°, what is not inevitable is that this geometry has been confirmed by the artist. St Paul's staff could have been at the same angle but in a different location, and thus not mark the top-left corner of the square. The church tower and also the pointed roof and window below need not have marked the right side of the square.)

3. From our knowledge of the geographical square derived from the Parchment cipher, we believe that it is now necessary to realign the square in the painting by rotating it through 15° about the top-left corner (Figure 5.7). Teniers has provided confirmation that this is the correct procedure: the upper side is

FIGURE 5.6 Teniers's *St Antony and St Paul* – the two staffs, which form part of the tilted equilateral triangle, also define a square.

found to pass through the head of the loaf-carrying raven – also at a tangent to the oval loaf – and onwards through the more remote bird above and to the left of the church (Plates 7c and 7d). Before we have even attempted to complete the square, it has become clear that an equilateral triangle, equivalent to the triangle derived from Parchment 1, has been drawn. The realigned square is now completed as shown by the dashed lines in Figure 5.7. When solving the Parchments, we had found various possible relationships between the triangle and the square; Teniers has shown us clearly which he had used.

4. The centre of the square we expected to 'mark the spot', but this is found to be below the left eye-socket of the skull; how satisfactory it would have been had the centre fallen decisively in the middle of the skull! However, the painting contains a reference to the 1½° 'error' identified in the Parchments, and to recur many more times: the crucifix is not aligned with the sides of the painting, but leans a little to the left. (In Figure 5.8 a bold line has been drawn to

FIGURE 5.7 *St Antony and St Paul* – the triangle and square constructed.

indicate this. In order not to obscure the details, the line is interrupted where it passes confirmatory evidence, and its right edge delineates the right side of the crucifix's upright, the well-defined corner of its base and the corner of the squared stone resting on the ground below.) Rotating the square anticlockwise by 1½° about the top-left corner to match the crucifix's alignment produces the result shown by solid lines. The centre of the square now falls precisely on the centre of the skull. (Even on the small scale of this illustration, readers may verify the accuracy by using a protractor.)

On the very clear evidence found in *St Antony and St Paul*, we can now be confident that the bearings from the top-left corner of the Parchment cipher square are correct in principle. We might now

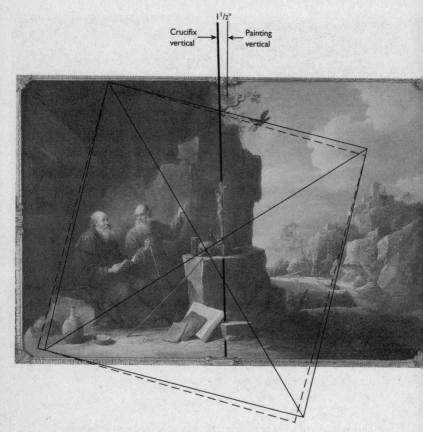

FIGURE 5.8 *St Antony and St Paul* – the crucifix indicates the 1½° correction.
When this is done, the centre of the square falls upon the centre of the skull.

consider referring to this corner as *La Croix*. But for the centre-point
we have two possibilities: if the 'cipher square' had been devised using
the Teniers method, it is patently obvious that the associated triangle
would have been too small and too far west to comply with the
Parchment 1 geometry. A glance at a map with the cipher square and
Parchment 1 triangle drawn in makes this clear (Figure 5.9). And, if
devised by some other method, could Teniers be so clear yet so wrong?

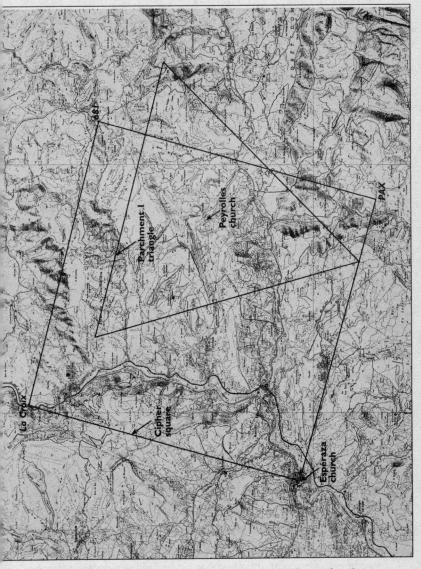

FIGURE 5.9 The cipher square and Parchment 1 triangle transferred
to the I.G.N. map.

The actual distance between the potential locations would be huge. A stunning thought then occurred to us: had the treasure been lost? And could this geometrical ambiguity be the cause?

An alternative method had to be found to resolve the dilemma of the two centre-points. Perhaps further study of the Poussin and the *681–La Croix* square would resolve the matter. Also, the Pope Celestine V painting needed to be investigated – assuming we could find it. Perhaps the 1½° alignment 'error' could throw some light on this problem also. What was really needed was further, completely independent corroboration of the correct geometric procedure. In the meantime, our earlier investigation of La Mort as the site for the 'treasure' was thrown into even greater doubt by the two possible centre-points. However, in spite of the apparent contradictions it raised, we were fairly convinced by the confidence and clarity of the message contained in Teniers's painting.

The Coronation of Pope Celestine V

Successful identification of the missing painting by Teniers gave us two of the three copies reputedly brought back by Saunière from the Louvre. We were left with a problem. This third copy was simply described as a 'Portrait of Pope Celestine V', with no artist named; and Celestine, we soon realised, was no ordinary Pope. Virtually forced into office, Celestine, a Calabrian hermit (another hermit!), was doubtless the most unusual and humble of candidates ever to fill the papal office. The history of his brief elevation to Holy Father was tragic. His simple origins ran counter to the political expectations of his calling, and there is historical confusion as to whether he resigned or was forced out of the papacy, each version differing according to the political stance of its author. In any event, it is clear that he died in captivity less than two years after his popular election. Given this background, we realised it was unlikely that Celestine would have sat in a glorified pose for a leading artist of the day; indeed, the artistic fashion of the late thirteenth century militated against such depiction. And his reign as Pope had been very brief.

A search of the Louvre catalogue under works of the thirteenth and fourteenth centuries turned up nothing. Celestine was not to be found. Faced with an impasse, we returned to the description given by de Sède. The answer was in his statement: if no artist was named, the work must therefore be anonymous. Celestine was found, within the works of the sixteenth century, in the 'Anonymous' section at the back of the catalogue. With the archive number to hand we placed a call to the R.M.N. in Paris – only to meet with further frustration. The catalogue picture, we were told, was far too small to be successfully reproduced and no negative of the original work existed. We were faced with a wait of several weeks – the time required to photograph the painting officially – but our request was met within twenty-four hours by the enterprise of the agency. Perplexed at the strange lack of a negative, one kind individual had searched the archives.

A negative had been found, and it was old – perhaps a century old – and hence its omission from the official list. We realised that Saunière himself may well have been the last person to receive a print from this negative, if it was not he who actually commissioned the photograph during his sojourn in Paris in March 1892. Provided with an excellent large photograph of Celestine's coronation by the R.M.N., we checked for the expected geometry. There are certainly enough lines to be seen. Let us start with the angle of the cross:

The three steps

1. The unknown painter of this papal coronation scene has been even more careful about concealing the geometry than had the artists of the paintings previously examined (Figure 5.10). The 60° angle is evident: the left side of the platform on which Celestine is seated and the shaft of the three-barred cross meet at this angle. But the axis of the geometry is not that of the picture frame: a secondary axis at an angle of 3½° to the frame has been established. This is

FIGURE 5.10 *The Coronation of Pope Celestine V* (artist unknown) – the triangle and square constructed.

defined by (working from left to right): an origin at the left corner formed by the edge of the upper frame and the right side of the false pilaster on the left (painted in grisaille – shades of grey); the top of the first cross; the top of the three-barred cross; the top of the arch over the throne, to which it is tangential; the upper edge of the bar of the next cross (actually the lobes on the top edge); and finally scrolls of the false pilaster on the right.

The result of this is that the lower-right side of the equilateral triangle, here defined by the edge of the dais, is not at 45° to the horizontal but at 41½°. The horizontal line has been clearly indicated by the joints in the floor tiles, which we have emphasised in Figure 5.10 with a line. As it is known that the final stage in the development of the geometry is normally an anticlockwise rotation by 1½°, how will we know what is required here? It is not enough to assume that the horizontal line in the floor is an east–west line, or parallel of latitude.

The other paintings and Parchment 1 all had meridional indications. Here, this function is perhaps performed by the shaft of the right-hand staff, emphasised by the dashed line, which will be recognised as being equivalent to the lines passing through the 'm over I' symbols of Parchment 1: it is at 7½° to the vertical. It is now clear that, instead of the final 1½° rotation, the required rotation will be 1½° plus 3½°: a neat 5° exactly. We already have a variety of interesting correspondences.

The upper side of the triangle is tangential to the crozier, Celestine's halo and the tip of the bishop's nose (! – the rather unhappy angle of his mouth appears to result from a wish to reflect the passing of this line), and terminates on the edge of the king's ermine-lined cloak. The left side of the first square is tangential to the jewel in the mitre of Bishop 2, and also to the oval clasp of his cloak – it runs down a fold in the skirt of his surplice – and terminates near the edge of the frame where it intersects the extended side of the triangle. Correspondences worth noting occur on the right side of the square, which grazes the forehead of the 'pageboy', his calf-muscle, and the tip of the scabbard. The line also passes through the intersection of two floor-tile joints, one of which is the 'horizontal' line identified above.

2. The square may now be rotated clockwise by 15° (Figure 5.11). The diagonals are drawn to locate the centre; one runs down the tassled fringe of the pope's dark garment. It is also interesting to draw a centre-line to this square. This line passes through the centre of the scroll rosette (part of the fake throne) and we may now appreciate that it was not bad draughtsmanship that causes this to 'float' above the dais. Its position provides a welcome confirmation that we are proceeding in the right direction.

3. Now comes the moment to apply the anticlockwise 'correction' of 5° which we had calculated previously, resulting in the square of solid lines (Figure 5.12). This has been 'crossed', and a centre-line drawn. We have avoided until now reintroducing the concept of the pyramid elevation found in Parchment 2, for it is time to demonstrate an interesting fact. The centre-line we had drawn is to be the base of the pyramid triangle, the apex of which falls on the top margin of the painting. The sides of the 'pyramid' are seen to touch, on the left side, Celestine's halo, and on the right, to run down one side of the king's sceptre.

FIGURE 5.11 *The Coronation of Pope Celestine V* – the square is rotated, and a 7½°
line identified.

As the diagrams show, the painting of Celestine V is important because
it reinforces the logic behind the 15° clockwise rotation, already indicated by the presence of the side of the triangle. In Appendix G we
have calculated whether this is geometrically precise or a close approximation; it is actually the latter, but so close as to have been negligible
in times past, when present-day methods of accurate calculation were
not available. There are various other details which help to locate the
position of the pyramid and its square base, but we shall not go into
them here.

FIGURE 5.12 *The Coronation of Pope Celestine V* – once the anticlockwise correction of 5° is applied, the pyramid geometry of Parchment 2 reveals a number of correspondences.

It must be assumed that the survival of Pythagorean esoteric geometry in the hands of various hermetic (secret) groups, coupled with the ancient and evocative symbol of the Seal of Solomon, gave rise to the adoption of this particular sequence of arcane geometry. In due course we shall explain why the Great Pyramid, the symbol of Egyptian knowledge, should reappear in a medieval context, and why it is integral to the Pythagorean veneration of the number five and pentagonal geometry.

It is disappointing that there is no confirmation of the final centre-point of the square. An argument to the effect that this would compromise the secrecy must fail, since the route to the solution is complex enough. There have been times when we questioned the validity of this painting in the context of the Secret, but when the correlations are reviewed, it is hard to dismiss it. The fact is that we are observing remnants that have 'slipped through the net'. It is possible that there was a companion painting which picked up the geometry at the point where this one stops; perhaps this one was considered adequate as it stands. But this is idle speculation, and other evidence awaits.

A quest for the Grail

Our search had originally been restricted to paintings named by de Sède. We now widened the remit, in the hope that paintings of earlier centuries would reveal something of relevance. A search lasting several exhausting months proved frustratingly unsuccessful. Occasionally we would glimpse an angle, a reclining staff, a peculiarity of composition; but all turned out to be false leads.

As we resigned ourselves to spending long hours in the Ashmolean Western Art Library, trawling through the complete catalogue of the Louvre in what might prove to be a fruitless search for other artists who had incorporated the geometry, a feeling of *déjà vu* became overwhelming. Somewhere another painting had been seen . . . And then, for no obvious reason, the mists cleared to reveal an image of a knight, a horse, a tree and a lance. All that was required was to reach out a hand and take down from a shelf in the Ashmolean a book on René d'Anjou – 'Good King René', as he was known during his lifetime and still is today.

La Fontaine de fortune (Plate 6) is the name by which this particular scene from the allegorical tale *Le Cuer d'amours espris* is known. Written by René d'Anjou and finished in 1457, this work has survived in three versions, though there must have been others since it enjoyed considerable celebrity. The Vienna and Paris versions share certain similarities, but the former is superior. It is clear that the Paris version was made as a direct copy, but that the copyist failed to observe the niceties. This was important to us in considering the precise arrangement of the painting, since it is now believed that King René not only wrote the story, but also commissioned the illustrations, supervised their execution and corrected the text. The Vienna copy is without doubt either the private copy of King René or one produced under his supervision, possibly that intended for the dedicatee, René's 'Cousin et nepveu Jehan Duc de Bourbon et d'Auvergne' (to quote the old French words).

Modelled on the *Roman de la rose*, the most famous of such tales, René's 'The Heart Smitten With Love' is a revival of knightly poetry, reflecting a quest for the Grail, in which the knight 'Cuer' (Heart), accompanied by 'Désir' tries to liberate and win the lady 'Doulce Mercy' by means of gallant deeds. In the scene shown in Plate 6, we see Cuer near the 'magic' spring, standing by a black marble monument that bears an inscription warning that the water is bitter, and of dire consequences should it be spilled. Désir rests near the horses. It is sunrise.

It should be mentioned in passing that in *The Holy Blood and the Holy Grail* there is an illustration of this picture – a coincidence that it should have been chosen to illustrate the concept of the underground stream of esoteric thought when it is so much more relevant to the mystery of Rennes.

It is hardly necessary to comment on the strange composition of this painting – it positively reeks of symbolism – and with our knowledge of the Parchment 1 geometry its significance could now be identified. And what stunning significance! Here we have not only a meticulous display of the geometry, but one executed under the direct supervision of one of the most celebrated men of his time. The significance of René d'Anjou as a man of learning, his influence on the Renaissance, and his role in establishing an esoteric elite among certain ruling dynasties, and consequentially among the great artists of the day, should not be underestimated.

La Fontaine de fortune examined

There are numerous oddities which catch the eye in this painting: the lance is the most obvious, angled at 75°. Also curious is the manner in which Cuer holds his hands: the left held out palm downwards, the other with the middle (or second) finger pointing, resting, on the back of the left wrist. He may appear (as others have described him) to be reading the inscription on the monument, his left hand pointing to the line he has reached. This is clearly not true: the hand is too far away from the text; it is normal to point with the forefinger; and, most obviously, his gaze is directed at his wrist – he is not looking at the inscription. He is, in fact, identifying a point.

In this painting, as in the Teniers and the second Poussin, the all-important 75° angle of the lance is the key to unlocking the now familiar geometry:

The three steps

1. With the lance so clearly indicating where to commence drawing the triangle, other clues to the placing of the other sides are readily identified (Figure 5.13). The tip of Cuer's finger indicates the point through which the lower-right side of the triangle is to pass, and this may be drawn at 60° to the centre-line of the lance. Having done this, it is clear that the top and right edges of the painting may locate the corners of the triangle. Drawing the upper side of the triangle at 60° to the lance's centre-line confirms this. (Note that the lower-right side is tangential to the armour roundel at Cuer's left elbow.)

2. The construction lines required to obtain the size of the square can now be drawn (as dashed lines in Figure 5.14) and the tilted square superimposed; its centre is found by drawing the diagonals. Confirmation of this spot is not immediately obvious, but it comes in a remarkable manner. The top, horizontal edge of the trough and the left, vertical side of the monument intersect at the centre of the square; they are like rectangular coordinates, or – transferred to a map – parallel and meridian. Another feature appears to refer to the spot: the shadow of the tree points in that direction, and a line from the centre of the

FIGURE 5.13 René d'Anjou's *La Fontaine de fortune* – the lance and Cuer's fingertip define the tilted equilateral triangle.

sun to the centre of the square runs down that shadow. This line is parallel to the lance – another 75° line.

3. The other triangle completing the hexagram might prove enlightening. In the Teniers it is confirmed by having the right side touch the oval loaf in the bird's beak (Figure 5.15). We may also note that, although St Paul's gesture with his left hand draws St Antony's attention to the bird, his forefinger and sleeve actually run along an axis of the hexagram.

   Completing the hexagram on the René is even more rewarding (Figure 5.16). The right side of the second triangle also passes through the point indicated by Cuer's fingertip – little wonder that he is staring at it so intently – and bisects the armour roundel at his left knee. The left side of the triangle bisects

FIGURE 5.14 *La Fontaine de fortune* – construction of the square, whose centre is confirmed by the intersection of edges of the trough and monument which correspond to a parallel and meridian.

the sun. That the centre of the sun is directly above the bottom point of the hexagram alerts us to a similar correspondence of great importance. The top corner of the hexagram is also on a near perpendicular, but this one is marked by the corner of the monument (and touches the oval of the dipper bowl's base) – which, it may now be noted, leans at 1½°.

FIGURE 5.15 *St Antony and St Paul* – the second triangle of the hexagram is confirmed by various correspondences.

The final line we drew on the hexagram proves to be extremely significant, for it is the same line that forms the meridian on Parchment 1, where the same corner–line intersection is found. René's picture appears to identify two meridional lines: one through the centre of the square, the other through the top corner of the hexagram. (The problem of these two lines of meridian will be seen to gain importance and will indeed be clarified, quite conclusively, in later chapters.)

It would be true to say that *La Fontaine de fortune* has indicated the hidden geometry so clumsily – the horse's head at an extraordinary angle to mirror the 75° angle of the lance – that the result is artistically one of the worst pieces of composition to have seen the light of day. Perhaps such eye-catching eccentricity was thought necessary to attract the attention of the *cognoscenti* (and this may be an important insight). However, new to the game as we then were, we could now spot the

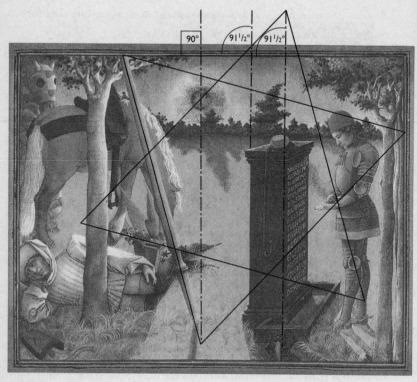

FIGURE 5.16 *La Fontaine de fortune* – the second triangle of the hexagram is
confirmed by various correspondences, and the 1½° tilt is indicated.

various elements of the geometry without needing such obvious point-
ers. An extraordinary thought occurred to us – could it be that this
work of King René was one of the first, perhaps *the* first, to attempt to
preserved the Secret by means of occult art? Comparison with the
same illustration from the Paris manuscript illustrates the point very
well, since the copyist (not knowing the occult significance) was so
appalled by the composition in various areas that he 'improved' René's
masterpiece – consequently ensuring that no outsider would be accidentally enlightened. A search for even earlier examples of an artistic
representation of the geometry would become a priority – but *La*

Fontaine de fortune did provide us with a mid-fifteenth-century date for the concealment of this most secret of secrets.

There are noticeable similarities of approach to the layout of the geometry between this painting and the Teniers. René also uses the 'frame', or border, to delineate certain features. But, considering the importance of the exact framing of the picture in relation to the hidden geometry – a millimetre or two here or there would render it indecipherable – the question arises as to whether the artists in question made allowance for this within their paintings. In the case of *La Fontaine de fortune* there was no danger that the geometry would be lost because a border was painted around it in the book. But such a fate could have befallen the Teniers if the painting were reframed at some point in its history, which indeed it was. However, in view of the precision with which it conforms to the geometry, the reframing must have carefully followed margins indicated by Teniers. This potential endangering of the preservation of the Secret was to become highly relevant in relation to the Poussin, as we shall see. When other similarities are noted, it is intriguing to consider the possibility that Teniers actually used *La Fontaine de fortune* as his prototype. Had it been in certain hands, this would have been quite feasible.

By now the possibility of a hoax, or even that the Parchments were nothing more than a game, had to be firmly discounted. We had to consider the implication that we had become immersed in an ancient mystery of tremendous import, and that the involvement of eminent personalities was to be expected.

Devonshire shepherds

Anxious for further data with which to complete the jigsaw, and encouraged by the utterly random discovery and success of René d'Anjou's *La Fontaine de fortune*, we wondered where else there might lurk a painting, a sculpture, a book; the work of an initiate. Although the works of Teniers had already been scoured while searching for the correct St Antony, the process was repeated, just in case, but without success. The erstwhile library of Good King René had obvious potential and could be expected to reveal much about the early preservation of the Secret – if a relevant work could be identified. This was pursued by ordering books on the king's life and art interests, and to these we shall return.

What of Nicolas Poussin? We had drawn a blank with *Les Bergers d'Arcadie II*, but were left with the uneasy feeling that this had more to do with our inability to understand the painting than with there being nothing there to understand. With Poussin, as with Teniers, there is a considerable body of work to examine, and not all his works are illustrated in the catalogues; there are also disputed paintings and a significant number of missing works. So why not commence with the most obvious painting? We returned to *Les Bergers d'Arcadie I*, the first painting by Poussin to incorporate the enigmatic phrase ET IN ARCADIA EGO, and another scene with shepherds and their staffs.

Famous as *Les Bergers d'Arcadie II* is, in comparison with the earlier version, at this stage of our investigation it was far less informative. The first version (Plate 4) has a much more explicit but less easily recognisable incorporation of the secret geometry. It has a novelty of presentation which at first hinders comprehension. From examination of previous paintings, we had come to expect the 'key' to recognition to be the left side of the triangle angled at 75° to the horizontal axis of the painting; the deduction of the 'squares' would then follow.

With this painting (Figure 5.17), Poussin has eliminated the 'triangle' and 'first-square' stages of the solution, and by means of the shepherds' staffs has indicated the location and orientation of the 'tilted square'. It is clear that the groove between the top slab of the tomb and the moulding beneath defines a diagonal – as does the further shepherd's staff – since a line drawn through this passes through the point of intersection of the two staffs. The best fit is obtained if the left side of the crook-staff is taken to define this line. By checking the angle that the square makes

16¹/₂°

Alignment of lower part
of crook-staff

FIGURE 5.17 Poussin's *Les Bergers d'Arcadie I* – the shepherds' staffs indicate the tilted square. Note the misalignment of the lower part of the crook-staff.

with the sides of the painting, it becomes evident that it is shown before its 1½° rotational correction. This is most readily observed at the right margin of the painting, where the angle is found to be 16½°. The limit of the paint is clearly visible where the light-coloured surface of the canvas, or underpainting, shows against the dark end of the tomb, and is a more reliable indication than the edge of a photograph, where 'cropping' often takes away the true edge of the painting. We have interpreted the point of intersection of the staffs as indicating the centre of the square, rather than one of its corners (which is an option), since this locates the whole geometric construction within the confines of the painting. This is clearly the correct decision, as will be shown.

Our decipherment of the arcane geometry did not result from a single line of investigation, and part of our difficulty in explaining its progress has stemmed from the great difficulty in conveying on paper the way it really happened. The brain is capable of jumping from one little detail, to a drawing, to a map, to a code, and back again in a way which would not make for good reading. And, like other parts of the puzzle, this first 'Shepherds' has some very important contributions to make.

The three steps

1. We had deduced from other sources that an essential part of the sequence was the final anticlockwise rotation by the small angle of 1½° which we have been referring to, perhaps erroneously, as the correction of an 'error'. Later we shall consider the possible motives for incorporating this rotation. Poussin has provided the most positive proof of this feature, in the shepherd's staff with the crook-end (Figure 5.17). If a straight-edge is placed against the very visible, upper length, it will be seen to be hopelessly out of alignment with the lower part, which can just be seen to the left of the bearded shepherd's right leg (it is most easily spotted by noting that it 'cuts off' the other shepherd's toes). An error, it might be surmised; perhaps rather an obvious one. But, not only is the lower part displaced to the right, it is also at a different angle. Is this angle 1½°? No, it is more subtle than that. Close examination of the actual painting revealed that this misalignment was no error, as Poussin has shown, just below the shepherd's hand, a sudden bend in the staff, which implies another bend in

the other direction out of sight below the shepherd's shoulder. (This detail is just about visible in Plate 4.) Seen on its own, the staff would be as shown in Figure 5.18.

2. If the whole geometric construction is now rotated through 1½° about the top-left corner of the square, as with the Teniers (Figure 5.19), the 'tomb' diagonal moves to align with the top of the slab and the crook-staff line along the right side, instead of the left as before. The square is now oriented at exactly 15° to the painting. However, it had been found with the Teniers painting that the suggested final orientation for the square is 1½° less than that.

3. If the square is now rotated a *further* 1½° anticlockwise (Figure 5.20), something remarkable occurs: the centre-line of the square (originally determined by the upper section of the crook-staff) is now perfectly superimposed on the lower, displaced, section of the staff. The substantial displacement to the right has been elucidated, and what had seemed like careless painting by Poussin has been confirmed as deliberate.

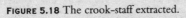

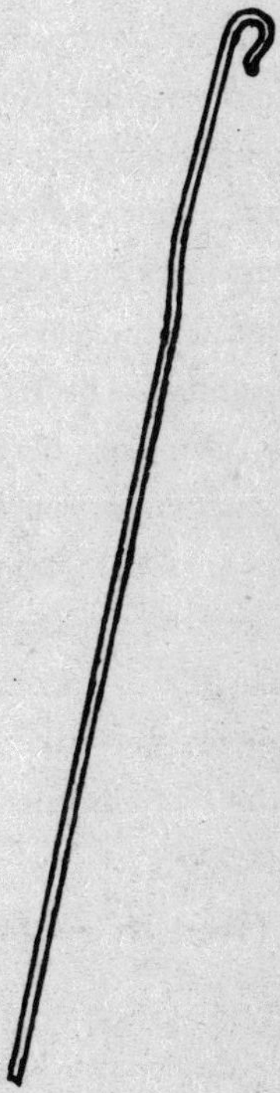

FIGURE 5.18 The crook-staff extracted.

The general effect of the geometry on Poussin's composition is evident in the sweep of the figures to the right, but also in details. A diagonal of the square runs down the shepherd's nose; the top edge of the square is marked by the broken end of a branch of a tree. Clearly these kinds of correlation are subjective, and there may be others which we have not noticed.

It should be explained that to determine the effect of rotating the initial geometry, we had drawn it on a transparent overlay which was rotated about a pin. Inaccuracies that may creep in if the geometry is repeatedly redrawn in different orientations were thus eliminated. For

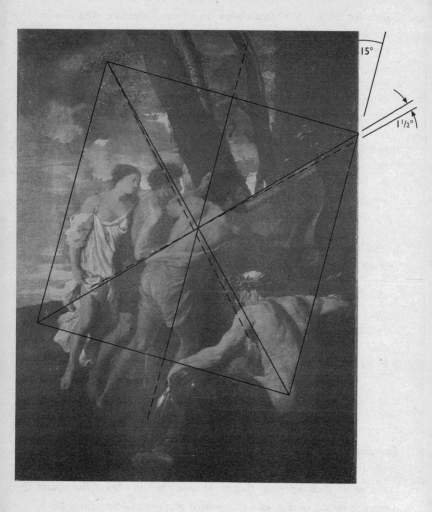

FIGURE 5.19 *Les Bergers d'Arcadie I* – a 1½° rotation is identified.

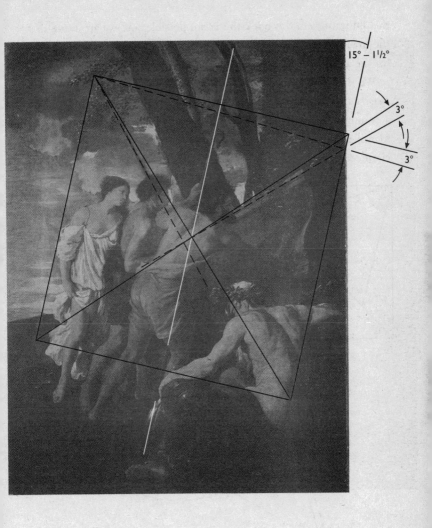

FIGURE 5.20 *Les Bergers d'Arcadie I* – a second 1½° rotation.

the illustrations in this book this is not possible, and we are aware that
the small size of illustration also does not assist in making the best case
for the argument; we had used copies three times this size.

We shall return to discuss further the implications of Poussin's *Les
Bergers d'Arcadie I*. But for now we had three paintings which displayed
a common geometry, and two 1½° anticlockwise rotations had been
identified (Figure 5.21). How these rotations are to be used would be
clarified later.

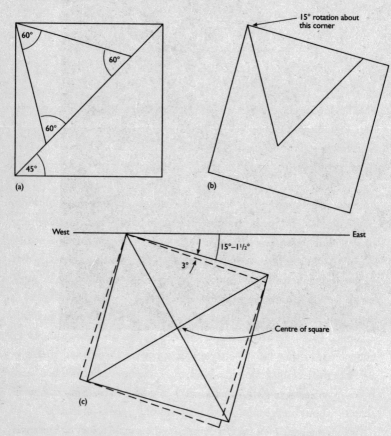

FIGURE 5.21 The main geometric elements identified as common to the three
paintings: (a) the square and equilateral triangle, (b) the square rotated through
15° and (c) two further 1½° rotations.

6
'X MARKS THE SPOT'

Having looked in great depth at the Parchments and paintings, we now had a host of geometrically interrelated figures – triangles, squares, hexagrams – and various angles. But what could be deduced and what did it mean? Was it simply an elaborate game designed to attract players and lead them around an unsolvable maze? The presence of an underlying geometric logic implied that this was not so, that a solution might be forthcoming with just a little more persistence. The painting by David Teniers had indicated a second centre-point, thereby casting further doubt on the process which had led us to La Mort. Perhaps this apparent discrepancy held a clue to the correct completion of the puzzle. With this in mind, we persisted.

In some respects, making geometric deductions is like working with a familiar language. Such familiarity encompasses abbreviations, slang, and perhaps other unconventional or specialist forms, and makes it possible to decipher poor handwriting, complete an unfinished sentence by inferring its sense, and identify a written word from its overall shape without the need to break it down into individual letters.

When the basic elements of geometry are as familiar as the elements of language, communication is possible. This may take the form of a complete statement, analogous to a grammatical sentence, or a shorthand convention may enable a concept to be effectively conveyed in a concise manner, without having to spell everything out. A simple example is the equilateral triangle, which we have met with. In the analogy the whole triangle is the complete sentence. But illustrate only two sides of equal length, with an included angle of 60°, and the whole triangle is easily worked out. A further degree of obscurity may be introduced by changing the length of one, or both, sides. The equilateral triangle might still be deduced, but with less certainty; and without any further input the scale of the triangle would remain unknown. Add another element, and the problem becomes solvable.

An extension of this concept may be likened to the use of abbreviations and acronyms in language. In a geometric context, we may see how a particular element may be used to represent the whole. More to the point, a line drawn at 60° to the notional horizontal of a page implies the geometry of the equilateral triangle; one drawn at 45° implies a right-angled triangle, or the diagonal of a square.

These concepts may be thought of as part of a whole grammar of geometry, the rules of which were established by Euclid and others, and which was later expanded to include the more obscure and esoteric. Here we have a glimpse of a language that is impenetrable to the layman, but a language nonetheless. And this is the background to the concealment of the Secret.

Euclid's theories are unlikely to be recalled by many readers; the geometric figures called polygrams which contribute so much of our evidence are unlikely to be familiar either. In-depth study of such shapes would comprise a book in itself, but it is enough to say that for the purposes of *this* book it is regular polygrams we are interested in (Figure 6.1) because these were the ones that intrigued our geometrically inclined ancestors. For those readers who require proof that we are not plucking shapes out of the air, a fuller analysis of esoteric geometry with particular regard to polygrams and Pythagoras is given in Appendix F.

However, other elements of geometry which would have been

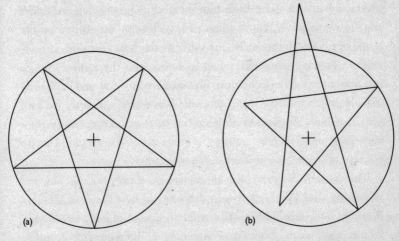

FIGURE 6.1 (a) A regular pentagram, whose points all lie on the same circle, and which has sides of equal length, and (b) an irregular pentagram.

considered esoteric a few generations ago may now be familiar to students of architecture, or philosophy, or even to the well-read amateur. The duplication of the square, otherwise known as Plato's theorem, is one such piece of geometry that might well be recognisable. That this should have a relationship with the equilateral triangle comes as a surprise. In the context of the geometry we have discussed previously, it is precisely this relationship that is important.

Geometric relationships

Many people do not understand how geometric relationships may be tested and proved (and why should they?), so we show here how one geometric figure may relate to another (or not), and how this relationship may be rigorously proved.

Unless a relationship is quite simple and the proof likely to be rapid, it is convenient first to test it by means of an accurate drawing. If this gives a promising result, it may then be worth attempting a (possibly) protracted analysis using Euclidean methods. The drawing itself does not constitute proof, but in times past, with some proofs beyond the scope of Euclidean theorems (and other methods not then being available), a drawing would have had to suffice and the relationship be taken as gospel. The techniques of trigonometry may not have been available at the time the secret geometry was conceived. Since we have yet to establish the first use of the geometry – at this stage our earliest date is the mid-fifteenth century, and René d'Anjou – we can make no assumptions about the abilities of the originator.

The example of the triangle and square has already arisen. Someone suspecting a relationship between them would have made an accurate drawing; if the relationship was identified, Euclidean logic would then be used to confirm it. Because a large number of theorems had already been established, it would be necessary only to select the appropriate one and proceed from there. So for the triangle and square it would not have been necessary to prove first that the centre of an equilateral triangle is on a line joining any corner to the centre of the opposite side at a point one-third of the way along that line (Figure 6.2); this may be taken as read. From this piece of information the rest of the proof follows easily. By studying the Leonardo da Vinci drawing (Figure 4.10 on p. 96), we may deduce the logic of the sequence he followed, and see how he made a mistake because the scale of his drawing was too small. This would not have mattered if he had then proceeded to check the result using geometric logic; whether he did or not we shall never know.

How does this relate to the map?

We have not yet drawn the Parchment 2 geometry on to the I.G.N. map at 1 : 25,000 scale, as there have been so many other leads to follow. Let us now have another look at the information derived from the Parchments and the paintings. We have two sets of geometry – one

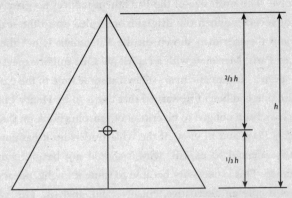

FIGURE 6.2 The centre of an equilateral triangle lies two-thirds of the way along a line joining a corner to the mid-point of the side opposite.

triangular, the other square – which relate to each other in a particular way such that if the triangle were to be drawn on the map in the correct position and the square derived from this (not forgetting the 1½° rotations), the centre of the square would represent the site of the Secret, or 'treasure'. In the best tradition of pirate maps, the point of intersection of the diagonals of the square would be the 'X that marks the spot'. The orientation of the triangle was clear – that much had been established from the paintings of Teniers, René d'Anjou and to some extent from the anonymous painter of Celestine. Also, the first Poussin painting of *Les Bergers d'Arcadie* had clarified the two separate 1½° rotations. And, of course, the cipher had also been instrumental in establishing the orientation of the square, but at the expense of confusion as to its size.

We ignored the size of the cipher square because we believed that other information would permit us to size and place the triangle. The lines radiating from Antugnac, and the clearly identified meridian, are tied to the triangle–square geometry. So, not only is the orientation shown, but the scale may be deduced from the relative distances of Antugnac to points on the meridian on the Parchment diagram compared with the I.G.N. map itself. There are, however, two problems left

to resolve. The small size of the Parchment induces no great expectations of accuracy when the diagrams are scaled up to the scale of the
map; and the meridian shown on the Parchment is not the present
Zero, or Paris, Meridian with a capital M. One might expect this of a
map – even a diagramatic map – drawn at some time in the past, and in
any case one had been forewarned that this is so by Henry Lincoln.

We have been obliged to be critical of Lincoln's book on the subject,
The Holy Place, and in view of the wide readership it has enjoyed we
feel it is essential to explain why it should not be given uncritical
acceptance. This is necessary because to some it might appear that this
book is simply an alternative, equally valid, analysis. This would be
understandable, since similar geometric figures appear in the two books,
but Lincoln's have *no* connection or relevance whatsoever to the present
work. His derive, we are forced to conclude, from the easily misinterpreted information with which he was provided, and from an
unsatisfactory methodology. This view, and the inference that he had
been used by others possessing a more comprehensive knowledge than
we had initially imagined, has been forced upon us since Lincoln draws
conclusions that are erroneous, but which – after much work – we have
found to derive from sound basic data.

Among his diagrams appears the one with lines radiating from
Antugnac (reproduced here in Figure 1.10, on p. 35), which was instrumental in signalling to us that a map lay hidden in the Parchments.
These lines, he deduces, intersect the Paris Meridian at equidistant
points, a fact he considers all the more remarkable since the Meridian
has been moved more than once – the last move ensuring that this
remarkable subdivision of the line had been perfected. This he regards
as suspicious, and since he proposes a prehistoric date for the conception and execution of his 'Temple' of invisible geometric figures, he
assumes that an *éminence grise* within the I.G.N. contributed to the
completion of an ancient pagan temple.

This is wrong on several counts, the chief of which is that the lines
he has drawn do not fall where he has indicated in his text; there is also

the point that, regardless of where a meridian line is drawn, it will always intersect a set of radiating lines at the same angles, with the same relative spacings of the points of intersection. This is a basic geometric truth, based on what are called similar triangles. By definition, any pair of meridians sufficiently close together and sufficiently far from the poles will, over a small difference in latitude, be parallel. This is all true of the small area covered by the map under consideration. Therefore the triangles within the 'fan' will remain similar to those of smaller or larger 'fans', and so will their related properties. But Lincoln had also drawn lines crossing the 'fan' and apparently intersecting on the Meridian. This surely confirms the precise location of the Meridian?

For one point on the Meridian near la Soulane, the bearing is shown as St Julia–Le Bezu, so we mark the point this gives on the Meridian. The other bearing is Antugnac–Couiza–(across the Meridian)–Sougraigne, and we mark that point on the Meridian. The two points are not coincident: they are about four millimetres apart on the map, or one hundred metres on the ground. For another point, the one Lincoln marks as I, the 'confirmatory' line crossing the 'fan' passes through Aven and Peyrolles. Never mind that the intersection at the Meridian is only approximate; could Peyrolles and Aven have been built to be in the required locations? Peyrolles – yes, but not Aven. On the map 'Aven' is marked next to a small dot, but it is not a town, a church, a *calvaire*, or a ruin, it is an *aven* – a swallow hole – a natural feature where a stream disappears into the ground. One could be forgiven for not knowing this; it does not appear in many quite large French–English dictionaries. This *aven* is implicated in another alignment – from Espéraza – in the most dubious of the intersections: at the point A, which relies on a back-bearing from Antugnac to Conilhac extended to the Meridian in the ratio 4:1, the two lines crossing at such a low angle that their actual point of intersection could be almost anywhere. This is very bad surveying practice. Our best efforts to justify the designated point gave nothing better than a position about a thousand metres west of the Meridian. But, if marked at all, it would not be by a swallow hole.

The Antugnac 'fan' re-examined

We can therefore rule out any conspiracy among the cartographers of France – at least on this particular point. But why did Lincoln draw the Antugnac 'fan' at all? It does not fit into the pattern of the other figures he had placed on the landscape; there is a suspicious lack of continuity. Yes, now *we* are suspicious. We have shown – and shall elaborate on this later – that there is indeed an excellent reason for drawing the 'fan' from Antugnac, but that it does not follow the equi-spaced pattern of Lincoln's version. And when one has taken the trouble to check the alignments, there can be only one conclusion: Lincoln was told that lines radiating from Antugnac are important, but did not realise he was being handed a key to the interpretation of the Parchments. Or was he misled into believing that the essence of the Rennes mystery is this invisible temple?

Lincoln is by no means alone in airing this type of theory in connection with Rennes. David Wood[1] has plotted similar vast figures across the landscape, and has the good sense to implicate ancient interstellar agencies in their creation. From his knowledge of surveying, he is aware of the impossibility of their creation (if that is the right word for something that does not exist) by an earthly prehistoric culture. Lincoln acknowledges Wood's contribution, but disapproves of his explanation which somehow involves the ancient gods of Egypt and displays an enthusiastic interest in the innermost, secret parts of the female anatomy. Gérard de Sède succinctly and delightfully despatched Mr Wood by referring to his theories as '*topo-gynécologie*'.

It might seem that we are being overly critical of the work of others. But it has taken some serious thought to arrive at the decision that Henry Lincoln's contribution is important but leads to the wrong conclusion. By his own actions he has made himself part of the Rennes-le-Château mystery; his personal involvement with Pierre Plantard and Philippe de Cherisey in the 1970s and his willingness to publish his views have put him in the firing-line. We are doing just the

same, and expect detractors. But we know that the steps we have followed are irrefutable. We have checked and rechecked every move and
have continued to be sceptical in the face of implications that seem so
remarkable. But the most fundamental difference is that Lincoln's theory has received no confirmation from any independent source. While
his diagrams are said to have been checked by 'experts', it is clear that
these referees checked them in isolation and did not investigate the
alignments Lincoln drew on the map.

It is fairly obvious by now that Henry Lincoln was given some complex information from some very informed sources. He would have us
believe also that substantial parts of this information, the Parchments,
and various other pieces of information disseminated by the 'Priory' are
substantially obfuscations, 'red herrings', and that to pursue them will
lead to confusion and failure. This opinion is based on a failure to
interpret correctly the information provided. We were to come to an
entirely different conclusion, finding that very little is superfluous.
Certainly, it is all intended to be puzzling and obscure, but hardly anything is included that is irrelevant or deliberately misleading. As we have
seen, and shall see again, it is the obscure that has to be sought out.

Geometry and the map: the test

So, enlightened and intrigued by the correspondence of the Parchment
lines and the Antugnac 'fan', we drew our geometry on to the map.
(Had the I.G.N. maps been instantly to hand to permit the checking of
Lincoln's work, before the discovery of the geometry within the
Parchments, it is unlikely that we should ever have pursued this affair –
so if obfuscation was the intention, it very nearly succeeded.)

The Meridian, we had learned, had been moved eastward from its
former origin at the Paris Observatoire to the cross on the dome of
the Panthéon; this occurred some time in the late 1800s. A street plan
of Paris provided the distance that this move represented. The

corresponding distance for the more southerly latitude of Rennes-le-Château was calculated to take account of the divergence of adjacent meridians as they run towards the equator. The difference turned out to be so small that it could be ignored for the scale to which we were working; nor indeed on the scale of the Parchments was the Meridian shift very great. Comparing this shift with the geometry on the Parchment showed the route of the Meridian to coincide, as far as scale permitted one to judge, with the centre of the right-hand side of the equilateral triangle – a point marked by a cross. At this stage of our investigations it seemed that the whole affair could have proved to be a hoax or just an amusing game, and it was in the latter context that we chose to proceed. So, if it appeared that the Meridian was intended to be in that specific location on the Parchment, it was assumed that that was where it was supposed to be.

The triangle was drawn on the map (actually on a transparent over-lay, to facilitate corrections) on this basis, and the size derived as described above. The angle that the right-hand side of the triangle makes with the meridian on the Parchment is, it will be recalled, not 45° but 46½°, so we chose the latter; the other sides followed suit, as did centre-lines and other constructional lines. Constant reference back to the Parchment and the proportions of lines enabled us to produce a 'best-fit' version. The point where the 46½° side of the triangle crossed the Meridian proved interesting, as on one side the line passed through a 'trig point', and equidistant along the line on the other side of the Meridian it passed through a feature marked 'Pierre Dressée' – a pre-historic standing stone. Whether this was intended it was impossible to say. As we drew, we would notice near-misses of lines passing features on the map. The same was true as we drew the other triangle to com-plete the hexagram, for we felt that there had been sufficient indication from the paintings that this was the intention. We resisted the tempta-tion to adjust the lines by even the slightest amount to make them go where we wanted.

Then came the moment to draw the square. Should it also have this

1½° shift, or should it be 'square' to the map? We elected to try the latter first, and so rotated the triangle about its top-left corner to give a 45° alignment with the Meridian. When we had done this we were astonished to find that all the near-misses had become direct hits. Centre-lines through the triangle now aligned with the trig point at the summit of la Pique and with a feature marked on the map as 'Cr^x.' – the same cross as *La Croix* of the cipher. The centre of the triangle which had fallen so tantalisingly close to the church at Peyrolles now coincided exactly with the circle part of the symbol for churches used on I.G.N. maps (with this circle-plus-cross symbol, it is the circle – not the cross – that marks the exact location). It may be recalled that when the centre-lines of the equilateral triangle had been drawn on to Parchment 1, one of them passed along the leg of the raised 'R', and we asked whether, with this concealed, the 'R' now looked like a 'P'. Would this be 'P' for Peyrolles? As the centre of the triangle when drawn on to the map falls on Peyrolles church, this surely had been the intention. In the Parchment diagram (Figure 1.12), the upright of the 'P' passes through the centre of the triangle: this point has to represent Peyrolles church. Considerable good fortune had caused us to draw the triangle almost exactly correct at the first attempt, or so it seemed, for all these correspondences were unlikely to be coincidental. And the second triangle of the hexagram also had a role to play, for its lower side had now revealed an orientation of considerable curiosity. Extended to the west, it passed exactly through the symbol for the church at Antugnac – it was another member of the 'fan' family!

To anyone who is thinking that all this smacks of the same type of 'line-finding' that we have so unmercifully criticised in others, we would point out that the latter alignment with Antugnac (henceforth we omit the word 'church' if the sense is clear) had not been suggested by the Parchments and could not possibly have been expected. It actually constitutes confirmation – and there is so much more to come.

'X marks the spot': the Site identified

We were greatly encouraged. The square was now drawn, and the point at which the centre would fall eagerly awaited; for if this should prove to be in a featureless tract of forest there would be no confirmation and nowhere to go from there. The centre actually fell on the side of a mountain about a hundred metres west of some rock outcrops. Then we remembered that the Teniers painting showed quite clearly that the square itself had to be rotated anticlockwise through 1½°; and the first Poussin showed that there were two 1½° components, the first of which we had already discharged with the triangle – so there was one more rotation to go. This done, the centre fell on a singular location; a point that *would* be readily identifiable on the ground because it is on a rocky outcrop on a mountain of otherwise smooth contours. The centre falls between two rocky features, the more southerly of which appeared to be a pinnacle, marked by a spot height on the map; the other, less easily interpreted from the map, was a large slab of rock. The name of this mountain was Cardou; and it lies a mere five kilometres from Rennes-le-Château. Could it really be so simple? Were we really so close to finding the 'treasure'?

Unfortunately it is impossible to show a reproduction of the geometry on a map of adequate size to confirm the features described. Figures 6.3 and 6.4, however, show details taken from the map of the entire area (Plate 11).[2]

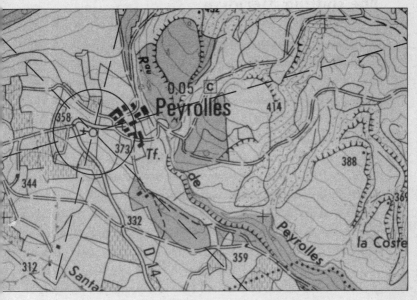

FIGURE 6.3 The geometry on the map – detail at Peyrolles.

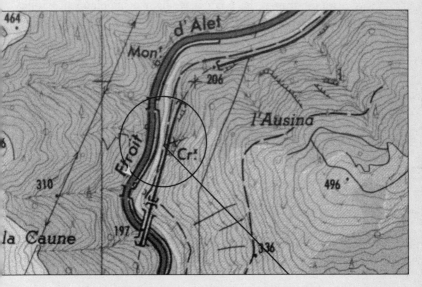

FIGURE 6.4 The geometry on the map – detail at *La Croix*.

The shifting Meridian

But what about Lincoln's information on the subject of the shifting Meridian? We decided to look at the paper by Lucie Lagarde[3] to which Lincoln refers. It became immediately obvious that Lincoln had made a serious mistake, probably caused by his incorrect translation of some fairly technical French. The origin of the Paris Meridian, having been established at the Observatoire in the reign of Louis XIV, has *never* since moved. The cross on the dome of the Panthéon had been adopted as the origin for the new triangulation of France, *not* as a new origin for the Meridian. This fact and the permanence of the Meridian are clearly displayed on the 'TOP25' 1:25,000 scale map of Paris, an enlargement of which is shown in Figure 6.5. So why had we still achieved an apparently correct result? We shall come back to this later. For the moment, it may be said that an 'old' meridian had been incorrectly identified as the Cassini Meridian of 1669 by Lincoln, or possibly by his informants.

We leave the map at this point as we have an appointment with a mountain. Its name – Cardou.

FIGURE 6.5 The Zero Meridian runs through the Paris Observatory – as it always has (detail from I.G.N. 1:25,000 map).

7
MOUNT CARDOU

It was late afternoon, and the time had come to visit the centre of our quest, the location on the side of Cardou mountain; but we needed to go there undetected. The hour of day, coupled with the hope that Sunday would keep any hill-workers and woodcutters away from the slopes, raised our hopes that we would be able to visit the Site without arousing suspicion.

Not for the first time we turned to our copy of the Cassini map. The mountains of Cardou and Blanchefort were recognisable, and the rivers and roads clearly identifiable. It was the roads that first drew our attention that afternoon, for what Cassini had to show differed substantially in detail from the modern maps of the I.G.N. The road which entered the valley below Blanchefort and Cardou did not cross the water at the juncture of the rivers Sals and Rialsesse, but further upstream at Serres. This placed the valley road to Rennes-les-Bains on the eastern side of the Sals, as opposed to its present-day course along the west bank.

Cassini had provided us with crucial and important information: this was, in all probability, the ancient road followed by the Romans and the Templars as they passed through the valley. We needed to approach the location via the same route if we were going to see the

Site as they did. Over the last couple of years we had received an enormous amount of help from people known and unknown to us in England and France, and we now received the indirect aid of the people of Haut Razès. Standing on the bank of the River Sals below Cardou, we saw that the local woodcutters, in their quest for access, had opened up the old Cassini road. We had resigned ourselves to a fairly arduous cross-country expedition, but now our approach would be a straight-forward matter. The previous day we had taken our first look at the Site (Plate 8) from across the valley, having climbed the steep path as far as Roc Nègre. The Cassini road now brought us to the south-west of the rock formation. This position left Roc Nègre at our backs, a hundred metres higher on the opposite side of the valley. The formation stood two hundred metres above and in front of us. As if stretched at the sides and compressed from above, the rocks had assumed an appearance which left us stunned (Figure 7.1).

An image of a sheer rockface from a distance can never prepare one for the sense of being totally dwarfed when close up. So it was for us when we finally reached the base of the rock. Surrounded above and to the sides by sheer pillars of rock, and with the valley far below, the feel-ing of being humbled by nature surpassed, for a brief moment, the realisation of where it was we were standing. This was where we had been directed, the exact position specified by the Parchments and the paintings. This was the location of the Secret – hidden and perhaps lost for centuries.

We stood in awe, and our eyes confirmed the unforgettable. The tri-angular formation far above seemed to blend with the base rock joining the left and right pillars. As the light faded, the colour began to drain away from the scene, and the angles of the rocks were thrown into sharp relief against the sky. Images of the many paintings we had pored over prior to our visit suddenly flooded back, for the right-hand edge of the rock on the left ran straight and true from summit to base, at an unmistakable angle from the horizontal. It ran at the angle of the shep-herd's staff in the Poussin, the staff of St Paul in the Teniers, the lance

FIGURE 7.1 The Site, viewed from a point on the foresters' road
opposite Roc Nègre.

in *La Fontaine de fortune* and the number given at *La Croix* – it ran at an
angle of 75°.

We could see that the rock formation before us, at the location we
had identified as the Site, would make an ideal hiding-place for a treasure, and it was clear what kind of excavation would be necessary to
conceal it. A small tunnel would be bored into the near-vertical rockface, leading to a chamber. An initial phase of the excavation would
have been to remove several metres of the loose eroded rock from the
'scree' slope at the base of the rockface. This would accomplish two
important objectives: it would ensure safe working conditions at the
mouth of the tunnel, and, once the treasure had been deposited, the
entrance could be hidden by piling the scree back to its original level.

Walking back down the forest road, we paused to examine a cutting into the heap of scree that sloped down from the sheer rockfaces above. Generally the material was quite fine, but our attention was drawn to a stratum of particularly coarse stones and small rocks concentrated in a bed about twenty centimetres deep below a thick layer of topsoil (Figure 7.2). This band was distinctive, and occurred *only* at this one level in the scree, to some distance either side of the Site. Beyond that it did not recur; in either direction (Figure 7.3). Could this deposit result from excavations carried out further up the slope?

At the junction of the rivers Sals and Rialsesse we halted below the heights of the Château de Blanchefort and looked back at the Site. We had with us a roll of film containing photographs of the Site taken as dusk approached. One exposure, taken hurriedly as the light had faded, would prove the greatest revelation of all. It showed the profile of the rocks at sunset against a darkening sky. The 75° angle, formed by the left-hand rock, had already been recognised as we stood dwarfed by the towering natural structure above; the remainder of the formation would combine to form a surprise which would astonish us.

Later we would compare this natural outline to the outline of a highly relevant painting we had tracked down. Not only would the match be exact, it would bring Jesus of Nazareth, quite literally, into the picture.

FIGURE 7.2 Cutting on the foresters' road – the layer of rock fragments below the Site.

FIGURE 7.3 Cutting on the foresters' road – typical deposit, with no layer of rock fragments.

8
THREE ERRANT PRIESTS

We were fairly sure we had found where the 'treasure' was believed to be located – but what it was remained elusive. There had to be some connection between the interested parties involved which could shed light on why this cache of such importance and perceived value had not previously been identified and dug up. It was becoming more and more obvious that the treasure was more valuable to some people left where it was. With this in mind we decided to take a more in-depth look at the *dramatis personae* so central to the events at the end of the nineteenth century.

Good working relationships between priests of neighbouring parishes in rural areas are not unusual. In order to ensure the efficient running of the services required by the Church, a group could undoubtedly exercise more control than an individual. But the legend of the area spoke of a more intense and indeed sinister collaboration between Abbé Saunière, Abbé Gélis and Abbé Boudet – the neighbouring priests of Rennes-le-Château, Coustaussa and Rennes-les-Bains.

Saunière was the junior of both Gélis and Boudet. Of the three, Antoine Gélis was the oldest: he was born in 1827, and had been priest of Coustaussa since 1857. Henri Boudet, born ten years later, had been the parish priest of Rennes-les-Bains since 1872. By the beginning of 1886, the year the Parchments were allegedly discovered, Saunière was in his thirty-fifth year, Boudet was approaching fifty-one and Gélis was awaiting his sixty-first birthday. That they were not of the same generation is neither here nor there, for legend has it that there was much else that brought them together.

Boudet and Saunière shared a close interest in the history and archaeology of the area, and both were tireless walkers. Gélis and Saunière apparently enjoyed a relationship of close confidentiality, if the stories of the correspondence between Gélis and the younger priest are to be believed. And all three had apparently been recipients of an unexplained windfall, for thenceforth none of the three was to endure the financial hardships associated with rural priesthood. But the apparent harmony between them was not to last.

The year 1897 saw not just the murder of Gélis, but also a rift in the close personal relationship between Boudet and Saunière. The triumvirate was broken by the death of the eldest of the group, and rumour has it that both Boudet and Saunière were visited by mysterious strangers in the days immediately preceding their own deaths, in 1915 and 1917 respectively. But the death of Gélis did not halt the supply of money to Saunière, and one can only assume that the older man's role had been secondary – an unfortunate, minor part in the larger drama. If Saunière is therefore seen as the central figure in the fortunes of the three, what of his known ambitions and the legacy he left? Having laboured long and hard to reach our conclusions about the true nature of the Parchments, it was now essential to ascertain whether Saunière had arrived at the same point and perhaps preserved his knowledge in some tangible form, leaving clues for posterity.

It is said that, towards the end of his life, Saunière entertained hopes of owning a car – a fantasy he was never to realise – and it is a little ironic that the road to his village is now used by multitudes of motorised tourists on their way to view his church and hear the official version of the carryings-on at Rennes. The Bérenger Saunière

industry is apparent everywhere: the shelves of shops are full of literature ranging from the more obscure esoterica to recently published
letters between the famous priest and his contemporaries. Demand
from the visiting public for information appears inexhaustible. In the
course of our research we had read much of this 'literature', but
remained largely unconvinced by what it had to say. Armed with our
own theories, we entered Saunière's church of St Mary Magdalene.

The terrible place

It is not just the gloom of the interior that lowers the spirit on entering this now famous church. Once the eyes have adjusted to the dim
light, the garish and tasteless decoration is almost overwhelming. Over
a period of years following his initial discovery of the Parchments,
Saunière 'restored' the fabric of the church, adding ornamentation and
detail, bizarre figures and gaudy carving. To any Catholic entering this
sanctum and wishing to cross his or her body with holy water, the font
provided is supported by perhaps the most unlikely figure of all, a well-
known gentleman indeed – the Devil himself (Plate 1). As a result of
our analysis of the Devil's Armchair, we now knew what no one
except Saunière and Boudet understood – the true reason for the
presence of this figure in the church and his uncomfortable, crouching
stance.

Saunière's lavish restoration has not withstood one hundred years of
exposure to the atmosphere of Haut Razès particularly well. The
brightly coloured plaster is badly cracked, suggesting subsidence of the
main fabric. The stations of the cross appeared to have weathered better. Impossible to overlook, the stations occupy a disproportionate
amount of space in what is not a large building. As others have shown,
they differ from the standard version in ways that suggest cryptic intention: the meanings to be derived from them undoubtedly refer to the
Secret, but so far have eluded a comprehensive analysis.

On 20 October 1891 Saunière commenced a reconstruction of the entrance and main door to the church, costing a grand total of 915 francs. He instructed the company of Giscard et Fils of Toulouse to incorporate to the left and right of the archway the arms of his bishop, Billard, and the holy father, Pope Leo XIII. The work was completed in 1892, preceding the stations of the cross and the holy water stoup by some five years; as if anticipating their eventual arrival, Saunière put the finishing touch to the entrance of his parish church. In the middle of the bas-relief directly above the door, the masons were instructed to carve an inscription which is probably unique in a modern place of Christian worship:

TERRIBILIS EST LOCUS ISTE

The declaration 'This place is terrible' had been employed in an early Christian church of ancient Rome, but had not proved popular since. Undoubtedly Saunière's knowledge of early Church history was the inspiration for this apparently cynical declaration. Having read the inscription above the entrance, one steps into the church to find the Devil offering holy water. It is surely no coincidence that the porch containing this inscription was completed the same year the Parchments were taken to Paris. Perhaps this message was a key to the darker side of his discovery? But if this was Saunière's place of discomfort, we were now to visit a place which brought him obvious delight and pleasure – his garden.

Saunière and his housekeeper

Photographs of Bérenger Saunière are common, but there is one in particular that has a charm of its own. Taken in his garden, it shows him sitting on the edge of the newly completed fountain, commissioned in 1897 and still, at this stage, empty. On the opposite side stands his housekeeper and confidante, Marie Denarnaud, hand on hip. Both subjects are smiling broadly as if anticipating the pleasure the fountain would bring. But perhaps Mlle Denarnaud looked content for rather different reasons. After all, not a single brick in the priest's newly completed residence, the Villa Bethania, belonged legally to her employer – it was all in her name. Saunière's sole legal claim to property was his burial plot, lying ready and waiting against the northern perimeter wall of the churchyard. But Saunière's generosity towards his companion did not stop there. Between 22 October 1898 and 4 April 1905 he purchased, in her name, no fewer than seven parcels of land adjoining the church and presbytery.

Marie Denarnaud's father, her mother and her brother had followed her to Rennes in 1892. This move prompted Saunière to restore the presbytery, enabling him to offer his housekeeper's relatives hospitality within his own home. By 1894 father and son were fully engaged on the restoration of the building and the adjoining churchyard. On an annual priestly salary of 900 francs, Saunière was to spend a total of 90,000 francs on the Villa Bethania and a further 19,000 francs on the terraces and gardens. This expenditure alone was an impossible amount of money for a man in Saunière's position to acquire – let alone spend – in the normal course of events: it amounted to more than 120 years of income from his salary.

If the only piece of real estate owned by Saunière was his final resting-place, then perhaps the grave itself could shed further light on the mystery. To deter treasure-hunters, a communal edict was passed in the years following the publication of the Parchments banning unauthorised excavation in the area. This move was necessitated by the perilous state of many of the old buildings in the narrow streets surrounding the Château d'Hautpoul, undermined by extensive tunnelling directed towards the ancient château and Saunière's church. In view of this edict, we had envisaged a picture reminiscent of the photographs we had seen from the 1950s – the graves of Saunière and Mlle Denarnaud, lying peacefully side by side. But we were in for a shock.

Clandestine use of pick and shovel had not been confined to below the streets of Rennes: an attempt had been made to break into the burial place of the priest and his female companion, and their graves were now protected by a substantial layer of concrete.

That these two graves should have been tampered with was unsettling, but not without precedent. Saunière and Denarnaud were not themselves blameless when it came to meddling with the departed, for they had been admonished during their lifetime for disturbing graves in the cemetery of St Mary Magdalene. On 12 March 1895 the municipal council of Rennes-le-Château wrote to the Prefect of the Aude, protesting that Saunière had displaced crosses, removed tombstones and destroyed old graves in the churchyard. During this period Saunière was engaged in the restoration of his churchyard; whether he concurrently pursued other, more sinister interests remains open to question.

The evening was drawing in, and we decided to leave the gloomy cemetery and its famous occupants. Passing through the iron gates of the cemetery, we walked down the narrow street and paused beneath the walls of the most imposing building in Rennes-le-Château, the Château d'Hautpoul. The gift of 3,000 francs which had enabled Saunière to start work on the altar of his church in 1886 had come from the Comtesse de Chambord, wife of the late pretender to the throne of France – the man who would have been Henri V. The restoration of the Bourbon line had been a cause close to the hearts of Saunière and the Marquis Amand d'Hautpoul. The assistance given by the Marquis had been considerable, and Saunière's sermon of 1885 – so vehemently anti-Republican – had evidently been noticed; hence the gift to the church of the initial sum.

With the light fading rapidly we left the village of Rennes-le-Château, reflecting on the alleged words of the late Marie Denarnaud:[1]

The people around here walk around on gold without knowing it . . . With that which the Monsieur has left we could feed

Rennes for a hundred years and there would still be enough left over . . . one day I will tell you a secret which will make of you a rich man – very, very rich.

Henri Boudet

As we assessed our findings that evening in the square of Rennes-les-Bains, we were conscious of being at the heart of the area studied by legions of treasure-hunters before us, all hungry for the breakthrough we had achieved over the last few months. For Rennes-les-Bains was Henri Boudet's home territory, and this close friend of Saunière had lived for years in the small presbytery opposite which we now sat. The square has changed little in the last century, and it was easy to imagine the learned priest, with his undisclosed and powerful connections, going about his daily business. There are many mysteries surrounding Boudet's life, not the least of which is the absence of surviving evidence *about* his life. There are no surviving photographs of him, and yet he is known to have been a keen photographer and apparently possessed a darkroom in his house. But perhaps his photography did not extend to personal pictures of himself and his friends. Perhaps the darkroom was used to provide copies of the Parchments for a select group? As far as we know, no likeness of him has ever been published.

The only clue to his appearance that we know of is to be found in the notes of Pierre Plantard's grandfather, recording impressions of his visit to Saunière at Rennes-le-Château on 6 June 1892. He wrote:

The Abbé Boudet, vicar of Rennes-les-Bains, the neighbouring parish, seemed to me as anxious to be extinguished as the Abbé Saunière was to be lit up. As much as the Abbé Saunière, a great dark fellow with dark eyes, of almost 1.80 metres, made an impressive figure, so the Abbé Boudet with his 1.70 metres, his slenderness and his lavender-blue eyes, did not.

This quotation is taken from Pierre Plantard's 1978 preface to a reprint[2] of the strange book *La Vraie Langue celtique* written by Henri Boudet. The only publicly known copy of Boudet's signature (reproduced in the same reprint) is a dedication inscribed in an original copy of *La Vraie Langue celtique* given to Plantard's grandfather (Figure 8.1). One might well question the authenticity of the previous quotation, and of other information contained in Plantard's preface, given the aura of fantasy that enshrouds the mystery of Rennes. Did Boudet really give a copy of his book to Plantard's grandfather, and is the signature really his? These doubts were essentially dispelled by our chance discovery in the Bodleian Library of a letter in Boudet's hand, and with it the original envelope (Figure 8.2). The signature and handwriting, clearly Boudet's best in the Oxford letter, are evidently by the same hand in the two examples.

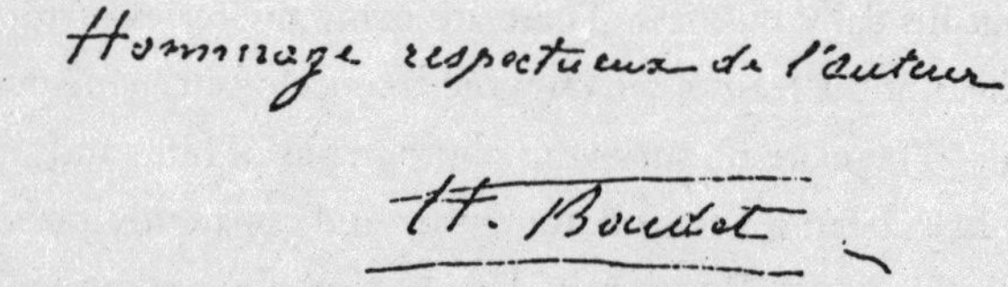

FIGURE 8.1 Henri Boudet's signature, as it appears in a personal dedication in a copy of his book *La Vraie Langue celtique*.

We had discovered the letter and envelope, addressed to 'The Rector of Oxford University', inside the cover of Boudet's book. The letter, written in good copperplate, had retained a freshness, having been protected from the light of day after probably being read only once and not opened again. Boudet had signed his communication with a flourish, posting the book and accompanying message from the small post office at Rennes-les-Bains; it had subsequently rested in the stacks of the very library we had left a few days previously in Oxford. We were quite possibly the first people this century to read its contents.

After the usual pleasantries, and an explanation of the book's content,

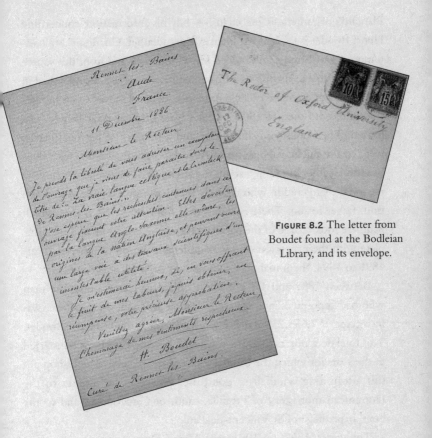

Rennes les Bains
Aude
France
11 Décembre 1886

Monsieur le Recteur

Je prends la liberté de vous adresser un exemplai...
de l'ouvrage que je viens de faire paraître sous le
titre de *La Vraie Langue celtique et le Cromleck*
de Rennes-les-Bains.

J'ose espérer que les recherches contenues dans ce...
ouvrage fixeront votre attention. Elles dévoilen...
par la langue Anglo-Saxonne elle même, les
origines de la station Anglaise, et peuvent ouvr...
une large voie à des travaux scientifiques d'un...
incontestable utilité.

Je m'estimerai heureux, Si, en vous offrant
le fruit de mes labeurs, j'puis obtenir, en
récompense, votre précieuse approbation.

Veuillez agréer, Monsieur le Recteur,
l'hommage de mes sentiments respectueux.

H. Boudet

Curé de Rennes les Bains.

The Rector of Oxford University
England

FIGURE 8.2 The letter from Boudet found at the Bodleian Library, and its envelope.

Boudet commends the work to the English in particular as being of immense importance. Rather strange – but then his thesis that all the languages of the world derive from Anglo-Saxon is fairly strange too. In sending a copy to one of the most celebrated universities in the world, we may recognise the same motive as was behind the sending of pamphlets to the Bibliothèque Nationale: it enabled it to survive. It is said that Boudet also sent a copy to Queen Victoria; she may well have been amused.

In his preface to *La Vraie Langue celtique*, Pierre Plantard outlines his theory that a message is hidden in Boudet's book. While interesting,

Plantard's argument is inconclusive, but his information concerning Henri Boudet is fascinating. Plantard's grandfather, Charles, was a contemporary of Boudet and indeed knew him well, and from this source Plantard is able to furnish us with some interesting facts. Boudet died in 1915 without direct heirs, a circumstance identical to that of his brother Edmond, who died in 1907 and in whose grave at Axat Boudet was buried. The books from his library and a number of personal papers went to the public rubbish tip in Axat. His account-books, with their beautiful leather bindings, caught the attention of a citizen of Axat who retrieved them, and in whose family they have since been passed down from father to son. These accounts date from 1885, the year in which Saunière took charge of the parish of Rennes-le-Château, and are complete with the exception of one considerable period of time, the years 1891 to 1894, the initial period of restoration work at Rennes.

Between 1885 and 1901, Bishop Billard of Carcassonne, the man who had appointed Saunière to his station at Rennes-le-Château, was in receipt of 7,655,250 francs from his junior in rank, Henri Boudet. This total does not include any sums which might have been transferred in the years for which the Boudet accounts are missing. The bishop put this astonishing windfall to good use, directing the monies to the Dominican monastery of Prouille, south of Carcassonne, and to the boys' orphanage of St Vincent-de-Paul.

The years 1887 to 1901 saw Marie Denarnaud in receipt of 3,679,431 francs from Boudet, money destined for the restoration of the church of St Mary Magdalene at Rennes-le-Château. Once again, this is not counting the period 1891–94, but these transactions follow a pattern consistent in the story. Bérenger Saunière was never the direct recipient of Boudet's gold francs – this was a service performed by Marie. Had the use of Marie as intermediary been a sensible precaution against the possible actions of a successor to Bishop Billard? If this were the case, then the action was fully justified when Beauséjour on his succession to the bishopric launched a full-scale inquiry into the priest's financial affairs (Figure 8.3).

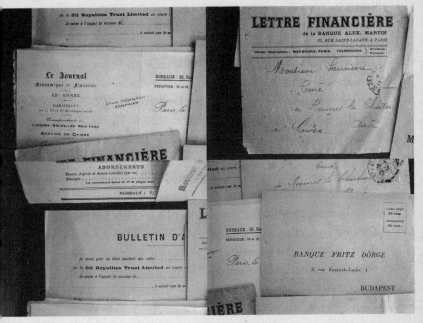

FIGURE 8.3 Evidence of Saunière's involvement in financial affairs beyond his station, preserved in the museum at Rennes.

With little money or property officially to his name, Saunière was unimpeachable. This left the investigation with the protracted task of condemning him of irregularity in his office as priest. In addition to the enormous sums of money made over to Denarnaud for the restoration of the church, Marie profited to the tune of a further 837,260 francs from the priest of Rennes-les-Bains between the years of 1894 and 1903. Boudet also paid Alfred, the Jesuit brother of Saunière, sums of 10,000 and 15,000 francs in 1901, and two further amounts of 15,000 francs in 1903. No reason or explanation has ever been given for this.

Proof of the high regard in which Boudet was held is to be found in the vestibule of the church at Rennes-les-Bains in the form of a large wall memorial inscribed with a dedication to him. It was hardly local disapproval that caused him to be buried at Axat. Many theories have been advanced to explain Boudet's somewhat strange place of burial, but one clue to the choice of brother over mother may lie in the contribution from Edmond to his brother's obscure and cryptic *magnum opus* – La *Vraie Langue celtique*.

Edmond Boudet had worked as the local notary, a job that entailed the study of all land transactions and manuscripts. This brotherly combination of priest and notary represented a potent power-base in a small community like Rennes. Indeed, it was Edmond who had drawn the detailed map included in *La Vraie Langue celtique* – an intricate work, executed with immense care and detail, which included the area of Cardou and Blanchefort – an area which we now knew to be crucial to the unravelling of the mystery. A close study of this map revealed some surprising inaccuracies.

Cardou was drawn further to the north than the position shown on the État-Major map, which would have been readily available to the brothers Boudet. If this were merely a case of technical error, or an attempt to avoid copyright problems, the fault had been compounded by the marking of the spot heights. Many contradicted the officially surveyed and recorded results.

Our formation of rocks on the side of Cardou, the rocks that so impressed us when we entered the valley, were distinguished on Edmond's map as a feature separate from the mountainside on which they are situated, and given the name 'Lampos'. Henri's explanation of the origin of this name is fascinating indeed:[3]

> This last rock, separated from Cardou and presenting several points reunited at the base, gave our ancestors the idea of small beings comprising a family . . . and poetically named these needles Lampos. This word derives from 'lamb', or 'to lamb', when speaking of the sheep.

Whether Boudet wished to convey the importance of the Site by the use of a name synonymous with Jesus Christ, we shall never know. There can be no doubt, however, that the name does not appear on any of the other maps, ancient or modern, that we had studied.

With this in mind, we turned our attention once again to Abbé Saunière. Perhaps a closer inspection of the museum dedicated to him would shed more light on the knowledge he inherited in 1886. The picture we had formed of him prior to the trip was beginning to emerge with greater clarity.

It was fairly obvious by now that Bérenger Saunière had been a man of complex and deep-seated convictions; a man who was dedicated to his role as priest, and generous to a fault. That at one point in his career he was in charge of two parishes is confirmation of his professional competence. The arduous year spent covering the two parishes of Antugnac and Rennes had been tackled with zeal; his sermons, rich and authoritative, displayed a strong grasp and understanding of both the Bible and the human psyche. A 'simple' parish priest, as the literature about his life so often describes him, he was certainly not.

Any air of naivety he undoubtedly cultivated intentionally, and probably proved essential when he was called to account for his financial affairs by Bishop Beauséjour, who had replaced Billard as Bishop of Carcassonne in 1902. This change of regime spelt trouble for both Saunière and Boudet. Saunière's attempt at explaining his immense acquisition of wealth to his new and highly unamused superior can only be described as laughable. It was apparent to us – having read the correspondence that passed between the two – that this was not simply arrogance on the part of Saunière, but a deliberate stalling in the face of a situation he knew he had little chance of explaining adequately.

Considering the vast sums expended on his building works and lifestyle, his explanations of a modest win on the lottery, tips from rich tourists and fees for saying masses (this was actually prohibited), and the other weak excuses he offered, were never going to carry much weight. When pressed by the persistent bishop, Saunière became too ill to correspond further. The matter finally went to the Vatican, and – astonishingly – Saunière was acquitted. This victory can but leave us wondering what his trump card might have been.

There existed an outside chance that, if he had discovered the secret geometry of the paintings from the Louvre, Saunière chose to preserve his findings in some cryptic fashion. But the chance that such evidence would have survived seemed remote. We, however, were fired with optimism by our recent discoveries, and we passed through the low entrance to the museum with a sense of expectation.

Further clues and impressions

Climbing directly up the internal wooden staircase leading to the small museum, we passed many photographs on the wall to our left. For the *aficionado* of 'the mystery of Rennes' this was a Mecca – the main props that had supported the Saunière affair were all present and accounted for. The most dramatic and colourful exhibit was Bérenger Saunière's priestly robes, preserved in all their glory. The richness of decoration seemed out of place in this humble village. But these were the garments of Holy Roman power – the official robes of the priest sent to the crumbling church of St Mary Magdalene in 1885 – and the brilliant colour of the brocaded cross shone out at us, undiminished by the passage of time.

We passed by the columns alleged to have contained the Parchments – they were exactly as we had seen them on our previous visit, and had nothing more to reveal. But armed with our knowledge of the Boudet brothers' complicity, the contradiction over the discovery itself did indicate one other possibility. Edmond, as notary to the area, would be as likely to have had documents relevant to the Château d'Hautpoul and the Blanchefort-Hautpoul-Fleury dynasty pass through his hands as would anyone else. Perhaps Edmond discovered the Parchments in the nearby château, or perhaps they had come into his possession in some other way. If Saunière *had* found them in his church – and no one else had been involved – why the apparent discrepancies? It was an interesting possibility, but it raised more questions than it answered.

As we were leaving, we were brought to an abrupt halt by one of the photographs on the staircase wall – a small, yet highly relevant illustration. In this museum where everything is commented on, this exhibit was conspicuous by its lack of museum analysis. Here, measuring approximately eight centimetres square and casually displayed, was a copy of Bérenger Saunière's *ex libris* – his personal bookplate (Figure 8.4). It readily caught our eye, attuned as we were to the geometry of the paintings and Parchments, for it contained a hexagram combined with a cross, an extremely strange arrangement for a Roman Catholic priest to favour.

With no hesitation, we took several photographs. Saunière had included in the bookplate's design the cross of Christ and a number of words and phrases which seemed at first glance insignificant. Not wishing to linger in front of such an intriguing piece of evidence, we resigned ourselves to a closer inspection of the details when the film was developed. We knew that we had come upon a piece of Saunière's own property which had a strong personal resonance. Just how significant it would prove we could not yet imagine.

We left the museum and took the well-trodden path to the Villa Bethania, now open and receiving visitors. In return for a few francs we gained entry to the home built for the famous priest and his housekeeper, which was now suffering visibly from the passage of the curious. The heady days when Marie Denarnaud had served guests with the finest wines, vintage Martinique rum and other costly delicacies were long past, and this was underlined by a computer screen flickering in one of the rooms we passed on the way through to the garden.

The state of Saunière's monument to personal fantasy, his Tour Magdala (Magdala Tower), reflects the present-day situation. It stands at

ASMODÉE

GRAVURE TIREE D'UN
LIVRE DE L'ABBÉ SAUNIERE

TRINUS ET UNUS ✱ TRIA SUNT MIRABILIA DEI
B. S.
CENTRUM IN TRIGONO CENTRI ✱ CENTRUM
HOMO ✱ MATER ET VIRGO

FIGURE 8.4 Saunière's personal bookplate, and a cutting of the Devil ('Asmodée') in chains found in his personal papers, framed together in the museum at Rennes.

the south-western end of the property, in complete architectural contrast to the Villa Bethania, and is similar to many of the neo-Gothic
follies of England. The square construction of the ground-floor library
supports a narrow circular tower with a spiral staircase leading to
rooftop battlements. Our intention was to enter the tower, climb the
staircase and look at the view enjoyed by Saunière. The door was ajar,
but our entry was undignified; we scrambled to the centre of the floor
across a mound of rubble. Each of the room's four corners disappeared
downwards into a cavity. Quite evidently, the ban on tunnelling
imposed on 28 July 1965 had not protected Bérenger Saunière's singular contribution to the architectural heritage of the Haut Razès:
treasure-hunters had been at work inside the building, undermining it.
The tower had been built at a cost of 40,000 francs, which would then
have bought a sizeable hunting-lodge. Despite the recent ravages, the
expense lavished on the tower was obvious: the library fittings, for
example, had been constructed by the finest joiners. The tower, completed in 1905, was erected on the site of a previous construction
which, according to legend, had exploded into the skies early in the
fourteenth century, several years before the first recorded use of gun-
powder in the West. We opened the staircase door and entered
uninvited, climbing to the battlements above.

Our reward was a remarkable view over the village and beyond.
The surrounding mountains were now fully visible, and one to the east
was particularly prominent – the dome of Cardou. Could it be that the
Tour Magdala was constructed by Saunière in order to view this one
specific location?

Later, as we walked down the road out of Rennes-le-Château,
avoiding the coach-loads of tourists, we thought once again of
Saunière's wish for a car. Had death come unnaturally, leaving this
desire unfulfilled? After all, cost was no object. Between 1896 and
1917 Saunière had officially dispensed a total of 659,413 gold francs.[4]
(One year after the death of her employer, Mlle Denarnaud officially
estimated her fixed assets at 100,000 gold francs.) That death had come

unannounced to the priest at the top of the hill seemed indisputable. It is reputed that Denarnaud had ordered Saunière's coffin one week in advance of his sudden and fatal stroke – her motives for this anticipatory move never explained. Equally strange, by all accounts, was the treatment of Saunière's corpse. Rather than being left in bed to receive the last respects of mourners, he was propped up in a chair downstairs (or on the terrace, according to some versions), wrapped in a cloth with a tasselled fringe – possibly even a ceremonial robe. Some mourners plucked tassels from his makeshift shroud, as mementoes. Why they should have taken this (apparent) liberty remains a mystery.

Thoughts of foul play reminded us of the Devil weighed down with holy water, and Bérenger Saunière's warning to those who entered the church of St Mary Magdalene. In the museum, quite apart from the extraordinary bookplate, we had also seen a curious cutting alleged to have been found in Saunière's personal papers (Figure 8.4) which showed Asmodeus in chains. As devils go, Asmodeus was the possessor of an interesting past: he had been employed against his wishes by King Solomon to assist in the building of the Temple of Jerusalem. The photofit with the Devil in the church was perfect. Thoughts of the Temple reminded us of the Knights Templar who had sworn their vows on the Temple Mount in *c.* 1120. The geometry and the presence of the hexagram in the Parchments, the paintings and the bookplate began to come together. A link was beginning to form in our minds about the extra-curricular activities of the priest of Rennes-le-Château, but it would be some time before conclusive proof was forthcoming.

An unsolved murder

The next morning we made a pilgrimage – a visit to the village and grave of Abbé Gélis. It was to be our first view of the last resting place of the murdered friend of Saunière and Boudet. The weather was suitably foreboding.

Coustaussa lies on the northern side of the Couiza–Arques road, which winds up the hill to the village; it is not dissimilar to the road to Rennes-le-Château, a mere two kilometres to the south-west. Antoine Gélis's grave is two-thirds of the way up the narrow cemetery (Figure 8.5). The graveyard is built on an incline, and the large and imposing headstone on the murdered priest's grave was succumbing to gravity. Much of the topsoil around the grave had been washed away, and the stone itself was badly frost-damaged, with pieces broken off. We stood in front of the grave, our feet sinking deep into the soft red earth – perilously close, we felt, to the body that lay beneath. The one word of his epitaph can just about be read on the disintegrating surface. It is chilling – *Assassiné*.

The official inquest into Gélis's death made much of the priest's reclusiveness and of his fear of danger in the form of persons known or unknown. Gélis spent most of his time alone in his presbytery behind the protection of a locked door which, when opened, triggered a bell. This was in direct contrast to the 'open door' practice followed by most priests of the time. That Gélis's assassin entered the house without the use of force, without activating this alarm, strongly suggests that they were acquainted. But the ease with which the murderer cornered his victim was not matched by the crime itself – a struggle ensued and the subsequent murder was violent and very bloody. Gélis did not go to his death as quietly as he had lived his life: the violence of the attack and his unsuccessful attempts at self-defence were tragically attested by the blood-soaked floor on which his battered body was later discovered.

The question of motivation remains a mystery, for while Gélis's killer had forced the lock of a deed-box – intent, it seemed, on recovering or discovering a document – the gold coin clearly visible on a chest of drawers was left untouched. But the attacker, whether intentionally or not, had left a calling-card: a packet of cigarettes with the curious phrase 'Viva Angelina' written on the front. To this day no one has determined the identity of the killer, though there is no doubt that in such a small village someone knew something or heard something.

FIGURE 8.5 The grave of Abbé Antoine Gélis.

Coustaussa is compact and intimate with narrow winding streets. It is impossible to believe that a murderer could infiltrate the village, commit such a crime and depart totally unobserved. Noise was the other factor prevalent in our minds. The crime had been brutal. It seemed that poor Gélis had struggled to reach the window after he had been battered with the fire-dog from his own fireplace. His attempt to summon help had been in vain, and he died under further repeated blows from an axe wielded from behind. Perhaps observing some obscure ritual, the killer had left his victim neatly arranged on the floor of the house.

It was time to visit Gélis's church. For such a modest and minor parish the church was large, and if the hopes of the clergy to fill all the seats verged on the optimistic, the money spent on the decoration was out of all proportion in such a humble location. The altar, of ogee sarcophagus form, rested on the ornately carved paws of a lion. The marble from which it was carved showed little sign of flaw, the fine, close matrix indicating both expense and quality. A symbol had been carved into the altar-screen's centre, and richly gilded for lasting effect. It was an equilateral triangle.

From behind the altar there rose twin wooden columns, supporting an oil painting between them which depicted another symbol by now familiar to us – the grape and the vine. The quality of the carving was indisputable. We followed the vine upwards as it reached to the full height of the column, the rich purple of the grapes still fresh in the sanctified atmosphere of this remote church. The complexity of this display, combined with the opulence of the altar, created an overbearing effect of garishness at odds with the simplicity of the rest of the interior.

Permitted entry to the vestry behind the altar, we pushed open the door and walked into the nineteenth century, for the room was exactly as it must have been in Gélis's time. The dust lay thick where Gélis would have robed himself for the ritual of the holy mass. In one of the cupboards we investigated, hanging in mute testimony to his role of priest and confessor, were the chasubles, and, like those of Bérenger Saunière, they were ornate and impressive. Gélis's obvious dedication to his faith was there for all to see, and evoked a poignancy when we thought of his fractured remains now lying beneath the hill above the village.

Our interest in the dusty remnants before us exceeded the patience of the verger who, by now alerted to our overt curiosity and showing much discomfort, ushered us towards the oak door of the vestry. By the door there lay a wooden object, no bigger than a book. Its shape was familiar – a Star of David, according to the verger. To us, though, this was clearly the same symbol that Saunière had incorporated in his bookplate, for here too the two triangles were superimposed, not interwoven in the way that the Star of David is conventionally formed. In any case, what was an ostensibly Jewish artefact doing in a Catholic church? Simply made, from two wooden triangles fixed together, and neither varnished nor painted, it was obviously not intended as a decorative item and certainly not meant to be on permanent display. We could only surmise that it had been made for personal contemplation, or for instructional purposes. This symbol had meanings quite apart from Christianity, Judaism, or even paganism. It had once represented the dual nature of the individual, part of a system of belief based on the ancient idea of life as a conflict of light versus dark. Had this ancient concept of duality been the inspiration for Saunière's bookplate design, and did its manifestation in the wooden star hint at activities beyond the realm of Catholicism?

Having concentrated on Saunière for much of our search, it now seemed that the death of Gélis and the symbols employed in his church and on his gravestone were leading us closer to a common thread between the various parties. One suggestion put forward by previous researchers is that the crime against Gélis involved the affairs of Rosicrucians, a theory which, as we progressed, was appearing to gain credibility. If the tripartite alliance – Saunière, Boudet and Gélis – had made considerable inroads into the Parchments during the three years of relative tranquillity before the documents were taken to Paris, then the involvement of Parisian paymasters, be they neo-Rosicrucians or illuminati of the Catholic Church, was highly likely. The prospect of acquiring knowledge of the true location of the Site would be, for any such organisation, a major coup. But had Saunière and his band of brothers fully succeeded in their efforts, and if so, had they conveyed the correct result to their superiors?

One hundred years on, the terrible murder of Abbé Gélis and the bizarre events surrounding the death of Saunière were still unsolved. If the Secret, which had been known to Boudet, Saunière and Marie Denarnaud, concerned the clues in the bookplate, in the church, at *La Croix* and at the Devil's Armchair, we would be well on the path to solving this strangest of episodes, the rebus within the greater mystery of Rennes.

The mind or minds which had conspired to create this grandest of all puzzles had employed codes, geometry, maps, obscure Latinisms and an intimate knowledge of the area. The cipher square, with its centre near La Mort, was therefore perplexing. This apparent misinterpretation of the geometry was surprising. Correct interpretation of the geometry of the Parchments and paintings had apparently not been achieved, and this presented several intriguing possibilities.

Had Saunière and Boudet fully interpreted the Parchments? Why the inclusion of the coded message which clearly indicated another site – the location near 'La Mort'? The suspicion that the message was a deliberate attempt to throw the investigator off the trail was growing stronger as we researched into the events surrounding the three priests.

9
THE POUSSIN
ENIGMA

On our return from Rennes-le-Château, finding ourselves at Toulouse Airport with some time and a few francs to spend, we decided to visit the bookshop. We noticed that the current issue of the magazine *Beaux Arts* carried an article on Nicolas Poussin, and were amazed to find it illustrated by a colour photograph of *Les Bergers d'Arcadie II*, *out* of its frame. Along the top of the painting was a wide brown band of uncleaned paintwork, which is normally concealed. That this was much wider than the normal amount of frame overlap was quite clear since the other margins were very small indeed – at most perhaps four millimetres. So, part of the painting had been deliberately concealed.

In time we obtained a slide of this photograph from the R.M.N., and it showed clearly that details of cloud and trees were included in the top band (Plate 9). The transition from the brown band to the clean paint is abrupt, and this concealed a 'fact' we were later to discover from the catalogue produced for the 1994 Poussin exhibition. We knew the painting had been cleaned between the taking of the black-and-white photograph and the colour photograph we had previously seen, but we were puzzled by the fact that this cleaning had been carried out without removing the frame – a most unusual practice, since it makes cleaning at the edges of the frame a difficult job. Or, if the frame had been removed, why had the whole of the painting not been cleaned? We shall return to this topic.

Shepherds unmasked

Having discovered why it had been impossible to find confirmation of the geometric sequence in *Les Bergers d'Arcadie II*, a new start was made with high hopes of success. This time, the 75° staff line would be extended across the uncleaned strip at the top of the painting to the edge of the painted surface. As Plate 9 shows, there is a narrow unpainted border around the canvas marking the intended limit of framing, an unusual feature since with such a narrow strip one would expect the artist to have painted to the edge. We decided that the edges of the paint area should determine the geometry of the preliminary square. Just enough of this was drawn – the top side and the upper part of the right side – in order to yield the diagonal which defines the 45° side of the triangle. The staff is already at 75° exactly, so no account has to be taken of the 1½° rotation at this stage.

The seven steps

1. The tilted square is drawn and its centre found from the diagonals (Figure 9.1), but there is no real confirmation from the painting: the point falls on the lower edge of the band of moulding below the level of the bearded shepherd's arm. There is, however, something exciting to note. We had previously remarked upon the angle of the second staff from the left, and how this had gone unnoticed by Lincoln and Cornford even though it is clearly at an angle of 72° to the horizontal (Figure 5.1, on p. 111). This had made us suspect the presence of a pentagonal figure such as a pentagram. The possibility had now become a probability, and indeed it was fairly clear what the arrangement was likely to be.

FIGURE 9.1 Poussin's *Les Bergers d'Arcadie II* unmasked – the triangle and square constructed.

2. Drawing a circle to circumscribe the equilateral triangle, which necessitated finding the centre of the triangle, we could see immediately that our hunch had been correct; for the second staff extended down to the circle hits it at a point perpendicularly below the centre of the triangle/circle (Figure 9.2). This staff is part of a pentagram symmetrically positioned with respect to the axes of the painting. We had now clearly found the intended triangle, and, consequentially, a hexagram and pentagram of common centre and common circumscribing circle.

FIGURE 9.2 *Les Bergers d'Arcadie II* unmasked – the suspected pentagram is confirmed.

FIGURE 9.3 *Les Bergers d'Arcadie II* unmasked – the third staff indicates the presence of a third polygram.

3. But Poussin has depicted a third staff. Is this of no significance? Let us go back to the tilted square, and look at part of it drawn together with the circle and the third staff, omitting other lines for clarity (Figure 9.3). The distances from the

staff to the centre of the circle, and from the diagonal (running from the top-left corner of the square) to the centre of the circle are the same; this is demonstrated by the small circle (radius R) inscribed so as to be tangential to these lines. If the staff is extended to the large circle (to become a chord of the circle) the length of this line is the same as the length of the equivalent line formed by the diagonal. What significance could this have?

Imagine that the shepherd brings his staff into a vertical position, but still tangential to the small circle (its length unchanged); this line, shown dashed in Figure 9.3, now cuts the circle at the same point as the diagonal of the square to form what could be the corner of a polygram with an included angle of 30°. The chord forming the sides of this polygram would have a length equal to both the diagonal and the extended staff; so it would seem that Poussin has obscurely indicated this by positioning the staff at 5° to the vertical, rather than vertical. Is there such a regular polygram?

It is a *dodecagram* – a twelve-pointed star – which proves to be more interesting than might at first seem. When studying the relationship between the equilateral triangle and the squares of Plato, it was remarked that the ultimate combination of these figures would be to place a triangle on each of the *four* sides of the inner square to produce a twelve-pointed star. But this figure would not be a true polygram (by our definition) for it consists of twelve separate triangles, each of them a polygram (*trigon*) in its own right.

The figure indicated by Poussin is a true dodecagram. Why has he not placed the staff representing it in the position of the square's diagonal? Clearly this is for reasons of composition. It had to be held by the third shepherd, and bunching three shepherds and three staffs to the left would have been disastrous. Making it vertical would have been out of the question. There would also have been a risk of being too overt; better to move it, change its angle. But to what angle? Why not 5°, an angle to appeal to any Pythagorean?

4. The dodecagram may be rotated around its centre to present various views. Aligned with the diagonal, it assumes a symmetry, with pairs of vertical and horizontal lines (Figure 9.4).

5. Aligned with the third staff, the dodecagram has no such symmetry; all the better to conceal it! But aligned so that it has a point at the top and a point at the bottom – perhaps the most obvious way to view it (like the pentagram) – it is found that it now has sides at 75° to the horizontal (Figure 9.5).

FIGURE 9.4 *Les Bergers d'Arcadie II* unmasked – the dodecagram is revealed. One of its points coincides with the intersection of the 75° staff with the circle.

6. There are some intriguing properties of the dodecagram, discussed in Appendix H. Suffice it here to say that it has properties which give it an unexpected relationship with pentagonal geometry. For example, superimposing the dodecagram on to the four triangles of the *pseudo-dodecagram* reveals that the chord of the former cuts off a segment of the circumscribing circle subdivided into five equal arcs by the points of the latter (Figure 9.6). So we find that Poussin has indicated three polygrams of common centre and circumscribing circle, eliminating any possibility of coincidence.

FIGURE 9.5 *Les Bergers d'Arcadie II* unmasked – when the dodecagram is rotated through 15°, so that it has a point at the top and at the bottom, one side becomes parallel to the 75° staff.

7. The centre of the square had received no overt confirmation from the painting. But there is still the final 1½° rotation to make. When this is done there is another revelation, for the centre moves upwards from the bottom edge of the moulding to the top edge, and sideways, to come to rest on the vertical line indicated by the joints in the stonework to which the third shepherd points with his index finger, and which grazes the second shepherd's thumb (Figure 9.7 and Plate 10).

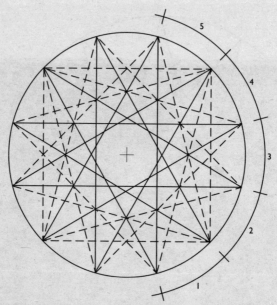

FIGURE 9.6 The dodecagram superimposed on the pseudo-dodecagram.

For the first time ever, the significance of the finger pointing at the line had been revealed. Poussin has shown us the vertical and horizontal lines of the meridian and parallel passing through the Site of the Secret. Later it will be seen that there is a specific designation for the point of intersection of these lines.

What justification is there for this final rotation, apart from the fact that it has been done so often? Why did Poussin paint his previous version, *Les Bergers d'Arcadie I*, unless to clarify the two 1½° rotations, in which the shift across the moulding at the top of the tomb was later to be paralleled in this painting of the shepherds? As we have shown, the dodecagram can be seen as a very special and very impenetrable secret indeed, ideal as the third lemon in Poussin's fruit machine! So, we had traced a stunning display of Pythagorean geometry, that combining the 'secret' geometry with the more standard – albeit, in its time, esoteric – pentagonal geometry. But we were due for another surprise.

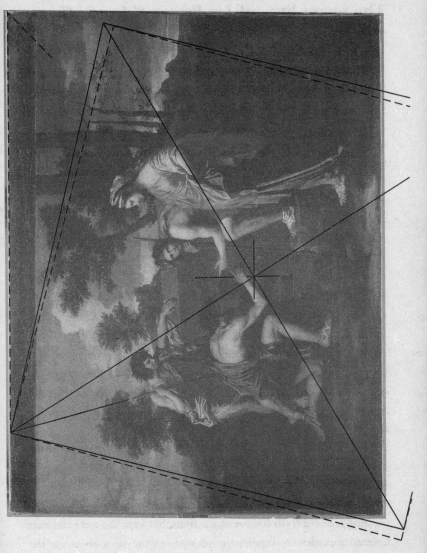

FIGURE 9.7 *Les Bergers d'Arcadie II* unmasked – the final rotation yields the meridian and parallel of the Site.

The secret lives of *Les Bergers d'Arcadie II* and *I*

According to the R.M.N. catalogue for the 1994 Poussin exhibition in Paris (repeated in London in 1995), the painting has been enlarged by 7 cm at the top (re-covered by the frame), 4.5 cm on the right and 2 cm at the bottom. The overall dimensions are given as height 85 cm, length 121 cm. The geometry works *with* extensions to the painting, but not without them. Poussin may have been responsible for the hidden part of the painting or he may not; the work may have been undertaken by an employee at the Louvre or by persons unknown. At this point it is impossible to decide one way or the other. So let us look at the alternatives in the light of the available information.

The catalogue description implies that the painting as originally executed by Poussin was of a smaller size, that it was subsequently enlarged by someone who thought they knew better than the master, and that it was later partly restored to its former dimensions by covering the top addition only. This scenario almost beggars belief. And now the significance of the dating of the other changes (that is, to the mountains) becomes evident. If we were to check the proportions of the engraving against those of the painting, we might be able to see whether the right and bottom extensions were present when the engraving was made – and thus, by implication, the top extension also.

Clearly, we have to visualise a more likely scenario – in view of the alterations to the mountains – that presents this modification as part of an attempt, not only to conceal the location depicted, but also to obliterate the geometry. In this scenario, someone, an initiate, has had the painting restored to its former dimensions, but kept the top extension covered in order to disguise the change. As the sizes given for the enlargements cannot be based on any knowledge of the original size of the canvas, the actual size of the painting in its original, or any intermediate, guise may not have been much different from its present size. (The geometry was checked on the limit of painting visible on the unframed canvas.) Thus, the frame may well have been reusable apart from concealing the top, rather wide (7 cm) strip. If true, this would prohibit the deduction of the painting's state when the early engraving was made, if the proportions were found to be the same. Of course, if they were found to be different, some deduction might well be possible.

In fact, from the reproduction in the catalogue, the print is found to be either narrower *or* higher than the painting, or both narrower *and* higher. Assuming the engraving to be a faithful copy – which it does seem to be – one may detect some differences at the margins. (When referring to the engraving, 'right' and 'left' will be used in the same sense as for the painting.) At the bottom, the distance from the woman's foot to the margin is greater in the print. On the right, the mountain ridge falls to the margin, whereas in the painting it rises, and it must be remembered that this part of the painting is an addition. The left side is not significantly different, and also the top margin touches the leaves exactly as in the painting. So what may be deduced from this?

The state of the print appears to reflect the original as-painted condition. But as the size difference is too small to be conclusive, and since the top is the same in both, the probability would be that the print was made after the first alterations. There is, however, one further possibility, and that is that the top of the painting was always covered. Do we know for sure that the top is an addition, or has this been assumed because of the dark paint? An examination of the painting unframed would answer this question.

An extraordinary comment made by the official guide at the Poussin exhibition in Paris contradicted the catalogue: he said that the covered top strip is original and that Poussin had indicated, by drawing a line, where the frame should come. Could this really be true?

An even stranger insight into the disturbing mystery of this painting was to be provided by Pierre Rosenberg, director of the Louvre, when present in London for the Royal Academy sojourn of the Poussin exhibition. In conversation with us he stated that the alteration to the top of the frame had been made by Louis XIV, adding that he (Louis) had often done things like that. These two comments from the guide and the director – though not agreeing on the who and when – support the likelihood that the top of the painting is not an addition, that Poussin had incorporated the full geometry and that it had been covered either for a long time (the Louis scenario) or ever since its first framing (the Poussin 'line' scenario).

From its style, the frame looks to belong to the seventeenth century, and Louis XIII at that: the condition and patination suggest this dating to be correct, rather than the frame being a later copy. Further evidence that the present frame could be the painting's original frame is provided by the clear signs of alteration, necessary if the covering of part of the painting is to be accounted for: a narrow piece has been inserted into the right side, near the bottom-right mitre. This has the appearance of a piece of the same carved framing, rather than a new piece made later to match, and suggests very strongly the correction of a cutting error made when the frame was being reduced because of the top overlap. In view of the age of the frame, it is possible that a later insert would have had time to attain the same degree of patination as the rest, and could therefore be a repair, but this is felt to be unlikely. A difficulty with this assessment is the problem of matching up the carving at the mitres if a frame is reduced. A frame of this quality would have the carving laid out to ensure not only that the carving detail matched on each side of the mitre, but also that this feature matched across all the mitres. This is not easy to achieve, since the proportions of the painting dictate the internal dimensions of the frame. The pattern of carving on the frame, for example, would need to be subtly elongated or condensed on the short side to achieve a match with the long side. The only way to suc-cessfully alter such a frame would be to remove sections some way from the mitres and then to restore the gesso (the layer of gypsum plaster applied to the wood) and gilding. This is what may well have happened here, only the one joint having moved sufficiently to have become visible.

Collectors and experts

Having found ourselves embroiled in these extraordinary complications, and struggling to find a realistic explanation of how an alteration (if that is what it is) to a renowned painting could complete the secret geometry, we next found ourselves dealing with a similar problem with the earlier painting, *Les Bergers d'Arcadie I*. For this too has been altered, at the top and left side. But this time a fascinating possibility presents itself. If the left-hand addition were to be removed, the extreme left corner of the tilted square would come very close to the margin of the painting. In other words, did Poussin paint the tilted square with its right and left corners touching the margins of the painting? Or, more interestingly, in view of the displaced staff, did the left corner fall on the painting's left margin when it had been rotated? Since he clearly intended to deal with the square 'up-front', he may have done either.

To help resolve when the additions were made, another painting comes to our aid. This is a portrait of Lady Anson, by Thomas Hudson (1701–79), and in her hand she holds a partly rolled copy of *Les Bergers d'Arcadie I*. Lady Anson was herself an amateur artist, and made copies of works by others. Enough of the copy is visible to reveal that the left-hand addition to the painting is not present (Figure 9.8).

Why did this portrait include a copy of *Les Bergers I*? The original Poussin is known to have been in the collection of the Duke of Devonshire by 1761, and almost certainly before 1751, the date of the Anson portrait. The Devonshire seat is at Chatsworth in Derbyshire, quite close to Shugborough Hall in Staffordshire, the home of the Ansons, whose family provided several earls of Lichfield. It is quite possible that Lady Anson had the opportunity, while on a house visit, to copy the original Poussin rather than another copy or engraving. This is considered to prove beyond reasonable doubt that the additions post-date the Anson portrait.[1] We have yet to see any evidence to suggest that the additions were made as a reinstatement of the original form of the painting.

FIGURE 9.8 Thomas Hudson's *Portrait of Lady Anson*. She is holding a copy of *Les Bergers d'Arcadie I* that shows no additions. The *Portrait* itself is based on occult geometry, as readers may wish to investigate for themselves.

Lady Anson was Elizabeth Yorke, daughter of the first Earl of Hardwicke, and wife of George Anson, the famous admiral who circumnavigated the globe. The couple spent a lot of time at Shugborough Hall, the home of George's elder brother Thomas, who was then Earl of Lichfield. It is clear that they all moved in an elevated stratum of society, so Elizabeth will have had the opportunity to make copies of many of the greatest works of art; one may well suspect the inclusion of the Poussin in her portrait to be for esoteric reasons.

The present earl is Patrick Lichfield, famous photographer and cousin of the Queen. His home is the seat of his ancestors, Shugborough Hall, where the intriguing marble bas-relief of *Les Bergers d'Arcadie II* is to be found. Hudson's portrait of Lady Anson was sold in 1967 by Christies for an unaccountably high sum[2] (both vendor and purchaser remaining anonymous). Also at Shugborough Hall in the 1970s was to be found a copy of the 'lost' painting by David Teniers, *St Antony and St Paul*, and Lady Anson's copy of *Les Bergers d'Arcadie I*. Visitors will find today that neither is on show. There is, however, a copy of the Anson portrait (school of Thomas Hudson), but in this version she holds an innocuous copy of an unidentified painting. Is it unreasonable to suspect that all items of esoteric interest – apart from the unmovable 'Shepherd's monument' – have been deliberately removed? Again, as so often with this mystery, pursuing one line of enquiry had opened up another. But let us return to the Poussin.

It would appear that Poussin's original brief was to execute one painting, *Les Bergers d'Arcadie I*, based on the geometry of the square, but not showing the sensitive relationship to the triangle. We can imagine Poussin at this stage as a novice member of the hermetic organisation that came to rule his life. The Louvre 'Shepherds' was to follow – much sooner than has previously been thought; the recent Paris and London exhibitions, allowing a rare opportunity for juxtaposition of the two paintings, resulted in a consensus closing of the interval to five to eight years.

Whether Poussin's rise through the ranks had by this time allowed

him to become fully cognizant of the esoteric geometry and the truth
of the secret it conceals is a matter for speculation only. If this were so,
it would explain not only the later introduction of the more occult
aspects of the geometry, but also the shift in atmosphere from the first
to the second painting upon which we have already commented. With
the completion of the analysis of the second painting, one may see an
interesting parallel with the Parchments – one 'square', the other
'hexagonal'.

Devising a chronology for the works of an artist whose records have
disappeared (if they ever existed) is not easy. The backlash over the previous Poussin exhibition in 1960 and Anthony Blunt's attempt to put
the exhibits in chronological order have been poignantly described by
the art historian and critic Brian Sewell.[3] That Anthony Blunt, univer-
sally accepted as the foremost expert on Poussin (with important, but
concealed, animosity from some quarters), had arranged the exhibits
incorrectly is not at all surprising, given that he constructed the order
on the basis of black-and-white photographs – all that was then available – many of which were of poor quality. He was the first to
appreciate his many errors in chronology the moment he set foot in the
completed exhibition. Before he had the opportunity to revise the display or to publish his own views, the pack was upon him.

If nothing else, the incident gives an insight into the latent savagery
in certain sections of the art world, and goes a long way towards clar-
ifying the extraordinary reluctance of 'experts' to pronounce on
matters that scream out for explanation. There can be no artist for
whom this is truer than Poussin. Later we shall take a closer look ourselves and, having no reputation to safeguard, will dare to open this
Pandora's box.

Sewell expresses his own reaction to the 1995 exhibition at the
Royal Academy thus:[4]

Thirty-five years later [after the 1960 Paris exhibition], on
entering the first room of the Poussin exhibition at the Royal

Academy, I can do no better than echo Mahon [Sir Denis Mahon, who had savaged Blunt's 1960 Paris chronology], word for word, for never have I been confronted with better evidence of blindness in the generation of Blunt's followers who teach art history today.

That there are great difficulties for art historians we have already acknowledged, but it nevertheless came as a surprise to discover how easy it is to overlook a 'glaring' piece of evidence. We had substantial opportunities to view both 'Shepherds', first in Paris and then in London. At the Royal Academy – where the security was no less strict – having first requested the attendance of a security guard, we were permitted to stand as close as we wished to *Les Bergers d'Arcadie II* and to examine the canvas with a magnifying glass. This enabled us to see that the present state of the sky/mountain junction at the right of the picture did not result from any repainting at the last cleaning; the significance of this has already been discussed. But neither such close scrutiny, nor viewing from a conventional distance, revealed something else of remarkable import. This was to be discovered from an enlarged projection of the excellent colour transparency obtained from the R.M.N.

Some coarse painting

Poussin was much concerned with the finish of his work during this particular period. He even on occasion used his thumb or fingertip to press down the paint surface when dry, but still pliable, in order to disguise brushmarks and differences in paint level, and this resulted in a virtually uniform, matt texture of fingerprints. The type of texture is clearly illustrated in enlarged photographs in Richard Beresford's monograph on *A Dance to the Music of Time*, a painting of the same period.[5] To find a large area of coarse, intrusive brushstrokes in a painting of the period is surprising, but this is indeed what is found in *Les*

Bergers II. Subsequent examination of all the other Poussins available revealed that none had an area of sky painted with such random, crude strokes.

Why this had not been visible to us when we were standing in front the actual Louvre painting of the shepherds is hard to say, for it is plain enough on the transparency. Perhaps something in the photographic process or the way the painting was lit for photography had enhanced the effect. The entire area of sky above the tomb and the shepherds has coarse brushmarks. They run at various angles, mainly diagonally, and sometimes crossing one another in a hatched pattern. They do not relate to the normal pattern employed by Poussin, whose brushwork tends to vary according to the object being painted. The only other areas where such haphazard brushwork is to be seen in *Les Bergers II* are small, isolated patches where it might be attributable to clumsy restoration, but also, more significantly, down the entire right edge of the painting where the added strip or repair has been painted in.

Enlarged to full size in the privacy of our own study, the painting was to reveal even more. Something that one cannot do with a real painting is touch it – let alone apply a straight-edge, make marks or measure angles – all of which may be done on a projected image. Thus we were able to find the exact point at the centre of the three polygrams and to check whether any trace of a perforation made by compasses had been left by Poussin when preparing the canvas. There is in fact a dark spot about three millimetres across at this very point.

We had some expectation of finding a perforation at this position, and had closely inspected the actual canvas at the Royal Academy with this in mind, but without success. Of course there would be no reason why a hole made by the point of a pair of compasses during the setting out of a painting's structure should survive the application of several layers of paint; also, underpainting may be detected only by X-ray photography. There is no doubt that a dark spot is to be seen at the key point we had identified, but would the X-ray photograph taken at the Louvre also reveal a filled hole behind it? Indeed it does. But it would be dishonest not to admit that there are several such dots to be seen, and the correctly placed one could be there by coincidence.

Whether or not the hidden top of the painting is original would surely be resolved by the records of restorations kept in the archives of the Louvre, but for the moment it had been quite enough to know that the painting had a secret life and that we had understood part of it. At the Louvre's research department, all photographic material was made available to us. This included photographs taken in normal, infra-red and ultraviolet light, plus photographs taken at low angles of illumination (grazing light). There were also enlargements of various details. Unfortunately there were no photographs of the back of the canvas.

We particularly wished to resolve the puzzling question of whether the top strip had been added after Poussin's time, but we could not see the back of the canvas. The grazing-light photographs, which show up surface undulations, were a help here. At the right edge, where a strip has been added and then overpainted, the surface is very rough; at the junction of the top strip it is completely smooth. Ultraviolet light is particularly useful for revealing any layers of paint added later, and also areas that the artist has reworked. Once again, this showed the right edge as having been overpainted, but not the top, which is quite clean. Closer examination of the right edge leads us to suspect that the extra strip of canvas is nothing more than reinforcement for a vulnerable point that can lead to cracking in old oil paintings: where the canvas flexes around the edge of the frame (this is further out than might be imagined, as the frame is 'releaved' on the inside to avoid painting across a hard edge). All this suggests that both the edges of the canvas that are involved in the geometry are almost certainly original; and the guide and M. Rosenberg are both vindicated to that extent.

But we were to make an even more significant find. Looking at the photographic enlargements, we came across one of the left-hand shepherd and his staff. Clearly visible down the left edge of the staff is a sharp line – probably scribed with a blunt knife – and this line is perfectly straight! (Plate 12). This is the 75° line. Poussin had ensured that, having scribed the line in the underpaint, it was not covered, or even partly obscured, by the completion of the staff. This clearly constitutes the best supporting evidence for the analysis of the painting, and the importance of the 75° line to the composition. Inspection of the other photographs taken in different light confirms that the staffs and the tomb details were the first features to be painted, and were then never again touched. This is in marked contrast to the figures, which received some considerable reworking. We consider the case for the occult origin of this painting now to be proved beyond any doubt.

If we are to consider it most likely that it was Louis XIV who had the top of the canvas concealed (as stated by M. Rosenberg), and possibly the mountain/sky alteration executed, we must consider it plausible that he had also ordered Colbert to have the original tomb at les Pontils destroyed. Why, one may ask, did he not have the entire painting destroyed? Quite apart from the sin of annihilating a great work of art, the answer is a matter of logic: if one had discovered the secret of eternal life, would one throw it away out of fear that others might utilise it? No, one would preserve it, in a secret format understandable only by a very few. Furthermore, we cannot be certain of the extent of Louis's involvement in, or indeed his knowledge of, the Secret, so to speculate at length on his motives would inevitably be inconclusive.

Another matter of keen interest was to discover whether Poussin had provided any other indications of the geometric trio of polygrams. The vertical centre-line that determines the lowest point of the pentagram, when drawn on a small-scale copy (A3 size), does not show the correspondences visible at full size; this line, which is parallel to the vertical joints in the tomb, passes along the 'I' of IN (from the inscription) and through the V and Λ shapes formed by pairs of leaves at the top and bottom of the leaf-laden branch. Enough evidence had now accrued to leave no doubt whatsoever of Poussin's involvement, and *Les Bergers d'Arcadie II* in particular, with the mystery of Rennes-le-Château.

10
THROUGH THE
PARCHMENTS
AND BEYOND

Investigation of the paintings had advanced our knowledge beyond our wildest expectations. While we breathed the conditioned air of the Louvre and Royal Academy, the origins of our enquiries had become remote, and, in retrospect, appeared slightly tarnished. But in fact the Parchments could now be reconsidered in a way that might previously have been thought somewhat rash: they could now be regarded as having a pedigree of some quality and age.

What may be deduced about the extent of knowledge of Bigou, or Boudet and Saunière, or Plantard and de Cherisey, if indeed any of them had a hand in the drafting or revision of the Parchments? Or, for that matter, what may be deduced (if anything) about the knowledge possessed by whoever was responsible for the Parchments? An eighteenth-century date, and the hand of Abbé Bigou, is claimed for the Parchments, so 681 as a spot height would be ruled out on the grounds of date. This theory – that the composition of the Parchments, and thus also the cipher, was the work of Bigou – has undoubtedly hindered previous attempts at decipherment. We are not convinced that style indicates a date any earlier than the nineteenth century, and we have already expressed doubts on other grounds. So, ignoring the date, let us check the theory.

The cipher message identifies a square to be placed on a map at an angle of 15° to lines of latitude and longitude. This we may now judge to be correct as far as the orientation is concerned, but there is no geometric justification for its positioning. Nor can we assume that this message indicates any knowledge of the role played by the triangle. Because we identified the triangle first and were then led to the square, this does not mean that other investigators would necessarily have followed the same route.

It is essential to appreciate that the letters making up the cipher in Parchment 2 are all additional to an original text. If these are removed, the text then reverts to its original Biblical form. In that form, the text of Parchment 2 would have contained nothing that would rule out a pre-nineteenth-century date, and the purpose of Parchment 2 would have been solely to augment the 'map' information in Parchment 1. On its own, Parchment 1 places an equilateral triangle in a geographical context. Parchment 2 initiates the logic of the geometric relationships, which to those in the know would have been easily used. Parchment 1 then confirms that there is an initial 1½° rotation to be noted, which establishes the 45° alignment of the triangle. That some other transposition is required may be deduced, as we did, but it is also clearly illustrated by Poussin in *Les Bergers d'Arcadie I*. This painting presents the geometry of the 'tilted square' without recourse to the triangle/hexagram. It is possible, therefore, to visualise someone having deduced the 'tilted square' with only an incomplete knowledge of the role of Parchment 1. That someone, searching for the square's location, would require some other data to break the deadlock. The other 'concealed' messages might hold the clue:

A DAGOBERT II ROI ET A SION EST CE TRESOR
ET IL EST LA MORT

That the *treasure* belongs to *Dagobert II* and is maybe *at Sion* and *it* (i.e. Sion) is *La Mort* represents a feasible translation of the message concealed in Parchment 1, and may be seen as settling the location of the square. It is also, of course, possible that this message was concocted by the nineteenth- or twentieth-century compiler of the cipher, in order to support the *681–La Croix* geometry. However, it is hard to believe that the location of *681* was a coincidence, particularly when looked at in conjunction with the other extraordinary coincidence of a railway bridge at 15° to the Meridian, adjacent to a cross, also in the required spot to align with *681* at 75° to the Meridian. There has to be some substantial logic behind this manipulation of the map, but to concoct the coded message in order to involve La Mort seems improbable, particularly as the only map to show this inconsequential farmstead had been superseded well before the date of conception of the cipher. The author of the cipher may have been aware of the Cassini map, but if his intention had been to preserve the Secret, it would have been pointless to use a system that relied on a map that was already out of circulation. It is one thing to be cryptic, another to be shortsighted.

If '681' is a twentieth-century addition to the map, the author of the cipher must have realised that this might be noted, and the authenticity of the Parchment questioned. That this is evidence for the manipulation of the I.G.N. map to suit the *681–La Croix* square is an inference that can be made; the Michelin road map does not show the spot height as 681, but indicates '680.'. As we had discovered on a visit to the Col de l'Espinas, 680 metres is the highest level of the pass, as marked by a sign at the spot (Figure 3.2, on p. 72). Such signposting is uncommon, and it is tempting to see this blatant contradiction of the map as 'making a point'. The Michelin map states that its copyright is the property of Michelin, and there is no acknowledgement to any other cartographical organisation. This almost certainly means that the maps are produced for Michelin by a cartographical organisation using data other than that supplied by the I.G.N. – or the spot height at Col de l'Espinas would be the same. And as it is unlikely that altitudes would have been determined independently by more than one survey –

the duplication of effort would be nonsensical – the probability is that 681 as given by the I.G.N. is wrong.

So, the deliberate alteration of one spot height on the I.G.N. map could well have been made by just *one* person in the employ of the Institute. After all, a high-level conspiracy among the mapmakers of France is fairly unlikely.

Interaction: the two Parchments

A scenario which is perhaps complementary to deductions about the placing of the cipher square unfolds from statements made by Pierre Plantard. These are to be found in the book *The Messianic Legacy* by Baigent, Leigh and Lincoln, in which events subsequent to the publication of their *The Holy Blood and the Holy Grail* are recounted. The relevant section is worth quoting in full:[1]

> During our meeting with him on 17 May 1983, M. Plantard elaborated on two of the paramount questions pertaining to Saunière's Parchments – and, in characteristic fashion, thereby created further mystification. The documents found by Saunière, he said, were *indeed only four in number.* Three of them were those to which various references had repeatedly alluded – a genealogy dating from 1244 bearing the seal of Blanche de Castille, an Hautpoul genealogy dating from 1644 and the Hautpoul 'testament' dating from 1695. *The fourth parchment,* he said, was the original on the basis of which the Marquis de Cherisey had devised a modified version. According to M. Plantard, there was *one coded message on each side of the page. In some way, apparently, the two texts interacted with each other – if, for example, they were held up to the light and viewed, as it were, in superimposition.* Indeed, it was suggested that M. Cherisey's chief 'modification' had simply been to *reproduce the two sides of the same page as separate pages, and not to*

the original scale . . . M. Plantard refused to comment on either of the Hautpoul parchments, or on the 1244 genealogy bearing the seal of Blanche of Castille. He simply asserted that the fourth parchment found by Saunière consisted of the two coded biblical texts, one on each side of the page. (our italics)

In the previous section, the authors give this explanation:[2]

In 1979, when we first met M. Plantard, we were told that both of the ciphered texts were in fact forgeries, concocted in 1956 by the Marquis de Cherisey for a short television programme. We challenged this assertion. [We have ascertained that there was no such television programme in 1956.] The staggering effort required to devise the ciphers seemed inappropriate, indeed ridiculous, for such a purpose. M. Plantard conceded that the forgeries were based very closely on the originals. In other words, they had not been 'concocted' by M. Cherisey at all. They had been *copied*, and M. Cherisey had made only a *few additions*. When these additions were deleted, what remained *were the original texts found by Saunière*. (our interpolation and italics)

From these statements it would appear to be possible to identify, not only confirmation of our interpretation of the interaction of Parchment 1 and Parchment 2, including the scale relationship between them, but also the origin of the *681–La Croix* square – the cipher square. These statements, having gone unremarked and ignored by others, were to us like bolts of lightning!

To anyone ignorant of the geometric content of the Parchments, the concept of viewing the texts *through* the parchment (all parchment is translucent) would suggest that the *letters* themselves interact. When this is tried, all one sees is a meaningless jumble. It would have been possible to have arranged for some shape to emerge in this way; such tricks are known. A present-day equivalent would be the posters of repetitive patterns – the 'magic eye' phenomenon – which, when viewed from the correct distance with the eyes relaxed, reveal an unexpected three-dimensional image.

Revelation of the double-sided nature of the single Parchment to anyone who had deduced the geometry of each side separately is equivalent to the discovery of the Rosetta Stone as an aid to deciphering hieroglyphs. The first deduction to be made from the fact that the texts on each side of a *single* Parchment interact when viewed held up to the light is that the lines at 7½° to the vertical – one on each side – would be seen to be at 15° to each other (Figure 10.1). This would be true only if the two texts had each been written the same way up, and with the lines of letters parallel, one side to the other. However, there

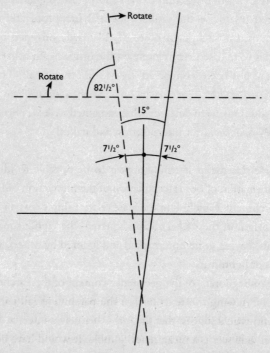

FIGURE 10.1 The geometry of the Parchment considered as a double-sided object. Alignments on the front are shown as solid lines, and those on the back are shown dashed. Here the two texts are assumed to be parallel.

is no reason to assume that this is the case, the only arguments in its favour being neatness and convention. Whatever the truth, there is still one obvious result. One text is seen reversed, and if the 7½° lines are already, or are to be, aligned, the geometry of one text would be rotated by 15° relative to the other (Figure 10.2). The difficulty of representing this relationship if only a one-sided medium is available is obvious; another method will be described later.

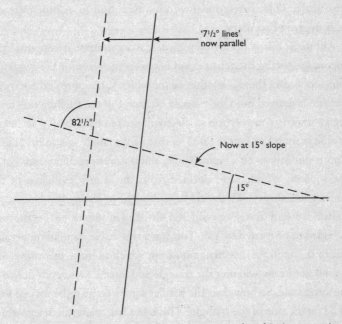

FIGURE 10.2 The Parchment's double-sided geometry, but this time assuming that the two sets of texts are inclined to each other by 15° – which makes the two 7½° lines parallel. As in Figure 10.1, alignments on the front are shown solid, and those on the back are shown dashed.

One might easily test the result of this relationship if it were known that the published illustrations of the Parchments are to the same scale. Some doubt about this is raised by the reference to de Cherisey having changed the scale, but this could mean changing the scale of both sides equally, rather than each side differently. The latter would not be a logical step unless confusion were intended. Fortunately, the Parchments (and now, of course, we mean de Cherisey's copies when we refer to 'the Parchments') are shown not only as black-line figures in *L'Or de Rennes* and *The Holy Place*, but also as photographs in *The Messianic Legacy*. If it could be shown that the relative scales of the two texts are the same in both forms of illustration, the probability would then be that they have been, in each case, illustrated to the correct relative scale. This correspondence does exist, and to an unexpectedly high degree of accuracy.

Although this is not to be regarded as a certainty, it certainly does encourage testing the relationship between the texts for the suggested interaction. But there is another factor which is far more convincing. If a square is derived from the triangle on Side 1 of the Parchment – using the geometric construction so clearly illustrated by Teniers – its length of side is found to be the same as that of the inner square on Side 2. This is unlikely to be a coincidence, and is a welcome endorsement of the squares, which were derived from the scanty evidence of the asterisk-like shapes. We should have thought of testing this before.

But we had always considered the larger square to be the one intended to be rotated by 15°. This was a reasonable assumption because it is in the appropriate orientation from which to make that move, and we did not know whether the triangle and squares were even drawn to the same scale. So how does the smaller square come to be rotated so as to lie on the side of the triangle? This is the last, masterful, trick, which *should* have made solution by an outsider impossible.

Wenzel Roritzer had published what he described as the masonic secret of the proportion of pinnacles. It is hard to see why it should be a secret. It is also hard to see why pinnacles should have their projecting decorative features sized on the basis of Plato's theorem – the duplication of the square. The *secret* is in the rotation of the inner square to be aligned with the outer one. When this has been done on the Parchment diagram, the smaller square is indeed ready for its 15° rotation (Figure 10.3).

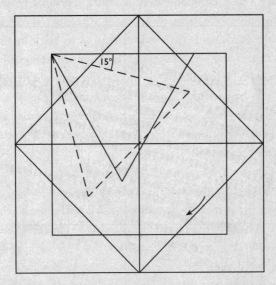

FIGURE 10.3 Rotation of the inner canted square to align with the outer one, as prescribed by Roritzer, brings it into the correct relationship with the equilateral triangle.

With the texts copied on to clear acetate and the geometry drawn on to its respective text (and with the smaller square in its new, aligned position), it is a simple matter to reproduce the effect of looking through the Parchment by placing the acetates back to back. (Of course, one may do this either with or without the texts, or with one and not the other, in the several possible combinations.) Sliding them around, it is apparent that there are only a limited number of potential arrangements which could be of any interest, and there is only one which is clearly correct. This is shown in Figure 10.4 (and also in colour in Plate 13). The 7½° lines – shown green on the plate – are parallel, the texts having been rotated.

If the lines of writing on both sides of the Parchment were originally parallel, this solution is not invalidated; the arrangement would probably have been as shown in Figure 10.5. Here we have assumed that the

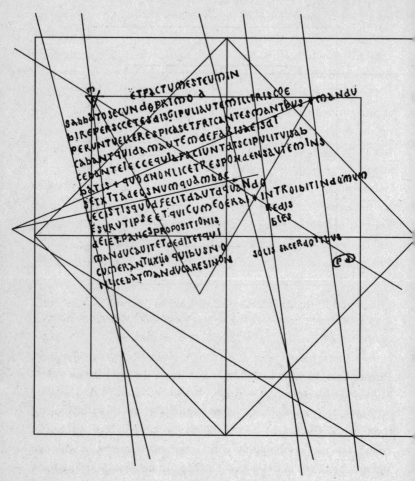

FIGURE 10.4 The Parchment's double-sided geometry – now clearly in the correct relationship.

top-left corners of the triangle and square would have coincided – as deduced from the paintings – but with the 7½° line of Side 2 converging with those of Side 1, rather than parallel to them. The angle between them is 15°, and the intention of a 15° rotation is evident since it is logical that the lines should be parallel. When this rotation is made, a corner of the triangle (on Side 1, remember) moves on to the green line of Side 2, thus confirming the move since the top-left corner of the triangle already has a similar line passing through it (refer again to Figure 10.4 and Plate 13). Some other ways in which this arrangement is confirmed are given in Appendix I.

Plates 13 and 14 show how the alignment of the green 7½° lines is also confirmed by the text. In Plate 13, the green line of Side 2 (the one on the right) may be compared with the text of Side 1: it is seen to run along the legs of two 'N's and is tangential to the 'b' of *sacerdotibus*, and to the oval flourish around 'PS'.

Looking through the Parchment to the other side (Plate 14, which has the Side 2 text reversed), the two green lines of Side 1 have much greater scope for acknowledgement from the script (there is more of it) and the result is remarkable, as readers may judge for themselves. The left-hand line in particular has clear correspondence with 'N's and 'T's, and two 'V's have the line run in the notches they form. But the clincher is the 'T' on the top line (here seen reversed, as 'T', actually the *last* letter of the top line). The green 7½° line on Side 2 – the one on the right here – had been defined by a similarly sloping 'T'. These two 'T's have been ringed. With the 7½° lines on the two sides of the Parchment now aligned, the other line passes through the last 'T' on line one of the text.

Plantard's statements, which have such revelatory consequences for the geometry, are also revealing in another way. It was said that de Cherisey had added to the Parchment. Why should he have done so? We now know the motivation and, by deduction, what it was he added. The motivation is a compulsion – or *obligation* – to contribute to the preservation of the knowledge. We shall expand on this assertion later, when additional supportive evidence has been introduced. So what did he add? The cipher message.

We have shown how the evidence for the dating of the cipher progressively reduces its age. The real clues are 681 and the railway bridge alignment. The spot height was not added to the map until the still current 1 : 25,000 I.G.N. issue. And the bridge as shown on the

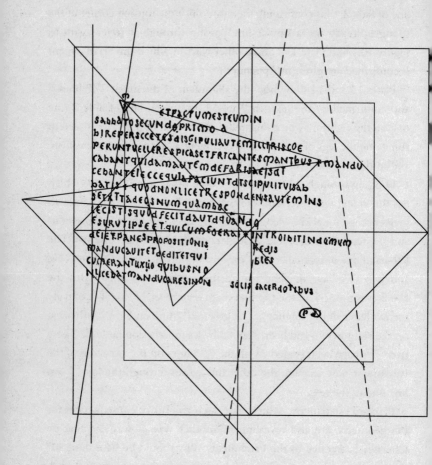

FIGURE 10.5 The Parchment's double-sided geometry – before the 15° rotation.

nineteenth-century État-Major map crosses the river at an angle that causes its orientation to be around 30° to the meridian! It will be recalled that the I.G.N. 1:25,000 map shows this as almost exactly 15°. We believe this to be conclusive evidence for a twentieth-century origin of the cipher.

Philippe de Cherisey (we shall hold him responsible until proved otherwise) must have understood the 'tilted square' of the Parchment geometry, decided to use this in his own way, and devised the cipher to produce the same end-result. There is absolutely no doubt that Side 2 of the Parchment contains additions: these are the letters that form the cipher. With them the text is unintelligible; surely in its original form the text would have made sense. And surely the originator of the Parchment would have been content, indeed satisfied, with the result he had achieved. The interaction of the two Sides is a masterly, occult, way of conveying the difficult transposition of the square relative to the triangle. Is it likely that the originator would have introduced the cipher and another square? This allows us to make a deduction of great significance: that the Parchment in its original form predates the input of de Cherisey. This is the first potential evidence for a pre-twentieth-century date – for the original parchment, not the coded message, of course. We have previously noted the lack of correspondences in Parchment 2 which one would have expected the originator to utilise: various dots and small letters, for example, have no role to play. One might also have expected the overall layout of the text to conform in some way to the geometry. These factors suggested that the alterations (made by de Cherisey) had eliminated some original correspondences; this may now be considered to have been proved.

(There remains a loose end to tidy away – one that may be beyond our ability to deal with. If the cipher were devised by de Cherisey, why does the Devil in the church at Rennes-le-Château draw attention to the Devil's Armchair? The role of the Armchair in the cipher is simply to have one look in the direction of Col Doux; it does not form part of the tilted square. We would suggest that the Armchair forms part of another scheme and was co-opted into the cipher.)

The possibility that the composer of the cipher had misunderstood the placing of the square and had arranged for its centre to fall as near as possible – most of the geographical features made use of not being

under his control – to La Mort, had been considered. We had done
M. de Cherisey an injustice. For the last four words of the message
demonstrate conclusively that he had solved the geometry correctly,
knew exactly where the secret is located: A MIDI POMMES
BLEUES.

11
FRESH CLUES
AND FURTHER
CONFIRMATION

The resolution of the Parchments had raised another question. If the geometry itself had been preserved in the paintings, but with no indication of where, geographically, it was to be applied, were the Parchments the sole surviving means of determining the location? The existence of the Parchments was substantiated only by photographs and hearsay (though the apparent tampering suggested some antiquity, rather than twentieth-century faking), so we could not leave the question unanswered. A reassessment of all the evidence was required, especially where Bérenger Saunière was concerned.

At this point in our research the whole Saunière affair was still no more than a signpost to the whereabouts of a secret location on Cardou. The legend of Rennes and the tales of its priest with unlimited funds were simply fascinating stories; hard evidence had so far eluded us. The time had come to look more closely at the photographs of Saunière's bookplate.

A hexagram combined with a cross may be regarded as a strange motif for an 'ex libris' label used by a Roman Catholic priest (Figure 8.4, on p. 182). It would be more at home in the library of an alchemist or a dabbler in the occult. But putting aside such subjective thoughts, there is nevertheless something about the arrangement of the small

circles supporting a cross, the centre of these circles marked with a dot
and a very small circle, that suggests there is more to the diagram than
at first meets the eye. There is also a dot at the centre of the cross. The
whole set-up speaks geometric volumes.

An examination of the basic geometry shows that the outer of the
two smaller circles which contain the words CENTRUM IN
TRIGONO CENTRI has a diameter equal to the radius of the inner
of the two larger circles – the one which circumscribes the hexagram –
it is, in other words, half its diameter. This relationship limits the geometric possibilities. However, the diameter of the inner small circle is,
superficially, arbitrary (the letters contained within the ring could be
almost any size), but may have been chosen for a specific purpose.

If a straight-edge is placed so as to form a line from the dot at the
centre of the cross that is tangential to the inner small circle, it is found
to be at 18° to the vertical, or 72° to the horizontal, indicating pentagonal geometry. This is the angle of the second shepherd's staff in *Les
Bergers d'Arcadie II*. A corresponding line may be drawn to the other
side of the circle, producing an included angle of 36° – so we know that
a pentagram is the figure to be drawn. This may be completed as
shown in Figure 11.1. If we need confirmation that a pentagram is the
intention, we find it provided by the appropriate placing of the letters
'O' of TRIGONO, and also 'H', 'O', 'T', etc. of the outer inscription.[1]

What does the phrase CENTRUM IN TRIGONO CENTRI mean,
if anything? Once again we have a Latin phrase without a verb. The sense
appears mysterious – 'the centre [is] within the triangle of the centre'. But
it becomes less mysterious when the diameter of the circle which would
circumscribe the points of the pentagram is found, for it is the same as
that of the circle circumscribing the hexagram. The centre of a circle of
the same diameter will be found at the centre of the triangle.

Is this all there is to be found? Perhaps a similar figure may be
deduced by reversing the roles of the cross and small circles.[2] The figure that one is thus compelled to draw proves to be a dodecagram
(Figure 11.2). The confirmation provided by several letters leaves no

PLATE 1   The Devil supporting the *bénitier* – the stoup for holding holy water – in the church at Rennes-le-Château.

PLATE 2 *Les Bergers d'Arcadie II*, by Nicolas Poussin, framed.

PLATE 3 *Et in Arcadia ego*, by Il Guercino.

PLATE 4   *Les Bergers d'Arcadie I*, by Nicolas Poussin.

PLATE 5 *St Antony and St Paul*, by David Teniers the Younger.

PLATE 6 *La Fontaine de fortune*, an illustration from the book *Le Cuer d'amours espris*, conceived and commissioned by René d'Anjou.

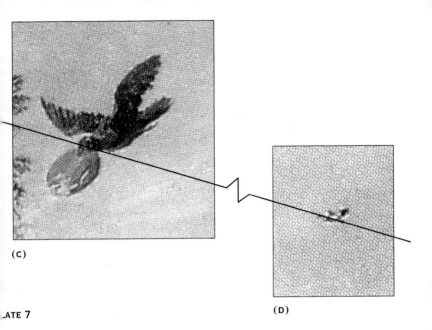

(C)

(D)

Details from *St Antony and St
Paul*: bowl, bread, church and
bird: showing how the lines of
the geometry are marked by
these features.

(A)

(B)

PLATE 8 Mount Cardou – the Site – as viewed from Roc Nègre.

PLATE 9 *Les Bergers d'Arcadie II*, by Nicolas Poussin, removed from its frame.

PLATE 10 *Les Bergers d'Arcadie II* – enlargement of the finger pointing at the line.

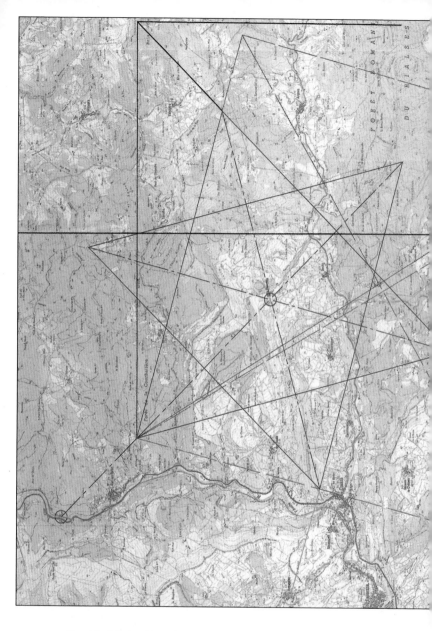

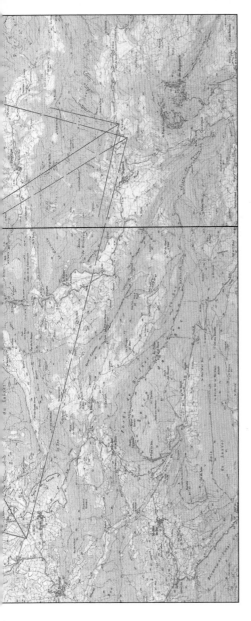

PLATE 11 Extract (at reduced size) from Sheets 2347 ouest Quillan and 2347 est Arques of the Institut Géographique National, 1:25,000 *Série Bleue* topographical maps of France. These two sheets join on the Zero Meridian of Paris, here emphasised by the black horizontal line. North is to the left. (This area is now also covered by a single sheet 2347 OT Quillan, at the same scale.)

The superimposed lines illustrate the 'Parchment geometry'. Blue lines are the two equilateral triangles of the hexagram from Parchment 1, shown after the first 1½° rotation; the right side of the first triangle is at exactly 45° to the Meridian; the lower side of the second triangle aligns with Antugnac church (one line of the Antugnac 'fan', shown green).

The derivation of the Parchment 2 square is shown by black and red lines. The centre of the square is at the intersection of the diagonals – shown before (dashed) and after the second 1½° rotation. The Site, on the west flank of Mount Cardou, is marked by the small red circle. The rock pinnacle, indicated by the 'château geometry', is cut by the diagonal (solid red line) and is slightly to the south-east.

PLATE 12 *Les Bergers d'Arcadie II* – enlargement of the first shepherd and his staff. The thin, perfectly straight 75° line may be seen at the left edge of the staff below his hand.

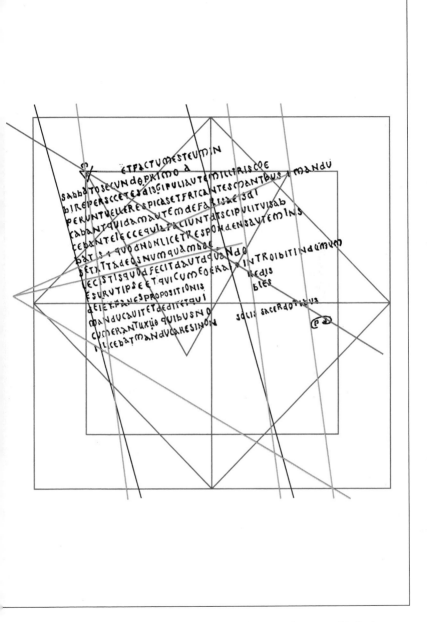

PLATE 13 The double-sided Parchment – showing the text of Side 1
– with the 7½° lines parallel.

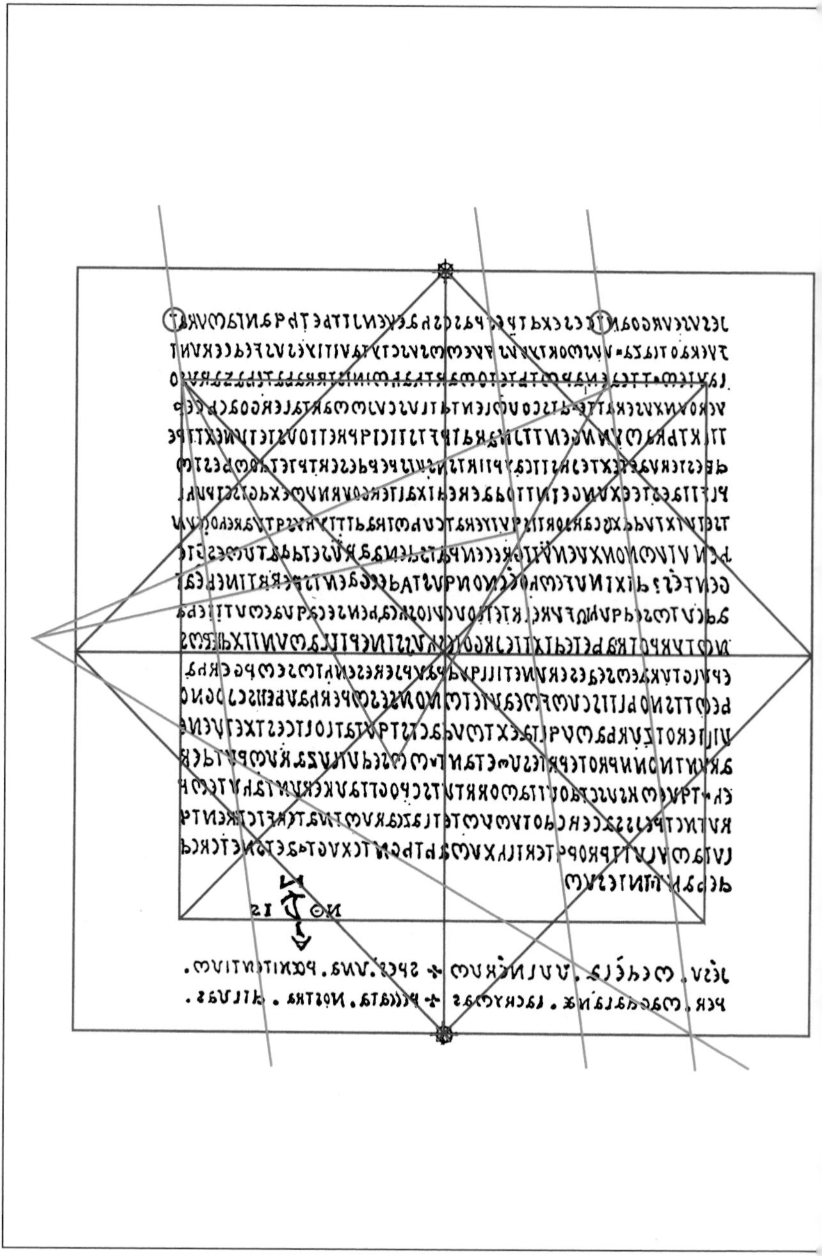

PLATE 14 The double-sided Parchment – showing the text of Side 2 reversed – with the 7½° lines parallel.

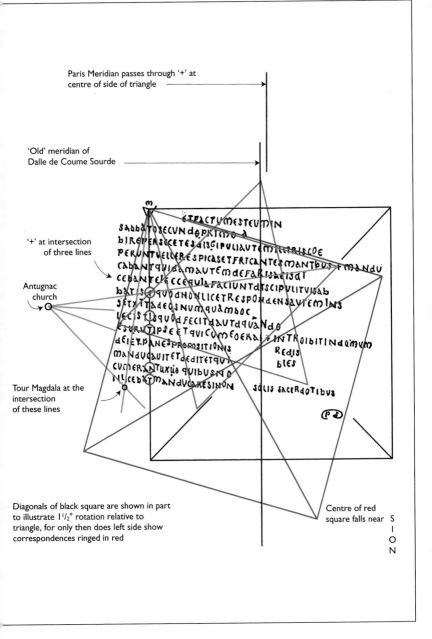

Paris Meridian passes through '+' at centre of side of triangle

'Old' meridian of Dalle de Coume Sourde

'+' at intersection of three lines

Antugnac church

Tour Magdala at the intersection of these lines

Diagonals of black square are shown in part to illustrate 1½° rotation relative to triangle, for only then does left side show correspondences ringed in red

Centre of red square falls near SION

ETFACTUMESTCUMIN
SABBATOSECUNDOPRIMOA
BIREPERSCCETESDISCIPULIAUTEMILLLIRISCOE
PERUNTUELLERESPICASETFRICANTESMANTBUSEMANDU
CABANTQUIDAMAUTEMdEFARISSACISAT
CEBANTELECCEQUIAFACIUNTdISCIPVLITVISAb
BATSEQUOdNONLICETRESPONdENSAVTEMINS
SETXITADEOSNUMQUAMBOC
LECISTISQUOdFECITdAUTddVANdO
ESVRUTIPSEETQVICVMEOERAT+INTROIBITINdUMUM
dEIETPANESPROPOSITIONIS REdIS
MANdUCAUITETdEdITETQVI bIES
CUMERANTUXUSQUIBUSNO
NLICEBdTMANdUCARESINON SOLIS SACERdOTIbVS

(P S)

PLATE 15 The main geometric elements on Parchment 1, and their geographical correspondences.

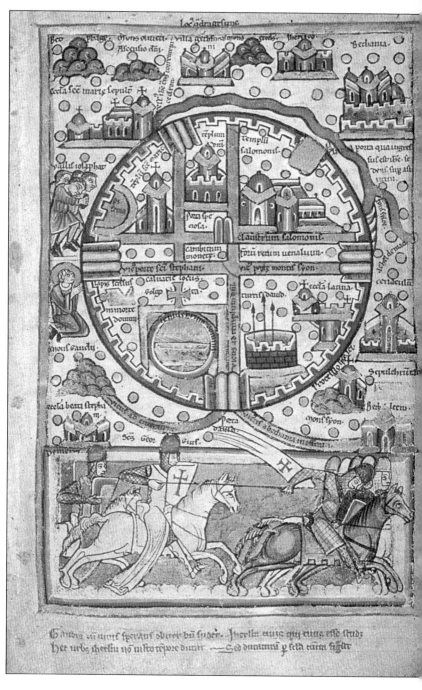

PLATE 16 'Circular map' of Jerusalem from the Royal Library at The Hague.

PLATE 17 Self-portrait by Nicolas Poussin.

PLATE 18   *Lord George Stuart*, by Sir Anthony Van Dyck. His staff (shepherd's *houlette*) is at 72° to the horizontal. A line joining the tip of his forefinger to the lower end of the staff is at 75° to the horizontal. The colours of his clothing may be compared with those of the woman in *Les Bergers d'Arcadie II.*

doubt that this is correct. On checking the diameter of the circumscribing circle, we find it is also the same as that of the hexagram.

FIGURE 11.1 Saunière's bookplate – the presence of a pentagram is indicated.

FIGURE 11.2 Saunière's bookplate – a dodecagram is also indicated.

Bérenger Saunière combined in his bookplate three polygrams, two
of them occulted. They are the hexagram, the pentagram and the
dodecagram. All may be circumscribed with circles of the same diameter. These are identical to the polygrams concealed by Nicolas Poussin
in *Les Bergers d'Arcadie II*. His also were circumscribed by equal circles,
but in this case their centres were coincident. The three polygrams do
not make an obvious trio, so now we can be fairly sure that Saunière
knew of Poussin's secret geometry.

It is possible to reconstruct the complete sequence followed either
by Saunière or a draughtsman on his behalf in producing the bookplate, and this is informative. Only sceptics and keen geometers need
follow the description, which is in Appendix J, but others may find it
intriguing also.

We had approached the Saunière story with an open mind.
However, it was becoming apparent that the nineteenth-century priest
did have connections with some markedly un-Catholic pastimes. We

had come across the twin triangles of the hexagram too often now – in Parchment 1 and the paintings, in Coustaussa church, in Saunière's bookplate – for us to reject the idea that he had been an adherent of Gnosticism. This religious philosophy is founded upon a concept of dualism, a struggle between opposing elements, and this is what is expressed by the two triangles. A principal tenet is that everyone has the ability to achieve a state known as Gnosis (Greek for 'knowledge') – a level of spiritual consciousness not dissimilar to the 'enlightenment' sought by the followers of Eastern mystic religions. As this bypasses church and priest as the route to salvation, the Catholic Church under-standably condemned Gnosticism as a dangerous 'heresy' – but here was its symbol, in Saunière's possession.

In the interval between our investigations of the priestly triumvirate in France and our work in England, much had happened in the life of the Saunière museum. Ownership of the estate had now passed into different hands. We were hopeful that a more serious policy would have been adopted. Perhaps more evidence had come to light?

Return to Rennes

Little had visibly changed at Rennes-le-Château during our absence, save the resurfacing of the approach road to the village. Much had happened, however, in connection with the famous priest. The museum had been enlarged to accommodate the vast amount of ephemera and documentation which had recently come to light, and the consequences were dramatic. The collection now on display was a revelation to anyone with an interest in the life of Saunière. Of all the new exhibits, the most significant were his personal notebooks.

Bérenger Saunière's handwriting was small and neat. Setting out his daily records with care, he had filled each page with the details of his movements and, most surprisingly, the weather. Such fascination with variations in the weather is perhaps not so extraordinary when one considers that for a year he was the priest of two parishes several kilo-metres apart, requiring him to undertake a strenuous hike over the mountains to perform his daily duties.

In view of the famous story about the discovery of the original Parchments, and the likelihood that they were not found in either the stone column or the wooden baluster, but that one of these may have *indicated* the actual place of concealment, there is one entry of more than a passing interest. It reveals that Saunière had, indeed, embarked on some exploratory works. On 21 September 1891 he made this casual-sounding entry (Figure 11.3):[3]

21 letter from Granes, <u>discovery of a tomb</u>, rained in the evening.

Saunière immediately halted work on the site of the tomb for three weeks, until 14 October when he recommenced, using different labourers. We shall never know why Saunière stopped the excavation and replaced his workforce, though we can make the reasonable guess that he wished to record the findings in secret. During the intervening period he was far from idle, as his journal entries for September show:

28 Depart for retreat—
28 trip to Carcassonne and Luc . . . 5,70 francs [from the accounts-book]
29 Saw Curé of Névian — to Gélis — to Carrière — Saw Cros and Secret

These entries throw up some interesting questions. Was this the dis-covery of the Marie de Nègre stone, the stone Saunière is alleged to have defaced? Or did this tomb contain the parchments, Saunière – anticipating their presence – completing the opening himself? Whichever, Saunière presumably realised the implications of the tomb inscriptions, for he decided to show them to his colleagues without delay. The week between 21 and 28 September would have been time

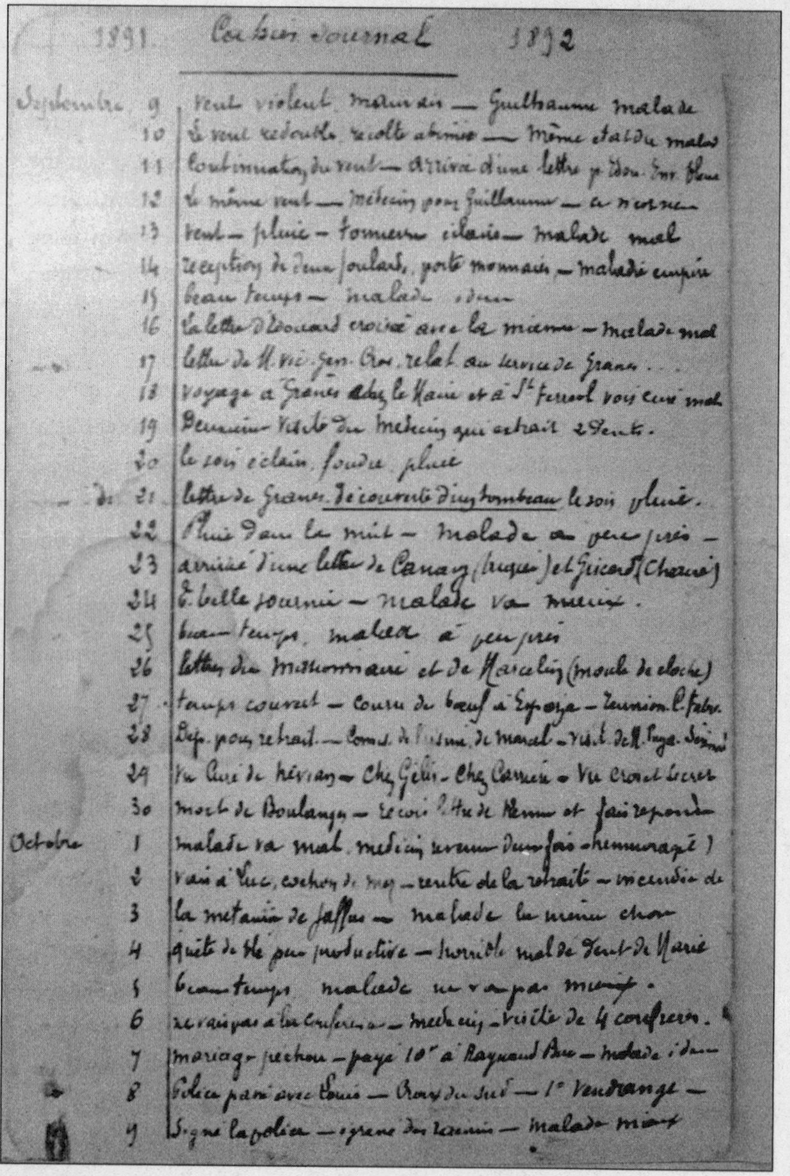
1891 Cahier journal 1892

Septembre 9 vent violent mauvais — Guillaume malade

20 le soir éclair, foudre, pluie

21 lettre de Granes. Découverte d'un tombeau le soir pluie.

24 belle journée — malade va mieux.

Octobre 1 malade va mal.

FIGURE 11.3 The page from Saunière's journal on which he recorded his 'discovery of a tomb' (shown here underlined).

enough for him to make copies, and Carcassonne, the seat of Bishop Billard and the location of Saunière's old seminary, would have been the logical destination for such incredible news.

His 'retreat' did not last long; by 2 October he was back at Rennes-le-Château, having met with his four confederates on 29 September, the second day of his 'retreat'. 'Chez Gélis' suggests he was at Coustaussa, Gélis's village, on the 29th, the trip to and from Carcassonne having therefore been made in a day. Cros was Vicaire Général of the diocese, second-in-command to Billard in Carcassonne, and the highest ecclesiastical authority in the immediate area. The clipped statement 'vu Cros et Secret' appearing after 'chez Gélis' suggests that Saunière was back in the vicinity of Rennes when he showed his findings to Cros.

Cros had 'seen' the Secret on 29 September. On 6 October Saunière, back at Rennes since the 2nd, received a visit from 'four colleagues', presumably the same four he had visited previously. It is apparent that if this group did indeed see the Secret at first hand, then whoever he revealed his knowledge to on the 29th while on his travels must have been shown a copy of some kind, in the form of either photographs or sketches.

Whether the discovery of September 1891 was that of the Marie de Nègre tomb, allegedly situated outside the church walls, must remain a mystery. What is revealed, however, is Saunière's fascination with the ancient tombs in his church and cemetery.

The grave of Marie de Nègre had been furnished with two stones: one upright, by way of a headstone; the other recumbent, covering the grave. The headstone is quite well documented; a drawing of it was made by members of the Society for Scientific Studies of the Aude during a field trip to the area in 1905, and printed, with a report on the trip, in the Society's journal. The drawing of the recumbent stone has a less reliable provenance, as it does not appear in that report. It is possible that this stone had become soil-covered by the date of the field trip and escaped notice.

The headstone was later defaced by Saunière, clearly with the intention of removing the rather strangely executed inscription. Some have questioned this story, but it is recorded that Saunière, accused by the Blanchefort descendants of defiling the grave of their ancestor, replaced the stone with a copy.[4] But the family was still not satisfied, for Saunière had changed the layout of the inscription, correcting the peculiarities. Their objections appear to have gone unheeded, so the priest's subterfuge succeeded. It would appear that Saunière had been unaware of the activities of the scientific society, and destroyed the inscription in ignorance of the existence of the drawing and of a photograph (now lost) taken some time before.

A new breakthrough: Marie de Nègre and the 60°

The inscription on the headstone of Marie de Nègre has been implicated, by other authors,[5] in the decoding of the cipher message of Side 2 of the Parchment. This could well have been its purpose, were it not for the fact that we had deduced the cipher to have been added to the Parchment long after Saunière's day. So, if Saunière was concerned to conceal its occult purpose, that purpose must have been related to something other than the cipher.[6] But what might this purpose have been? What secret did the Marie de Nègre stones hold, and what were the chances of cracking any coded message they might contain? With the experience we had gained from studying the Parchment and paintings, our ability to interpret relevant data had improved. We now turned our attention to the two gravestones of Marie de Nègre d'Ablès, Dame d'Hautpoul de Blanchefort.

The recumbent stone (Figure 11.4) bears a Greek version of ET IN ARCADIA EGO:

ET IN A + PX AΔ + IA EΓΩ

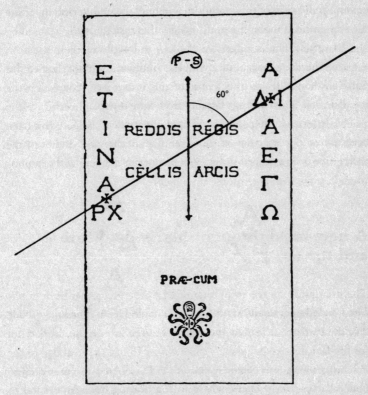

FIGURE 11.4 Inscription on the recumbent stone of the tomb of Marie de Nègre d'Ablès, from a drawing of unknown date.

It actually offers the better possibility for progress, for it contains a vertical line, terminated with arrowheads; also there are '+' symbols, and these had been instrumental in solving the Parchment; perhaps they have a similar function here? A straight line drawn through these crosses cuts the existing vertical line at 60°. There is good reason to find this intriguing: the angle is precise – it is not approximately 60°, it is *exactly* 60°. But this precludes the line from being part of the triangle–square geometry (although this is the interior angle of the equilateral triangle, it is not an angle that any line makes with a meridian or parallel), unless, that is, some rotation of the stone is intended. But there is no obvious indication of this intention, and one is forced to conclude that the way ahead is more direct, if, indeed, there is one at all.

The vertical line is suggestive of a line of longitude – a meridian – the arrowheads perhaps indicative of a continuation of the line to the north and south. If this is so, a line crossing it may well indicate a bearing. But, if it is a bearing, a bearing from which point?

The letters forming the Greek transliteration of ARCADIA have been split into two groups on opposite sides of the stone and, furthermore, have been grouped in a strange manner incorporating the crosses:

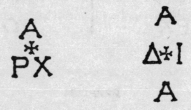

The word has been split to read A–RC and A–DI–A. The line joining the crosses passes through the centre of ARC – or should that be ARQUES?

Placing navigator's parallel rules on the I.G.N. map at the suggested angle enables one to check where such a bearing from Arques might lead. If it is to be from the town, the most likely point would be the church, but this certainly does not give a line passing even near the Site, or near anywhere else remotely interesting. No other building or feature within the town yields a line of any interest. Is there anything else?

The most prominent landmark near the town of Arques is the Château d'Arques, with its magnificent keep, which we had seen in photographs. The gravestone has a potential reference to the château, although the Latin is obscure and ambiguous:

REDDIS	RÉGIS
CÈLLIS	ARCIS

The vertical line divides these words, so it is impossible to know whether one is supposed to read them across or down; but, in Latin, the order is not that important. Individually the words may mean:

REDDIS: you give back, restore, return, give up, resign, offer, assign, repeat, recite, represent, render, make, answer; or, it might be the ancient name for Rennes

RÉGIS: you rule, or of the King

CÈLLIS: with, or to, the cell, cellar, storehouse, pantry, shrine (in a temple), chapel servant's room, honeycomb

ARCIS: of the stronghold, citadel, castle, palace, temple, defence, refuge (the word is ARX, ARCIS; *not* arca, arcae or arcus, arcus)

So it is clear that there is some scope for various translations, but if one considers these in the apparent context, it would appear most likely that a reference to the Château d'Arques, not the church or town, is intended. An informative meaning of REDDIS RÉGIS eludes us, but a possible translation of CÈLLIS ARCIS might be 'to the storehouse of the castle', in which case this most likely refers to the castle keep; for the Latin for 'keep' is the same as for 'castle' – ARX, ARCIS. Therefore, if one wished to say in Latin 'to the keep of the castle at Arques', the same Latin word would be used three times!

The I.G.N. map shows the Château d'Arques to have a wall enclosing a bailey yard, at the centre of which there is the outline of a square enclosure, but in the south-west corner, shown in black, is a building, and nearby is noted a '*donjon*', or keep. This, as the most prominent feature, may be the point through which the line of the bearing should pass. This line is found to run very close to the rock pinnacle adjacent to the Site. If the line is drawn so as to follow the 60° bearing, but passing exactly through the pinnacle, it then passes through the centre of the square in the middle of the bailey. If the line is drawn so as to pass through the pinnacle *and* the black square marked *donjon*, the bearing is about half a degree off 60°. We suspected that this black square is not the keep, and that it is the central square – the normal position for a keep – which gives a precise result. (On visiting the château, as is explained later, we discovered that '*donjon*' has been incorrectly placed on the map, and the keep *is* the square at the centre of the bailey.) This is too remarkable to be a coincidence, but without a comparable bearing from another point the Site is not pinpointed; perhaps this is the purpose of the headstone.

The headstone has no lines or crosses, as had the recumbent stone, but it does bear other clues (Figure 11.5). The drawing of this stone shows it to have had a triangular top – the edges are drawn at approximately 59° to the vertical sides. It is quite possible that this angle was

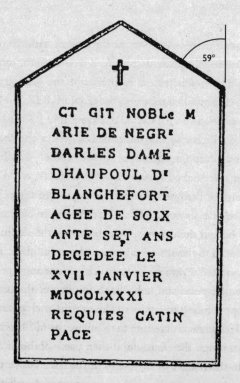

FIGURE 11.5 Inscription on the headstone of the tomb of Marie de Nègre d'Ablès, from a drawing made in 1905.

actually 60° on the stone itself, for the drawing has the sides converging slightly towards the bottom (they are not parallel); most likely, published versions of the drawing are based on a photograph taken without the focal plane precisely parallel to the plane of the headstone. A small error in both the horizontal and vertical alignments would have produced the result seen. Admittedly, this does not prove that the angle was 60°, only that it may well have been.

A number of strange mistakes in the inscription have been noted by previous researchers.[7] However, it appears that they perform more than one function, for the P has dropped out of the SEPT (seven) leaving SET, which is meaningless in French; so 'sixty-seven' is perhaps to be read as 'sixty'. Could the other bearing also be 60°? Perhaps, but from where?

There are two places named in the inscription: ARLES – which is so far away as to be improbable and is in any case an error for Ablès – and BLANCHEFORT, which is far more likely. If the bearing is to be from the Château de Blanchefort, the point to be used is clear, for the ruin is small and its centre is marked by a spot height. The line drawn from this point at 60° to the meridian passes exactly through the spot height at the top of the pinnacle. Thus the two gravestones combine to locate the pinnacle at the Site (Figure 11.6).

Realisation that the Site was identifiable from the information on the gravestones must have come as a shock to Saunière. There can be little doubt that, having deduced the purpose of the de Nègre stones, he would have effaced the inscriptions, so blatant was their message. The story of his vandalism, we saw, was gaining substance.

One question remained: could the significance of these bearings have been appreciated before an accurate map was available? There is certainly no difficulty in sighting the pinnacle from Blanchefort, as it is just across the valley. This fact, and the discovery of the interesting angle of the bearing, may have given rise to the use of a similar bearing from the other direction, the two combining to pinpoint the Site. So can the Site be seen from the keep of the Château d'Arques, or vice versa? It

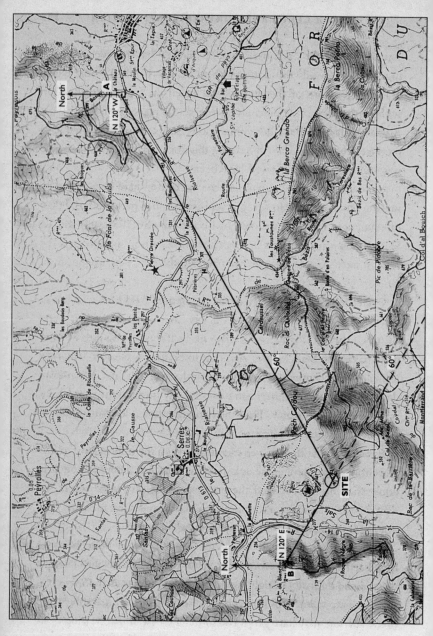

FIGURE 11.6 The bearings of the Site from the châteaux at Blanchefort and Arques, as indicated by the de Nègre gravestones.

cannot − as Mount Cardou intervenes. But the line passes almost exactly through the summit of the mountain. Standing on this point, it would be possible (vegetation permitting) to take a sight in both directions and establish the bearing. That the keep, or an even earlier structure, had been constructed on this particular spot in order to define the location of the Site is intuitively unlikely. It was, however, hard to visualise the location of this building as a coincidence. The improbability of major buildings being erected for the purpose of defining the Site was a matter we would be forced to reconsider. For the moment at least, the case for the Site is seen to have been substantially reinforced.

The Château d'Arques

Arques had featured very little in our investigations until the discovery of the geometry implied by the de Nègre gravestones. It had now taken on an extremely important role in relation to the Site, so we decided to pay it a visit.

The Château d'Arques is an imposing structure. A substantial part of the bailey wall and the gateway are complete; and, as we should have expected, the *donjon*, or keep, is within the bailey (Figure 11.7). The 'black square' is a minor building compared with the towering keep of four storeys; the cartographer had made an error in the placing of the *'donjon'* label.

We had already discovered that a 60° line drawn through the pinnacle at the Site passes through the centre of the square building shown on the map, and this was now confirmed as the keep. That this was the intention of the gravestone inscription cannot be doubted.

The château has an interesting history. Most of the present structures, including the keep, were constructed by order of Pierre de Voisins in the thirteenth century. Debate continues locally over the origins of the site. It is not easy to defend as it occupies only a gentle rise

FIGURE 11.7 The Château d'Arques.

in the landscape, and its massive walls were necessary substitutes for the natural defences enjoyed by fortresses occupying more commanding positions. Even so, why did the château need such an exceptionally high keep? An obvious explanation lay in the advantage to sighting afforded by such a high tower.

On further fact stood out. The western and northern curtain walls of the bailey yard had been constructed from a stone different to that of the works by Pierre de Voisins. This, and modifications caused by his work, point to the existence of an earlier construction; indeed, it had been stated that there was previously a monastery on the site.[8] Had Arques been a repository of sacred knowledge? The persistent recurrence of ARC, ARCA, ARCADIA, in our researches certainly suggested something more than a coincidence of name.

Now that the precision of the 60° bearings indicated by the

gravestones had been confirmed, we decided to work out whether the buildings in question had been erected as permanent survey beacons, or markers. We had already seen how the churches at Antugnac and Peyrolles had so remarkably fitted the Parchment geometry when drawn on to the map, and now the Château d'Arques had become involved. A more detailed examination of features on the map and on the ground would be our next task.

Survey beacons

The Marie de Nègre gravestones had provided bearings from two locations which intersected near the Site – actually with great precision on the pinnacle of rock that on the I.G.N. map is just five millimetres, or 120 metres on the ground, south-west of the point indicated by the Parchment geometry. That these two completely independent sources are intended to mark the same location is undeniable. What is not clear is which is the more accurate.

The natural pinnacle is a remarkable feature, virtually indestructible and always recognisable given a rough indication of its location. However, the entire arrangement of the rock outcrops on the flank of the mountain is so remarkable, incorporating the great rock whose south-eastern flank is at an angle very close to 75°, that the Site is more likely to be between the pinnacle and this companion rock. This view is reinforced by the existence of the central triangular rock that marks the mid-point between them (Figure 11.8). This is the location indicated by the Parchment geometry, which probably refines the siting indicated approximately by the pinnacle. However, there are possibly two schools of thought.

These bearings were N 120° E and N 120° W, or at 60° to meridians passing through Blanchefort and the Château d'Arques, respectively. We also knew from the Parchment and paintings that Peyrolles church had an important role to play because it lay exactly at the centre of the

FIGURE 11.8 The Site, viewed from Roc Nègre. A point on the rockface below the central, triangular rock is the location indicated by the Parchment geometry; the pinnacle to the right is suggested by the de Nègre gravestones. Which is correct?

hexagram, but did it have a role to play in relation to Arques and Blanchefort? We decided to see whether an angular relationship existed, by tracing these points from the I.G.N. map and measuring the bearings of each point from the other. The result (Figure 11.9) was surprising: to an extraordinary accuracy, far better than half a degree, the angles were found to be as follows:

ARQUES–PEYROLLES–BLANCHEFORT: 90°
PEYROLLES–BLANCHEFORT–ARQUES: 60°
BLANCHEFORT–ARQUES–PEYROLLES: 30°

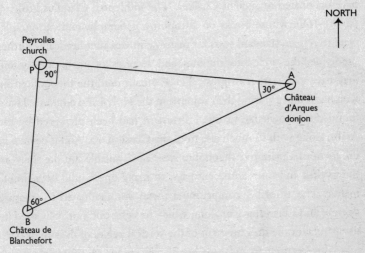

FIGURE 11.9 The châteaux at Arques and Blanchefort and the church at
Peyrolles mark the corners of the 30–60–90 degree triangle ABP.

The result is surprising for two reasons. Firstly, the angles are of the
'30–60 degree' family, as are the gravestone bearings. Secondly, they
produce a '30–60–90 degree' triangle, one that is extremely useful and
familiar to anyone with a knowledge of technical drawing. But, the real
significance lies in the implication that these angles represent the result
of accurate surveying. Considering the dates of the buildings, this is surprising but not impossible. The most important question to investigate
now was whether this was by design or coincidence. We needed to
look at the methods and instruments available at the time the buildings
were constructed, between the twelfth and fourteenth centuries, to
see if they were sufficiently accurate to produce this result.

Land survey and the ancient legacy

The principle of angular measurement was certainly known in very
ancient times. The division of the circle into 360 degrees is thought to

have originated in ancient Chaldea. The influential Claudius Ptolemy (AD 90–168), whose books on astronomy, geography and cartography were to remain standard texts for many centuries after his death, further subdivided the circle into 'minutes' and 'seconds' of arc, but this system may have even earlier origins.[9] The Romans used the theodolite; the Knights Templar during their sojourn in the Holy Land could well have found that knowledge of this instrument had been preserved by the Arabs, along with so much else from the Classical era. And if devices in the form of a primitive theodolite were not available 'off the shelf' in the twelfth and thirteenth centuries, to make one would be a simple matter. The astrolabe, comprising a metal disc graduated to measure degrees and a pivoting arm along which to sight, and normally used by navigators for the measurement of the vertical angles of the sun or stars, may also be used to measure horizontal angles. A simple mariner's astrolabe is shown in Figure 11.10. Arab astrolabes of great precision and sophistication survive.

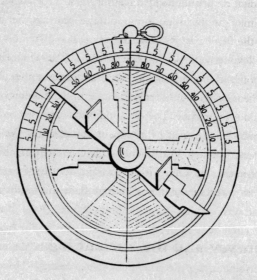

FIGURE 11.10 A mariner's astrolabe, used for taking bearings and measuring elevations.

The crucial question remained one of accuracy. Our enquiry revolved around the basic instruments available to the medieval mason or carpenter – the straight-edge, dividers and square. A draughtsman of the Middle Ages would have employed, together with his T-square, two set squares, one of which would have been the 30–60–90, and it is this relationship which is significant.

Some angles are more readily obtainable than others, in the absence of a graduated protractor. The most obvious is 90°, which is easily bisected to obtain 45° with great accuracy. An angle as large as 45° is of limited use in surveying, so will require subdivision. Accurate bisection is a simple matter using dividers; whereas division into three, for example, is not and may be achieved only by methods of successive approximation. But halving to 22½° introduces the inconvenient half-degree in what is still quite a large angle, and further halvings yield fractions of increasing inconvenience. There is another family of angles that is easy to obtain with comparable accuracy, and which permits greater subdivision before the half-angle appears. This is '60–30–15', all of which may be obtained using only compasses, or dividers.[10] Moreover, the familiar 7½° comes from bisecting 15°.

The well-known 'points' of the navigator's compass, before the incorporation of the magnetised needle, existed in another incarnation as the mariner's 'wind rose': a diagram indicating the points of origin of the observed principal winds. The number of points so indicated has varied through the centuries; the present standard is to show the four cardinal points – N, E, S and W – with successive bisections of the angular divisions to produce thirty-two points. But a wind rose of twelve points 'was accepted throughout the Roman Empire from Egypt to Spain and was common throughout the Middle Ages'.[11] A rose that divides the circle into twelve has intervals of 30°. If the bearing from Blanchefort to the Site had been found to be 60°, why not employ that angle and its siblings for the other definitive geometry? However, there is another important consideration.

For bearings to be taken it must be possible to sight from one location to the other. Study of map contours had given us a fair idea of the visibility between the various locations, and it was apparent that the proposed lines of sight are not all clear: there is high ground between Peyrolles and Arques. For the 30–60–90 degree triangle to be established there would have to be one or more intermediate stations positioned so as to permit triangulation of these points. Such stations would not need to be permanent, but maybe a desire to make it possible for the survey to be repeated would have prompted the construction of monuments whose very nature would minimise the risk of later destruction, substantial remnants of which might therefore have survived into the twentieth century. Other châteaux must be primary candidates for such structures, and one in particular, which is tall and suitably located – the Château de Serres. This is shown on the I.G.N. map as a small rectangle, oriented approximately NW–SE. Traced on to our diagram and with lines drawn between the Château de Serres (S), Peyrolles church (P) and the Château de Blanchefort (B), S is seen to be equidistant from P and B to a remarkable accuracy. But what of the bearings from these two spots? Astonishingly, the angles formed are as follows:

PEYROLLES–BLANCHEFORT–SERRES: 30°
BLANCHEFORT–PEYROLLES–SERRES: 30°

These angles are accurate to within half a degree when the lines are drawn to intersect on the centre of the château. However, intuition suggested drawing these lines not to the centre, but to the corner most readily visible from Peyrolles and Blanchefort, and that is the western corner. When this is done the angles are precisely 30°, as shown in Figure 11.11. (The point on the I.G.N. map taken as marking Peyrolles church is the centre of the circle of the symbol, and for the Château de Blanchefort the centre of the principal ruin which is marked with the spot height 476.) A further line drawn from Peyrolles to a point X on the line AB shows that the western corner of the Château de Serres is

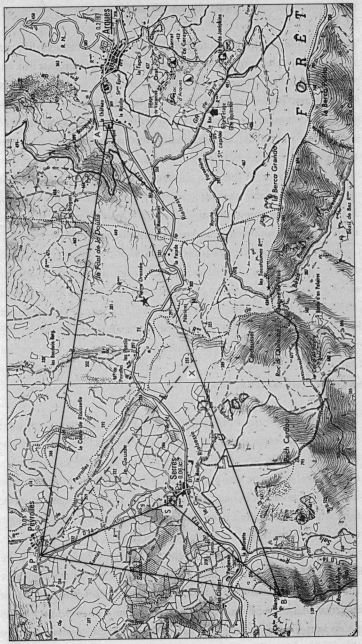

FIGURE 11.11 The location S of the Château de Serres in relation to the triangle ABP suggests that it played a role in triangulation. (I.G.N. 1 : 25,000 map)

at the centre of an equilateral triangle (Figure 11.11). Point X, although
not marked in any way, falls on a location well sited to be part of a triangulation survey. The remarkable relationships between Arques,
Blanchefort, Peyrolles and Serres – all based on 30–60–90 degree
geometry – argued so strongly for the *constructed* features having been
deliberately and painstakingly located, that all we needed was one more
feature and the matter would be clinched.

The importance of this new configuration, which for brevity's sake
we shall refer to as the 'château geometry', is that it moved the evidence
away from coded messages of unspecified age and provenance, and
from grave inscriptions that are no longer to be seen; we were leaving
a world of shadows and half-truths. This new plan – albeit geometric in
a way – was rooted in real objects in the landscape. But there still had
to be a way to preserve it and pass it down. The time had come to take
a close look at the western corner of the Château de Serres to see
whether there was anything relevant about the building itself.

The conclusive test

Relieved for once not to be heading for a graveyard, our anticipation
increased as we approached the final bend in the road leading up to the
Château de Serres. We knew that if there was nothing distinctive about
the western corner, it was back to the drawing-board. As the château
came into view from behind a group of trees, it seemed that our worst
fears would be confirmed, for our first sight was of an uncompromis-
ingly 'square' building. And then we noticed it.

Distinct from the remainder of the building, a turret rose from the
western corner (Figure 11.12a). Of a different stone to the walls, the
circular shape and the corbelling reminded us of another turret, that of
the Tour Magdala at Rennes-le-Château (Figure 11.12b). There could
be no better confirmation of a survey-point. At the precise point of
geometrical intersection, the turret rose above the supporting walls

(a)   (b)

FIGURE 11.12 The turrets of (a) the Château de Serres and
(b) the Tour Magdala.

and terminated in a stone dome, complete with a stone ball finial. To
anyone in the tower, on the intersection marked by the finial, Peyrolles
and Blanchefort would have been visible, enabling them to confirm the
angles by observation.

With the confirmation of this feature came relief, and the realisation
that this was surely vindication of the theory. We leaned against the
sun-warmed corner below the turret and used the Magellan G.P.S.
handset to fix our position. The possibility of chance was rapidly

dwindling, and this strange structure on the western corner of the château appeared to be the prototype for Saunière's tower at Rennes. If Saunière, as we supposed, had correctly interpreted the Parchment, and therefore correctly identified the location on Cardou, what better final touch to his home than a square construction, a library, complete with a round tower – a replica of the crucial sighting-point necessary to understand the geometry complementary to the de Nègre stone?

Having taken a G.P.S. fix at Serres, we decided to repeat the process from the Peyrolles graveyard facing the southern prospect of Blanchefort, Cardou and the Château de Serres. Later, our readings would enable us to confirm the bearings so far obtained only from the I.G.N. map. Standing in a break between cypress trees, we looked southwards to the valley, the clarity of the air rewarding us with a view to the distant Pyrenees. The mountain of Blanchefort, a stark white against the green of the surrounding slopes, guarded the entrance of the valley leading past the Site and the approach to Rennes-les-Bains. We looked for the all-important western corner of the Château de Serres. To the naked eye it was just visible, and with great relief we trained our binoculars carefully on the tower, focusing on the finial and the top windows below the roof. Then, using a prismatic compass, we sighted the finial on top of the turret at Serres; we did the same for the ruin at Blanchefort. Subtracting one bearing from the other, we were left with 30°. We had the proof we needed.

Correlations: the château and Parchment geometries

With this substantial backing for the château geometry came the realisation that there need not be just a single method of preserving the location of what was undeniably an important treasure. Peyrolles had first come to our attention in its role as the centre of the hexagram in the Parchment geometry, and therefore featured in both methods. We thought of Antugnac church: while not implicated in the 'château geometry', it was very much part of the Parchment geometry. We wondered if it too had been built to suit a geometric layout, or whether it was simply found later to have a convenient location. Peyrolles, Serres and Blanchefort are not that far apart, but Antugnac church is comparatively remote. Could its location have been surveyed at the early date indicated?

Investigating this possibility, we found a clear line of sight from Rennes-le-Château to Antugnac church, across the wide valley of the Aude and along the valley of the tributary Ruisseau d'Antugnac. This is most easily appreciated when standing (this is not recommended!) on the tiny turret of Saunière's Tour Magdala, and this may be no coincidence as the tower lies on a 45° bearing from Antugnac church: the extreme westerly (and, presumably, inconvenient) siting intended to achieve that very fact. Surely it is no coincidence that Saunière (or his masters) had designed a square tower with a corner turret, like the one at Serres, and to perform a similar role. This 45° line from Antugnac is the one so clearly indicated on Parchment 1 and now known to pass through Saunière's tower. (A line parallel, it should be noted, to the *La Croix*–Peyrolles church line.)

We must refer back for a moment to the Parchment 1 diagram as it relates to the map. We had drawn on the main components of the diagram, but in our rush to have a result – a site for the 'treasure' – the various other lines were forgotten. It is now that we can see something significant emerging, for the 7½° line drawn through the top-left corner of the triangle on Parchment 1, when drawn on the map, is found to pass through the Tour Magdala! The intersection of the 7½° and 45° lines falls exactly on the tower (Plate 15). We consider this to prove, beyond reasonable doubt, that the original Parchment was at least contemporaneous with the construction of the tower, and probably predated it, since the site had formerly been marked, it is said, with a cross, and before that a tower. We cannot prove the former existence of the cross, but there must have been a tower at, or very close to, this spot; the outer defence works of the château would have demanded it.

Before moving on, there are further extraordinary relationships to be noted. The geometry we have been referring to as the 'Parchment' or 'Parchment and paintings' geometry was, as will be evident by now, related to the map on the basis of the scaled features from Parchment 1, and confirmed by the geographical features that are found to conform with it. This was how we did it, but this may not be how it was derived. Quite independently we had deduced the 'surveyed' layout of the châteaux at Arques and Serres and the church at Peyrolles. When these two independent sets of geometry are seen together – super-imposed – a relationship appears.

A circle inscribed within the Parchment hexagram has a radius equal to PB, the distance between Peyrolles church and the Château de Blanchefort (Figure 11.13), a fact we were unaware of during the original plotting of the geometry on the map. Also, the Meridian passes right through the point of intersection of the line AB and the hexagram's centre-line (this point is ringed on the map) – possibly a coincidence, but by now there are so many!

Then we see that the château geometry is that of a putative hexagram, rotated about P through an angle of 6° relative to the Parchment geometry. This 6° rotation gives rise to the 36° relationship (Figures 11.13 and 11.14). Now, 36° is a 'pentagonal' angle and generates another set of geometry, part of which has already been introduced into the 'data-bank' of the Secret, but which, as we show later, had been inaccurately copied and had become unrecognisable. This is the Coume Sourde diagram – the means of conveying this geometry and relating it to the Meridian. From the arrangement of these lines, other sets of polygonal geometry may follow; and one has to consider the possibil-ity that this is intentional, though there is no guarantee.

How these polygonal figures interrelate, and how new ones may be implied by a subtle variation, reinforces our opinion that Pythagorean-ism has been a major influence in the work of the initiates of the Secret. It is regrettable that this book's page size does not permit clear –

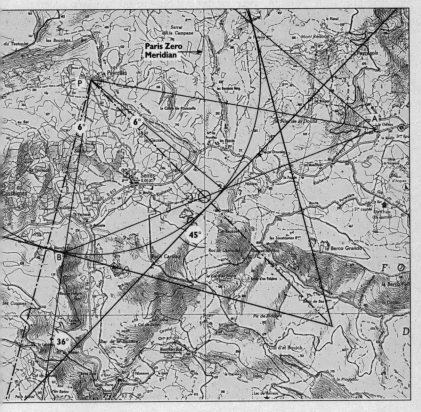

FIGURE 11.13 The Parchment and château geometries combined on the I.G.N. 1:25,000 map.

and truly convincing – illustration of these relationships. When they are superimposed on the I.G.N. map at 1:25,000 scale, the Parchment triangles have sides 338 millimetres long. If one looks at this length on a tape-measure, one can see the potential for accuracy.

To achieve the required level of precision for a treasure-map, one would first need to decide on the accuracy necessary to locate a feature on the ground. If the feature is so remarkable that no great precision on the ground is required, then the same applies to the required accuracy of the map. The placing of permanent features on the ground can be problematic. Sometimes, 'less than perfect' has to do; sometimes, 'less than perfect' is perfectly adequate. The object of our next visit would prove to be in the latter category.

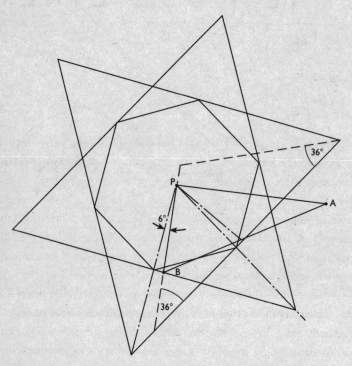

FIGURE 11.14 The Parchment and château geometries and their relation to the triangle on the Dalle de Coume Sourde, shown by dashed lines.

12
THE GRAVE ON
THE ROSE LINE

We now had within our grasp a second and equally conclusive method of locating the Site, adding further weight to our conviction that the formation of rocks on Cardou was the most secret of hiding-places and the location of the 'treasure' of Rennes. As morning broke over the town of Rennes-les-Bains, we had a very short trip to make: down the main street, across the square, through the church portico and into the graveyard. We walked along the rows of graves, gravel crunching beneath our feet, eyes searching for just one name: Boudet.

We knew from the image we had built up of this secretive priest that the gravestone he erected to his mother and sister would be consequential, but what we saw was rather strange (Figure 12.1). The early-morning light threw the rough granite facing of the tomb into relief, and viewed from the front the tombstone seemed devoid of inscription. Madame and Mademoiselle Boudet lie beneath a fine recumbent slab of white granite speckled with black crystals. That it appears to be blank may be deliberate: the crystalline structure, the lack of a polished finish and the random distribution of crystals all contribute to confuse the eye. We peered closer to see what it had to reveal. The stone does bear inscriptions: separate epitaphs to the two women. One is on the left and one on the right, and dividing the two – as on the de

FIGURE 12.1 The tombs of Henri Boudet's mother and sister (left) and Jean Vié (right) in the graveyard at Rennes-les-Bains.

Nègre stone – is a vertical line with an arrowhead top and bottom. Henri Boudet had duplicated the system used by the composer of the de Nègre inscription, and indicated a meridian.[1]

Suspecting that Boudet may well have placed this grave in a significant position, we checked its position by using the G.P.S., which showed that, to within the accuracy of the system, the grave lies on a meridian running close to the Site. Reference to the map shows that the grave would need to be further east to be on a line through the pinnacle of rock, but also that it conforms very closely to the location of the Site as determined by the Parchment geometry. The difference is no more than a millimetre on the 1:25,000 map.

Pierre Plantard[2] discusses a meridian which runs between Serres and Peyrolles, and thus very close to the grave. He pointedly refers to this as *le méridien*, but he also shows that he knows perfectly well that the Zero, or Paris, Meridian runs to the east of Mount Cardou, nearly 1,400 metres away. He is deliberately confusing two meridians. A meridian through the graveyard at Rennes-les-Bains runs between Serres and Peyrolles; the Zero Meridian runs well to the east of Serres. This is quite revealing. Firstly, since it appeared that Plantard knew the location of the Zero Meridian, he may have introduced the confusion to highlight the route of the other meridian, which he goes on to call the 'rose-line'.[3] We might also deduce from Plantard's red herring that he knows the location of the Site. But if he does, would he have published information so dangerously close to the truth? Secondly, because of the difficulty of extending a meridian from one location to another at some great distance, considerable error would result if only primitive methods and instruments were available. But the occasional need for local surveys – such as the resolution of boundary disputes and the partitioning of land for inheritance purposes – could give rise to the establishment of a local meridian. This is a straightforward matter since such a meridian would not require to be fixed relative to any other. Local surveys proliferated, and so did local meridians.[4]

There would have been no incentive whatever to embark on the arduous task of extending a meridian from one part of the country to another by means of a triangulated survey unless this were to be the basis for a national survey. (The first such survey anywhere in the world was carried out in France by Jean-Dominique Cassini and his colleagues.) As so often with the Rennes mystery, a detail would emerge later to undermine our preconception.

The implication of a meridional line in the Boudet tomb inscription received added support when we continued our study of the monument as a whole. The 'cross' that stands on the vertical slab was different to any we had seen before. Engraved upon it is another cross of unusual form, the top of the upright and the ends of the arms ending in arrowheads. This could represent only one thing: north, west and east. Other references to the Rose Line are to be found among the Priory

Documents. One, under the name 'Nicolas Beaucéan' (clearly an alias, since Beaucéan was the name given to the Templars' flag) quotes – almost certainly apocryphally – the deceased Abbé Courtauly thus: 'If the parishes of Peyrolles and Serres are the twin children of St Vincent, the parish of Rennes-les-Bains guards the heart of Roseline', and goes on to explain the Meridian as the 'red line, in English: *Rose-Line*'. The repeated references to the Rose Line as the Meridian clearly establish its role in locating the Site, so for the Site to be fixed geographically it remained only to establish the line of latitude running through it. If this were to be regarded as an east–west 'Rose Line', the two Rose Lines would form a 'Rose Cross'. This could actually be the origin of this enigmatic designation. Indeed, the parish of Rennes-les-Bains would then 'guard the heart of Roseline', for the heart would be the point at which the Rose Lines *cross*. Remember that Poussin had a shepherd point out the Rose Line.

There is one more item to note about the Boudet cross. Its sides are not parallel. When we checked the angle, we found each side of the cross to be at 1½° to the vertical.

Further implications

The Boudet grave is located next to that of a Jean Vié. This location was considered to be important by Pierre Plantard, who notes[5] that a reference to that recurring date, 17 January, may be implied by the sound of the name Jean Vié (Janvier) and that the fact that the date on Vié's grave is given as '1er 7^{embre}', meaning 1 September, in the manner of abbreviation frequently seen on graves of the nineteenth century, thus producing the '17'. Other occurrences of this date include the feast day of St Antony the Hermit, the date of death given on the gravestone of Marie de Nègre, and the date of Abbé Saunière's fatal stroke. Another saint to have that feast day is St Sulpice. In the fine Paris church of St Sulpice, a brass line set into the floor marks the meridian;

not *exactly* the Zero Meridian that runs through the Observatoire – it is just a little too far west – but not too far off perhaps for those who have an obsession with meridians and enjoy allusions to them.

That St Antony also shares the same day might therefore have been an adequate reason for selecting him as the subject of the painting by David Teniers. The apocryphal descent of Godfroi de Bouillon from this saint may also be noted. It appears that this possibility was debated, but not resolved, in former times. We have not pursued the delicate question of whether the necessary procreative act was performed before the saint's conversion or was a slip-up during a particularly arduous session of temptation.

The date on the de Nègre stone may not have been the true occasion of the lady's death, though the registry entry in the hand of Abbé Bigou himself attests to this date. And, if we are prepared to consider that Saunière's 'stroke' was the result of a murder attempt that was less than instantaneous in its result, the same date may well have been selected for his demise. We may add to these instances: Nicolas Flamel (one of the alleged Grand Masters of the Priory of Sion) is said to have performed his first successful alchemical transmutation at noon on this date; and a statue of Charles de Lorraine (another purported Grand Master) was unveiled in Brussels on 17 January 1775.[6] This unveiling of Charles would seem to be of some real significance since in 1761 he had become Grand Master of the Teutonic Order. Even the year of the event may have been selected, for it includes not only the 17 again, but also 75 – the key angle of the secret geometry.

The peculiarities of the siting of the grave aside, the choice of the graveyard itself comes as no surprise. The same may not be said of Henri Boudet's choice for his own place of last repose. Had the information on the tomb been the reason for Boudet's burial at Axat, and indeed for that of his brother? Boudet's mother and sister had died before the two men. A double inscription following the format of the de Nègre stone was therefore an ideal way of commemorating the two women.[7] This would date the stone to the later death, that of Boudet's sister Adélaïde in 1896; Marie Antonia, his mother, died in 1895. Boudet's brother Edmond did not die until 1907, and was buried in the town of Axat – a fairly obvious decision, as this was the place of his retirement. Henri, who outlived them all, followed the example of his brother and also left for Axat, where on his death in 1915 he was interred with Edmond.

There has been much speculation over the reason why this priest, with forty-two years of faithful service at Rennes-les-Bains, was not laid to rest in the churchyard of his adopted parish, alongside his mother and sister. Our observations had provided a glaringly simple explanation: as custom dictated family grouping, the burial of Henri at Rennes-les-Bains would require a change to the headstone which would nullify the message it bore. Henri Boudet's will has – unsurprisingly – never come to light, but one can confidently assume that it stipulated Axat as his final place of rest.

As we left the graveyard, our thoughts returned to the Rose Cross. If the Rose Line had been established, what of its east–west counterpart? What features might be found along the line of latitude, or parallel, that runs through the Site? The de Nègre stones had designated the pinnacle of rock close to, but not coincident with, the Site as marked by the Parchment geometry. We cannot say which is the more correct identification.

We returned to the I.G.N. map, and placed a straight-edge parallel to the east–west grid-lines, thus marking a line of constant latitude, passing through the spot height at the pinnacle. Nothing is to be found east of the Site, neither close by nor even at the furthest edge. To the west, the finger tracing along the straight-edge found nothing until it had travelled a scale 8.15 kilometres, when it stopped abruptly. It had stopped in Espéraza, at the symbol designating the church, through which the straight-edge passed precisely.[8] This was a surprise, and led to an extraordinary thought. If Espéraza church marks the south-west corner of the cipher square, should the circuitous route *PAX–681–La Croix* around the square lead us not to deduce that La Mort was its centre, but rather to arrive at the church and await further instructions? In arriving at the church we had completed the square, the 'guardian spirit' – the remaining part of the cipher message being A MIDI POMMES BLEUES: not 'at midday' but 'at the meridian', or even 'to the meridian'. So, from the church in Espéraza we were to take the most direct route to the meridian in question (by remaining at the same latitude) in order to arrive at the Site. But of course it has to be the correct meridian – not the present Paris, Zero Meridian, but the 'Rose Line' to which our attention has been so persistently drawn.[9] We were being directed to the centre of the 'Rose Cross' where will be found *pommes bleues*, the grapes – the body of Christ, perhaps?

13

THE KNIGHTS
TEMPLAR AND
THE PLACE OF
THE SKULL

We were fully aware that the events surrounding Saunière, still within living memory, had been the starting-point for *our* story, but it was fairly obvious that they were not the starting-point for *the* story. The gravestone of the Boudet ladies, and its prototype, the de Nègre gravestone, had come as a wonderful addition to the information contained in the Parchments. The gravestones not only confirmed the geometry and its correct placement on Cardou, but threw the origin of the preservation of the Secret back in time to well before the nineteenth century, to the origins of the châteaux at Blanchefort and Arques. The time had come to investigate the previous residents of the area to see if a connection could be found. But what could possibly link the original landowners with a group of Catholic priests at the end of the nineteenth century?

From the map it was evident that one location in the area of Rennes would provide us with a clear view of the Site and its surroundings, and perhaps a clue as to the former guardians of the 'treasure'. Blanchefort Castle gave us one of the 60° lines that cut through the Site. From this location we would also be able to observe Peyrolles church and the Château of Serres, both crucial to the château geometry. Climbing the steep path to the ruins of Blanchefort, we looked across the valley to the Site, with its distinctive rock formation, massive and dark in the shadow of the western side of Mount Cardou.

The Château de Blanchefort and the Knights Templar

Blanchefort, with its legendary associations with the Knights Templar, had been woven into tales of treasure much embellished by conjecture over the years. The fortunes of the Knights Templar had risen dramatically when the founding members returned to France, not least because of the decision taken by the Council of Troyes in 1129 granting the Order recognition by the Church. While this explains the change in their spiritual status, it does not account for the change in their fiscal status. As before, however, evidence was to come to our aid.

Much of the Templar wealth was amassed over the years through the inheritance of land and property, donated either by initiates or by those wishing to support an increasingly influential and potent force in the affairs of the French kingdom. Many of these land transactions, written in Latin, survived the destruction of the Order in 1307, and whereas much of the Templar 'history' in the area is little more than fiction, we found vital documents which did indicate their very real presence on and around this strategic mountain.[1]

According to a document dated 20 May 1130, the Templars had been present in the area since 1127, the year in which their first Grand Master, Hugues de Payens, had returned from Palestine.[2] This document confirms the transfer of the locality of Peirois or Peyrolles into the hands of the Order, whose master 'after God' is Hugues de Payens.

The second document comes from the same archive and is equally relevant to our story. Spanning a period from late March to early April 1134, it is also a land transaction, recording a gift from one William of Aleniano to the Knights of the 'Temple of Solomon'. But it is the surname of Blanchefort, one of the Templar witnesses to the signing of this document, that is of real interest.

Earlier researchers who studied Albon's *Cartulaire général* (a compilation of Templar transactions) had described the 'Blanchefort' in this document as possessing the Christian name of Bertrand, thus identifying him with the sixth Grand Master, elected in 1156.[3] The Château de Blanchefort was thus elevated to dizzying heights on the back of this assertion, declared as having belonged to the sixth Grand Master, Bertrand de Blanchefort; concealment of 'treasure' could therefore have been conducted under his protection.

However, closer study of the source of this identification reveals a discrepancy. It is not a *Bertrand* who is recorded but a *Bernard:* Bernardi de 'Blanca Fort'. This destroys at a stroke the documentary 'evidence' that Bertrand the Grand Master of the Knights Templar had anything to do with the area of Rennes. The index of the *Cartulaire* concerning the Rennes area confirmed this. Of Blanca-Fort knights, there were three mentioned: Arnaldus, Bernardus and Raimundus. There is no mention of a Bertrand. Aware that the Templar connection made by a previous book was wishful thinking, we were now thinking that the château was devoid of Templar connections, thereby undermining our theory. Was there really nothing else? Turning again to the document about Bernard, one witness stood out: Raymond, Abbé of Alet-les-Bains.

At the centre of Alet-les-Bains stand the ruins of a Benedictine abbey. The Rule of the Templars had been modelled on the Benedictine rule of poverty, chastity and obedience; knowing this common link, we researched the ownership of Alet Abbey. One source[4] told that it had been in Templar hands from 1132 to 1180. This was a real breakthrough, for we knew[5] that on 19 June 1119, ownership of the Château de Blanchefort had been transferred to the Abbeys of St Gilles and Alet-les-Bains by order of Pope Calixtus II. So, unless the château had been transferred to another owner between 1119 and 1132, it was, during the early years of the Order, a Templar possession.

This document therefore established that both Peyrolles and

Blanchefort were, from the years 1130 and 1132 respectively, both under Templar control. Moreover, the Abbey of Alet had come under their control in the same period. But what of our theories about early surveying and the château geometry? Did the church at Peyrolles have an earlier and more secular origin as a Templar barracks or *commanderie*? This seems possible, by reason of its isolation from the rest of the village and its position on the ancient highway as marked on the Cassini map. This route used to run from south of Alet-les-Bains eastwards through La Mort to Peyrolles church, before striking south past the Château de Serres. From Serres it crossed the river and then curved around the base of Mount Cardou to reach the base of the Site (Figure 13.1). Later study of the church at Peyrolles did indeed show that substantial additions had been made to an earlier building. This was apparent in the south-facing wall, where the top half of a filled-in archway demonstrated the existence of a large arched entrance in the original construction.

Peyrolles was visible from Blanchefort, which meant that the Templars could easily have monitored movement around the area of the Site on Cardou. If the Templars were associated with the concealment of the 'treasure' on Cardou, then the Château de Blanchefort, by virtue of its position, could easily have fulfilled the role of observation-post.

Sentinels of the Secret

The more we considered the strategic positioning of the Château de Blanchefort, the more we came to realise the obvious. This castle served no village as protector. The time and effort involved in leaving the mountain and reaching the road below ruled out any possibility of successfully halting undesired guests. Blanchefort, as demonstrated in the de Nègre stone, was perfectly placed for the visual protection of the Site, and an ideal signalling-post from which to summon assistance against anyone approaching Cardou.

Putting ourselves in the place of the medieval sentinel guarding the

FIGURE 13.1 The 1750 Cassini map, showing the route of the old road, the 'foresters' road'.

Site, but with the modern advantage of binoculars, we studied the road beneath us, Cassini map in hand. We picked up the old highway as it came out of the hills to the west of Peyrolles church. Here, as if accentuating the strategic importance of the Peyrolles site, it turned to the south-east, curving round as it passed through the closely packed vineyards heading for the outlying buildings of the village of Serres. The entry of the road into the village was obscured by the Château de Serres, with its sighting-tower clinging to the western corner of the main building, distinctive even without the aid of binoculars.

Visitors would have entered Serres watched by the guards of the château. This small village was of great significance in the days before the construction of the modern east–west highway connecting Arques and Couiza. The modern road heading south to Rennes-les-Bains crosses the Rialsesse river just before it joins the Sals, below the Château de Blanchefort. The Cassini map shows the river-crossing at Serres.

We searched for the old crossing-point. Bright in the light of the sun, a white construction stood out in contrast to the weathered stone and the various greens of the vegetation. We were looking at a newly re-constructed bridge across the river, at the point where the ancient medieval crossing had stood, as marked on the Cassini map, but which had been destroyed by floods. This restoration might just indicate the starting-point of the old road which continued around the northern side of Cardou, thus confirming the original route. We followed the track leading from the bridge, and its direction soon became apparent: there was little doubt that this was the old route. Its course continued up to the turning at the entrance to the valley under Blanchefort, where it joined the foresters' recently cleared roadway. The entire route matched that marked on the Cassini map. When we had stood in front of the Site on the foresters' road, with the Roc Nègre at our backs, we had assumed our elevation to be that of the old road, and our view of the Site to be that seen by the Templars and their predecessors. The Cassini map had suggested this to be the case, but we were now presented with solid confirmation that the remnants of this access to the valley, guarded by the garrison at Blanchefort, still existed.

The discovery had an added significance. If this crossing at Serres was medieval, the chances were that it had exploited the site of an older ford – that used by the Visigoths and the Romans in passing from the plains of Peyrolles to the Sals valley, leading south to Rennes-les-Bains. Contemporaries of Christ would have entered the valley along this route, and the Knights Templar, in time, would have followed in their footsteps.

The Templars' association both with the area and with the Parchment geometry had to be verified if the Order was to be identified with the Secret of Rennes. Peyrolles, Blanchefort and Alet-les-Bains had all yielded proof of possible Templar involvement with the key physical points of the château geometry. We had lacked a more tangible link between the Order and the secret geometry until our study of medieval surveying techniques (and, in consequence, medieval maps) provided us with an unexpected but perfect candidate. We found what amounted to the earliest representation of the Parchment geometry. This was a plan of Jerusalem, which proved to be a map within a map.

The Templar map

Our study of ancient mapmaking had shown us that the normal European techniques and practices of the period in which the châteaux were built would not have permitted the degree of precision we had identified. But the organisation we suspected of being responsible had received instruction from an unexpected quarter.

Pondering the origins of the secret geometry and how it first came to be used as an occult map, it is inevitable that questions should arise. When was it first used as a map? Whose idea was it? Where might the earliest surviving example be found? Could the Templars have had the expertise? Why did René d'Anjou use the geometry in *La Fontaine de fortune*, when the painting contains insufficient data for it to be used as a map? If a map had been made before the fifteenth century, what form would it have taken – parchment, perhaps, or stone? And so on. A brief look at medieval mapmaking is required.

One of the founders of modern geography was Claudius Ptolemy, who in the second century AD formulated many of the principles still applied today. He specified that maps should be oriented with north at the top and east at the right. In his *Geographia*, the first book to deal specifically with cartography, he laid down these and other rules, and published his maps. His were the only (European) world maps with a scientific basis to survive into the Middle Ages, and were to provide the pattern for later mapping in the age of discovery. He proposed the arrangements of lines extending around the world – lines of longitude and latitude. A grid system not unlike this, but for use over much shorter distances, had long been in use by the Roman surveyor. He would first establish two lines at right angles to each other called the *kardo maximus* (KM), running north–south, and the *decumanus maximus* (DM), running west–east. So the principle of meridian and parallel has an ancient and authoritative origin.

In the early 1200s (this is for extant examples – the practice could be older) European maps began to feature a direction-indicator for the cardinal points in the form of a cross. The earliest have a decorative elaboration of one arm of the cross, indicating east, and pointing *downwards* – Ptolemy's advice having been forgotten, no single convention had yet been adopted. When one considers the abilities of the Romans in the third century AD, one might expect to find a steady progress in surveying and cartography from then on. But in the early seventh century we find the whole of the known world reduced to a simple diagram: the 'T–O' map. We have Isidore, Bishop of Seville, to thank for this; Figure 13.2 shows an example from an eleventh-century copy of his *Etymologies*.[6] From then until the Renaissance, this childishly simple representation of a flat 'disc-world' was the norm. Attempts at realistic mapmaking in this period were rare, and indeed any attempt to depict the world as it actually was could place the would-be cartographer in danger. What had gone wrong?

A comprehensive answer to this question would require a discussion of myriad factors, but one may be singled out as the principal culprit –

FIGURE 13.2 A medieval 'T–O' map of the world: the 'T' divides the known world, the 'O', into three continents; north is to the left.

the Christian Church. The Church's 'patristic', formative period found it struggling to resolve questions of theology and doctrine. For some time the new religion co-existed with the culture of the Classical world into which it had been born. Indeed, apart from the abandonment of the ancient pantheon of gods, there need not have been conflict with the ancient philosophies and associated fields of learning. But this was not to be.

Visions of the form of the world described in the Scriptures became matters for debate. They could not be reconciled with the spherical world of the Greeks and Ptolemy. Ludicrous diagrams were devised in which all semblance of logic was abandoned in a vain attempt to reconcile the conflicting descriptions within the Scriptures themselves. Inevitably, the Holy City appeared as the centre of the world on T–O maps of about 1110 because, according to the 'Word of God', 'This *is* Jerusalem: I have set it in the midst of the nations and countries *that are* round about her.'[7] And there it remained until about 1450, when cartographers were forced to respond to the discoveries of Marco Polo and other explorers.

Meanwhile, the Arabs had became the custodians of Classical wisdom. They had a high regard for Claudius Ptolemy, correcting some of his errors, and during the Dark and Middle Ages of Europe they preserved his books. The precision of astronomical observation achieved by the Arabs during this period was quite remarkable, as were their achievements in mathematics. We may well imagine the culture shock awaiting the invading armies of the Crusaders, coming from the cultural wastelands of northern Europe. We may also imagine that not all of the crusading noblemen looked upon the knowledge of the Infidels with a barbarian distaste. Some will have been inspired to learn from them.

The implications may be considered. Although the Order of the Knights Templar had arisen out of the success of the First Crusade, and their remit was to protect the pilgrim routes, the fact that they took several years to establish the numbers of men and the infrastructure necessary for such an undertaking raises doubts about their real motives. Whatever their motives may have been, they did absorb all they could of the Arabs' acquired and enhanced knowledge of the ancients. The Arabs, in effect, provided them with a link to their severed inheritance. They would ultimately stand accused, along with other crimes, of becoming tainted with the 'heresy' of Muhammadanism, so immersed in the culture of the Arabs had they become. There is no doubt that they became well versed in aspects of mathematics and geometry unknown in contemporary Europe, and secretly preserved their discoveries. A Templar chapel at Montsaunes in the Pyrenees, close to the Spanish border, has wall paintings that testify to this. Gradually the Templars acquired the knowledge denied to them and to the rest of the Western world by centuries of the vested interest of the Church of Rome.

Meanwhile, people continued to make maps. In the Islamic world, a technique of geometric mapping had been devised which dispensed with any naturalistic representation of geographic detail: towns became circles; countries and land-masses became arrangements of geometric components. Figure 13.3 is from a Persian copy of a tenth-century atlas.[8] At the bottom is north-west Africa, and the semicircle above it is southern Spain (the equilateral triangle will not go unnoticed).

The Holy City, Jerusalem, was itself mapped with some success in a realistic manner. After all, there should be little objection to a true plan of a city which owed its appearance mainly to the hand of man. But in most medieval maps Jerusalem also receives the circular treatment; Figure 13.4, from the thirteenth century, is typical. East is at the top, so the David Gate (now called the Jaffa Gate) is at the bottom. The Golden Gate is at the top right, and within the circular, crenellated walls are the Holy Sepulchre, Golgotha – marked by a cross (bottom left), the Temple of Solomon (top right) and just beyond this and to the left is the Dome of the Rock. The Latin Church is shown in the north-west quadrant, close to the central road junction. This example is in the British Library

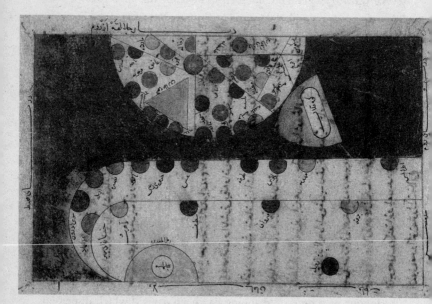

FIGURE 13.3 An Islamic 'geometric map' of the western Mediterranean.

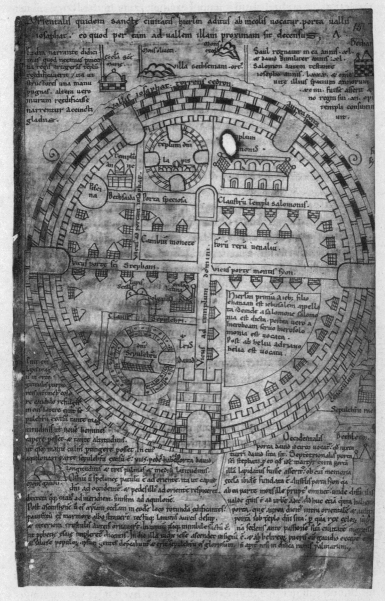

FIGURE 13.4 A typical 'circular map' of Jerusalem, from the thirteenth century; north is to the left.

collection.[9] Another, more splendid example, kept in the Royal Library
in The Hague, is shown in Plate 16. This has been dated to some time
in the thirteenth century,[10] and is immediately more interesting as it has
a depiction at the bottom of knights in combat, popularly called crusaders, but referred to by some as Templar Knights.

When this map was made, there would have been a major Templar
presence in Jerusalem. But there is only one 'Templar' pictured – or at
least only one knight in white vestments bearing the legendary red
cross – and above his head is written 'Saint George' (Latin *Scs. Geor-
Gius*). After the suppression of the Order, any document celebrating
Templar exploits would have become an embarrassment. Most will
have been consigned to the flames, as were many of the knights themselves. But a beautiful and extremely valuable manuscript such as this
may have suffered no more than a little refurbishment, a small amend-
ment here and there to appease the censor. The knight whose horse's
nose is just crossing the border on the right is not a Templar, nor,
clearly, are his companions. He wears a suit of mail, but not the long
garment of the pursuing knights. Templars were obliged to wear a long
white habit – this was an original rule of the Order, instigated several
years before it was ordained that they should emblazon this and their
shields with the famous red 'cross-pattée'. Behind 'St George', the
other knight also rides a white horse with red bridle and has the same
long garment streaming behind, but this is green and his shield is green
with a red border. Templar clerics wore green, but we feel fairly sure
that his shield has been altered so as to make 'St George' unique. Of
course, the real St George also bears the red cross – the red cross of
England, the red cross of the Order of the Garter. But is that red cross
a cross-pattée? We do not believe so. These knights are (or were) both
Templars. There is other evidence of alteration. The Templar on the left
has had his lance removed; all that is left is a faint light-coloured line.
Parts of the drawing that it covered have been carefully reinstated, but
his thumb still grasps a non-existent weapon. Even if he was no longer
allowed to be a Templar, why disarm him? There may have been other

alterations, but none is evident, and it may be safely stated that the alterations we have noted are of great antiquity.

There are other anomalies. The gates to the city are represented here, as in other plans of the time, by arched openings; the Golden Gate (slightly damaged) is shut, as was usual, while the others have their doors thrown back. Here we can identify a simple drafting error: the doors, as expected of a pair closing a single round-arched doorway, each have a quarter-round top, since they meet in the centre, but the archways are shown with two half-round arches – as if there were a centre-post. The Porta Speciosa within the city has both its red doors closed, and the gateway is shown with twin arches. The gateways would be expected to open on to a street centred on the arch. At the David Gate they do, and, remarkably, this street appears to have two traffic lanes, marked by a centre-line. The left-hand lane soon turns left, or north, and heads towards Golgotha and beyond. However, expectations of a 'one-way' system around the narrow streets are short-lived – this lane soon turns left again to terminate at the city wall. The right-hand lane terminates at a dead-end at the city wall, unlike on the previous map, where it terminates at the Porta Speciosa T-junction. Other streets are single lanes, but strangely are not centred on gateways.

This may be seen to be deliberate, for the lines that fall in the centre of the gateway and correspond to the centre-line of the arch – hence the peculiar shape – are actually diameters of the outer circle that encloses the city, and their point of intersection is the centre of the circle. The road width has then been drawn to be on one side of these lines, not equally on either side.

It was time to have a good-sized copy made and mount it on the drawing-board, because the diameters suggest, not only N–S and E–W lines, but also that there is an implied square to be drawn around and tangential to the circle. We set up the picture so as to have the principal roads 'square' to the drawing-board, and drew in the enclosing square, as shown in Figure 13.5. (Note that here we have drawn lines of a thickness equivalent to the thinnest of those in the original drawing.)

Figure 13.5 The 'circular map' of Jerusalem from the collection at the Royal Library in The Hague. A square has been constructed upon it.

We have not yet commented on the many golden discs which litter the background of the painting. They are not villages; these are shown as buildings, as can be seen from the depiction of Bethlehem. The discs appear to be purely decorative.[11]

When the square has been drawn, we begin to suspect the purpose of these gold discs, for the left side is tangential to two of them, as are the right side and the lower side. The upper side is tangential to one, and if extended to the left, to another also (Figure 13.5). The two that this line touches are on either side of the cross on the little church at the top left of the painting. The corner of the square falls on this cross. It is not unreasonable to suspect that we are looking at the prototype for the Saunière Parchments, where 'O's are favoured indicators of lines, as are various round and oval objects in the paintings. But this is far from proven so far.

It is rather much to hope that the triangle is represented here, but it is easy enough to check whether the square is to be rotated by drawing the top line from the cross at 15° to the horizontal. This line is tangential to four discs. Surely this leaves little doubt that we have before us a stunning and controversial document: a thirteenth-century map, possibly a Templar map, of the secret location. It is not even necessary to complete the drawing (which, of course, we shall shortly do) to see where the Site is located. It falls on the calvary, the golden cross-pattée, at Golgotha – the 'Place of the Skull'. Thinking back, Teniers had also made the centre of the tilted square the place of the skull. And Golgotha, in this map and unlike the other, has been shown immediately above the sepulchre – the former burial place of Jesus.

But we have jumped ahead, for there are questions to be asked and answered. And the geometry should be completed. We have a good idea what to expect from the geometry, and this will speed the process, but one must beware of imposing a desired result.

The six steps

1. Lines joining the upper corners of the tilted square to the centre of the
   Golgotha calvary should be the diagonals of the square – they should meet at
   right angles. They do. One touches two gold discs; the other no less than five
   (Figure 13.6). But it is immediately evident, when the drawing is on the board
   and an adjustable set-square is used, that these lines are not at the angles to the
   axes of the drawing that one might expect. These should be 60° and 30°. They
   are, in fact, 61½° and 28½°. Yes – incredibly – they are rotated clockwise
   through 1½°. So the orientation of the picture should have been different to
   the obvious way we had chosen. Is there an indication of what this should have
   been? Of course there is. We have already taken a close look at the features all
   around it. It is 'St George's' lance.

   The knights and their horses and equipment are all very well drawn – by the
   conventions of the period. There is an almost obsessive attention to detail. The
   fleeing horseman wears a mail suit (inadequate protection from the lance thrust
   which has pierced his back; blood flows from the wound), but his legs are protected by chausses of bezante armour, made from small discs riveted on to
   leather, and retained by a series of fastenings behind the leg. The pursuing
   Templar has a mail suit, but plain chausses, suggesting plate armour with plate
   'sollerets' on the feet. This is an innovation more commonly seen in the early
   1300s, so one might deduce a date in the late 1200s for the map and state-of-
   the-art leg protection for the Templar. The horses are carefully drawn; it is clear
   that both pursued and pursuers are mounted on Arab steeds, from their fine
   heads and dished faces. Although this military action is clearly taking place in
   the Holy Land, the map has been painted in Europe (after the fall of Outremer,
   as the Holy Land was known to the Templars), as the foes do not look in the
   least like Saracens. This, and the other evidence of a date later than the late
   1200s, perhaps after 1300, is intriguing. The fall of Acre in 1291 marks the end
   of Crusading in the Holy Lands, and the Templar arrest warrant was then only
   fifteen years off. With Christian pilgrimage no longer feasible, the *raison d'être*
   of the Templars – protection of those pilgrims – had gone, and if they were
   beginning to see the 'writing on the wall', the need for written records of the
   Secret would have become pressing.

   With such care exercised in the drawing of the armour and horses, one
   might expect similar care to be exercised in the drawing of the lance. But it has
   no substance – it is a mere wand. It is a line, at 1½° to the horizontal. The
   other pursuing knight has lost his lance, but one may still clearly see where it

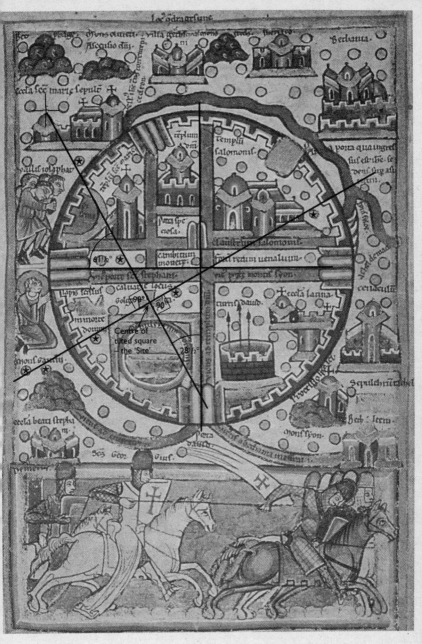

FIGURE 13.6 The Hague map – the diagonals of a square, centred on the cross-pattée, display a 1½° rotation.

was once grasped in his mail-clad hand. This lance was also a line, but one which was horizontal. The two together illustrate the 1½° shift in orientation to be found in the map; so now it is clear why the lance was removed. It would have been better, but not possible because of the pennant and the resulting nonsense of the composition, to remove the other lance. Safer that the manuscript had been destroyed.

2. Further explicit elements of the geometry have been added to Figure 13.7, which summarises the normal relationships. There are rather a lot of lines on this one diagram, but they should now be somewhat familiar. All the lines receive the expected confirmation by being tangential to gold discs, and we even find that, where possible, when lines cross the written notes, the letters reflect the line in the same manner as on the Parchments. (We have highlighted with a bold line the discs and letters that mark the geometry, but have been careful not to adjust any positions.)

3. Letters reflecting the line are most notable where the 75° and 76½° lines cross the word 'ferifuf'; the letters sloping backwards to match the lines (Figure 13.7). Correcting the left side of the original square by 1½° shifts it so as to touch the left sides of gold discs, where it previously touched on the right; it also has letters which correspond, and now runs down the edge of the unidentifiable dark band to the left of the knights.

4. A 72° line passing through the Golgotha calvary is marked, so the pentagonal geometry is represented and the relevance of this line will be endorsed by later revelations.

5. Surely, if the 72° alignment had been from the very earliest times an integral component of the map, it should have appeared elsewhere. Let us look again at the second earliest representation in our possession – La Fontaine de fortune. That we should do so is appropriate in any case, as the means used to confirm the location of the Site – at the centre of the rotated square – may now be thought, in the light of subsequent revelations, to be all the more remarkable: the edges of the monument and trough are meridian and parallel. But, we are looking for an indication of the 72°. A 72° line passing through the centre of the square – the Site – is found to be tangential to the disc of the sun (Figure 13.8) and leads to another polygonal figure which reinforces this correspondence (but we shall not pursue this now).

FIGURE 13.7 The Hague map – other lines, in configurations by now familiar, are added.

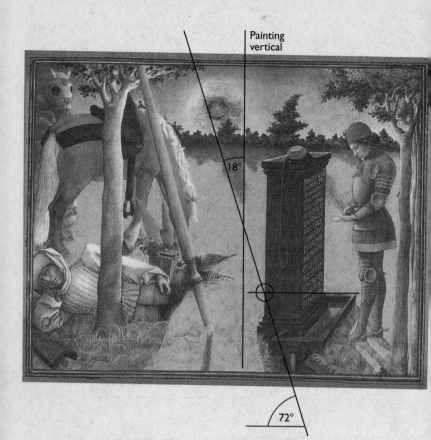

Painting vertical

18°

72°

FIGURE 13.8 *La Fontaine de fortune* – a 72° line from the position indicated for the Site is tangential to the sun's disc.

6. Returning to the Jerusalem map, the centre of the equilateral triangle is identified by a meridian and parallel – the centre-line of the shorter E–W road and the line just above the words 'Porta Speciosa' – this point corresponds, of course, to Peyrolles church. Perhaps the church in the painting to the left of this point is intended to be just that, but this is hardly conclusive. There is no sign that the Château de Serres had been marked.

But at the intersection of the 30° and 28½° lines, which falls on the edge of the second N–S road, there is a tower – shown corner-on, thus providing its own centre-line – and this corresponds precisely to the location of the *donjon* of the Château d'Arques.

The precision of the angular measurements is striking, for when the square is re-aligned to suit the 'lance' orientation, the 28½° becomes 30°, of course, and the 30° becomes 28½°. The latter bearing measured on the map is 29°. We should not perhaps expect an accuracy better than around half a degree, and may surmise that when realistic allowances are made for attainable accuracy these angles were both intended to be 30°. This is an altogether unhoped-for confirmation of our deduced preference for the 30–60 degree family.

Regardless of the gold discs, the most convincing confirmation of the map's validity is the accuracy of the bearings. From the rock pinnacle at the Site to the corner of the square the angle is 61½° on the I.G.N. map, just as shown on the Jerusalem map. This surely must be the true origin of the 1½° 'error', the small rotation required to make the angles fit the convenient 60° family. (Other details of the Jerusalem Templar map are discussed in Appendix K. While intriguing, they have no further effect on our conclusions.)

The Templars and Cardou

The evidence for this map being the prototype for the Parchments, paintings and gravestones is quite clear, and the manner of its conception apparent.

Steeped in the Arab-preserved knowledge of the work of Claudius Ptolemy, and having seen how a location may be precisely recorded using geometry, the Templars combined these to form the most secure document yet devised, as a means of preserving the knowledge of the whereabouts of the 'secret treasure' of Rennes-le-Château. Most significant of all, the Templar map of Jerusalem contained the most direct evidence we had unearthed to date about the Secret's nature.

The clues were many: the symbolism of the body inherent in the message *pommes bleues*; Henri Boudet's curious name for the Site (*Lampos*, or the Lamb); the statue of Christ at Antugnac, gazing at the Site; Dagobert's treasure, the 'he' who 'is there dead . . . at Sion'; and the lines on the Marie de Nègre and Boudet tombstones giving the meridian bisecting the Site, which had in turn led us to the Rose

Cross. All these clues had gradually combined to suggest something which the Templar map of Jerusalem now supported: that the Secret concerned the fate of Jesus Christ, whose body, according to accounts in the New Testament, had ceased to have an earthly existence following the Ascension into heaven from the hills of Jerusalem some twelve hundred years previously.

For us this was the moment of conviction. We felt that the Templar map had removed any trace of uncertainty about our interpretation of the nature of the Secret. Whether or not the Templars had been instrumental in the act of concealment, the map – interacting as it did with the Parchments, paintings and gravestones – indicated to us that the body of Jesus resides not at the right hand of his father in heaven, but in the Languedoc, in the side of Mount Cardou.

What could be more appropriate than to use the plan showing the site of Christ's original sepulchre – the circular (inherently geometric) plan of Jerusalem – to show the site of Christ's *new* sepulchre. The standard representation even shows the sarcophagus (from the Greek, meaning 'flesh consumer') within a circular representation of the sepulchre (from the Latin *sepelio*, meaning 'bury'); a *cavern*. Instant occultation results from the unstated change in orientation from east to north, and the obscure geometric placing of buildings and *calvaires* in France corresponding to features on the Jerusalem map completed the record of what constituted the most hazardous knowledge in Christendom.

The evidence of Templar complicity in the Secret of Rennes was now substantially strengthened. We had a map, with the geometry, and an allusion from various sources to a spiritual treasure of immense consequence. We also knew from our investigations into the origins of medieval mapmaking that the rose and the cross were connected. If the Templars portrayed the cross on their mantle, what evidence existed for their association with the rose?

The Rose and the Cross

The Knights Templar had chosen a simple and striking uniform of a white surcoat emblazoned with a red cross-pattée. With our discovery of the relevance of the meridian of the Site, and the unusual cross on the grave of Boudet's mother and sister at Rennes-les-Bains, we now looked upon the cross-pattée of the Templar Order with new interest. Why had they adopted such an insignia, and why the particular colour?

The island of Cyprus and the city of Paris both provided important clues. On display in the Cluny Museum in Paris is the lid of a tomb belonging to one Raoul Sarrazini, a thirteenth-century knight. The lid is vast and carved in a highly distinctive manner. The skilfully cut bas-relief includes large roses which fill each section of the cross. Sarrazini's gravestone was the first solid evidence we had seen of an early allusion to the rosy cross, as distinct from the later Rosicrucian symbolism, which emerged from the revivalists of the seventeenth century. In the bowels of the museum lay two complete sarcophagi, retrieved from Cyprus and Templar in origin. Despite the dim light we could make out the bas-relief in the sides of the stone. The detail was simple in design, singular and unmistakable. Each tomb was embellished with the symbol of the rose.

The Templar association with the Rose and Cross was now becoming clearer. Their adoption of the 'rosy cross' was displayed on their surcoats, for the 'rose' is visualised as the *red* rose, and a rosy cross is therefore a red cross. If the red cross of the Templars held such significance, what had been the sequence of events? Had certain Templars discovered the body of Jesus in Jerusalem, or had they inherited the location which contained the secret treasure on their return to France? While it is impossible to ascertain their motives for adopting a red cross as their symbol, it is certain that they had used the geometry in the Jerusalem map and that the abnormal placing of a road on this map emphasised the Rose Line passing through the calvary cross. It was appropriate that at this point in our deliberations we should come across some information that – perhaps appearing superficial – would so neatly tie together the loose strands.

At Rosslyn in Scotland is the seat of the Sinclair family. They trace their ancestry back to the St Clairs whose arrival from France is associated with the migration of Templars away from countries where the destruction and persecution of the Order was taken seriously. The Masonic connections to be identified in the extraordinary chapel at Rosslyn undoubtedly relate to the probable Templar connections with the 'Scottish Rite' of Freemasonry.[12] But it is the etymology of the name Rosslyn that so amazed us. Conventionally, this stems from the Celtic words meaning 'promontory' and 'waterfall', but the Sinclairs identify in it the red stream – the Blood of Christ – 'which is personified in Saint Roseline, a little-known saint, much favoured by the Grail family'.[13] Until the nineteenth century, the name had been written as Roselin or Rosline.

As we had stood at Peyrolles and verified the angles between the sighting-tower at the Château de Serres and the heights of the Château de Blanchefort, we had pondered on meridians and the Boudet tomb at Rennes-les-Bains. Our path had now led us indirectly to the Knights Templar, to the true meaning of the rosy cross and its real significance in the story of Rennes-le-Château. Our discoveries linked the cross with roses to the Site at Cardou in a way which was undeniable, drawing two thousand years of history into the frame, and answering many of the questions raised during the course of our investigation.

It was now evident that crosses, either carved on tombstones or free-standing in the countryside, were being used to help preserve the location of the Site. We therefore turned to the I.G.N. map to see whether there were any local *calvaires* that might be relevant. We found one, marked above Montazels – the village where Saunière was born.

As we rounded the bend of the road above Montazels, we fully expected to find another *calvaire* of the nineteenth century, similar to *La Croix* at Alet-les-Bains. Not for the first time, we were surprised. Rising no higher than a metre from a low concrete base stood a cross, apparently many centuries old and an almost perfect match with the cross carved into the lintel of the western doorway of the Château de Serres. It was of the pattée form associated with the Knights Templar (Figure 13.9). From its elevated position it enjoyed a commanding view. Blanchefort and, beyond, Cardou were to our left; Rennes-le-Château, closer, lay to our right. Closer inspection confirmed our first impression: the Montazels cross was much older than the late nineteenth century, but it had been placed on a more recent base. Despite our enquiries locally, no one could be specific about when it had been moved to its current position.

Had Saunière placed this ancient Templar cross above his home village, a place with the Site in view, to mirror its companion above the

FIGURE 13.9 The cross above Montazels is an ancient cross-pattée. In the distance Mount Cardou rises on the left, and Rennes-le-Château is situated on the high ground on the right.

lintel at Serres? If the Templar cross on the lintel was genuine, and dated from the fourteenth century or earlier, then the involvement of the Templar Order at Serres would receive solid confirmation. Had the château been built on the site of an earlier Templar building, and the lintel re-employed by the new master?

We had one last task before leaving the Montazels cross: to take a bearing on the heights of Blanchefort. This cross had been placed at around 103° from the château, and roughly the same from the Site. Allowing for a magnetic deviation of about 2° since the 1890s, it appears that an angle of 75° was intended, which when added to the adjusted bearing would give 180°. The number 75 had appeared again: the number which the coded document found in Saunière's personal papers emphasised with the word 'danger'. Why was it so dangerous to priests in particular, and what did the priests of Rennes have in common?

We had recently discovered information relating to the use of the *calvaire* by the Rosicrucians in a book published in 1879.[14] They had used these wayside crosses as an important means of preserving secret knowledge. The book depicted a *calvaire* showing the symbol of the rose at its centre, and left us in no doubt that we had stumbled upon a little-known piece of information. The *calvaire* had been specifically used as a means of celebrating the knowledge of the Rose Cross.

In ancient times, red roses had been placed on the graves of those who had led exemplary lives, and this fact took us back to Gélis's unstable headstone, adorned with a rose. This, the flower of the Rosicrucians, we now knew to hold a double meaning. A rose placed on a gravestone symbolised the arrival of premature death – which in the case of Gélis was undoubtedly true.

There are two stained-glass windows at the entrance to the Villa Bethania, showing the Sacred Heart in two versions. The first is wholly conventional, surrounded by thorns and topped by a cross. The second is very different: pierced by a dagger, and encircled with roses. We were now certain that the factor common to the three nineteenth-century priests was Rosicrucianism, and that the Secret was heretical and concerned the fate of Christ. The Site, on the Rose Line, held the Secret of Rennes. Another clue to link the rose and cross with the ultimate 'treasure' was not long in coming.

14
ET IN ARCADIA
EGO

When Abbé Bérenger Saunière was assigned the parish of Antugnac pending the appointment of a new priest, he kept a record of his pastoral activities, and noted the strain he felt through having to walk so far between Rennes-le-Château and Antugnac in order to conduct services and tend flocks in two parishes. These notebooks and papers have been collected and published under the title *Mon Enseignment à Antugnac*. They give a vivid picture of the life of a priest at the turn of the century.

At the back of the book are some photographs of the church, the nearby chapel at Croux and the *calvaire* on the slope of the hill northwest of the village. The *calvaire*, which is marked on the map by the usual '+' symbol, is at the fork of two roads, and is shown in the photographs to be not just a cross, but to have a statue of a standing Christ adjacent, the two separated by an evergreen bush. Studying the photographs, it looked as though the figure of Christ were facing the general direction of the Site. The possibility that the statue and the cross may together indicate the Site – maybe even provide a means of sighting as with the back and front sights of a rifle – meant that a visit would be required. We found the *calvaire* standing inside the fork of the road, but it was the statue, separated from the *calvaire* by tall shrubs and undergrowth, that caught our immediate attention.

With shoulders turned and head gently lowered stood a life-size figure of Christ (Figure 14.1). His arms were outstretched, but his supplicant stance ended in the jagged hollows of broken wrists, for his hands had broken off – or had *been* broken off – and were nowhere to be seen. The terracotta of his body was streaked from years of rain, and the plinth elevated the figure high above its surroundings.

Standing behind the statue, we looked across his shoulder to see what he saw. Lying before his and our gaze stretched a vista that included the village of Antugnac immediately below and to the right, and a panoramic view of mountains in the distance, including Mount Cardou. Where does Christ direct his gaze? Not towards the church, but to the village and to the right of the summit of Cardou. We were astonished to see that he looked towards the Site, only just visible beyond the nearer range. This we confirmed by means of a compass, which when aligned with the rectangular base of the statue gave a bearing of N 105° E, or S 75° E. This was checked on the spot against the map, and found to be within a degree or so of the bearing to the Site. Rather than establish the orientation of the figure to the precise bearing, it would appear that 75° was considered close enough and ensured recognition of the esoteric concept. Fifteen degrees to the line of latitude, 75° to a meridian: the geometry of the tilted square had been used again, in yet another location.

Our attention now turned to the cross (Figure 14.2). The orientation of this was very different to that of the statue, and the compass showed it to be approximately magnetic east–west. The inscription also proved to be revealing. At the top is the conventional IN RI, except that the 'N' had been carved in reverse, thus: 'Ͷ'. Its angle was checked, but found to be inconclusive. The reversal of the capital 'N' is not uncommon in semi-literate writing. In particular, the mistake can occur when an effort has been made to draw it carefully, perhaps before engraving it or painting it large on a sign. However, some authorities

FIGURE 14.1 The *calvaire* at Antugnac – a life-size figure of Jesus.
Roses grow nearby.

see in this reversal (generally speaking, that is, not referring to this case) the signposting of an occult intention. Be that as it may, the cross had more in store.

Below IN RI is carved the year – 1838, and below this the letters 'B D'. The numbers of the year are strangely formed. Each '8' is composed of two separate circles with a distinct space between them, crying

FIGURE 14.2 The *calvaire* at Antugnac – the cross.

out (to us, that is) for a line to be drawn between them. The '3' is of the 'two-straight-lines-and-a-semicircle' variety, but very distorted. The two straight lines are conveying an angle. Application of the protractor showed the angle to be 75°, to an accuracy which, considering the medium and the age of the monument, should satisfy the most hardened sceptic. Together, the statue and the cross leave no doubt about the direction in which Christ is intended to look. But to specify the location of the Site another bearing would be required – from another fixed point far enough away to ensure an angle of intersection of the two sight-lines which is not too acute to pinpoint the spot. We had quite recently observed an indicator of just such a bearing – the Boudet monument at Rennes-les-Bains, though this is not necessarily the original partner of the Antugnac cross.

It is most likely, if not certain, that the cross and statue were oriented with the aid of a magnetic compass. Magnetic north deviates from true north by an amount which is constantly changing, the amount and rate of change depending on the geographical location. When the cross was erected this deviation would have been greater than at present. If one wished to know when a magnetic bearing of 75° would have been correct for the Site, it is possible to calculate this, but not with any precision as the rate of change also varies. It seems likely, then, that the intention was to establish the *calvaire* with a suggestion of the direction of the Site, but with a clear and specific reference to the secret geometry.

The date on the Antugnac *calvaire* is intriguing: 1838 is earlier than most nineteenth-century dates in the story. Could it have been erected then? Possibly. But . . . if one were to subtract 1 from 8 and then 3 from 8, one would have a 7 and a 5: 75, perhaps? Remember the dates on the cross by the railway at *La Croix*: 1876 minus 1801 equals 75.

We could now take stock. We had returned to France confident of the location of the Site, but with some details to check and more photographs to be taken. The Antugnac *calvaire* and the Boudet monument at Rennes-les-Bains had provided independent confirmation, and we now felt quite sure we had found a statue of Christ *looking towards his own place of burial*. If this were not actually the truth, there could be no doubt that those responsible for all of the corroborative evidence for the location firmly believed it to be so. And could there be any doubt that his body, or the knowledge of its location, is the Holy Grail – in Old French the *Sangraal*, or *Sangreal*, the *Sang Réal* perhaps, the Royal

Blood[1] that flowed from the body of Jesus, from the grapes that symbolise his body – the *pommes bleues*!

If Jesus Christ, whom the Church had declared resurrected, lay under Cardou, and Poussin's shepherd was seen to point to the meridian of the Site in *Les Bergers d'Arcadie*, then the meaning of ET IN ARCADIA EGO [SUM] – which had so long eluded us – also became clear. We had been left with the anagram

ARCAM DEI TANGO
I touch the tomb of God

which still left four letters over: E, I, S and U. These can form the word ESUI, 'of his', but this would be grammatically superfluous. If one checks off the letters of ET IN ARCADIA EGO SUM in order, however, to verify their presence in the anagram, one finds that the four letters appear in this order: I, E, S and U. Which leaves only one possibility: IESU – that is, *JESUS*. And so one arrives at:

I touch the tomb of God, Jesus

15
ONE ERRANT
ACADEMIC

With a substantial body of evidence linking the preservation of a great Secret and independent confirmation of the Secret's location, it may seem that there is little more to be known. But it is not in our nature to be easily satisfied, or complacent, and there remained some small details which we wished to clarify. In particular, we would have liked to identify the origins of the de Nègre gravestones, and of the Parchment, and also to finally settle the date of that document. We were also aware that throughout our investigations named conspirators had been somewhat absent – perhaps an understandable reticence, bearing in mind the heretical nature of the 'treasure' as we now understood it, but none the less frustrating. Our awareness of the organisations which had played their part, and the roles of certain nineteenth-century Catholic priests, was gradually gaining clarity. Individuals, particularly from secular walks of life, had largely eluded us. In the course of our investigation of the mystery various items of potential interest were identified, but put to one side for later consideration. To one of these we now turned in the hope that it might cast some light on shadier areas.

The 'Matri Deum' cippus

Among the illustrations in Eugene Stublein's *Pierres gravées du Languedoc* ('Engraved Stones of the Languedoc') are to be found depictions of Roman altar-stones of the pre-Christian era. Also illustrated are the two gravestones of Marie de Nègre and other miscellaneous engraved stones. The authenticity of this document has been much disputed, and its true authorship never satisfactorily resolved. Superficially, the stones illustrated may or may not be genuine; may or not exist or have existed at the time of original publication. Even the extant copies of the work purport to be a re-issue under the auspices of one Abbé Joseph Courtauly, and *his* involvement is also doubted. What possible value could this document have?

We may suspect the same motivation behind this work as for the Priory Documents; indeed, it may be included justifiably within that designation, and as such may be 'good in parts'. That it represents a juxtaposition of items intended to establish a concept, or pedigree, or authority is clear: we may thus expect that there are reliable parts, included to add substance to the document and bolster the impostors.

The Marie de Nègre gravestones make strange bedfellows for the Roman items. The drawings of the Roman stones are copies of originals made for the academic work *Inscriptions antiques des Pyrénées* commenced by the notable barrister and antiquarian Julien Sacaze, completed by others after his death and published in 1892. So we may go to this work for definitive examples of these drawings. We were pleasantly surprised to find a scarcely used copy in the Taylor Institute – a wing of the Ashmolean Museum in Oxford.

The most striking and workmanlike stone in the Stublein set is the one we shall refer to as the Matri Deum stone, from the first line of its inscription. Sacaze describes it as 'Cippus [short column] in white marble . . . found in the ancient cathedral church of Alet [les Bains] and taken to the Toulouse Museum' (Figure 15.1). The drawing, made by

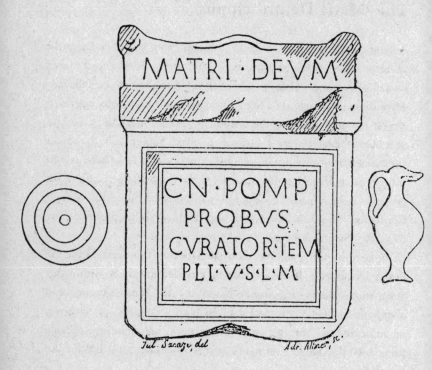

FIGURE 15.1 The Matri Deum stone, as drawn
by Julien Sacaze.

Sacaze – his name is to be seen at bottom left – shows the front
elevation, and to the left and right the bas-reliefs found on its flanks.
The original purpose of this stone, as with many similar ones illustrated
in the Sacaze book, was to serve as an altar; more specifically, a place
which saw the ritual pouring of wine to a named deity – in this case the
'mother of the gods', Cybele. The objects depicted were used during
such ceremonies. The jug contains the wine. The 'patera' of concentric
circles was often a purely decorative architectural feature, but in this
context it appears in its original role as the dish into which the wine

was poured during the ceremony. The many different examples to be seen in Sacaze's book show this and other paterae to have become stylised; others are shown realistically, often with handles. The arrangement of circles is thus variable.

The inscription follows a standard format which includes the name of the deity, the name of the patron, and an appropriate phrase of thanks and dedication, this often related to some perceived act of kindness by the god. Many examples are crudely executed, perhaps because the stone-carver did not mark out the letters before carving. Even the most basic planning of the inscription would have achieved better results than are generally seen. When such sloppiness is evident it is usually because the work was rustic and produced for a low price. The Matri Deum stone therefore presents an anomaly.

Others have remarked on the letter 'M' which crosses the moulded border; Sacaze deduces from this that the work is provincial and crude – a theory negated by other examples in his book which are cruder. It is also apparent that the 'M' did not have to cross the border. That it is equivalent to the 'M' of the Dalle de Coume Sourde – indicating a meridian – is possible, and suggests that the geometry may well be present. This is soon found to be true.

There could, of course, be many reasons why this is not possible – how could an indication of a meridian be present on an altar of the pagan period, well before the concept was established, let alone achievable? Objections were soon overridden by the emergence of the familiar geometry. This was fortunate, for if the geometry had not so readily revealed itself, we would never have visited the museum where the altar-stone itself resides. But this visit allowed the troubling question of the meridian on the pagan altar to be answered in no uncertain manner.

A full analysis of the drawing provided by Sacaze proves to be highly rewarding, answering some questions that had lingered at the back of our minds, and reinforced conclusions we had arrived at from other evidence. The importance of this is so great, excluding any doubts about intention, originator or precision, that the complete analysis has been provided as Appendix L. These are the reasons why we were so confident:

1. Sacaze had *falsified* the drawing of the real altar in order to accommodate the geometric features that are now so familiar. This extraordinary fact was to become evident from the moment we first set eyes on the photographs of the altar held at the Musée Saint-Raymond in Toulouse. The differences were clearly not due to careless copying, because the particular alterations made in the drawing are the very features that provide the geometry. The altar itself is not available for inspection as it is in store, ruling out the risk of a casual observer noticing the discrepancies with the Sacaze drawing.

2. The various elements are rigorously substantiated by their interrelationship. The drawing is so meticulously executed, with *fine* lines, that this cannot be due to chance.

3. The drawing incorporates features which, recognisable to the initiate, provide a happy 'masonic handshake' of acknowledgement. Indeed, the initiate would only need a small nudge in the direction of the drawing; small wonder that Sacaze has mentioned, in his text, the wayward 'M'.

Solving the geometric puzzle, in effect following the mental processes of Sacaze, proved to be an extraordinary experience. In Appendix L the analysis of the drawing is followed by a comparison with the altar itself. Here we show some of the features that ensure enlightenment, and demonstrate the discrepancies between stone and drawing as we proceed. The drawing and the stone are illustrated side by side in Figure 15.2 to aid comparison. All the alterations serve a purpose.

An indication that the geometry is present is the angle of the right-hand leg of the 'M' of MATRI. It is at 75° + 1½° to the horizontal (the latter being determined by the border moulding). The tops of the letters of MATRI DEVM define the top of the 'square', and the left side of the 'square' is a vertical line from the top-right apex of the 'M'. This vertical is found to coincide with the inner vertical line of the

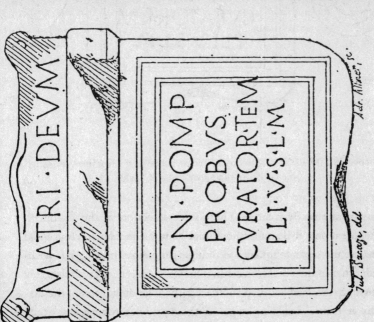

FIGURE 15.2 The Matri Deum stone – (a) Sacaze's drawing compared with (b) a photograph.

border (Figure 15.3). From this auspicious start, the solution proceeds with relative ease.

We have seen that a difficulty experienced by the compiler of these occult maps – of which this drawing is very clearly another example – is the incorporation of the angles through which the components of the

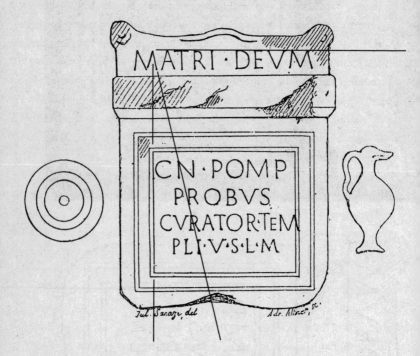

FIGURE 15.3 The Matri Deum stone – construction of the first lines, showing the corner of the square and a 75° angle.

diagram are to be rotated. The double-sidedness of the 'Saunière' Parchment provided an ingenious solution to the problem, as one could visualise the separate square and triangle geometries moving relative to each other in the correct manner. The 1½° 'corrections' were less ably shown. Sacaze had adopted another method: he drew parts of the diagram at 'before' and 'after' stages. Without prior knowledge, this would be very hard to follow. He has provided some assistance by drawing all the uprights in the letters of MATRI DEVM at 1½° to the vertical: they all lean to the left.

The layout of the inscription on the altar-stone is quite competent – better than in Sacaze's drawing – and reveals a serious effort to achieve a harmonious, workmanlike effect. There appears to have been a genuine accident at the end of the third line which resulted in the small size of the 'E' and the unfortunate excursion of the 'M' into the border moulding. Unlike the 'M' in the drawing – which *could* have been squeezed into the frame, but kicks its leg out an an angle – the 'M' on the stone is more discrete and keeps that leg parallel to the moulding. (It is interesting to consider the relationship between the stone-carver and his client in this circumstance. Was there a discount agreed for sloppy workmanship?)

If the assumption about the 'M' crossing the border is correct, this designates one of the inner pair of lines as the 'old' meridian (the one indicated on Parchment 1 and the Coume Sourde diagram). Of these two lines, it will probably be the right-hand one, as this is the extent of the leg of the 'M' (Figure 15.4). This line extended passes through a 'chip' just below a cornice which does not exist on the stone. One may suspect that the leg of the 'M' is indicating the point A at which the 45° right-hand side of the triangle is going to cut this meridian. (Having already noted the incorporation of the 1½°, this must be considered for each line that is drawn.) If a line is drawn through the point A at 45° minus 1½° to the horizontal, and the top side of the triangle drawn in at 15° + 1½° to the horizontal – this passing through the corner of the cornice at B, the triangle is completed. The subsequent unravelling of the diagram is summarised in Figures 15.5 and 15.6.

The line assumed to be the 'old' meridian, extended upwards, passes through the apex of the second triangle, as demonstrated elsewhere (in *La Fontaine de fortune*, for instance). The moulding lines apparently indicate old *and new* meridians – an important feature to ensure correct solution (Figure 15.7). This tedious complication of the meridians –

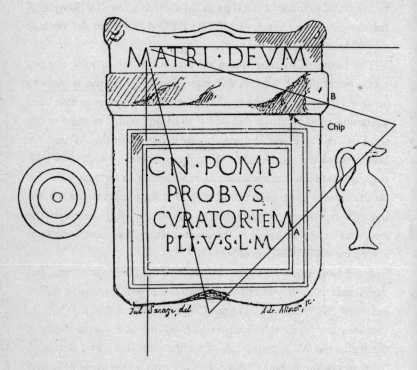

FIGURE 15.4 The Matri Deum stone – the equilateral triangle appears.

not of our own making – has caused others to fail in their quest for the correct result.[1] So let us note that the *new* meridian is the present Paris (Zero) Meridian; the *old* meridian is shown on the paintings and Parchment and runs as stated above. Neither of these is the Rose Line; this being an imaginary north–south line running through, or very near, the rock pinnacle of the Site. Before we saw the photographs of the altar, it was this feature that clearly cast doubt on the age of the stone: it could not possibly be Roman. We had had to assume that we were dealing with a fake stone, the likelihood of an academic faking the *drawing* being remote.

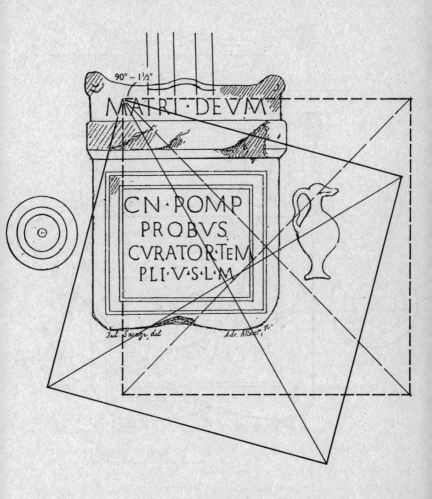

90° – 1½°

MATRI · DEVM

CN · POMP
PROBVS
CVRATOR·Tem
PLI · V · S · L · M

FIGURE 15.5 The Matri Deum stone – the left side of the tilted square is
confirmed by the 'M' of MATRI.

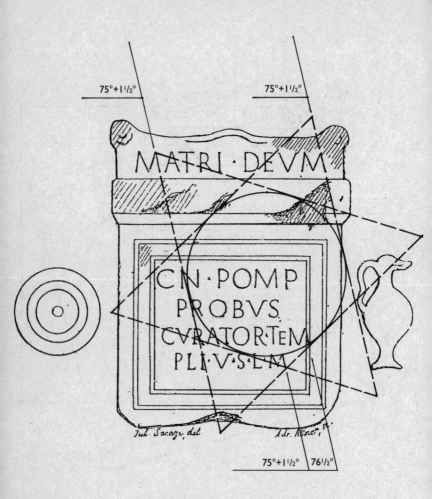

75°+1 1/2°   75°+1 1/2°

MATRI · DEVM

CN · POMP
PROBVS
CVRATOR TEM
PLI · V · S · L M

Jul. Sarage del   Adr. Riscri sc.

75°+1 1/2°   76 1/2°

FIGURE 15.6 The Matri Deum stone – the right side of the second triangle is confirmed by the 'M' of DEVM.

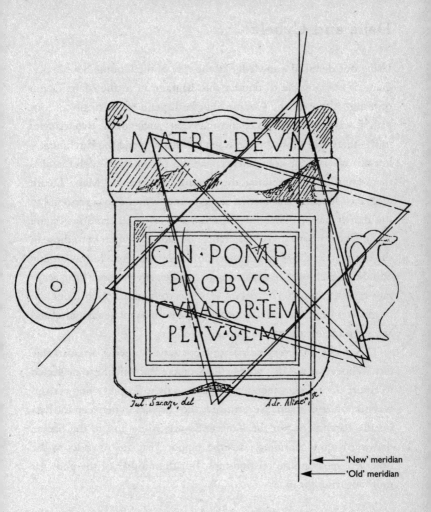

FIGURE 15.7 The Matri Deum stone – the hexagram is rotated by 1½°, and the patera confirms the new position of the second triangle's left side. The 'old' and 'new' meridians correspond to lines of the moulding.

Dalle and Cybele

Using our deduced knowledge of the role of the Coume Sourde diagram, it was possible to transfer this diagram on to the Matri Deum drawing. Although the Coume Sourde diagram set us firmly on our path, it was not possible to confirm the exact angles of the two triangles in it – there was a disparity between the diagram and the Parchment – but this was of little consequence, and did not interfere with the ultimate solution. Combining the Coume Sourde and Matri Deum diagrams elucidates this matter, as the former is found to correspond to the drawn 'frame', or border, around the lower inscription (Figure 15.8). The proportions of this 'frame' are radically different to those of the original on the stone, the need for correspondence to the Coume Sourde diagram presumably having overridden any pretence of an accurate representation. The details leave scarcely any doubt about the original concept and its relationship to the permanent geographical and architectural features we had already deduced.

This is not only very satisfactory, but actually reveals a remarkable fact. Whoever it was that redrew the Saunière Parchment had neglected to ensure the accuracy required to maintain these features – and perhaps was not aware of them. Nevertheless, the correlation between the data on the Parchment, on the Coume Sourde stone and in the Sacaze drawing is quite stunning, as is the support that this provides to the observed geographical relationships. But the mother of the gods has more surprises for us.

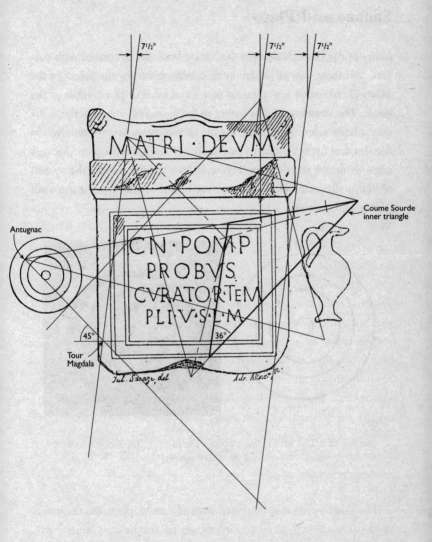

FIGURE 15.8 The Matri Deum stone – the geometry of the Dalle de Coume Sourde and some other familiar lines are confirmed. The patera plays a role in locating the Tour Magdala.

Sacaze and Plato

Many of the Roman altars in the Sacaze book are decorated with paterae, and these vary in design quite considerably, but the patera of the Matri Deum stone is composed of a set of circles like no other in the book. The drawing of this patera may be singled out as perhaps the most blatant falsification of all, for the carved patera on the stone was in the simplest form possible: a succession of equispaced circles. Sacaze's carefully drawn set of circles (Figure 15.9) is an analogue for the squares of Plato's theorem. This was recognised quite intuitively, but the truth of it is easily shown.

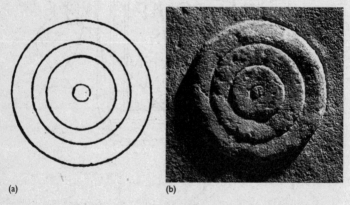

(a)   (b)

FIGURE 15.9 The Matri Deum stone – the patera in (a) Sacaze's drawing and (b) a photograph.

The inner square may be drawn with its sides tangential to the innermost of the three large circles. Its corners fall on the next larger circle. If this is repeated for the larger square, the same is seen to be true. The equilateral triangle may also be drawn – and, of course, its corners fall on the outer circle (Figure 15.10). The patera thus provides an independent symbol of recognition for the sacerdotal, and in addition points to the geometry to be found in the main body of the drawing.

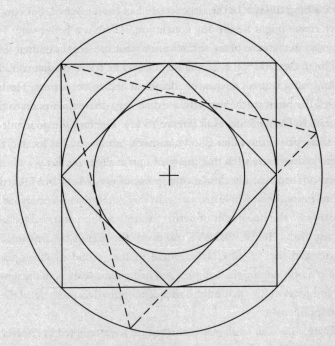

FIGURE 15.10 The Matri Deum stone – Plato's squares derived from the circles of the patera as drawn by Sacaze.

We were now aware that Sacaze had utilised all manner of nuances in his incorporation of the geometry in the drawing of the stone, and another possibility now occurred to us. The derivation of a sequence of squares, each one twice the area of that preceding – in accordance with Plato's theorem, is a process that may be repeated *ad infinitum*. Perhaps Sacaze has arranged for the patera squares to be in this proportion to the large square of the main diagram. In other words, if one were to start with the larger patera square and work upwards in size, in accordance with the theorem, would one arrive at a square the same size as that in the main diagram? If so, this would provide yet another endorsement for the derivation of the whole geometry.

This theory could be checked by drawing all the squares until one

approaching the size of the large square had been reached, but cumu-
lative errors might negate any conclusion. There is a better way. The
2:1 ratio of the areas of the squares means that the lengths of their sides
will be in the ratio √2:1. So the theory may be tested mathematically;
in Appendix L it is conclusively demonstrated to be correct. Having
proved the point mathematically, we then drew these squares on to the
diagram to illustrate the result (Figure 15.11). The final square is indeed
the same size as the other (shown dashed), but Sacaze has located the
centre of his patera such that this final square aligns perfectly with the
other, one side passing through the point of the 'M' of MATRI, the
pivotal point of the whole geometry. In this extraordinary endeavour to
incorporate the maximum of detail, Sacaze has also contrived to have
the leg of the 'R' of PROBVS run down the side of the first smaller
square, and the 'C' of CN tangential to the second smaller square.
One can only admire the complex and meticulous work – all the drawing and redrawing – that must have been required to produce all these
correspondences.

There is another small matter that Sacaze has attempted to resolve; at
least, this is what we deduce from a curious feature. Following our policy of 'honesty' (with ourselves as much as with anyone else), we have
drawn the illustrations for this book as accurately as possible with the
finest lines appropriate to the original illustration and compatible with
clear reproduction. By taking another look at a diagram similar to
Figure 15.5, but this time on a larger scale, an odd feature becomes
apparent (Figure 15.12). The square's diagonal from top left to bottom
right passes close by and almost parallel to a sloping line of the last 'M'.
It would have been nice if these lines had coincided, but they did not.
Even odder is the fact that, but for an adjustment of ½° the diagonal
would pass exactly along that line – it is at the correct orientation for
this to occur. This is suspicious.

Assuming for the moment that this is intended to be the correct
alignment, what happens when the final 1½° anticlockwise rotation of
the square is made? This is shown in Figure 15.12. The centre of the

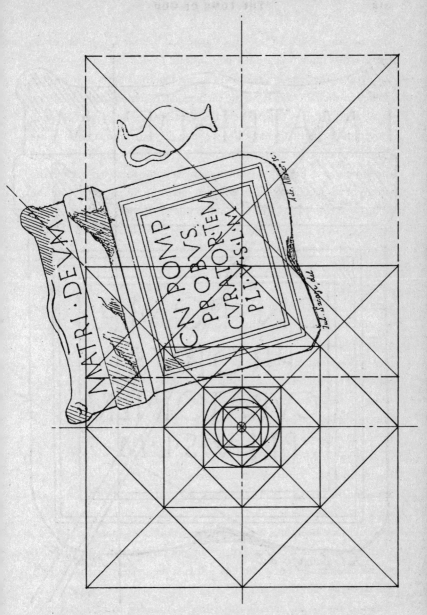

Text visible within the figure:
MATRI·DEVM
CN·POMP
PROBVS
CVRATOREM
PLEV·SLM

FIGURE 15.11 The Matri Deum stone – expanding the squares associated with the patera in accordance with Plato's theorem leads to some interesting correspondences.

MATRI · DEVM

CN · POMP
PROBVS
CVRATOR · eM
PLI · V · S · L · M

Jul. Sacaze, del

Adr. Alis..

1½°

½°

FIGURE 15.12 The Matri Deum stone – Sacaze has corrected the Parchment geometry so that the centre of the square now falls on a meridian passing through the pinnacle, the Rose Line, and this is clearly marked.

square now falls on a vertical line passing through the end of the leg of the 'M', and this vertical line also runs up the upright of the second 'P' of POMP and through the point of the 'V' of DEVM above. There can be no doubting this intention, as it explains why the 'P' has been moved to the left, away from the moulded border – compared with the stone itself.

Can it be that Sacaze has indicated a correction to the basic Parchment geometry? The small discrepancy between the centre of the square and the pinnacle of rock has already been noted, so one may check this on the full-size map. Sure enough, a further ½° rotation added to the 1½° brings the centre of the square exactly on to a meridional line passing through the pinnacle.

Slightly disappointed that we had not found the altar to be a fake, and thus have the geometry preserved in stone, we had nevertheless come away from the museum with photographic evidence of the nineteenth-century activities of the Rosicrucians, and this time we could pin a name on a conspirator. We had come a long way from our first tentative identification of the Parchment as a map.

Meridians resolved

Just like the 1½° rotation, another element that has dogged our steps is the Meridian. Or should that be meridian, with a small 'm'? We had used some information that proved erroneous, but had achieved the correct answer. Certainly there was an element of luck in that the Parchment diagram was drawn on the I.G.N. map in the correct place, but this was due more to our prevailing attitude at the time than to the dubious information. The scale of the Parchment made it impossible to determine with any real accuracy where the 'revised' Meridian was supposed to run, relative to the Parchment text, other than it was a small distance to the right, or east, of the one indicated. It was the co-incidence that this brought it very close to, or even on to, the centre of that side of the triangle that made it worth trying – and, of course, that point is marked by a cross. We did not tell ourselves that this was the correct, inevitable deduction; it simply had to do for the time being. The manner in which it was confirmed by the geographical features has already been discussed at length. And, of course, other independent confirmation has since been forthcoming. But we should try to deduce the truth behind the strange misinformation provided by Henry Lincoln.

That he introduces the paper by Lucie Lagarde[2] as evidence of the Meridian shift shows either that he had wished to verify this for himself, or that his attention had been drawn to this paper for another reason, and by others. In either event, we may only conclude that he was told about the shifting Meridian, for there is no probability that he would have considered it of his own volition; why would he? (Indeed, why would anybody?) The extreme illogicality of a country retaining a national Meridian in the face of an international movement to adopt another, and then to move the origin of that national Meridian a small distance away from the national observatory, should have alerted us to the problem before. As we have already said in our own defence, the very public nature of the route of the Paris Meridian renders statements on this – in print – beyond suspicion. That an author (Lincoln) should have made the (apochryphal) shift of the Meridian the basis for a conspiracy theory further ensured the acceptance of this erroneous 'fact'. Remember also that he was not associating this shift with the Parchment, merely joining dots on the map. The only scenario that makes sense to us is that he was provided with information which fell short of being explicit, was misinterpreted and got squeezed to become the Invisible Megalithic Temple posited in Lincoln's *The Holy Place*. An extraordinary outcome is that the purpose of the informant was most likely achieved! We must explain.

Nobody who has read this far will have failed to wonder at the inscrutable purpose behind the disclosure of the Parchment and associated data. If it is such a great secret, why even hint of its existence? One has to invoke the 'nuclear stand-off' concept. The possession of weapons of guaranteed mutual annihilation ensures peace (albeit a rather nervous, insecure peace) only when the potential combatants are aware of each other's capability. Similarly, there is little point in being party to a great, power-inducing secret without other sacerdotal groups or individuals being aware of this. In spite of Lincoln's mishandling of the information, his books and television documentaries have ensured that the point has been made. More importantly, his evidence (the Antugnac 'fan' of bearings, the basic geometric concept of the Parchment, and the existence of an earlier meridian) has been enshrined in books.

Has the desired result been achieved? We do not know, nor may we ever. Nor may we ever know or even deduce what the aim may have been. (Perhaps the best one can say is that the motive may well be political, with aims that begin at a parochial level – France – and with aspirations of worldwide influence. The 'evidence' for this may be read in a multitude of published works whose contents we have largely passed over in the present book, as being too far removed from the core topic.[3])

But we have drifted away from the discussion of the problematical Meridian. One may suspect that the reference in the Lagarde paper upon which Lincoln's attention was supposed to have been concentrated was not the Panthéon triangulation origin, but the reference to the strange eulogy on the Paris Meridian appearing on a map of 1753 by R.J. Julien.[4] This illogical statement may be making a plea for the Paris Meridian to be regarded as 'le premier Méridien' because of its relevance to the location of the Site. Regardless of this, when the references to the Rose Line are taken seriously, there are no fewer than three positions for a meridian in the vicinity of the Site to be considered. Why? The Paris Meridian, running as it always has through the Observatoire, happens to run through the centre of the right side of the first triangle before its 1½° rotation. This is a remarkable enough occurrence, but, yes, it could be a coincidence. What we maintain puts it beyond the realm of coincidence is that the relationship of triangle to

Meridian is also marked in another way. Look again at the triangle after the 1½° rotation, when the right side is at 45° to the Meridian (Figure 15.13). The point of intersection of the triangle's centre-line with the Meridian is also passed through by another line: a side of the 30–60–90 degree triangle forming part of the 'château geometry' – the line joining Blanchefort and the Arques *donjon*.

Could this have been deliberately contrived? Is there any evidence that the line of the Meridian and the location of the Observatoire were carefully established, or simply placed at a point of convenience or availability? The latter question can be answered positively:[5]

> On the 21st. of June, 1667, the day of the summer solstice, the members of the Académie assembled at Fauborg St Jacques, and with great pomp and circumstance *made observations for the purpose of 'locating'* the new observatory and establishing a meridian line through its center, a line which was to become the official meridian of Paris. The intention was that this should become the standard meridian of longitude for all nations. (our italics)

The italics are ours, but the inverted commas around the word 'locating' are Lloyd Brown's, for he was quoting the original report.

There can actually be no means of, or purpose in, 'locating' an observatory except with the intention of placing it on a parallel or meridian (or both), predetermined by some other location. 'Location' or 'place' is always relative: it has no meaning without reference to some other place, even if this is simply 'next to the river' or 'under the tree' or some other such designation our forebears may have considered important in selecting a site for a dwelling (or a temple). But this would not have required observations of a scientific nature as implied by the activities of the Académie Française.

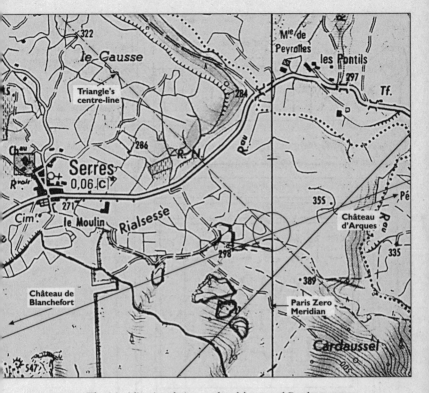

FIGURE 15.13 The Meridian in relation to the château and Parchment geometry.

The Rose Meridian

A further look at the drawing by Julien Sacaze is now required, because it has more to say about the meridian problem than we had first appreciated. It had already been noted that the 'old' and 'new' Meridians (as we had then chosen to call them) are indicated in his drawing as the vertical lines of the border emphasised by the positions of the legs of two 'M's. To these we have added a third, also indicated by an 'M'. This is marked in Figure 15.14, along with the others.

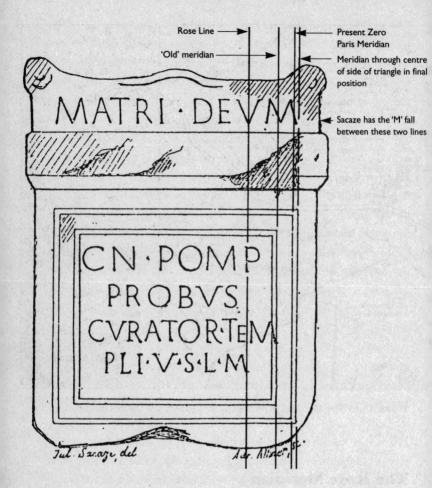

FIGURE 15.14 The Matri Deum stone – Sacaze has clarified the relationships between the three meridians.

As we have seen, this third meridian is not merely suggested by the last 'M', but also confirms itself by passing along the ends of the horizontal lines of the 'E' of TEM, along the upright of the second 'P' of POMP, and through the point of the 'V' of DEVM. This is clearly the Rose Line since it passes through the Site as marked by the pinnacle.

This may be seen to be true from its relationship to the centre of the square – all the more so, since Sacaze showed the additional ½° correction to bring this on to the Rose Line. Sacaze has used the same feature of the 'M' three times to illustrate the three relevant meridional lines. Not only does this preclude coincidence – if by this time one were still apprehensive – but it also confirms the antiquity of the first and second meridians. The centre one, which passes through the apex of the second triangle, is seen to do the same in René d'Anjou's *La Fontaine de fortune* and in Parchment 1. (Did Sacaze make an error in drawing the 'M' of DEVM? If the central point of the 'M' had been very slightly to the left, the 'old' meridian would have passed through the point, as with the letter 'V' to its left.) We must reiterate that the Coume Sourde diagram and its attendant Latin inscription also identify this line, and we have shown that the diagram's derivation from the geographical arrangement endorses this on the large scale of the 1 : 25,000 map. That it also does this in the Sacaze drawing is beyond chance.

So, what could have been the origin of the central of the three meridians? The question might be regarded as academic at this stage, but for the fact of its appearance in Parchment 1. Why the official Paris Meridian should not have been indicated on the Parchment is a mystery, considering this meridian had been in existence since the early 1700s. It is known that local meridians were established for the purposes of parochial mapping, so the line in question may well have been chosen for its esoteric connection, but for this to be retained as late as the twentieth-century copying of the two sides of the Parchment (to become Parchments 1 and 2) implies a further document – one that preserves the relationship between this local meridian and the national Meridian. Such a document is the Sacaze drawing of the Matri Deum altar – and there may well have been other, earlier examples.

It would not be unreasonable to ask why the Rose Line, as the meridian passing through the Site, was not chosen to be the Zero Meridian, but remained an occult concept. This question has effectively answered itself. For it to have been anything other than occult would have been hazardous. If the Zero Meridian were to run through the remarkable rock formation on the flank of Cardou, it would surely not go unremarked, and if another small clue were solved the Secret could well have been out. Such a clue was to be found in the de Nègre gravestones (or just one of them), which addressed the identification of the Site in a manner far too overt for safety. Clearly this was Bérenger Saunière's opinion, for he destroyed them!

Such a tidy resolution of the exhausting affair of the meridians came as a welcome relief. On reflection, it was hardly surprising that over several hundred years the well-intentioned 'polishing' of the 'map', and the proliferation of its forms, should have caused some confusion. Then again, some of the confusion may well have been intentional. Finally, with all the data we had accumulated, we were in a position to take an overview of the historical timespan.

16

THE SECRET AND
ITS GUARDIANS

The unravelling of the Rennes mystery can be compared to the work of an archaeologist excavating a site. The archaeologist has an already complicated job made harder by the activities of later occupants of a site having disturbed deeper and therefore earlier strata, old and new becoming mixed together over time. We have examined all the evidence that has come our way, but unlike the shards from a dig, most of this evidence was on the surface. This made the chronology unreliable and the origin of much of the material highly dubious. Our first tentative trowel-probes had been into disturbed strata, the detritus of previous excavations. But at least we were aware of this, and could catalogue the finds with a certain amount of caution. Continuing to dig brought us not only welcome, undisturbed material, but also some remarkable new evidence.

The methods used to conceal or contribute to the preservation of the Secret have been numerous and varied. They have called upon talents in the fields of literature, painting, geometry, architecture, engraving, sculpture, surveying, antiquarianism, cryptography, and cartography. It is an extraordinary enterprise, which has not only spanned the centuries but has, in the hands of some very different personalities, shown some remarkably different facets. The methods of concealment have evolved down the centuries, but have always been rooted in the same geometric basis.

The earliest manifestation of the Secret that we have uncovered is the Hague map of Jerusalem 'officially' dated to somewhere in the thirteenth century. There may well be earlier or other contemporary examples of such maps contrived to indicate the secret location; we have examined several published examples of T–O maps of Jerusalem, but without exception they all lack even a trace of the geometry or the appropriate juxtaposition of features which would suggest a knowledge of the Secret. This, in itself, enhances the singularity of the Hague map. If there had been a consensus in the thirteenth century about where the holy places within Jerusalem should be placed on a T–O map of that city, the proliferation of maps with this layout would have caused a variant to come under suspicion. But as they all show variations, sometimes large ones, the peculiarities of the Hague map would not have attracted comment.

It is probable that other copies were produced at the time. Surviving examples may have remained in the possession of families whose sacerdotal tradition has ensured the concealment of these and other occult works. Royal libraries have a habit of becoming accessible to the citizens at times of revolution or social change; at such times private collections stand a much greater chance of remaining private. But the need for strict security, which restricts access to such documents, has an enemy: destruction – either by the elements or by deliberate vandalism. The burning of books is a time-honoured expression of barbarianism. Accidents also happen. So how did the caretakers of this most secret of secrets safeguard against such catastrophes?

Assuming the Templars to have been the concealers, and thus the first mappers of the Secret, one copy each for the founding members would have sufficed; their ability to pass on the knowledge verbally would have been an adequate fall-back in the event of an enforced destruction of documents. Their rapid rise to great influence at the highest levels – giving them the power to make or break kings – must

have given them the confidence that no further proliferation or diver-
sification of recorded data would be necessary well into the foreseeable
future. During this period the Secret was religiously guarded (the cliché
is appropriate in this case), but an aroma of sacred, secret knowledge
must have wafted through the courts, to be detected in due course by
the court poets and emerge as the Grail romances.

That fateful day in 1307 when an attempt was made to arrest every
Templar was the beginning of the end of the Order. Five years later it
was formally suppressed. Armed resistance was not an option, because
of the Templars' vow not to take up arms against fellow-Christians, but
the move against them had not taken them completely by surprise.
Some knights escaped with documents and valuables. Those who
remained in France presumably hoped that all was not lost for the
Order, and that the historic support of the Papacy would alleviate their
current difficulties. It may be safely assumed that copies of secret maps
were spirited away with other incriminating documents and came to
rest in countries sympathetic to the Order and perhaps even under the
rule of adepts. It is possible to picture the evolution of a hierarchy of
sacerdotalism in which various degrees of knowledge would be permitted. Such a development over the years would have conferred
various benefits on the parties concerned.

The aspirant desires access to an exclusive club, one that by repute is
the sole guardian of a Great Mystery. The appeal is timeless. Modern
Freemasonry exudes an aura of exclusivity, of sacerdotalism, that many
find irresistible. The promise of enlightenment and the desire to
'belong' are powerful traps which close with a snap. Once inside, the
novice is bound by threats of dire retaliation should the secrets be
revealed. This itself lends a *frisson* of excitement and reinforces the
recruit's belief in the importance of the meagre knowledge that he
will be permitted to acquire. Of course, there are today remarkably few
disembowellings of wayward Freemasons. There is no need: the majority of Freemasons know little or nothing of great secrets. Not even at
the highest levels attainable by rising through the ranks is sacerdotalism

to be achieved. And so would it always have been. Only by the decision of the invisible, uppermost echelon would a rank-and-file member of special ability be selected for enlightenment – a burden of intolerable weight for some.

It is well documented that during the twelfth and thirteenth centuries the Templar ranks swelled considerably. Such mass recruitment may well have been a deliberate policy, aimed at protecting 'the knowledge' and providing an occult substructure available in times of need. It would only take one sacerdotal head of state, whether king or duke, to ensure protection for members at the highest levels. A secret of this magnitude would have guaranteed a loyalty that transcended geographical divisions and barriers of nationality.

By 1306 or even earlier, the potential for disaster would have become evident to the Templars and their supporters. The time had come to put Plan B into operation. On the day of the mass arrests, no documents or treasures were to be found. The Templars of knightly rank who remained to face their accusers would stand up to the worst excesses of the Inquisition, confident in their own ability to endure the pain of torture to keep the Secret safe. The Templar ranks, of sergeant and lower, had only the vaguest concepts of the Order's secrets, as their confused and conflicting testimonies demonstrate. The worship of a head is a common element in these testimonies, but the descriptions vary widely: it was blue; it had two faces; it was terrifying.

With the escaping Templar knights went their documents, maps among them; or perhaps these items had preceded them into exile and were already in safe hands in territories such as Scotland, Lorraine and the Low Countries: states outside the control of the French king and therefore havens from the worst excesses of persecution. In some cases, the response to the papal directive was so desultory that years were to pass before the matter was addressed, and by this time the remaining Templars had melted away into other orders such as the Teutonic Knights, or simply gone to ground.

The bitter quest

The next example of tangible preservation of the Secret shows a development that would predominate until the nineteenth century. It is not possible to say whether *La Fontaine de fortune* was the first new concept after the Jerusalem map, but it clearly marks the divorce of the geometric from the geographic.

The Jerusalem map, for all its obscurity, *is* a map, and the risk of the geometry being associated with the geography must have been problematic. In future the geometry would be preserved independently and some other means found to ensure recognition of the geographical location. Between the demise of the Templar Order and the next appearance of the secret geometry, two hundred years were to pass. We have found no clear example from this period, and it seems likely that in a time of religious suppression in the area of Haut Razès the Secret was forced even further underground. It may have been transmitted only verbally, and only at the highest level of initiation.

There is, however, an indication that René's tale of Cuer was intended to do more than include one reference to the secret geometry. *La Fontaine de fortune* is just one painting from a series illustrating *Le Cuer d'amours espris* – 'The Heart Smitten With Love'. The book had spaces in the text left blank for the insertion of the illustrations; forty-one were intended, of which only sixteen were completed in the definitive Vienna version. What conclusions can be drawn about René's intentions in producing this book, on which he lavished so much personal care?

Although clearly modelled on earlier romances, René's has peculiarities that make it unusual. The story is of Cuer's quest for the lady Doulce Mercy – 'sweet grace'. It is a sad tale of unfulfilled love; the bitter waters run through the story, first seen rising as the bubbling spring at the fountain and then flowing through the narrative as the river that symbolises the quest. Another recurring element is Cuer's lance, which makes other overtly geometric contributions in addition to that at the

Fountain of Fortune. Had all the paintings been completed it is probable that an informative geometric sequence would be discernible. But there is another compelling element to be noted. As Cuer and his squire Désir follow the trail, they pass through many different topographies, and it has been said that these are illustrated so explicitly that one may identify the regions of France through which they pass.[1] It is a truism to state that the tale is 'allegorical', but this is as much as most commentators attempt and it is hardly informative. Never do they elaborate on this statement in other than the broadest philosophical terms, despite the fact that the elements and symbolism of the tale offer a wide range of interpretations.

All are agreed that the clear precedent for such an allegorical quest is Le Roman de la rose, which is in two parts.[2] The second, written by Jean de Meung in approximately 1277, is incontestably hermetic, conveying hidden meanings to the enlightened. Jean was eventually to be denounced as a troubadour with leanings to Catharism (see Appendix A).

But perhaps this quest for the unattainable has its strongest parallel in the quest of the Grail and in Lancelot's ultimate failure to succeed due to his imperfection. In the Arsenal collection of the Bibliothèque Nationale is a manuscript book of Lancelot's quest. One illustration catches the eye (Figure 16.1), for the scene mirrors characteristics of the landscape surrounding the Site. Lancelot is despondent, reclining against a black rock (Roc Nègre?); across a river (the Sals?) lies a mountain (Cardou?). Nearby is a wayside cross, and above it the Grail – unattainable by Lancelot – is held aloft by two angels. The displacement of the Grail to one side of the cross suggests an angle; it is 1½°. The other features of the tree supporting the leaning lance, and the grazing horse, are clearly derived from – or are the origin of – the features found in La Fontaine de fortune (Plate 6). The latter is the case, for the provenance of this work may be traced back to the Duc de Berry, who purchased it from a Parisian bookseller in 1406; of its earlier history there is no record. Which is unfortunate, for when the various places

FIGURE 16.1 Lancelot despondent, from the *Roman de Lancelot* (c. 1400), Bibliothèque Nationale, Paris.

visited by Cuer seen in the other paintings in René's book are reconsidered, they are seen to relate strongly to places on the Grail quest of King Arthur's knights. Perhaps the quest is the same in both cases.

In view of our discovery of the Secret and how it has been preserved, we can now see the allegory of Cuer's quest as that of the Grail, or the Secret, and the form of René's book as an illustration of the route to be taken in order to pinpoint the precise location. It is a pity it was never completed.

'The Poor, the Sick and the Unlucky'

There is another book that has a remarkable bearing on the preservation of the Secret. This 'book of Hours' (a costly, profusely illustrated prayer-book) was auctioned by Sotheby's in London in 1974 and now resides in a private collection in Belgium. Fortunately a set of good photographs had been taken before the sale, and may be inspected at the Courtauld Institute, London.

One picture is without precedent, for it covers a two-page spread, when miniatures in books of Hours normally occupy just part of one page. Before examining this picture, we shall look at an earlier work on the same theme. This is a sketch – possibly for a wall painting – from the sixteenth century, and shows 'the poor, the sick and the unlucky helping Christ to carry the cross' (Figure 16.2).[3] A curiosity is that, although Christ is carrying his cross, he has already been crucified – as proved by the holes in his feet. Notice also that there is a figure in a gown on the right helping to carry the cross who does not appear to be one of the named helpers.

The source of this theme has been established, beyond reasonable doubt, as René d'Anjou.[4] Otto Pächt declares this 'votive image' to be highly unusual; René was running counter to the Church's theological and artistic norms, which visualise Christ alone with his cross. The assistance provided by the poor, the sick and the unlucky implies the gnostic belief in resurrection for all. Pächt has called this theme René's 'spiritual property' and traces his fascination to the early years (1420–34) he spent in Alsace-Lorraine.[5]

We may now turn to the painting (Figure 16.3) in the book of

FIGURE 16.2 *The Poor, the Sick and the Unlucky Helping Christ to Carry the Cross* (sixteenth century), version from the Bibliothèque Nationale, Paris.

Hours 'of exceptional quality' auctioned by Sotheby's. The book dates from around 1500, some twenty years after René's death, but it may well have been executed by an artist formerly in his 'studio',[6] for the painting reflects a theme originally described by him in 1435. In addition, René commissioned a painting on this theme for the Celestine Order's church at Avignon in later life.[7]

There are differences to be noted between this and the previous version. The feet are now discreetly covered. One of the helpers has a staff which inconveniently drags on the ground. And the figure on the right is no longer walking, but holds on to the cross while kneeling. Why has all this changed? The cross is now at the correct angle to be the top side of the tilted square. The staff is at 72° to the horizontal, the angle made by the second shepherd's staff in *Les Bergers d'Arcadie II*, and

FIGURE 16.3 *The Poor, the Sick and the Unlucky Helping Christ to Carry the Cross* (sixteenth century), version from a private collection in Belgium.

also found in *La Fontaine de fortune* and in the Templar map of Jerusalem. So the occult geometry is represented. But the other changes are more extraordinary. Christ's gown has its right edge at an angle reminiscent of the right edge of the rock at Cardou – the one on the left or north of the Site. The figure on the right – now so strangely crouching – has taken on the form of the right or south rock from which rises the pinnacle. By now, of course, we do not expect these correspondences to be coincidences. And if we take a tracing of the photograph of the Site taken from the old road opposite the Roc Nègre, adjust the scale to suit the illustration, and superimpose it on the painting, the fit is extraordinary (Figure 16.4).

So, King René's master-plan was not so much to divorce the

FIGURE 16.4 The extraordinary fit of (a) the profile of the Site with (b) the disposition of the figures in the Sotheby's copy of *The Poor, the Sick and the Unlucky*.

geometric from the geographic, but rather to impose on them a trial separation. It seems that the separation was considered a success, for subsequent appearances of the geometry in art up to the nineteenth century have no overt geographic references that we have been able to prove. Another development that may be tentatively credited to René is the elaboration of the geometry from the Jerusalem map arrangement – of lines at 30° intervals radiating from a corner of a square – to incorporate the esoteric relationships of the squares and equilateral triangles. The language of occult communication was evolving.

But perhaps René's most enduring contribution to the preservation of the Secret was the idea of art as the medium of greatest safety. This was sound, for works of art, if not invulnerable, have a better record of surviving destruction than books. In future, adepts would employ professional artists to paint pictures with an occult intention. These artists were trusted novices of varying grades, sometimes even uninitiated, who worked to layouts provided. Occasionally the artist would rise to full cognizance and experience a profound change in his life. The possession of occult paintings or other works of art became an end in itself – the symbol of personal enlightenment and an ever-present 'hermetic handshake'. Perhaps the divorce of geometry from geography was so complete that many of those cognizant of the geometry knew of its esoteric status but not its purpose.

It might appear inevitable that it should fall to René to take up the challenge of preserving the knowledge. We may assume that if he were not already an adept of the great Secret, he was to become so after his marriage to Isabelle de Lorraine, eldest daughter and heiress of Charles II, le Hardi, on whose death René was to become Duc de Lorraine. For it was to Lorraine – a sovereign state not subservient to France – that so many Templars had fled. It is unlikely that in the intervening hundred years the dukes of Lorraine, having so generously granted a safe haven, would have failed to gain the respect of the Templars. It follows that an increasing level of initiation would have taken place between host and guest.

The world of King René

In spite of the wealth of knowledge which has survived about René –
a good, likeable, but unlucky man, with an impressive list of kingdoms,
dukedoms and other titles – there is a noticeable absence of detail
about his education. Particularly lacking is information on the influences and events that led to him becoming such a prominent figure of
the 'proto-Renaissance'. For instance, when only three years old, he
had been taken to the monastery at Marcoussis – the Celestine house
that was later to yield the painting of the coronation of Pope Celestine
V – and he was to maintain a close association with the monastic order
of the Celestines throughout his life. To what extent they were responsible for his education we can only guess.

There is no doubt that René, in Italy for six years in a vain attempt
to hold his Kingdom of Naples against Alfonso of Aragon, maintained
a friendship with the Sforzas of Milan, and through them Cosimo de'
Medici. It was Cosimo who had masterminded the rebirth of learning
in Western Europe. He founded the Library of San Marco in 1444,
instigated the translation of Pythagorean, Platonic, Gnostic and
Hermetic literature, and inaugurated the Platonic Academy. His illustrious grandson, Lorenzo the Magnificent, was to continue this support
for the arts and learning at an unprecedented level, a strategy which
would effectively break the Church's stranglehold on learning.

René d'Anjou was a contemporary, albeit an older one, of Leonardo
da Vinci, and it is not inconceivable that they were acquainted. They
certainly moved in similar circles. One of Leonardo's patrons was
Ludovico Sforza, a close friend of René and an original member of
René's ill-fated 'Order of the Crescent' – ill-fated in that the Church
eventually ordered its dissolution. There has been much speculation
about the nature of Leonardo's religious beliefs: he was a heretic of an
unspecified leaning according to his biographer, Vasari, and an early
Rosicrucian according to others.[8] These are murky waters, but our discoveries have allowed a little light to filter through. Leonardo's interest

in aspects of the secret geometry appears less coincidental when one considers the company he kept. As far as documentary evidence of his esoteric activities is concerned, Leonardo appears to have kept a very tidy house – or perhaps someone tidied for him? He certainly managed to keep one step ahead of the Inquisition.

René, on the other hand, has left us a wealth of truly puzzling evidence of his esoteric interests, as we have seen. Other commentators have been obliged to hurry past his symbolism. Even his motto, *En Dieu en soit*, inscribed on a billowing sail hung from thorns, is described as 'obscure'.[9] This is surely an understatement, since no one has any idea what he meant by it. The main stem of the thorn on which the sail hangs is cleanly cut into three pieces, for reasons unknown. The point is that René's works simply exude occultism. The device he adopted as his personal emblem has caused much speculation, but with little progress, as to its origins and symbolism. This is the Cross of Lorraine, the double-armed cross that became so familiar as the emblem of the Free French forces during the Second World War. Why this was adopted by Charles de Gaulle as an appropriate symbol is not known. Why René adopted it is not known. Why should a cross have two bars? We believe we now know the answer to these questions.

The Cross of Lorraine is not the cross of the crucifixion, it is a cross-staff. This is *exactly* what it looks like. It is a surveying instrument, an early device for measuring angles, used for example to ascertain altitudes and take bearings. We believe that this cross is symbolic of surveying, and thus of the concealment of the Secret and the preservation of the knowledge of its location by means of triangulation and the establishment of the meridian and parallel of the Site.[10]

Death and Arcadia

King René stood at a pivotal point in time between the Middle Ages and the Renaissance. His yearning for the age of chivalry was counterbalanced by his desire for learning. So, on the one hand he commissioned the magnificently illustrated *Livre des tournois*, a treatise on the conduct of tournaments; on the other he wrote the pastoral poem *Regnault et Jeanneton*, which transparently describes the love of René for his second wife, Jeanne de Laval. This poem is of great interest since the rural idiom he chose is that of Virgil, and the setting, in spirit if not actually stated, is that of Arcadia. This more than anything shows René to have been a man of the Renaissance ahead of his time. The charming representation of René and Jeanne as shepherd and shepherdess may not have been the direct inspiration for Nicolas Poussin, but it certainly encourages the idea of a theme adopted by an hermetic association.

On the subject of human mortality, however, René shows a side of his personality which was firmly entrenched in the Middle Ages. Although the *memento mori*, the association of objects such as skulls with the inevitability of death, was to remain a powerful symbol well into the eighteenth century and arguably beyond, the extreme representations of the results of death and decomposition were first and foremost a medieval preoccupation. And René was more obsessive than most in this regard.

A painting in a monastery belonging to the Celestines at Avignon, now destroyed, attributed by tradition to the founder of this particular house, King René himself, represented the body of a dead woman, standing, enveloped in a shroud, with her 'head dressed and worms gnawing her bowels'. The first lines of the inscription at the foot of the picture are these:[11]

> Once I was beautiful above all women
> But by death I became like this,
> My flesh was very beautiful, fresh and soft,
> Now it is altogether turned to ashes.

So the medieval remnant of René's rapidly expanding world still demanded the realistic depiction of the horrors of death. He was to have himself depicted as the King-in-Death in his other book of Hours, the *London Hours of René of Anjou*, and again in 1450 by his artist Coppin Delft in a fresco above the tomb René had designed for himself in the Church of St Maurice at Angers.[12]

It is the 'wistfulness of remembrance and the thought of frailty in itself'[13] that one finds in later references to mortality; lurid details give way to the simple *memento mori* of the skull and the phrase *Et in Arcadia ego*. But it is with René d'Anjou that we first find the esoteric preoccupation with death and Arcadia.

Nicolas Poussin

When Poussin was commissioned (for it must be assumed that he did not embark on such a venture without instruction, or at least tacit approval) to paint the first of his pictures incorporating the secret geometry, there would have been a clear set of guidelines. Not only would the pattern of the geometry determine the layout, but also the mode would reflect the esoteric wisdom of the secret society. And since this had evolved as part of the rebirth of the Classical pagan culture, it would mean a leaning towards a Classical idiom. A Christian theme would be inadvisable on two counts. Any subject overtly related to Christ or Christianity would be hazardous in combination with the Secret, smacking as it would of heresy. So the philosophies of the Stoics, neo-Platonists, Platonists and Pythagoreans, and also that of Hermeticism, all with their misty origins in much older beliefs and traditions, would require a language in art that reflected the language of the philosopher. A vocabulary of motifs would need to be evolved. In the works of an intellectual painter like Poussin one finds allusions that can make his paintings impenetrable to the layman, and a minefield for art commentators. Arcadia with its nymphs and shepherds would be a suitable theme, as it provided a vehicle for the portrayal of the human condition in a setting far removed from normal existence. So it is that simple country folk – shepherds, tenders of vines – are made, notably in the *Eclogues*, or Pastoral Poems, of Virgil, to discuss indirectly matters of philosophical import: 'Landscape is no longer mere decoration in Vergil [*sic*] but an integral background for tragic thought, where the fate which is so insistent a theme in the *Aeneid* is discerned beneath the conventional traits of a shepherd's existence.'[14]

And, of course, it is in Poussin's vision of Arcadia that one meets the elements combined: the *memento mori* of the skull, the nymph and the shepherds, the elegiac inscription on the tomb. In *Les Bergers d'Arcadie II*, the move away from overt, vulgar references to death is complete: the skull no longer appears; the audience has become more sophisticated.

Glimpses of the personalities behind the scenes of the hermetic coterie come and go in a flash when the sources of this iconography are sought. Other glimpses – into the parallelism of the imagery – are more enduring. The pastoral poem by Virgil, *The Golden Age Returns*, was regarded as a precognition, a prediction even, of the Jewish Messiah:[15]

> The Church, as it gained strength in Rome, was quick to claim Virgil as one of nature's Christians before the time of Christ. When the Emperor Constantine in the fourth century established Christianity as the state religion, he identified the Child of Virgil's Prophecy with Christ.

As we show later, there are other parallels between the Classical and the Christian to be noted in the *oeuvre* of Nicolas Poussin.

Giovanni Francesco Barbieri (1591–1666), known as Il Guercino, the first artist to employ the phrase '*Et in Arcadia ego*', was self-taught and so drew from many sources, including Annibale Carracci, whose *St Francis in Meditation* has the saint before a skull and crucifix. There is also an inscription:

Io imago de[lla] morte

mezza da[l] Paesaggio

ottantcinque

F[E]CIT

This has been translated as 'I, image of death, in the midst of the landscape,' which clearly corresponds in some degree to the Guercino
phrase. But more than this, the concept of *Paesaggio* may be seen as a
transposition of the Biblical garden, or Paradise. Judith Bernstock of
Cornell University made the point well:[16]

> it may refer to the wilderness, not only of saintly retreats, but also
> of refuge prepared for the true Church . . . which . . . through
> spiritual and moral subjugation and cultivation . . . [could]
> become a garden or Eden of the Lord

A closer comparison of the Carracci and Guercino phrases reveals them
to be identical in all but the substitution of 'Arcadia' for 'Paesaggio'.
The 'image of death' is the 'I' of both phrases, but in the Guercino the
obvious has not been stated; the skull (Plate 3) is more than adequate to
clarify who 'I' is. So 'Paesaggio' and 'Arcadia' are, perhaps, inter-
changeable. The implications of this become momentous when seen in
the context of Paesaggio being a refuge for the true Church which
'through spiritual and moral subjugation' could become an Eden of the
Lord. This is undoubtedly an example of the Christian/pagan parallels
that were later to become an essential part of the iconography of
Poussin. Would it not also be reasonable to see in this 'Eden of the
Lord' an implication of the quest for Gnosis?

Guercino's painting *Et in Arcadia ego* is first recorded in an inventory
of Cardinal Antonio Barberini's collection, dated 1644. While there is
no documentary evidence to suggest a commission or the date it was
painted, Barberini may have bought it himself from Guercino when
he was in Bologna in 1629 and 1630. It was in the 1630s that he

commissioned important works by Guercino which were sent back to Rome. Another possibility is that Antonio's uncle, Pope Urban VIII, bought it soon after his accession in 1623. The Barberinis acquired some of Guercino's greatest works during Urban's papacy. In any event, it was in 'Barberini hands' when Poussin saw it before painting his *Les Bergers d'Arcadie I* around 1630.[17]

There is not necessarily any occult significance in the symbolism of the Guercino. The goldfinch on the tree is a symbol of the passion and death of Christ, and hence of immortality; the tree itself is an allusion to the cross, the eternal tree of life on the hill of Golgotha; the skull is a reminder of Golgotha, the place of the skull; even the bee is a symbol of the honey that is Christ and, significantly, never sleeps. The mouse, like Time, gnaws at the skull, exposing even Death's vulnerability – to the resurrection of the spirit. Observing the scene are two shepherds (one of whom has been seen as a representation of Christ). All the elements are there for Poussin to adopt as he sees fit; but in that adoption a transformation as resonant as it is invisible will occur.

In view of our discovery of occult geometry in paintings by Poussin, it did not surprise us to learn that even in his own lifetime there were those who came to doubt his religious convictions. 'It has been suggested that Poussin was influenced by Jesuit ideas, that he was a Jansenist, that he was connected with the Compagnie du St Sacrament, that he was touched by Protestant doctrines, or that he was a *libertin* . . . the idea that Poussin was not in sympathy with the Catholicism current in the Rome of his day' was how Anthony Blunt summed up the possible directions Poussin's unconventional beliefs may have taken.[18]

The revelation of the geometric nature of some (it is not possible yet to say 'all') of Poussin's paintings may well curtail any further discussion of his religious leanings; all those influences listed by Blunt may be applicable, or none of them. The most apposite tag yet applied to his philosophy is Stoicism. The Stoics had roots in ancient Greece, and believed that virtue and happiness could be attained only by submission to destiny and the natural law. A Stoic revival had begun in France in

1584. Yes, he was certainly a Stoic, but also a Pythagorean, a neo-Platonist, a Gnostic. These appellations are not mutually exclusive. What is lacking is a blanket term that embraces all of these and perhaps more: could this be 'Rosicrucian'?

Poussin and the ancient world

Gnosticism has been described as 'Platonism run wild', also as an 'acute Hellenizing of Christianity',[19] and it is this latter comment that is the key to Poussin's preference for Hellenic, or Graeco-Roman, allegories of Christian themes. When Poussin paints Bacchus (also known to the Greeks and Romans as Dionysus) he means us to see Christ. The perceived parallels that make this allegory pertinent are not obscure. The paramount role of wine – and intoxication – in Bacchic festivals has a rather different role in the blood/wine transubstantiation symbolism of Christianity; the bunch of grapes may also be prominent in any painting involving Bacchus, and thus constitute a symbol for the living Christ, or indeed the occult symbol for the body of Christ that we have encountered elsewhere. And Bacchus was the son of a god: the greatest of the gods, Zeus, the master of the sky. To complete the parallel, Bacchus's mother, Semele, was a mortal woman.

Such Hellenic, pagan parallels were not considered shocking to the Church of Poussin's time, and it would be wrong to infer any great occult significance in them. But as an acceptable vehicle for the portrayal of Christian themes, it provided an entirely appropriate (and recognisable to the initiate) genre into which hermetic themes could be imperceptibly introduced.

When Poussin was not working in Arcadian, Bacchic or generally Hellenic mode, he confirmed his intellectual independence by selecting his own iconography. In the *Sacraments* he dressed Jesus and the Apostles throughout in the pallium (a special cloak worn by early Christians), a depiction without parallel in Poussin's time. Such a reference to the period predating the struggle for a universal catholic church – leading to the departure of the Eastern Churches, the dominance of Rome, and the triumph of the Pauline creed – may now be thought of as harking back to the purity of the original message of Jesus, and the period of peaceful coexistence of the new faith with the Classical tradition. Poussin's references to religious affairs in his letters are scant. According to Blunt, 'all display a surprising tone of flippancy'.[20] On hearing of the death of Pope Urban VIII, Poussin wrote 'God grant that we shall be better governed in the future than in the past.'[21] With such insights into the Poussin genre, and by implication into the manner of fraternity he served, it is fair to say that his theme became that of Gnosticism for initiates. And these initiates were both secular and ecclesiastical.[22]

We have seen that there is a shift in emphasis, or feeling, between Poussin's two Arcadian paintings. There is also a remarkable change to be seen between his two self-portraits, but in this case the difference is due not to a change in the artist's perception, but to the necessity of accurately portraying his personality and preoccupations. Poussin's 'jealous and difficult'[23] friend, Paul Fréart de Chantelou, commissioned the portrait. He had not wanted a self-portrait; it was Poussin who suggested this in a letter of April 1647, claiming that nobody in Rome could paint a good likeness. He commenced work with little enthusiasm for the task, and was dissatisfied with the result. The second attempt was started and finished in less than a year. 'He sent the first to Pointel [another client] and commended the second to Chantelou [with this illuminating message] "I assert that this portrait shall be a sign to you of my avowed subservience, in so far as I should not have undertaken anything like this for any other living person".'[24] In the first self-portrait the sitter has a somewhat whimsical expression, clearly lacking the intensity of emotion so essential in a definitive portrayal of a man and his spirit. The second self-portrait is a powerful, undoubtedly accurate likeness, and an intense and revealing exposure of his devoted but troubled soul. But the changed expression is not the only difference between the two portraits: one might wonder whether there were other considerations behind the new approach.

The radically different approach to the composition is the more extraordinary in view of the carefully considered composition and symbolism of Self-portrait I (shown as a reversed engraving in Figure 16.5) as painstakingly analysed by Oskar Bätschmann. The strangeness of Self-portrait II, with its backdrop of framed canvasses overlapping and forming a rectilinear pattern, is a radical departure not only from Self-portrait I, but also from any precedent (Plate 17). That the frames behind Poussin form only right angles with each other and with the frame of the portrait itself, and that the ring he wears is square with a pyramidal diamond, are enough to arouse suspicions of a Masonic connection; the fragment of painting visible at the left reinforces this impression. The single eye in the woman's diadem is the eye above the pyramid on the U.S. dollar-bill – a well-known example of Masonic symbolism (Figure 16.6).

According to Bätschmann, the pyramid-cut diamond ('in emblems as in reality it was a prerogative of the nobility') preserved its importance as an indication of permanence, honesty and indestructibility. These are the virtues of Stoicism, which in Blunt's view could have been Poussin's motivating philosophy.

Searching for enlightening commentary on the work of Poussin is a frustrating business. One would expect to find a plausible analysis of the two self-portraits that not only casts light on the composition and iconography of the first, but also speculates on the change between the first and the second. But this lack of analysis applies to most of Poussin's works. Bätschmann may be credited with an attempt to fill the vacuum, but even he, along with most commentators, fails to address the elements in Poussin's *oeuvre* that most demand explanation. One is reluctant to include Anthony Blunt in this blanket condemnation, for he did not shrink from confronting the problems and, in spite of errors, his works still make him a major figure in Poussin studies. One cannot resist the feeling that he knew more than he was prepared to say.

FIGURE 16.5 Poussin's Self-portrait I, as engraved by Jean Pesne.

FIGURE 16.6 The reverse of the Seal of the United States of America.

Poussin and the modern art world

The recent Poussin exhibitions in Paris and London to mark the 400th anniversary of his birth, and the subsequent lectures and presentations, represent the current state of Poussin studies. In view of this it was surprising to find very little commentary on the symbolic themes inherent in Poussin's work.

Examples of geometric elements that find their way, often inexplicably, into Poussin's paintings are the sphere and the pyramid. In some cases their presence is legitimate on architectural grounds, but often they defy logic and are invariably ignored. An example of this is to be found in *Moses Saved From the Water* (*c.* 1651), in the background of which is seen a building, pink in colour, with curvilinear walls and rows of 'windows' or openings, resembling nothing more than a 1970s multistorey car park, and of about the same size.[25] But the most extraordinary feature is the sphere that sits on top of the building. This is grey, and presumably of stone, and from the clear perspective of the painting it must be almost 10 metres in diameter and weigh around

1,000 tonnes. Apart from the size problem, the arrangement is illogical. Clearly there must be an occult purpose.

The incorporation of pyramids at almost any opportunity is more readily understood in the Platonist–Pythagorean context that we have already discussed. *The Finding of Moses* (c. 1638, in the Louvre), quite naturally in this case, has one prominent pyramid, its lower part concealed behind a slope, and its reflection seen in the water of the Nile. Seen in the water are the reflections of two figures standing on the bank, facing the place of rescue. They watch with more than casual interest. These figures or their equivalents recur frequently, and may be regarded as representative of the philosophers often depicted by Poussin in a 'philosopher's grove'. Identified by Anthony Blunt as being similar to the figures in *The Grove of the Philosophers* by Salvator Rosa, they are always extraneous to the theme of the painting, and cast an eerie but not unbenevolent eye over the proceedings. These are Poussin's acknowledgement of the schools of philosophy so instrumental in the creation of his own persona and that of previous and contemporary adepts. That they should be occultly framed by the reflection of the pyramid is clearly apposite. The river-god in this painting is, of course, the Nile. In his cornucopia are exotic fruits and a fir cone. It is hardly necessary to point out that fir cones are far from common in Egypt; this was common knowledge even in the 1600s. The fir cone, which appears elsewhere in the *oeuvre* – notably one of huge size in an entirely deciduous grove wherein *The Triumph of Pan*[26] is riotously celebrated – is a Bacchic and Gnostic symbol.

Some breaths of fresh air were to waft into the stuffy atmosphere of Poussin studies in a lecture given at the Royal Academy on 13 March 1995. Martin Clayton, the curator of the Royal Collection of Poussin drawings, revealed that the backs of certain drawings have markings – dots and indentations – that have so far defied analysis. In his presentation he emphasised the lack of knowledge of Poussin's working methods. His initial, conceptual drawings have survived in good numbers and in many cases may be indisputably related to the finished painting. But there are often substantial differences between the concept and the finished article. There had to have been intermediate drawings, possibly with a geometric format, that were to be transferred to the canvas prior to painting. These comments were made without any knowledge (quite obviously) of the discoveries we had made in the case of two paintings of *Les Bergers d'Arcadie*; the need for continued silence on the matter was a cause for some frustration on the part of our art-historian researcher who attended the lecture on our behalf. Martin Clayton's friendly comment to her to the effect that if she were to find out what the reverse-side markings meant, would she be kind enough to let him know, may have been prophetic! We have as yet had no opportunity to examine the drawings in question, and cannot say whether our discoveries will throw any light on the matter, but we certainly intend to find out.

In the light of this examination of Poussin's influences and beliefs, is there anything more to conclude about *Les Bergers d'Arcadie II*? Having examined the allegory and symbolism employed by Poussin, the new role of the female figure may be re-examined. Her pose, manner and dress show her to be a Hellenic muse. The mental activity of the three men is anchored by her stoic authority. She clearly personifies Wisdom; she is Sophia (Greek: *sophos*, 'wise'), the 'Baphomet' revered by the Templars, and the supreme symbol of gnosis. One might suspect that the lady Doulce Mercy – 'Sweet Grace' – of René d'Anjou's quest is also Sophia. Having attained gnosis, one would certainly have achieved a state of sweet grace.

The re-dating of this painting to be contemporary with the *Baptism* from the first *Sacraments* series of paintings,[27] of 1638, reinforced our initial impression that the scenery of both is similar. Curiously, the rocky mound with its evergreen trees at les Pontils on which the tomb used to stand – out of view in the 'Shepherds' – actually seems to make its appearance in the *Baptism*. The group of figures on the mound, observing but not participating, are the philosophers.

Also re-dated during the London exhibition was *A Dance to the*

Music of Time, brought over from the Wallace Collection for one hour only on 24 March 1995 (it cannot be loaned): formerly put at around 1639, this was found to fit the artist's style of 1634–35. This painting had always been associated with a group of paintings, belonging to Cardinal Rospigliosi, thought by some to include *Les Bergers d'Arcadie II*, and all essentially contemporaneous. One wonders if the revised date for the latter (1638) should not also have been nearer 1635. In any case, the interval between the two 'Shepherds' of, say, five to eight years could correspond to the period required for Poussin to reach full initiation.

Sir Anthony Van Dyck

In the course of our investigations we were to discover a connection between Poussin and another of the great painters of the day, Anthony Van Dyck (1599–1641), which opened up a whole new perspective on the Secret. The starting-point for the trail had a very familiar ring to it.

There used to be an engraving of a painting by Van Dyck hanging in the church at Rennes-les-Bains. It was a *Lamentation of the Dead Christ*, and its presence in the church, by implication, was significant. Just like the Parchments, whose originals have never been seen, and the de Nègre gravestones, destroyed a hundred years ago, the Van Dyck no longer hangs in the church. Did it ever hang in the church? Indeed, is it important whether it did or did not? Whether it would be worth while to pursue this lead it was impossible to say, but, ever hopeful, we investigated.

There are two *Lamentations* painted by Van Dyck that had contemporary engravings made of them. The 1634 engraving, by Lucas Vosterman, was dedicated by Van Dyck to his English friend, the Anglican cleric George Gage. The 1636 version was engraved by Schelte a Bolswert. It is cited in two exhibition catalogues as being different in dimensions and detail to the original painting, but in neither publication is an illustration of the Bolswert version provided, or a reference to its present whereabouts given. Both paintings were commissioned by Abbé Cesare Allessandro Scaglia, who held the intriguing posts of diplomat to the dukes of Savoy in Rome (1614–23), Paris (1625–27) and London (1631–32). Scaglia, a Franciscan, was anti-French, and one may safely assume that along with his religious calling and diplomatic postings he combined espionage. This is a reasonable assumption, as political intrigue was rife during this period, and the Catholic clergy was as involved then as it has been in more modern times. In 1634, in addition to the *Lamentation*, he also commissioned Van Dyck to paint a portrait of himself and a devotional religious painting.

The dukes of Savoy had become custodians of the Holy Shroud in around 1453. One of the yearly public exhibitions of the Holy Shroud in the seventeenth century occurred in the presence of the princesses Maria Adelaide, Maria Anna and Maria Louise of the House of Savoy. The Vienna manuscript of King René's *Le Cuer d'amours espris*, after Duc Jean de Bourbon, had belonged to Catherine de Lorraine, Duchesse de Bourbon, sister of King Henri IV; then to Duc Eugène de Savoie, entering the Imperial Library of Vienna in 1738.

The Van Dyck *Lamentations* display obvious compositional similarities to the *Lamentation* painted by Poussin around 1655–57. It was in 1656 that Nicolas Fouquet sent his younger brother, the Abbé Louis, to Rome, where he met Poussin. Following this meeting he was to write an incriminating letter to his brother about Poussin's 'secret' which, he stated, even 'kings would have great difficulty extracting from him'.[28] Poussin's patron for the *Lamentation* of this period is not known. The two painters had a mutual circle of friends, and it is strange to find no evidence of them having met. They missed meeting in Rome by a few months in 1623. Poussin was in Paris from mid-December 1640 to October 1642; Van Dyck was also there between January and May of 1641, and again on 16 November and 4 December that same year, in attempts to win commissions for the decoration of the Louvre Palace.

Neither of Van Dyck's applications was to be successful. Van Dyck returned to London, deeply depressed and unwell. He died suddenly in his studio five days later.

Poussin, having been named First Painter to the King in 1640 – a position he had neither sought nor wanted – was responsible for, but unhappy about, the Louvre decorations, which brought him into open conflict with the other artists under the patronage of Louis XIII. Who it was who made the decision not to use Van Dyck is unclear.

Van Dyck's fortunes had been rather better in 1632, when he arrived in England to take up a royal appointment. Immediately knighted, he was installed in a house at Blackfriars and granted an annual pension of £200. From then until his death in 1641 he worked almost exclusively for the court, and had an immense influence on portraiture in Britain. His desire to seek employment elsewhere may have stemmed from a perception that all was not well in Britain: Charles I had been defeated by the Scots in the 'Second Bishops' War' of 1640; the House of Commons made its 'Grand Remonstrance' to Charles in 1641. With friends in diplomatic and other high places, he might well have been aware that the time was right for a move; there may, of course, have been other factors.

It is extraordinary that we have been unable to find any record of a connection between the two painters, Van Dyck and Poussin. Two artists of such stature would surely have had, and expressed, a view of each other. They shared a biographer in Bellori,[29] who was given information on Van Dyck's life by the latter's close English friend Kenelm Digby on the occasions of Digby's visits to Rome.

Sir Kenelm Digby (1602–1665) was certainly a memorable figure. He was a Catholic with a breadth of intellectual interests that charac-terised the Stuart court; he was a founder-member of the Royal Society; he was the Royal Agent on a number of missions to France on behalf of the Catholic Queen Henrietta Maria (a 'Christian neo-Platonist'[30]), wife of Charles I and sister of Louis XIII. He also travelled in Italy and Spain. He had been a pupil of Thomas Allen, a mathematician and student of the occult at Oxford; it was to Digby that Allen bequeathed his library and it was with Digby that Van Dyck is supposed to have dabbled in alchemy.[31] (In this period alchemy was often among the interests of the learned and influential.) Digby has been named as a Rosicrucian.[32] There is an engraving printed on silk showing the occasion of the exposition of the Holy Shroud in the presence of the princesses of Savoy, to which we referred above. This is in the collection of Sherborne Castle, Dorset, since 1617 the seat of the Digby family.

George Gage met Van Dyck in Rome, where he moved in the same ubiquitous circle of political agents and art connoisseurs as Scaglia. Van Dyck dedicated the 1634 *Lamentation* to him, referring to him as 'the Agent of Charles I'. The complexities of court life, and the opportunities for espionage, and therefore for the promulgation of an underground stream of esoteric Christianity – the formation of allegiances that transcend national, or doctrinal frontiers – may be glimpsed in these accounts. (Our continuing researches have reinforced this view of a hidden force, but our net has spread beyond the scope of this present work.)

It was in 1636 that Van Dyck painted King Charles I in the robes of the Order of the Garter. The order had been founded by Edward III around 1348 on the model of the Burgundian Order of the Golden Fleece, with the intention of cementing the union between the leading nobles and the Crown. Charles was, however, in the words of Elias Ashmole, 'the greatest increaser of the honour and renown of this most illustrious order'. The Golden Fleece connection is interesting, as around 1626–27 Sir William Vaughan had written the first work in English which 'can fairly be described as a Rosicrucian tract',[33] entitled *The Golden Fleece*. This was dedicated to Charles I, and it was in 1626, the year after his succession, that Charles had decreed that all knights should wear the Garter badge embroidered on the left side of their cloaks. The badge is the red cross of St George. The aureole of silver rays, in imitation of the French Order of the Holy Spirit, was added later.

Two portraits by Van Dyck are particularly exciting, considering the evidence for some secret link between him and Poussin. These are of Lord Wharton (1632) and Lord George Stuart, Seigneur d'Aubigny (c. 1638) (Plate 18), and both depict the sitters in the 'Arcadian' mode. The style of dress and the colours induce a shock recall of the figure of Wisdom in *Les Bergers d'Arcadie II*. Once more, one finds Arcadia as a common thread.

David Teniers the Younger

Contemporary with Poussin and Van Dyck, Teniers is nevertheless in a different league; his vast output scarcely ventures into the cerebral regions that characterise the work of Poussin, or the perceptive mastery of Van Dyck's portraits. He was highly successful and technically quite competent, but one must judge him an unlikely candidate for induction into elevated hermetic circles. The virtual absence of any complex symbolism in his work, or even the duplication of his one singular venture into the field of esoterica in *St Antony and St Paul*, indicates that he must have been working to express instructions on that occasion. Indeed, the overt portrayal of the geometric secret suggests the slavish following of a plan drawn up by someone else; that person certainly sacerdotal but lacking the artistic ability to appreciate the scope for subtlety. In this event, it is worth investigating his patrons for potential sources of the occult knowledge.

Teniers was born in Anvers in 1610, and died in Bruxelles in 1690. His first wife came from a family that had produced two eminent painters; she was Anne Brueghel. They were married in 1637, and she died on 11 May 1656. On 21 October of the same year he married Isabelle de Fren, daughter of André de Fren, Secretary to the Council of Brabant. This was surely a worth-while connection; the dukes of Brabant had formerly been called the dukes of Bouillon and traced their ancestry directly back to Godfroi de Bouillon, who captured Jerusalem as leader of the First Crusade, and thus liberated the Holy Sepulchre. This must rank high on the list of potential connections to the Secret.

But Teniers was blessed with his own excellent connections. The Archduke Leopold William, governor of the Low Countries in 1647, was a powerful protector who gave Teniers the title of Court Painter, Chamberlain and Conservator of his gallery. More than this, he sent works by Teniers to several crowned heads with his recommendation: to Philip IV of Spain, William II of Orange, Christine of Sweden and Don Juan of Austria, natural son of Philip IV, who succeeded Leopold William in the Netherlands in 1656. So he was not without patronage, and the commission for the occult *St Antony and St Paul* could have come from almost any one of these. Past critics have been perplexed, for his meteoric rise in no way matched his talents. Perhaps there was a hidden side to David Teniers, and we have misjudged his esoteric connections.

In 1663 there was a curious development. He requested to be admitted to the ranks of the nobility, claiming ancestors of the name d'Ath. More curiously, his request was granted on the condition that he produced no more paintings for money. It seems that he did not persist.

Teniers may not have received any more commissions for occult works, or, if he did, these have remained securely out of profane view. But at least one other adept had appreciated the content of *St Antony and St Paul*, and had a copy made. That copy once resided at Shugborough Hall, the seat of the Ansons. It will be recalled that they clearly held Poussin in some esteem, for in the grounds is the marble monument version of *Les Bergers d'Arcadie II*; and in the Hudson portrait of Lady Anson, she holds her own copy of *Les Bergers d'Arcadie I*. Perhaps it was less Poussin than the occult message that they valued. The Ansons must have had an adept within their fold in the eighteenth century, if not earlier.

At some point in the late seventeenth century the artistic connection appears to have died out – perhaps to go further underground, but certainly it has eluded us. When it next appeared the mode of concealment was different again, the Secret becoming more closely associated with death, and tombstones the medium. There are several reasons why the use of art might have become unpopular at this point.

Social upheavals caused a change in the relationship between client (or patron) and painter. The process of social change was accelerated by the Revolution in France, with inevitable repercussions throughout Europe. This client–painter relationship was of extreme significance in the case of non-initiates like David Teniers and even in the case of Poussin who, while clearly an initiate, was invariably painting under commission from others. The market for the works of the great, and not so great, artists would eventually be found primarily with the *nouveau riche*. The perceived status associated with owning an occult painting by one of the great artists appears to have diminished with this change in the market.

Art had started to become accessible to the masses, and so was perhaps no longer regarded as safe; or, in the case of new occult works, this made it necessary to guard them more closely. It is worth noting the wealth of unseen art, regarded today as minor (even if not thought so by the patron), which languishes in private collections. For example, though not in the remit of this book, there are many overtly pornographic works by the great masters, never placed on public show either then or now. These were commissioned, kept concealed and shown only to fellow *amateurs*. And when one considers the small number of works that we have identified from a period of some three hundred years, it has to be admitted that, of the many, these are the few that have slipped through the safety-net.

It is of course possible that we have not been looking in the right direction, despite having scoured countless art catalogues covering the last three centuries. While more examples undoubtedly exist, for the time being we have a wealth of material, enough for a small gallery of the esoteric, and enough corroborative symbolism to rule out simple coincidence.

17
THE BONES OF
THE PROPHET

Reeling somewhat from the results of research which had led us to a
site we believed to be of world importance, we took stock of our findings and considered the wider implications. In particular, there was the
role of the Christian Church, the organisation that had dominated the
politics and thinking of Western civilisation since the time of
Constantine the Great. What we needed now was context – a framework – and the final piece of the jigsaw might well slip into place.

We had uncovered a hidden world, with a membership as surprising
as it was unexpected. Throughout our study, heretical symbolism –
whether hermetic, Gnostic or Rosicrucian – had hovered on the side-
lines. It was now necessary to investigate the origin of such alternative
systems of belief and assess, not just their points of divergence from
more 'acceptable' thinking, but also the points of overlap. Clearly, our
findings digressed markedly from official Church history, and, realising
that we should not shoot the messenger, we decided that an examination of the origins of Christianity was necessary. It is worth stating at
this point that the survey about to be undertaken ventures into areas
where there is conflict among Church historians and theologians;
indeed, some recently expressed views are so dramatic and disputed that
they may not be reconciled in this century, or even in the next. We

have endeavoured to present the most authoritative and the most logical of views. For some the account will be too simplistic, for others outrageous; for a few it will seem inconclusive, but in view of the nature of our findings the debate must be opened.

When we looked in more depth at the history of the Church, various questions arose which had a direct bearing on our findings in France. What had been the real message of Jesus? How different was he to the other messiahs of the time? Was he elevated to the stature of 'Christ' entirely because of the Resurrection? Most importantly, if Jesus' body had remained on earth and we had discovered its whereabouts, what would this mean for Christianity? Resolving these questions required us to begin in first-century Palestine, and with the man whom the Parchments, paintings and tombstones referred to so clearly: Jesus of Nazareth.

The occupied Palestine into which Jesus was born was both complex and volatile. The Roman Empire was still in a state of rapid expansion, and the alliances the Romans sought to further their empire-building were highly complex. As with all forced occupations, the support of the ruling dynasties, whose authority the Romans eventually wished to usurp, was a valuable short-term asset. The result was a web of uneasy, flawed alliances. But the greatest threat to peaceful Roman rule arose out of divergent beliefs within Judaism, in particular Zealotry. Palestine was a country with a religion, and indeed a spiritual outlook, very different from that of the pantheistic Roman Empire. The difference inevitably led to conflict as the irresistible military force of Rome came up against the immovable object of the law of the Hebrews – Mosaic law. The aristocratic Roman historian Tacitus was explicit about this difference, and the tone of his prose is a good indication of the intolerance of the Roman army. When talking of the Jews in general, he does not mince his words, declaring that Moses 'in order to assert for the future his authority over his people, introduced a cult that was quite novel and opposed to that of other mortals.'[1]

Describing their different approach to all matters of life, including

diet and sexual practice, he makes another significant observation. The
Jews, he states, were given to burying their dead and not cremating
them. Anxious to underline all differences, Tacitus continues:[2]

> their God is supreme and eternal, unchangeable and indes-
> tructible . . . They pay no such honour to their kings nor to
> Caesar.

The Gnostic inheritance

In the first century AD, Palestine, lying as it did at the eastern end of the
Mediterranean (Figure 17.1), was a zone of interchange between the
civilisation of ancient Greece and the Roman Empire, and the territory
of the Euphrates delta – the heart of ancient Persia. From Persia had
come the religion of Zoroastrianism, and in this faith, which saw the
earth as a battleground between forces of light and dark, lies the possible origin of 'Gnosis', or Gnosticism. This belief, which had become
increasingly relevant as our study progressed, was prevalent in Jerusalem
at the time of Jesus of Nazareth, and indeed predated him by many
centuries.

So, Persia offers itself as the strongest candidate for the origins of
Gnosticism, though this is still a subject of debate and may never be
resolved. Judaism is another contender: monotheistic, it would have
provided a suitable basis for the more esoteric approach to God and his
creation contained in Gnosticism.

Inherent in Gnostic belief is the concept of dual creation, or 'dualism', a concept which both Saunière and Gélis had apparently embraced,
despite its obvious conflict with the doctrine of the Catholic Church. In
this 'dualistic' view of the world, the divine cosmos was divided from the
lower world, the earthly existence of man. It had been the work of
God's angels to create human existence, and the result had been less than
satisfactory. Man had issued forth from creation inherently evil, and

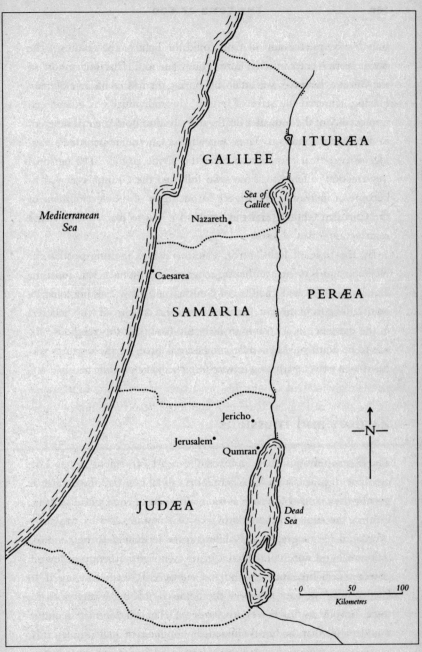

FIGURE 17.1 Map of the Holy Land at the time of Christ,
showing the provinces.

only by the intercession of God could the light of the cosmos – the divine spark – enter into the human body and soul. This intercession, so the Gnostics believed, was attainable during the natural lifetime of man. Having achieved the state of 'gnosis' the individual was guaranteed immortality of the soul after death, and salvation from the evil inherent in the human condition. Thus, at death the Gnostic 'resurrected', leaving his corporeal existence to enter the divine cosmos. The personal 'resurrection' offered to those who followed the Gnostic way was to become of increasing importance in our study of the development of the Christian Church, and the emphasis it was to place on *one* man's resurrection – that of Jesus.

By the time of Jesus' birth, Palestine was a melting-pot of the Hellenic and Roman pantheistic religions and monotheistic Judaism. The long-established tradition of Gnostic thought was also holding its own: hailing from the east, mature in itself and open to all who believed in the existence of a cosmic or heavenly God. But this religious mix was to be dominated by a different external force, for the territory was ruled by a power with an overwhelming military capability.

Zealots and messiahs

The Roman Empire had annexed the heart of ancient Israel. The province of Judea, with Jerusalem as its capital city, had the extensive port by then named Caesarea as the main point of entry into Palestine. Galilee, the most northerly province of Palestine, had by this time overcome its geographical isolation from Jerusalem to become an influential and important district in its own right, a centre of Jewish power and a breeding-ground for sedition. Routes converged at Galilee from the four points of the compass, making it important to trade. Beyond its north-western borders Hellenism dominated, and it is undeniable that the Greek influence upon the rich and commercially active lakeside region was still considerable, adding to the contempt in which the Jewish authorities in Jerusalem held their northern cousins. The Jews of Jerusalem, who influenced the politics of the religious council of the Temple, were for the sake of maintaining their power prepared to uphold the *status quo* that existed between their Roman masters and themselves. The same could not be said of their brethren in Galilee.

Discontent with the Roman invader fomented in this hot and humid area. But the Galileans, despised by the priesthood of the Temple, were at least willing to put their convictions to the test. The year AD 6 saw the beginning of an armed struggle by the Zealots against the authority of Rome. (The Zealots were those Jews who, since the second century BC, had been fighting for a homeland free from foreign oppression and united under strict observance of the Mosaic law.) Judas of Gamala, a Galilean patriot, led a revolt which, though unsuccessful, set the pattern for conflict in Palestine. Although the role of Judas is considered to have been largely non-violent, the Roman response to his protest was anything but. Judas was killed, and over two thousand of his followers were crucified. The destruction of the participants did not, however, eradicate the cause. Judas had a son, Menahim, who was to continue in the footsteps of his father, though this time with sword in hand and the vision of messianic inheritance firmly at the forefront of his mind.

Menahim was one of several self-proclaimed messiahs of first-century Palestine. This desire to embrace and manipulate the future of Israel via religion is evident in the number of prophets who fuelled people's expectation of the coming of a new age, and protesters who aggravated an already precarious social and political situation. Dominic Crossan, in his work *The Historical Jesus*, lists the numerous types of unrest in Palestine at the time. The list is extensive, underlining the complexity of the situation. His protesters number seven between 65 BC and 4 BC; ten prophets appear between AD 30 and AD 73; bandits he counts eleven, and messiahs five – starting with Judas the Galilean and ending with Simon bar Giora.

It is therefore clear that, before Jesus ever set foot in the city of

Jerusalem, the appearance of various messiahs and the use of crucifixion as a form of punishment were familiar to both the Jews and the Romans living out their uneasy coexistence in Palestine.

The 'holy ones' of Qumran

Judaism, seeking to maintain its integrity in a Hellenic world, had also to contend with the forces of Gnosticism and of the pagan Roman invader. In addition, there had for some time been Jewish dissatisfaction with their own Temple priesthood. In the second century BC, when Jerusalem was under Greek domination, a group of priests had broken away from the Temple and retreated into the wilderness at Qumran, close to the shores of the Dead Sea. They saw the adoption of the lunar calendar by the dominant Hasmonean Temple priesthood as making it impossible to calculate the correct days of sacrifice in the Jewish calendar. In other words, the core of their belief had suddenly become flawed in the eyes of God.

Since 1947 this Jewish breakaway sect, known to history as the 'Essenes', a name derived from the Syriac for 'holy ones' has left scholars eager to associate the community with the roots of Christianity. For this was the year in which, hidden in the many caves that pierce the escarpment above the settlement of Qumran, the Dead Sea Scrolls were discovered.

These documents, manuscripts bound and preserved in jars of terracotta, are a priceless inheritance from the past, and throw light on the events, and indeed the hopes and fears, of the age. They help to illuminate the daily influences on the person who is central to our story: the Galilean whose name, when translated from the Greek or Hebrew, means 'God is salvation' – Jesus. The 'holy ones' wished for a return to the old order of Israel, with a descendant from the line of David established on the throne and the old priesthood back in command of the Temple and upholding the highest traditions – strict observance of the Torah, the law of God and Moses.

The majority of the scrolls, for years jealously guarded by the Jesuit scholars first placed in charge of their translation, are now in the hands of the Israelis and on display in Jerusalem. With the publication of the revised edition of his book on the Dead Sea Scrolls, Geza Vermes, the leading contemporary authority on the subject, has provided the general public with information of stunning relevance to the origins of Christianity.[3] One of the scroll fragments deals with the coming of the Messiah, and reinforces the aim of the Essene community:[4]

> I shall be his father and he shall be my son. He is the Branch of David who shall arise with the Interpreter of the Law to rule in Zion at the end of time.

A second fragment requires no further explanation, when we remember that it predates the birth of Jesus by several generations:[5]

> . . . the heavens and the earth will listen to His Messiah,
> And glorious things which have never been the Lord will
>   accomplish,
> For he will heal the wounded, and revive the dead, and bring
>   good news to the poor.

It is apparent that the prototypic vision of the Davidic messiah existed in Qumran from the first century BC. But the prophecy remained unfulfilled. One man, who would later walk the hills of Galilee, encapsulated the requirements of the prophecy, but was it the Essenes themselves who promoted Jesus to the task, or did Jesus act independently, simply influenced by the desert community?

In the absence of documentary evidence, this question cannot be directly answered. It remains beyond doubt, however, that the writings of the New Testament contain similarities with texts found at Qumran which predate the life of Jesus. If Jesus or his disciples had contact or involvement with the Essenes, this would explain the coincidence.

We would later visit the former home of this reclusive desert group and see for ourselves the environment which provided the backdrop to their aims and hopes. But for now we focused our attention on the figure so central to our quest: Jesus of Nazareth, the man whose physical remains we believed to be buried deep within Mount Cardou. In the light of our findings we would have cause to re-examine the circumstances of his death; for now we turned to the circumstances of his brief but influential life.

Jesus' life

The multi-religious and multi-factional world into which Jesus was born was far removed from the simplistic Jews-against-Romans scenario promoted in the New Testament accounts. Certain Jewish sects had awaited the arrival of a Davidic messiah, but to many he was just another in a long line of would-be prophets. Jesus, though, was unlike any other pretender to the throne. Menahim, who predated Jesus by a generation, had epitomised the popular image of the saviour of Israel, though the factors which had contributed to this – his ostentation, and indeed the Zealot company he shared the stage with – were to contribute greatly to his downfall. Jesus, on the other hand, could not have been more different.

The entry of Jesus into Jerusalem in the days preceding the Passover of AD 33 marked a significant point of achievement for the man who, by personal intervention in the daily affairs of the people of Judea, had gained a reputation for upholding the message of the Old Testament. While pursuing an active campaign to inform and assist the poor and oppressed of Judea, he maintained his own servile position: an example of extreme altruism by the messianic standards of the day.

Unfortunately for Jesus, the occupying powers saw him rather differently. To them he had all the hallmarks of a troublemaker. In their eyes he was mixing religion with politics, and they were not alone in this view. His behaviour in the Temple precincts when he had over-turned the tables of the money-lenders had not endeared him to either the Sadducees or the Sanhedrin, the council of the Jewish Temple. The Sadducees, a religious group which had achieved dominance in the Sanhedrin, collaborated openly with the Roman authorities and it was their business venture in developing a taxation scheme for the sacrifice of animals that had so publicly met with Jesus' wrath. But Jesus' final act of provocation occurred during the preparation for Passover. By enter-ing Jerusalem, acclaimed by his supporters, at a time when the major political players on the Palestinian scene were congregating in the city, he illuminated the gulf that existed between his message of liberation and the stance taken by the established hierarchy.

If the arrest of one more self-proclaimed messiah was considered dis-astrous by his followers, they should have expected no less, for Jesus played into the hands of his enemies in a way that confirms the view that he was intent on fulfilling the prophecy of a Davidic messiah to the full. His end on the evening before the Sabbath, as a victim of the established order, was another statistic to add to the long list of un-desirables who had taken their last breath at Golgotha – 'the place of the skull'.

Jesus' death

If Jesus' punishment was identical to that meted out to numerous other radicals, upstarts, protesters and petty criminals during this volatile period, it is not unreasonable to assume that his personal message of liberation would have been consigned to the dust of Judean history at the same time. Since this is not what happened, it is essential to inves-tigate the days immediately following the crucifixion to ascertain why events took the course they did.

The tomb to which Jesus was consigned after crucifixion was, according to the Gospels, new, and therefore presumably unused.[6]

We know from the Gospel accounts that this tomb belonged to Joseph of Arimathea, and that he had been instrumental in obtaining the release of Jesus from the cross and conveying him there. Jewish tombs of the period required a considerable amount of work by a stone-mason. A tomb consisted principally of a single antechamber hollowed out, cave-fashion, from the rock, with horizontal shafts cut into the interior walls to accommodate the deceased. Several bodies could thereby be incorporated in the same tomb, simply by cutting more shafts.

If a family was wealthy enough, after decomposition the remains of their dead were taken out of the shafts, stowed inside a terracotta jar or ossuary, and then replaced. The Roman custom of leaving the crucified on the cross to be picked clean by carrion birds would have undoubt-edly speeded up this method of final preservation, a fate which Jesus (whether dead or alive) was spared, as it is recorded that he was taken down early from the cross due to the impending Sabbath.

The entrance to the tomb would have been sealed by a large stone or by the erection of a temporary wall, so that the burial chamber could be re-opened if and when circumstance demanded. Whether Joseph had transported Jesus to a tomb which was destined for family use and unfinished we shall never know. It seems probable, however, that a main chamber at the very least was completed. The technicalities of the tomb aside, what about the fate of the body? What rights were accorded to the family and friends of one so summarily and publicly dealt with?

We know from the Gospel accounts that Jesus was subjected to cru-cifixion, but is there any archaeological evidence for this process of punishment or for the disposal of a crucified body? In 1968, the area of Ha-Mivtar in north-eastern Jerusalem yielded the world's first and so far only example of a victim of crucifixion. The remains of Yehohanan ben Hagkol came to light, guaranteeing him a niche in history far removed from the dark interior of the burial cave in which he had rested for almost two thousand years.

Yehohanan was Jewish, and in his twenties when he died. Records have not survived as to the nature of his crime, though it was known that he was high-born and related to a master-builder of the second Temple of Jerusalem. His remains are highly revealing. The nail hammered through the joint in his right heel had found a knot in the timber as it exited the flesh, leaving the bent piece of iron testimony to the frustrations of the executioner. The family on retrieving the body had obviously been similarly plagued by the obstinate nail. With a portion of the cross still attached to the remains of their relative, they had taken the body away for burial in a tomb until decomposition would permit final burial in an ossuary.

The skeleton of Yehohanan, bearing evidence of his terrible death, was discovered by Vassilios Tzaferis of the Israel Antiques Authority. It is the method of burial that is of most relevance to the story of Jesus. Reburial in an ossuary was not the norm – it was a luxury few could afford. The family of Yehohanan ben Hagkol had evidently wielded some influence in order to retrieve his body for a decent burial, a similarity to the story of Jesus which is quite remarkable. This parallel with the recorded fate of Jesus is significant, as it demonstrates via archaeological evidence that a victim removed early from the cross could have had a decent burial, and that such evidence could survive for almost two thousand years.

The Resurrection

The work of the Jerusalem disciples who filled the vacuum left by Jesus after his crucifixion was intense but short-lived. The situation in which they found themselves was complicated by the speed of events: they had seen the arrest, trial and execution of their leader within a single day. The enigma surrounding Jesus' physical departure from the scene must be studied from two opposing viewpoints:

1. If he had indeed succumbed to his ordeal, what became of his body?
2. If he had been revived through the services of Joseph and his women helpers, what became of him in the remaining years of his life?

The concept of bodily resurrection was not an issue for the surviving members of his group – not, that is, until Paul and the apostles saw the immense potential of the idea.

The disappearance of Jesus' body from the tomb and his alleged reappearances to his disciples fall within the authority of the New Testament. According to Biblical accounts, the tomb was found empty, and the shroud purchased by Joseph was the only evidence that Jesus had occupied the chamber at all. Considering the lack of information about the fate of Jesus, whether alive or dead after the crucifixion, one question is paramount. Why should an empty tomb be a matter of such importance to the Gospel writers? The answer may be found in the radical decision taken by the early Church which confirmed that the bodily Resurrection of Jesus should symbolise the sacrifice by God of his only son. This was a major departure from the concept of a Christ destined to fulfil a prophecy by re-establishing the line of David, thus securing the future of the new Jewish messianic age centred around the Temple at Jerusalem.

Through the medium of the New Testament, the message of the early Church was reinforced to provide a simplistic view for the masses. Jesus the Messiah had sacrificed himself for the sinners of the world, and his body had been physically resurrected. Confirming the bodily Resurrection from the tomb, the Church proclaimed this act of sacrifice as universal, applicable to Jew and Gentile alike, and by doing so they projected the story of Jesus far beyond Jerusalem and into a worldwide arena. But the message did not spread itself. It was one man in particular who dictated the direction of the early Roman Church, and it is to him that we must now turn.

The role of Paul the Apostle

The actions of Paul following the 'death' of Jesus illustrate the existence of a clear agenda for the spreading of the message of Christ. Several years were to pass before Paul, on the road to Damascus, received his instructions in a blinding vision. Suddenly, the way forward for Paul and for the Christian message was clear. Paul, who had never met Jesus, completely reversed his attitude. His conversion on the road to Damascus turned him from a persecutor of Jesus' disciples to the most ardent champion of the new faith. His campaign took him to the centre of the Empire – to the gates of Imperial Rome – a long way geographically and ideologically from Jerusalem and the established guardians of the Judaic faith. The success of the Church owes more to this one man and his ministry than to any other.

Paul, the son of a Pharisee, was born in Tarsus around AD 10. He was destined for the rabbinnate, and made his first visit to Jerusalem at the age of eighteen. While proud of his Jewish ancestry, Paul's father passed on his Roman citizenship to his son, effectively providing him with a foot in both camps. The city of Tarsus, provincial Roman capital of the north-eastern Mediterranean area, retained the Hellenisation of its ancient past, giving Paul an upbringing that was truly cosmopolitan. The Pharisees, whose name derived from a Greek word meaning 'the separated ones', had distanced themselves from the Temple, as had the Essenes at the time of the unsuccessful resistance to the Greek occupation of Palestine.

The Pharisees took the middle-ground between the Zealot Essenes and the openly political actions of the Sadducees, who had formed alliances with the Romans. They advocated passive resistance to the Romans, while retaining much of the Hellenistic inheritance discarded by the Sadducees and the Essenes. This inheritance, in the context of Paul and the future structure of the early Christian Church, was the most significant factor in the politico-religious ferment in Jerusalem. The Pharisees, of whom Paul was initially a vociferous example,

believed in the existence of spirits and angels, and thereby in intercession between God and man on earth. But their most relevant belief –
in terms of the path the Pauline Church would later take – had to do
with the future of the individual after leaving the physical world. For
the Pharisees believed in the resurrection of the soul after death and in
the development of the soul by the furtherance of good works on
earth. Here are strong similarities to the fundamentals of Gnosis.

Paul drew upon this religious inheritance, discarding points of doctrine which were exclusive and incorporating those which enhanced his
vision of the Christian message in the future. He saw Christianity as
addressing all religious shades of grey. Jesus provided the perfect answer
to all men, be they Greek, Roman or Jew. Jesus was God and Messiah
in one. This carried Paul's training as a Pharisee into the Church of
Christ, creating a resurrected Messiah and thereby leaving the beliefs of
the Pharisees, the Essenes, the Sadducees, the Zealots and the Romans
to be eventually consigned to the pages of history. The Pauline Church,
eventually to become the Roman Catholic Church, survived. One
further group, the disciples, the daily companions of Jesus, were also
side-lined by the dynamic work of Paul. This conflict of interest holds
the real key to the questions surrounding the messianic status of Jesus,
the Resurrection, and the Gentilisation of a religion which had in its
'Christ', or anointed Messiah, a traditional Jewish foundation.

Paul rose to his new role as the spokesman for the Christian cause
with considerable zeal. His vigorous suggestions for the spreading of the
new faith led him away from the more orthodox line that had been
taken by the Jerusalem disciples. Paul gradually parted company with
James, Jesus' half-brother, and abandoned the hard faction of disciples –
the 'Nazarenes' – who remained in Jerusalem, intent on furthering
what they believed to be the true message of Jesus. This separation was
a crucial moment in history, and determined the future course of the
Roman Catholic Church and the fate of millions down the centuries.
For Paul's version of Christianity was to effectively whittle away at the
heart of the matter: the Jewishness of Jesus.

The early church, Paul, and the Resurrection

So, if the role of Paul presents us with a scenario for the manipulation of at least one fact about Jesus, the significance of his ancestry, it must also cause us to question another 'fact' about him: that his body had disappeared. And if mystery and confusion surrounded his physical remains, what of his closest followers – those who really did know Jesus during his lifetime? What path did they follow in the wake of Jesus' 'death'?

After the disappearance of Jesus from the Jerusalem scene, James, his half-brother, is known to have inherited the leadership of the first Christian Church of Jerusalem. James's personal example of sanctity and rigid discipline with regard to the laws of sacrifice and circumcision improved his status accordingly in the eyes of those Jews who had converted to the Christian way. Paul had other ideas – in his opinion, the Church should be open to non-Jews. The admission of Gentiles into a church regarded by many as the province of circumcised Jews therefore aroused much debate. Should the influence of Hellenism be allowed to bear on the Jerusalem Church, with all the perils that such expansion into the Gentile world would inevitably bring, or should the sole custodians of Jesus' message be members of a Church fully confirmed in the old faith of their Jewish forefathers? By the year AD 49 the issue had come to a head. James, by now the senior of the elders of the Jerusalem Church, ruled on the dispute which threatened to split the followers of Christ for ever.

Paul arrived in Jerusalem from the Syrian city of Antioch, spokesman for the Christian community, anxious to repeal the uncompromising laws upheld by the elders of Jerusalem. By this time, fully converted and active in his role as an apostle, Paul championed the cause of the non-Jew to be allowed to receive the message of Jesus and enter the ranks of the Jerusalem Church. James conceded with a compromise: Gentiles would be admitted, provided they abstained from fornication, from eating the meat of strangled animals, and from offering food to idols. Circumcision, viewed by the Jerusalem Church as a prerequisite to salvation, was left off the agenda, leaving Paul and his companion Barnabus victorious in their desired aim: Christianity had become officially accessible to every citizen in Antioch and in the Empire. This achieved, Paul set off to continue his work abroad.

By the time of his return to Jerusalem eight years later, attitudes had hardened, as James himself was the first to recognise. The following passage from *Acts* reflects the fear and distrust with which the work of Paul was regarded in Jerusalem in AD 58. James warns:[7]

> . . . how many thousands there are among the Jews of those who have believed: they are all zealous of the Law, and they have been told about you [Paul] that you teach all the Jews who are among the Gentiles to forsake Moses, telling them not to circumcise their children or observe the customs.

This passage illuminates the very real gulf that existed between the closest of Jesus' followers and the later converts such as Paul. Paul, upon his arrival in the city, took heed of James's warning, submitting himself to a week of purification and sacrifices in the Temple, in the company of four others whose sacrifices he himself financed. Before the end of the seven days, Paul was recognised and accused of entering the Temple with Greek Gentiles – and only the intervention of the guards prevented his lynching. Obviously ignorant of the depth of feeling against him, Paul's next move can only be described as unfortunate. Called to account before the Council, he attempted to divide his Pharisee and Sadducee accusers by claiming, as the son of a Pharisee, to be a Pharisee himself, and as such a believer in the resurrection of the dead, a doctrine completely at odds with the views of the Sadducees. With such a divisive defence, Paul was removed from the council chamber and returned to the Fortress Antonia. The Romans, aware of a plot to kill him, removed him to Caesarea where he languished in prison for more than two years.

A change of Roman procurator emboldened the Sanhedrin to persuade the Romans to return Paul for trial in Jerusalem, which left him no alternative. Knowing that Jerusalem meant death, he appealed as a Roman citizen to the Emperor of Rome. Festus, the new procurator, was absolved of any further decision as to his fate, and Paul was destined for trial in Rome. The autumn weather had set in and the wandering ex-Pharisee, citizen of Rome and ardent Christian once again, came close to his maker in a near-shipwreck. House arrest in Rome was followed by further travels, with his relentless drive directed towards his particular interpretation of the Resurrection of Jesus, the message he believed should be embraced by Jews and Gentiles alike.

A parting of the ways

By the time of his death at the hands of Nero in AD 67, the destiny of James, half-brother of Jesus and leader of the Jerusalem Church, had also been fulfilled. Festus, the procurator who had dispatched Paul to Rome, had not lived long, and upon his death the Sanhedrin closed in on the Christian sect of Jerusalem. James was arrested and summarily executed by being thrown into the valley of Kidron from the top of the Temple wall. With his death there disappeared what was perhaps the true message of Jesus, for James's Jerusalem Church had failed to widen its net beyond the narrow confines of an elite group in the Holy City. Paul, on the other hand, had conducted a political campaign of some foresight in disseminating the message of a resurrected Christ to an ever wider audience throughout the Empire.

From the moment Paul walked out of Jerusalem for the last time to begin his own pilgrimage towards martyrdom in Rome, the Christian religion effectively left the city of Jerusalem, destined to flourish abroad before making its bloody return to the narrow streets of the citadel one thousand years later, under the sword of the First Crusade. With this departure the body of Jesus and the true story of his fate was consigned to the unknown. Jesus, whether entombed somewhere within the rocky surrounds, or at liberty in places unknown, had left a city divided. His spiritual status was also obscure. To many of those sympathetic to his movement and his message, the memory of the teacher was sufficient unto the task which lay ahead, a task which had not lost the Jewishness of its objective: the reinstatement of the Righteous in Jerusalem and the vanquishing of evil.

In the light of history, we can see that Jesus' name and the cross upon which he suffered would not have circumnavigated the globe by the mid-sixteenth century had it not been for the strenuous efforts made by Paul of Tarsus, the balding man of quick temper and short stature, possessed with a single-minded purpose. But Paul did not invent the idea of bodily resurrection – the concept was already established on the periphery of Jewish beliefs. As a physical occurrence, we were intrigued to find a curious record of it from five hundred years before, in the writings of the historian Herodotus:[8]

Aristeas, they said, who belonged to one of the noblest families in the island, had entered one day into a fuller's shop, when he suddenly dropped down dead. Hereupon the fuller shut up his shop, and went to tell Aristeas' kindred what had happened. The report of the death had just spread through the town, when a certain Cyzicenian, lately arrived from Artaca, contradicted the rumour, affirming that he had met Aristeas on his road to Cyzicus, and had spoken with him. This man, therefore, strenuously denied the rumour; the relations, however, proceeded to the fuller's shop with all the things necessary for the funeral, intending to carry the body away. But on the shop being opened, no Aristeas was found, either dead or alive. Seven years afterwards he reappeared, they told me, in Proconnesus, and wrote the poem called by the Greeks *The Arimaspeia*, after which he disappeared a second time.

The 'return' of Aristeas is highly relevant to the concept of resurrection established by the early Christian Church around the figure of Jesus. The key elements in the tale of Aristeas and the New Testament account of Jesus' Resurrection are very similar. In both cases no body was found when witnesses returned. There was then, in both cases, a reappearance. The Greeks apparently expected little more than enlightened literature from this apparent miracle, and as such Herodotus made no claims to greatness for it. In the case of Jesus, in the context of a turbulent and expectant Palestine, the reappearance was ideal for the further claims to greatness soon to be made about his brief but radical life.

Jesus and the Essenes

But what about the other group who had figured in our early studies – the Essenes of Qumran, the breakaway sect who had not only awaited the arrival of a messiah from the line of David, but had preserved their hopes in the form of the all-important Dead Sea Scrolls? The former home of this group had to be visited.

Qumran lies some thirty kilometres outside Jerusalem. The road to it leads quite literally through the wilderness – a desolate, sun-scorched wasteland. The many paths that rise up to the caves in which the Scrolls were found are as narrow and precipitous as they would have been two thousand years ago. The settlement itself stands on a natural platform jutting out towards the shore of the Dead Sea, a platform which can be reached only by climbing an extremely steep track from the road which follows the shore. We spent many hours among the caves and rocks of the escarpment, from where we could view every detail of the excavated ruins of the settlement perched on the plateau below.

The ingredients are all present for the ultimate place of spiritual refuge – remoteness, inaccessibility and an absence of worldly distractions. We could think of nowhere else in the world, at any moment in history, where there had existed such perfect conditions, and in such close proximity, for the creation of a messianic message as there had been at Qumran almost two thousand years ago.

The first century AD had seen Jerusalem, with its glorious mono-theistic past, occupied by foreigners who worshipped a multitude of diverse gods and goddesses. No doubt mirroring the dissatisfaction of many, the Essenes followed their convictions and left their fellow-Jews in Jerusalem for the wilderness of Qumran. To survive in the desert, let alone pursue an occupation, would have been far from easy. To prosper as the Essenes of Qumran had so evidently done, the community must have worked together with a powerful sense of purpose. Standing in the fierce heat, we were lost in admiration for the tenacity of these idealis-tic people. The record of the community's rules, beliefs and prophecies, written on dried goatskin, spoke of an almost incredible achievement in the face of the elements. The survival of the scrolls themselves over the centuries seemed nothing short of a miracle.

The Essene community had been dispersed by the Roman army fol-lowing the destruction of the Temple in AD 70. The Roman soldiers who moved into the buildings of Qumran which had once been occu-pied by scribes were presumably unaware of the scrolls hurriedly concealed in the numerous caves up on the escarpment. We knew that even in the twentieth century it was highly probable that further scrolls lay concealed in collapsed caves. Indeed, three months after our visit in November 1995 the Israelis were to announce that they had located several new man-made caves in the escarpment upon which we now stood.

We thought about the fate of the people who had lived at Qumran and the alternative lifestyle that it offered. Would new scrolls shed fur-ther light on the Essenes and on the Jerusalem of the first century? We were aware that 'civilisation' and the temptations of Jerusalem were but two days journey to the west. But then, as now, the remoteness was complete. We were convinced that this was the perfect territory for the development of prophecy and the preparation for a messianic age. It remained significant that the apostle Paul had departed from Jerusalem towards the west, to Rome and the heart of the Empire. In the opposite direction, to the east, lay more wilderness and the desert, a place of little potential for the expansion of the message he wished to convey.

There is no concrete evidence that Jesus was himself an Essene, although Barbara Thiering puts forward a convincing argument that he was.[9] If Jesus had been influenced by the messianic expectations of the Essenes, then he had played out the role of Davidic messiah to the point of tragedy. But the Essenes had awaited a messiah who would restore the rightful ritual of sacrifice to the Temple, and Jesus had clearly not achieved this, and perhaps had not attempted to.

However, there is no doubt that the example Jesus set during his own lifetime, and the core of his teachings, appeared to have much in common with the tenets of Gnosticism. And the Essenes can be described as being influenced by certain aspects of ancient Gnosticism, as is evident in their description of the forces of light and dark in the War Scroll, found in the caves above Qumran. We left the site at Qumran more aware of the distinction between ancient Gnosticism and Christian Gnosticism; our thoughts then turned to the Jerusalem Passover of AD 33, when Jesus had been condemned to die on the cross.

The fate of Jesus' bones

If Jesus *was* crucified, as reported in the New Testament, did he succumb to the punishment, and what happened to his body afterwards? The only answer to the first question is provided by the New Testament, as no alternative account of the passion and crucifixion has survived. Josephus, the Jewish Zealot commander turned Roman historian, wrote a history of his people, *The History of the Jews*, and it is here that we find possibly the earliest, and most significant example of the manipulation of original texts to further the resurrection story of Jesus.

The origin of the Josephan texts has come under intense scrutiny. There are those who suspect that Josephus's eyewitness accounts of events in Herodian Judea were later edited by Christian publishers; they certainly have a suspiciously pro-Christian bias. Such a bias is completely out of context with the experiences of a man who was by first choice a Jewish Zealot and subsequently – out of an instinct for survival – a convert to the Roman Empire. The standard Josephan text, translated from the Greek by Christian scholars, describes the life of Jesus in the following way:[10]

> About this time there lived Jesus, a wise man, if indeed one ought to call him a man. For he was the one who wrought surprising feats and was a teacher of such people who accept the truth gladly. He won over many Jews and many of the Greeks. He was the Messiah. When Pilate, upon hearing him accused by men of the highest standing amongst us, had condemned him to be crucified, those who had in the first place come to love him did not give up their affection for him. On the third day he appeared to them restored to life, for the prophets of God had prophesied these and countless other marvellous things about him.

The year 1971 saw a major find in the continuing search for the truth behind the Gospel accounts. Shlomo Pines, of Jerusalem's Hebrew University, identified a discrepancy between this Christianised version of Josephus and a tenth-century version written by Agapius and preserved in the Arab book *Kitab al'Unwan*. While we knew of its existence, we had little success in tracking it down in either the Taylor Institute or the Bodleian Library, but a copy was located for us in the University Library of Haifa. Pines has done an immense amount of work into early manuscripts found in Middle-Eastern monasteries, but his work has received little publicity – hence the problem of getting hold of his work in England. The photocopies of the relevant sections duly arrived and did indeed confirm the existence of an early interpretation of Josephus's work and some subtle but highly significant differences. The passage quoted above is presented as follows:[11]

> At this time there was a wise man called Jesus. His conduct was good, and he was known to be virtuous [or his learning/ knowledge was outstanding]. And many people from among the Jews and the other nations became his disciples. Pilate condemned him to be crucified and to die. But those who had become his disciples did not abandon his discipleship. They reported that he had appeared to them three days after his crucifixion, *and that he was alive*: accordingly he was *perhaps the Messiah*, concerning whom the prophets have recounted wonders. (Crossan's interpolation; our italics)

There are three possible explanations for the difference in tone between the two passages: an Arabic bias as to the status of Jesus; the benefit of several centuries of hindsight; or a reflection of the original words used by Josephus. The last of these was to gain considerable substance as we delved further.

The Arabic version is significant as it retains the detachment of the author in a style consistent with the rest of his 'histories.' The discrepancy in tone between the two exposes the first Western text to accusations of tampering, and the deliberate promotion of a doctrine established as the central pillar of faith in the Church of Christ: that is, the truly Messianic status of Jesus of Nazareth, fully proven by his Resurrection from the kingdom of the dead. The existence of the Agapius version of Josephus also clarifies another area of possible doubt. It would seem highly unlikely that this document, which included the accounts of the destruction of the Temple and the siege of Masada (now substantiated by archaeological excavation), would include an episode of history which was totally false. We can therefore deduce that the crucifixion of Jesus *did* take place, and that his disciples promoted him as the long-awaited prophet from the line of David. The existence of a later altered version of the same text can only add proof to the former's originality.

Judged solely on the basis of historical evidence, the Agapius translation of Josephus possesses a far greater claim to authenticity than the Christianised version. The claim that Jesus rose from the dead is cast in doubt, as Agapius makes it quite clear that following the crucifixion Jesus was seen *alive*, but not that he was *restored to life*. So, if Jesus did not die but survived, what became of him? And if he did die on the cross, where was his unresurrected body subsequently taken? If, as we believed, his remains had found their way to southern France, it was now time to consider the various options.

Three hypotheses

1. Jesus survived the crucifixion and travelled in person to the Languedoc.
2. His embalmed body was brought to the area by family and friends.
3. His burial place in Jerusalem was discovered by the Knights Templar, and his remains brought to France on their return from the Holy Land.

If the family of Herod had ended their earthly days familiar with the landscape of the Languedoc,[12] the thought that Jesus of Nazareth had followed in their footsteps seemed, in the light of the possibility that he had survived the crucifixion, increasingly plausible. With such eminent figures arriving from Palestine shortly after AD 33, who would find anything unusual in the passage of one more Jew to shores which had offered sanctuary to the exiled and the fallen?

Even if Christ had not reached the heights of Rennes alive, legend and tradition had it that his body, in form unresurrected, did. Protected by his family, the embalmed body or his bones could perhaps have been successfully transported and concealed from the knowledge of all but a select few.

His burial in Jerusalem and retrieval by the Knights Templar was the third possibility. The unexplained excavations conducted by the Order under the Temple Mount have over the years pointed the finger of suspicion at the Order's true motives in establishing their organisation on that site in the Holy City. If nothing else, this episode demonstrated a marked predisposition towards tunnelling, an activity which we now believed was essential if the location given on Cardou was to conceal such a valuable treasure. And the Templars had of course provided us with a vital clue in the form of the map of Jerusalem containing the secret geometry: a map within a map which tied the empty sepulchre of Jesus in Jerusalem with the *new* sepulchre of Jesus on Mount Cardou.

If the remains of Jesus of Nazareth had since Roman times been hidden in Jerusalem or in the area of Rennes-le-Château, could they have survived the years leading up to the Templar era, and where had they been concealed in the interim? The use of embalming was widespread and fully developed at the time of Christ. Jerusalem lay at the hub of the great trading routes which entered from Syria, the Lebanon and Jordan, with Mesopotamia and the Indian subcontinent beyond. Herbs, spices and the aloe which Joseph of Arimathea is said to have taken to the tomb of Jesus would have been abundant in the markets of first-century Jerusalem.

Aloe and myrrh were commonly used for embalming. Embalming involved the introduction of preservatives into the body once it had been drained of blood and the vital organs removed. Following this process, the body would eventually become mummified. We knew from our own researches that the Templars were familiar with a sophisticated version of this practice, for in the nineteenth century a tomb of a Templar knight was opened in Britain. The lead-lined sarcophagus revealed a surprise to the Victorian correspondent of the *Gentleman's Magazine*.[13] The onlookers observed the body of a youth, perfectly preserved, floating in a liquid which tasted of catsup. Whereas the thought of tasting the embalming fluid employed by the Templars might offend even the coarsest of sensibilities today, this episode illustrates the expertise utilised by the embalmer of the fourteenth century, a science undoubtedly inherited if not enhanced by the knights during their sojourn in the Near East.

But aloe has a more common application, which is still practised today: it is well known for its capacity to heal heavy bruising and in assisting in the alleviation of trauma. If the first hypothesis – that Jesus survived the crucifixion – is correct, then Joseph must have exerted himself greatly in the days immediately following, as he is said to have carried to the tomb no less than thirty kilograms of the herb mixture, certainly enough to administer to a body, badly bruised and shocked to the point of death.[14]

Exit of a Messiah

Whether Christ had succumbed to the ordeal of crucifixion or had survived to die in another place would make no difference to his embalming, provided the experts, the materials and the instruments were at hand. It is possible that the Templars had inherited the mummified body, preserved and hidden at a location such as Arques; hence, perhaps, the name ARCA, and the many allusions to forms such as 'Arcadia' and its adoption in Poussin's *Les Bergers d'Arcadie*. The inclusion of Arques in the de Nègre gravestone geometry had come as an additional and tantalising clue that the Château d'Arques held secrets waiting to be uncovered. Legend has it that the land on which the château is built had a previous occupant – a monastery. That later in its life it was sold to a Templar *commanderie* at Peyrolles was also significant. Had the remains been held in the environs of the monastery, later to be moved to a safer and more controllable location by the Templars themselves?

The evidence of archaeology, the study of the most recently discovered fragments of the Dead Sea Scrolls, and one's personal experiences of mortality do not support the idea of the bodily Resurrection. The study of various motives which lay behind the behaviour of the founding members of the Christian church reinforce this logical conclusion. The evidence given by Josephus about the survival of a personal friend when released from the cross following his intervention establishes a solid historical precedent for a triumph over death, not by resurrection but by *resuscitation*. Barbara Thiering, in her work *Jesus the Man*, categorically states that Jesus survived the crucifixion and lived to enjoy the fruits of old age. Thiering approaches the New Testament with a remarkable theory, the use of the 'Pesher' or coded message concealed within the words of the text.[15] Thus a simple statement from the New Testament can, according to Thiering, have another, precise meaning. From her studies she claims to have established that Jesus did leave Jerusalem following his crucifixion and that he (and his family) may have found refuge in the south of France, on Herodian estates, thus giving rise to the legend of the Grail.[16] In her most recent book,[17] following further research, she claims that Jesus died and was buried in or around Rome sometime after AD 70. If Jesus had indeed been the recipient of life-saving ministrations by Joseph of Arimathea, his future would have been decidedly insecure in a country where he was well known. While the Romans and the Sanhedrin believed him dead – a problem dealt with and, quite literally, buried – spies in the province abounded, and the even more rural area of Galilee, which would have shown much sympathy to a native son, would still have been dangerous. Logic would therefore suggest a departure from the scene.

By the first century, travel within the Roman Empire was relatively straightforward. The commercial influence of the Empire had spread to every area of the Mediterranean coastline, and in many cases, as with the province of Narbonne, further inland. The movement of armies and the development of trade had resulted in an efficient network of routes both overland and across the sea. Roman commercial shipping provided the main means for transporting goods around the Empire. Despite the risks inherent in travel by sea – shipwreck, piracy, and capture by enemy vessels – by the time of Christ the Mediterranean area was so well controlled by the Romans that shipwreck was the only significant risk faced by entrepreneurial shipowners. The appetite of Rome for rare goods, foodstuffs, raw materials and manpower was voracious, and the number of ships plying the waters rose to fill the increasing demands. These vessels, small by modern standards, coursed the length and breadth of the Mediterranean and provided an alternative mode of transport for travellers unwilling to embark on longer journeys by land.

The development of underwater research around the Mediterranean coast in the twentieth century has yielded a more complete picture of Roman shipping. Entire ships with much of their hull still intact have been found in the sand on the bottom of the seabed. In some cases their cargoes of foodstuff sealed in amphorae have been found perfectly preserved. Such finds testify to a minority of unsuccessful voyages, but given favourable winds, ideally during the summer months, most maritime traffic reached its destination. There is no doubt that the Roman shipping network could have plucked an exile from the dusty shores of the eastern Mediterranean and released him at a port in southern France with discretion and ease.

If Jesus had survived the crucifixion, to walk out of Jerusalem and into exile, the western end of the Mediterranean would have been an excellent destination. It was well served by merchant routes, and the colony which had grown up and spread inland from the port of Narbonne was home to a large and influential Jewish population. (The presence of Jews in the Languedoc of the first century was not unusual; Jews at this time made up about a tenth of the Empire's population.) A rapid expansion into the interior of Gaul, a country spacious and rich both agriculturally and in mineral deposits, had attracted Jewish entrepreneurs. The conditions for Jesus' continued survival were certainly favourable, and this leads us on to another of the theories about his post-crucifixion status – that he arrived in the Languedoc with the pregnant Mary Magdalene, thereby establishing a bloodline – later to become the Merovingian dynasty – which exists to this day. The legendary treasure of King Dagobert II, King of the Merovingians, and his marriage to Gizelle de Razès on the site of Saunière's church at Rennes-le-Château, now came under our scrutiny.

Much has been written about this union, not least in *The Holy Blood and the Holy Grail*. The historical verification rests upon the authenticity, or otherwise, of the 'Lobineau' documents, registered in the Bibliothèque Nationale in Paris. The theory proposed by the authors of the above book – that Jesus arrived *en famille* in the Languedoc and that the later Merovingian dynasty helped perpetuate his line – is not one which bears any relevance to our story, except to concur with the theory that Jesus enjoyed all the faculties of a mortal human being. Having found no supporting documentary evidence apart from the Lobineau documents, we concluded that the story surrounding Dagobert was, like the claims to the bloodline, unsubstantiable. Similarly, the association of the Merovingians with Arcadia seemed to contradict well-established research. The Merovingians' ancestors, according to archaeological evidence, came from an area east of the Rhine, and had struck west towards France where they established their dynastic kingdoms.[18] There is no evidence to support their own folkloric belief in their origin in Troy, or – as the author of one of the Priory Documents would have it – Arcadia. For us, therefore, these claims of bloodline were irrelevant to our own investigation, not least in respect of our own accumulation of evidence surrounding the mystery of Rennes. This pointed not to a bloodline but to the basic element without which all other conjecture was superfluous: the true history of the crucifixion and the subsequent fate of Jesus, and what his survival or death meant to the expectant Jews of Judea.

The message of Jesus had struck a chord of hope and liberation. The assumption that his body remained in a physical state would have been acceptable to the Hellenic Judaeo-Christians; the requirement for his body to have undergone physical resurrection was not a prerequisite for belief in his teaching. To guarantee the success of the movement, however, the belief that God had intervened and raised Jesus from the dead, leaving an empty tomb, had obvious potential, but then the reappearance of a body would prove a huge embarrassment. This argument adds weight to the need for the removal of Jesus from the scene, either dead or alive. If Jesus had died at the Passover, his Jewish family and friends and *not* the Romans would have been responsible for the disposal of his corpse; the task could have been allocated to Joseph of Arimathea, but this is impossible to prove as there are no accounts other than those in the Gospels.

As we studied these events and the early origins of the Christian Church in the light of our discovery of the Secret, we came to appreciate that the teachings of Jesus contain the essence of ancient Gnosticism – respect for the individual and the right to self-determination, based on personal responsibility. James's Church of Jerusalem and the followers of Jesus who had not been influenced by Paul and his doctrine of the Resurrection had returned to the legacy of Gnosticism, and from this remnant grew Christian Gnosticism.

The Christians who followed Paul and the New Testament ardently believed that Jesus had bodily resurrected. The Christian Gnostics, by contrast, were under no such illusion: to them, Jesus was the mortal son of Mary and as such his spirit would have left his body on death to return to the cosmos. Jesus' importance to the Christian Gnostic was in no way diminished by this – he was still the single figure of their adoration as the enlightened prophet who spoke the wisdom of God. Indeed, as he had been filled by the divine spark, he was the mortal manifestation of the God of the cosmos. This would explain why the existence of his body became of such importance to select groups of people such as the Templars and the Rosicrucians in succeeding centuries.

How did the established Church react to such heresy within its ranks?

The preservation of Christian Gnosis: the gospels of Nag Hammadi

Today, the Church prefers to remain silent on the question of Christian Gnosticism; indeed, most Christians are unaware of this aspect of the origin of their faith. The discovery this century of the Gnostic gospels of Nag Hammadi has revealed that, for many of the early Christians, the road to Roman Catholicism had not been a question of choice. During the second and third centuries, the early Roman Church waged a fierce battle against the people they recognised as the real proponents of heresy: the Christian Gnostics.

The battle was fought to protect the cornerstone of early Church doctrine – the belief in Christ as the resurrected son of God – and as such necessitated the exclusion of the more esoteric meanderings of philosophy and self-resurrection exercising the mind of the Gnostic.

To the Christian Gnostics of the second and third centuries, Jesus was a figure of importance. They believed that Jesus was a Divine Being, filled with the spark of divine knowledge, which had allowed him to fulfil a role of instruction to others who searched for the Gnostic way, and thus achieve communion with the supreme being, the God of the cosmos. To the Church of Rome this stance was heretical to the core, challenging as it did the basic tenets of its doctrine. As the bishops of Rome rose to positions of power and influence in the provinces of the Roman Empire, so the Gnostics suffered, and their message became subdued.

The discovery in 1945 of the Nag Hammadi gospels in Upper Egypt uncovered a precious and illuminating record of this long-forgotten battle, casting new light on the possible fate of Jesus and the condemnation of Gnosticism by the Church of Rome – condemnation which has lasted to the present day.[19] The Nag Hammadi library, preserved like that at Qumran in jars of terracotta, consists of fifty-two separate tracts, and was first published in English in 1977.[20] The process of translation was frustratingly protracted, and if scholars were dragging their feet it is easy to see why. Typical of many, the Gospel of Thomas is startling. This mixture of parable, proverb and prophecy, dated to the first century of the Christian era, mirrors the events later to be described in the New Testament of the Pauline Church. The Gospel of Thomas, however, contains one instruction that Christians of Pauline persuasion would certainly not wish to reproduce or repeat. In the twelfth saying, the disciples question Jesus on the future:

We know that you will depart from us. Who is to be our leader?

The response of Jesus is telling:

Wherever you are, you are to go to James the righteous, for whose sake heaven and earth came into being.

If this gospel is repeating the true words of Jesus, there can be no doubt of his own intentions for the future Church: James was to lead it, and his stance as upholder of the Mosaic law – which excluded the Gentiles – was unambiguous. When the disciples ask what death holds for them, Jesus says this:

Have you discovered, then, the beginning, that you look for the end? For where the beginning is, the end will be. Blessed is he who will take his place in the beginning: he will know the end and *will not experience death*. (our italics)

Resurrection of the spirit, *during one's natural lifetime*, is the clear implication of this message. Resurrection of the body, and in particular the body of Jesus – the message of the Gentile Church of Rome founded by Paul – is a concept far removed from the scenario of such Gnostic Christianity. The message we had received, as investigators of the history surrounding the affair of Rennes, was clarified by this extraordinary gospel. These documents, which contravened the doctrine of the Roman Church to the point of heresy by questioning the status of Jesus as the physically resurrected son of God, had survived the diaspora of the early Church of Jerusalem and highlighted the difference between Gnostic and Pauline Christians. The existence of the physical remains of Jesus must therefore have become a burning issue to enquiring minds.

18
IN THE NAME
OF JESUS

With the facts surrounding the crucifixion reappraised and the alternatives investigated, what light could the record of the early Christian Church, and the Roman Catholic Church it subsequently became, throw on our findings? How had Christian Gnosticism, and its belief in the unresurrected Jesus, managed to survive? For survive it had, despite the drastic and unremitting efforts of the Roman Church over the centuries. The hunt for heretics began well before the Middle Ages. In the earliest centuries of the Christian Church, the Christian Gnostics and many other small groups of Christians who had placed their own diverse and individual interpretations on the messianic behaviour of Jesus found themselves directly in the firing line of the Roman Church. The fourth century was a busy period for the ecclesiastical pen, and the records it left allow us an insight into the crucial years of the social establishment of the Church of Rome – a period in which the religious course of the West would be set for the next sixteen hundred years, and greatly influence the society into which we ourselves have been born.

By the fourth century after the birth of Jesus, the Christians established in Rome had found that wealth accompanied influence. After the initial years of persecution they became, unlike their priestly and distant desert cousins, materially enriched. The fourth century saw the writing of *The Ecclesiastical History* by Eusebius, who eventually became bishop of his adopted city, Caesarea. This work, which forms the pillar of early Roman Catholic history, was written in the same century as the concealment of the Nag Hammadi gospels, and less than three centuries after the concealment of the Dead Sea Scrolls, one hundred kilometres to the east at Qumran. The Dead Sea Scrolls and the Nag Hammadi gospels would together provide a dormant testimony to the true origins of Christianity.

Eusebius had begun a search for heretics, and the Christian Gnostics were firmly in his sights. History was to demonstrate that heresy was not, however, to be eradicated by mere propaganda for the Church of Rome. If elements of rogue Christianity existed, casting doubt on the Resurrection of Jesus, sterner action would be needed to dampen Gnostic spirits. But a secret will always find someone to covet it, and the suppression of Gnostic belief pushed the heretical thoughts of the Jerusalem Church of James into the underworld of hidden knowledge – an underworld the medieval Church would be quick to label as diabolic.

During the first and second centuries the Christian Church prevailed against attacks on its belief, as well as serious physical persecution of its adherents. The reign of Constantine has long been promoted by Church historians as the turning-point in the Church's fortunes. There can be no doubt that it marked a watershed in the survival of the Roman Catholic Church, guaranteeing a doctrine that stood in stark contrast to that of the Jerusalem Church. Constantine, who succeeded to the throne in the early years of the third century, inherited an Empire well populated with Christians. These Christians, despite their differences of opinion with the pagans and the intermittent persecution of their number, had succeeded in establishing themselves within the framework of Roman law. The reported conversion of Constantine had followed the battle of Milvan Bridge in the year 312, a battle which saw the defeat of Maxentius and allowed Constantine unrivalled succession over the whole of the Western Empire. The removal of Lucinius, ruler of the Eastern Empire, was to follow in the fullness of time, leaving Constantine sole emperor and ruler by the year 324. Constantine's action after Milvan Bridge surprised all his subjects, including the Christians. It was presented by theological historians as a battlefield conversion to Pauline Christianity, but the truth is somewhat different.

Constantine had declared before the battle that if victory was to grace his efforts he would embrace the religion of the Christian cult, and he had his reasons. Prior to the battle, the god Sol Invictus, pagan god of the sun, had filled Constantine's religious horizon to the exclusion of all others. With victory came thanks, and recognition of the power of Christianity. His subsequent conversion to Jesus was no more than a shift of deities; Constantine, as emperor, was still the regal and mortal intermediary between the people and their supreme maker. The monotheistic structure of Christianity was recognised by Constantine as possessing an intrinsic political strength, giving him an advantage over the rival kingdoms which surrounded the Empire. His choice was to be thoroughly tested over the succeeding centuries, and the adoption of Christianity proved to be fortuitous for the emperor and his successors.

The inheritance of the apostle Paul – the concept of Jesus as the risen son of God – provided the basis for a better-defined creed, or set belief, in the Church he had generated. By the reign of Constantine, disagreement between the bishops of the Church concerning the precise nature of this creed had reached a climax. The argument raged around the definition of God and the status of his son, Jesus Christ. The Council of Nicea was duly convened in 325 to address the thorny issue. Did Jesus, as the Arian faction (the followers of the priest Arius) held, derive from God as a part of overall creation, or was he, as the more biblically motivated bishops maintained, a manifested part of a single Godhead? The biblical lobby won the day, and the creed which was declared as final has formed the backbone of Christian theology to the present day. The son Jesus was declared to be:[1]

> True God of true God,
>
> Begotten, not made,
>
> Being of one substance with the father.

This declaration left scant leeway for discussion, and no room for a Gnostic view of Jesus as having more earthly, human origins. It effectively contradicted the Gnostic interpretation of Jesus' life as a shining example of one man's, one *mortal* man's, ability to achieve the ultimate state of grace within his own lifetime. Jesus, the Church eventually declared, was not conceived naturally, and therefore the 'knowledge' he had achieved was not available to all; indeed, it would become the grossest heresy from this point on to say that it was.

It was in the face of this intransigence that the concealment of the Nag Hammadi gospels can be more easily understood, for they did portray a very different interpretation of the life of the Messiah. Pauline Christianity, which offered the promise of salvation following death, held the believer to moral ransom. Jesus, the Church declared, had died to expiate the sins of the world. The true Christian was therefore beholden to such a sacrifice made on his or her behalf. The Roman Catholic Church, with a 'Pope' or father at its head, represented the word of Jesus on earth and as such expected the obedience of the populace. It was therefore inevitable that the growth in the power of the Church was matched by a growth in fear of the Gnostics and of the secret truths they held concerning the Resurrection and the sayings of Christ.

The balance established by Constantine between Church and state was set to endure until the Reformation and beyond, with varying degrees of oscillation. But the incorporation of the Church within the highest levels of state business came with a price. Guilt would become the common currency of the Church. If, prior to the battle of Milvan Bridge, the pagan Western kingdoms ever possessed a sense of humour, it was destined to vanish with the acceptance of Pauline Christianity. Original sin would be the next cudgel with which to beat the free-believer. The destiny of Western man passed in a single moment from the Hellenic vision of the free individual bound to personal destiny to the moral strictures of state Christianity. During the break-up of the Roman Empire and the turbulent years of the Dark Ages, the Church of Rome successfully consolidated its control by converting the new leaders of the Western kingdoms. Constantine had opened the door to the Christians. The gateway to Gnostic self-realisation, which had begun to close at this moment, became, like the knowledge of the gospels of Nag Hammadi and the writings of the Dead Sea Scrolls, firmly barred – save to a very few.

But what of Jerusalem, the Temple Mount, the other places that had rung with the voices of Jesus, James and Paul? Constantine was quick to see the need to provide his people with 'proof' of the life of Jesus through the medium of shrines and sacred places. Until this point the last resting-place of Jesus had not been a place of worship, or indeed of much interest at all. At Constantine's instigation the empty 'tomb' of Jesus was officially discovered, and pilgrimage to the city and the holy sites much encouraged. This open-door policy to the consecrated sites of Jerusalem continued for many years after the death of Constantine. It was only in the seventh century that it came to an abrupt halt when the Islamic conquest of Jerusalem removed the Holy City from Western juridical influence, a situation which was to last until the Crusaders broke through the walls in July 1099.

The Christian Son of God

The interval of the Dark Ages and the Islamic conquest of Palestine had removed the threat of any remnants of Judean Gnostic heresy infecting the doctrine of the Pauline Church. One other change, central to the development of the medieval view, resulted from this involuntary exile: the 'Gentilisation' of Jesus was successfully engineered by the Church. Jesus was no longer to be confused with the Jewish messiah who may have followed the path of an Essene Gnostic, upholding as he did so the Mosaic law of his forefathers, and attempting the fulfilment of a prophecy. Jesus, indeed, was no longer a Jew – he was the Christ who had suffered at the hands of the Romans, and whose fate had been sealed by the duplicity of the Jews.

In this historical vacuum which separated the Near East from the West, the New Testament, with its uniform accounts of the life and passion of Jesus of Nazareth, reigned supreme, unchallenged by any unauthorised and heretical Gnostic texts that might have survived from the time of James, the brother of Jesus. This stance was to be revised and enhanced at the end of the eleventh century, when the Catholic Church launched the First Crusade. This call to arms followed the conquest of Jerusalem by the Seljuk Turks, whose indiscriminate attacks on Christian pilgrims forcibly ended an era of relative tolerance by the Arabs towards the passage of pilgrims travelling to the Holy City, which had been under their control for the previous four hundred years.

One group would suffer greatly from the mad enthusiasm which followed the call to arms by the Pope. These were the original occupants of Jerusalem and Judea, now also dispersed throughout the Western kingdoms – the Jews. If heretics were accorded a trial, albeit a mock one, the Jews were accorded none. The history of the First Crusade, which gave rise to the Templar Order, encapsulates the indiscriminate cruelty of the age. The behaviour of the crusaders, much documented by both sides in the conflict, provides a vivid background to the establishment of the Order of the Knights Templar in *c.* 1120, at the Temple Mount in Jerusalem.

The Knights Templar

There are many legends surrounding the Knights Templar, certain of which – the ownership of land around Rennes-le-Château, and their curious adoption of the Rose Cross – had been found to have a very relevant bearing on both the location on Cardou and the nature of the 'treasure' itself. It was now appropriate to consider further what they were alleged to be defending in Jerusalem, and what, in time, they would come to defend in France.

The considerable influence they wielded has led to much speculation about their actual role. From the moment of its foundation, the Order had special privileges which set it apart from the rest of society. The Templars' charter bound them to the role of protectors of the pilgrim routes to Jerusalem. Their vow of chastity, poverty and obedience also confirmed the Order in its declaration of loyal service to its Grand Master and fellow brothers.

The image of the Order caught the imagination of monarchy and subjects alike, and special dispensation from taxes and duties followed swiftly wherever the Order established *commanderies* or recruited members from the community. The increasing power of the Templars rapidly outgrew their initially modest aspirations. Delicate diplomatic tasks were assigned to members of the Order, leading to contact with the enlightened minds of the Arab Empire from which they undoubtedly prospered, learning of the sciences of the ancient Greek and Roman worlds – knowledge either long forgotten or deliberately subdued.

In the aftermath of the capture of the Holy City by the crusading knights of the West in 1099, Hugues de Payens and Geoffrey de Saint-Omer established a headquarters for their new Order within the palace precincts on the Temple Mount. By the time of the Order's inauguration during the reign of Baldwin II, King of Jerusalem, a nucleus of men around Hugues and Geoffrey formed a centre of power. Jerusalem and its environs lay literally at their feet. The exact date for the founding of the Templar Order still remains in doubt today, with references to a 'milice du Christ' present in the Holy City by 1114, and conflicting evidence from chroniclers.[2] For the first nine years of its existence, the Order expanded little beyond the original band of nine knights who had sworn loyalty and obedience to their Master and to the Pope.

The Templars, although small in number at the time of their return to France in 1127, were soon to become an extremely effective military force. However, they had not confined their activities in Jerusalem to the fight against the Saracen. Another activity had captured their imagination – they had learned to excavate.

Within a generation, the leading Templars, in the company of their first Grand Master, Hugues de Payens, would leave Palestine to further the cause of their brotherhood in Europe. They left Jerusalem having conducted excavations under the Temple Mount itself, evidence of which still exists today. They were no longer the 'Poor Knights' of the Order's full title; and there has been much conjecture over their excavations and the treasure they reputedly found. So what did the Templars discover during their digging? In the absence of conclusive evidence, one can speculate that they found wealth in the form of gold coin or other treasures, which would certainly have improved their economic circumstances. But they were not lacking in rich patronage, as the bequests from sympathetic individuals testify. The mystery that surrounds the Order to this day, combined with the very real clue they left in the map of Jerusalem, implies a very different sort of discovery.

Jerusalem in the twelfth century would have contained ancient sites and cemeteries dating back to the Roman era. Jewish cemeteries, containing tombs from the Herodian dynasty, would have been identifiable as such to the twelfth-century visitor, and disturbing them would have posed little in the way of moral dilemma to the Templar: the inhabitants were 'pagan'. If it was not the remains of Jesus that the Templars found under the Temple Mount, had they – by accident or design – uncovered the entrance to a tomb of the first century, and did this tomb contain an ossuary that would provide them with proof as to the fate of Jesus, a fate which differed greatly from the Gospel accounts? Not only did the Templar map of Jerusalem tie the Order directly to the secret location on Cardou, but the centre of the square when drawn on to this map fell above the sepulchre of Jesus. This had confirmed our suspicions that certain undefined elements of the Order had participated in the preservation of the Secret, which we were now certain alluded to the remains of Christ, preserved and concealed, locatable by secret geometry and attested by the Gnostic teachings so assiduously repressed by the Church.

The Templars and Gnosticism

In the embryonic stages of the Church, Paul had made allowances for heresy, declaring it a useful way of marking the believer from the unbeliever, but by the twelfth century such woolly liberalism had either been forgotten or was simply ignored. However, the departure from the message of Paul held grave consequences for the future of all European Christian nations. It heralded a descent into intolerance which had only one possible outcome: the stifling of social progress and the continuing repression of the individual's right to self-determination. The Albigensian Crusade against the Cathars in the twelfth century marked the beginning of formal religious conflict between Christians, conducted with the backing of state power, that would culminate in the wars of religion in the sixteenth and seventeenth centuries. So what had gone wrong?

Why had the Church, with a figurehead as exemplary as Jesus of Nazareth, entered so enthusiastically into the oppression of fellow-Christians? Part of the answer lies in the origins of the Christian Church and the problem of putting Jesus' words into action. There can be little doubt that Jesus was a revolutionary, and that the message he promoted was so highly altruistic that its full acceptance in any hierarchical society would prove impossible because the very hierarchy would be undermined. His fine and egalitarian ideals suffered the moment they were extended into the community. Christianity could claim success, but did it reflect the true message of Jesus? For many, from the Judaeo-Christian Nazarenes to the Cathars of the Languedoc, the true message had died with the election of the first pope of Rome, and the real tragedy of the life of Jesus was the manner in which his words had been distorted.

Our research had uncovered the use of coded information which led us through the mystery of the Parchments found by Saunière. The Templars themselves had employed a cipher at the highest level of their organisation. The Atbash cipher, identified by the late Hugh Schonfield, has provided us with the intriguing possibility that the Templar leaders had been exposed to the influences of a Christian Gnosticism still surviving in the Near East. By using the Hebrew alphabet, the Atbash cipher made possible a systematic conversion of words which completely disguised a message. The use of this subterfuge was simple, and shows much in common with the Pesher code employed in the Dead Sea Scrolls. In relating a simple, innocuous story to the uninformed reader, it was possible to offer the initiated the true facts of an alternative event at the same time. The cipher permitted a superior informed group to be granted access to information concealed in the manuscript.

During the trial of the Knights Templar in 1307, an accusation was levelled at the Grand Master and other senior members of the Order. The inquisitors asked for an explanation of the use of the word 'Baphomet' during closed ceremonies of Templar initiation. Despite the use of prolonged torture, the trial judges had to satisfy themselves with their own inference that the Templars were invoking a corruption of the name of Muhammad, while at the same time spitting on the holy cross. The answer, as we now perceived, was different but equally condemning. The Atbash method applied to the word 'Baphomet' converts it to 'Sophia', the female figure familiar as a symbol to those of the Gnostic way. In Greek, Sophia means 'wisdom', and as communicator between light and dark she remains central to the development of individuals wishing to experience the resurrection of the soul within their earthly lifetime. The Nag Hammadi library includes a Gospel of the Sophia of Jesus Christ, so the Templar use of such a bizarre word as Baphomet is less perplexing. By the twelfth century, allusion to

Gnosis was perilous in the extreme; hence the use of the Atbash cipher.

By the beginning of the fourteenth century, less than two centuries after their humble beginnings, the Templars wielded power and influence on an international level. Power had also brought envy, and to the French monarchy the supposed wealth of the order had become irresistible, particularly for a king like Philip-le-Bel, who would later direct his avarice and powers of persecution towards the Jews of the Languedoc. The papacy, despite its intimate links with the Templar Order, withdrew support, leaving the king free to pursue the destruction of the Order. In 1307 he struck, arresting all Templars in France – or at least arresting all those he could get his hands on, for a number, sensing the tide was turning against them, had previously fled to territories more sympathetic to their cause.

The Celestines

In 1260, forty-seven years before the demise of the Templar Order and at the height of its influence and power, a Calabrian hermit founded the Order of the Celestines. In 1294, after a period of two years in which the papal throne had been vacant, he was elected Pope. This saintly man of humble origins, born Pietro da Morrone, became Pope Celestine V, the portrait of whom Bérenger Saunière apparently had in his baggage on his return from Paris in 1892.

Whoever had commissioned the painting of the coronation of Pope Celestine V had recognised the Gnostic qualities of Celestine's life, deeming it to be a highly appropriate subject in which to preserve the secret geometry. In view of the tragedy that would later befall him, Celestine can, in the light of history, be judged the victim of his own saintly virtues.

The beginning of the century had seen the suppression of the Cathar heresy under the might of the Albigensian Crusade and the establishment of the Dominican Order as the new 'Militia of Christ' – the spiritual shock-troops of Rome. The Church was still on the attack against declared or suspected heresy, and any hint of Gnosticism was to be eradicated. The Cathar belief was firmly rooted in the Gnostic belief in self-fulfilment that had so alarmed the fathers of the early Church of Rome. The seeds of heresy had spread westwards from the ruins of the Byzantine Empire, through Italy and into southern France, and by the latter half of the eleventh century the heresy had gained a firm hold in the mountainous regions of the Languedoc. In the year 1176, Raymond, Count of Toulouse, described his city as being overrun with heretics. This marked the beginning of a coalition of forces to combat the situation, backed by Rome and endowed with a terrible and far-reaching mandate. The resulting act of war waged on fellow-Christians was named the Albigensian Crusade due to the great number of Cathars living in and around the city of Albi. Between 1208 and 1256, the 'crusaders' of the Pope rampaged through the 'infected' areas of southern France in a murderous attempt to wipe out the heresy of Catharism for ever. While largely successful, the Church was quick to see that the problem needed to be dealt with once and for all. To this end the first Catholic Inquisition was set up, under the evangelical leadership of St Dominic. The method of the Inquisitors was one of infiltration: to take their tribunals into the mountainous villages of the Languedoc and extinguish any remaining embers of the dualism which rejected the message of Catholic Rome for one of personal salvation.

At the time of the election of Celestine V in 1294, the memory of the Cathar heresy, which had affected Italy as well as France, was still fresh in the mind of the Church. The election of such an unlikely candidate – a monk and former hermit – was therefore seen by the more heretical elements of Christian society as the fulfilment of heavenly prophecy. The Joachimites, followers of Joachim of Fiore, like Celestine a Calabrian, had been awaiting the year 1260, for which there had been prophesied a change in the established order of a Church which they considered, as had the Cathars preceding them, to be corrupt and unrepresentative of the true message of Jesus. The election of Pietro da

Morrone had therefore raised this particular heresy to new heights of expectation. The brief and tragic papal career of this devout man lasted but three and a half months, imprisonment and death following soon afterwards. As his spirit had faded and died during his incarceration in the tower of Fumone, so too had the hopes of the Joachimites for a new era of love and eternal hope, free from Roman Catholic influence, an era they had looked upon Celestine to initiate.

The centuries which saw the rise and fall of the Knights Templar had been a turbulent period in the development of the Church of Rome. Eight crusades had been undertaken, and Jerusalem had come under direct Christian kingship for the first time in history, only to be lost to the Saracen less than ninety years after Godfroi de Bouillon had established his presence on the Temple Mount. The destructive force of the crusades had been turned on fellow-Christians of the Languedoc, and the power of the Inquisition had been directly experienced by thousands. Pope Celestine V had risen to the most powerful position in the Vatican, from where, because of the division among the cardinals of the Church, his very different background and Gnostic leanings might have disturbed the established Church hierarchy, had it not been for his advanced age and lack of political ambition.

The Church had emerged from this hiatus further entrenched, suppressing any challenge to its authority with force. The era of the independent military order was also over, and from that time on the individual monarchies of Western Europe built up their national military strength, a development that would guarantee monarchical supremacy until the advent of the industrial revolution.

The painting of Pope Celestine V by an anonymous sixteenth-century French artist had hung in the Celestine monastery of Marcoussis until the French Revolution and the final dissolution of the Celestine order. The monasteries of this order had flourished after the death of its founder, and enjoyed the patronage of the French nobility to an unusual degree. René d'Anjou was taken to the monastery of Marcoussis at an early age, and continued to have a close association with the Celestines throughout his life: it cannot be coincidence that this man, who was later to become King of Sicily and then titular ruler of Jerusalem, and another alleged Grand Master of the Priory of Sion, would himself perpetuate the secret geometry found in the Parchments.

It seemed likely that an unknown element within the Templar Order had taken the knowledge with them in their flight, and more than just coincidence that the following events should then occur: Templars had reached the safety of Lorraine; then King René, who inherited the duchy by marriage in 1431, commissioned a miniature which contained geometry identical to that found in the Jerusalem Templar map.

The Priory of Sion

If we were looking at the perpetuation of a 'secret' within Templar ranks, then what historical evidence was there to confirm the mysterious 'Priory of Sion' as having had anything to do with the Templars themselves, or for that matter with the secret geometry? We had seen the word SION on the Parchments found by Bérenger Saunière, but what of the evidence for the existence of a 'Priory' with such a title?

Its existence is in fact well documented. Their original name and organisation are mentioned in a charter of 1152, and also in a fourteenth-century copy of an earlier parchment dated 1178.[3] The organisation is reputed to have been founded under the name of the 'Order of Sion', the title Priory of Sion being adopted in 1188. It is reputed to have been a breakaway group from within the ranks of the Knights Templar, though this is disputed. This separation of the Order of Sion in 1188 from the main body of the Templar Order is alleged to have occurred in a legendary episode known as 'The Splitting of the Elm'.

While no Templar link is apparent by way of contemporary

documentation, one connection does remain. René d'Anjou had clearly illustrated the split elm in manuscripts of his own – it occurs in a picture we shall shortly investigate – and some Templar knights had found refuge in the lands of his inheritance.[4] The Priory of Sion had apparently adopted a secondary title, though we doubted the historical accuracy of this claim. This was 'The Order of the Rose Cross Veritas' – similar to the inscription on the porch of Bérenger Saunière's church. However, prompted by this information, we had examined with renewed interest Templar sarcophagi decorated with roses in the Cluny museum in Paris. And Templar inscriptions on the wall of a church at Montsaunes in the Languedoc quite clearly bore the inscription 'Rosa' around the Templar cross.

René d'Anjou and the split at Gisors

We had come to suspect that René d'Anjou may have utilised his artistic interests to leave a clue to the provenance of the geometry incorporated in *La Fontaine de fortune*. Research into surviving documentation brought us to the work of the late professor Otto Pächt, a twentieth-century expert on King René. Pächt had accumulated a wealth of material, and his 1977 work 'René d'Anjou – Studien II' brought the breakthrough we sought. We had read of this document some years before, but since it only exists in its original German form it was not easy to track down. After a wait of several months we obtained a copy from Vienna. A page of a manuscript kept in a St Petersburg museum immediately stood out: depicting the coats of arms of King René and his second wife, Jeanne de Laval, the illustration was revealing (Figure 18.1).

On the left was a split elm, the split running from the top of the tree to the wide base. The top of the dead tree was capped by a black rock from which sprang a new and vibrant shoot. Spreading across the top and towards the right of the painting, the new branch passed through the handles of a chalice from the top of which a flame burned.

This illustration, if not René's own work then certainly of his commission, contained not only the split elm of Gisors, but also the black rock of the Grail painting – suggesting Roc Nègre on the spur of Blanchefort – and the chalice we knew to be the most prized of all René's possessions, the porpyhry chalice reputed to have been used by Jesus during the wedding feast at Cana. This indicated that René had inherited knowledge of the split at Gisors in 1188 and the legendary separation of the Priory of Sion from the Knights Templar. There also existed a link between this and the Lancelot 'Grail' miniature. The black rock against which Lancelot had rested in despair in the latter held the rebirth of the knowledge, depicted in the René manuscript as the flourishing shoot. If Lancelot had turned his gaze to the opposite side of the Sals valley in desperation, fully aware that his state of imperfection prevented his full realisation of the Secret, René by contrast had celebrated the rebirth of the Secret in a way that would be fully explicit to the initiate.

The union of houses through marriage to the youthful Jeanne de Laval had been immortalised in this extraordinary illustration, from which can be drawn only one conclusion. Their personal union had enabled René to complete a picture which had remained divided since 'The Splitting of the Elm' at the field of Gisors. If René was indeed a Grand Master of the Priory of Sion, had his marriage to Jeanne given the Order information they, rather than the Templars, had lost at Gisors? If this was the case, then the conclusion was straightforward. The Templar Order had retained certain information at Gisors for themselves. We knew from the Jerusalem map that the Templars had known of the location, the secret geometry being clearly demonstrated. *La Fontaine de fortune* was completed for René during his second marriage, and contained the secret geometry. There now seemed little doubt: René had reunified a fragmented knowledge – the knowledge of the location at Cardou which contained the Holy Grail, the remains of Jesus Christ.

FIGURE 18.1 The coat of arms of René d'Anjou and his second wife, Jeanne de Laval, and a depiction of a green shoot coming from the 'split elm'.

If the Christian Gnosticism with which the Templars had come into contact, and the secret it held for the initiate, had been suppressed for many centuries under fear of extreme persecution, what of the internal crisis within the Roman Catholic Church itself during the sixteenth century, the crisis that would eventually lead to the Reformation, a time when dissension reached a climax? Was this not a time when circumstances were right for confronting the Church with the greatest of all questions – the whereabouts of the body of the Messiah? The answer to this lies in the aims of the Reformers themselves, and a dissension of a very specific nature.

The Reformation

The passing of René d'Anjou marked the end of an era. The early years of the sixteenth century saw continuing warfare between the realms of the Christian West, a struggle which was to consolidate power and influence in the hands of the principal monarchies, reducing the autonomy of lesser princes such as René. With this shift towards national unity came an increased role for the Church of Rome. If the heresies of the Languedoc had caused the Church such immense concern in the thirteenth century, the advent of the printing press and the consequent increase in the dissemination of information that this innovation brought about was the realisation of their worst nightmare. If the Bible could be translated into the vernacular, printed with relative ease, and become accessible to all, so too could criticism of the Church and its doctrine. The power of Biblical and New Testament interpretation, for so long the unchallenged territory of the priests of Rome, was under threat from the very people who maintained the power of the Church – the Christian believer.

The Reformation was a direct result of the continuing discontent that no argument presented by the Roman Church could dispel. However, the threat posed by the Reformation in Europe differed greatly from that posed by the early Church. The doctrine of the Resurrection was not under threat, nor was the status of the Virgin Mary in doubt. The conflict actually arose out of papal profligacy. The opulence of the Vatican, very visible by the sixteenth century, caused great offence to many a devout and committed Christian, and the printed word added fuel to the fire. Doctrinal disputes followed close behind. What the heretical Gnostics of the thirteenth and fourteenth centuries had failed to achieve, the Reformation movement accomplished with the aid of new technology, and the resulting rift between Protestant and Catholic remained permanent despite all the efforts of the Counter-Reformation.

Although the Protestant breakaway from the Church of Rome was founded in the dissatisfaction of many Christians who regarded the Roman Church as being corrupt, the Protestants were not Gnostics. While the rift in the Church would continue to manifest itself in persecution and war between the two sides for several centuries, the fundamental Pauline doctrine upon which the Church of Rome had established its supremacy remained unchallenged.

Christian Gnosticism, or any allusion to self-determination in any openly manifested form, continued to be successfully repressed by both the Catholic and the Protestant churches. But the concept of individual liberty had never been extinguished, and it emerged again, in central Europe at the beginning of the seventeenth century, in a movement known as the Rosicrucian enlightenment.

19
THE ROSE CROSS:
ITS REBIRTH AND
BENEFACTORS

If Gnosticism had to remain underground throughout the years of the Reformation out of continued fear of persecution, the political and religious situation was soon to change. While the symbolism used by the Templars derived from the Rose Cross, linking the very meridian which passed near Rennes-le-Château with the mortal remains of Jesus, would remain hidden, the wider knowledge of Gnosticism *per se* was not so secret as to prevent it from appearing in print.

The Rosicrucian movement which flowered in Europe owed its origins to an intellectual desire to investigate the inheritance of ancient philosophy and take up the eternal quest for the true origins of the human condition. Rosicrucianism, in the form in which it is known today, announced its rebirth with the publication of the so-called *Rosicrucian Manifestos*, two short tracts which appeared in Germany in 1614–15. Detailing the achievements of one Christian Rosencreutz, described as the founder of the ancient order of the Rose Cross, the publications caused a considerable furore.

This revival of the rosy cross was a bold attempt to illustrate the more esoteric components of Gnosticism. During this revival it found new expression in the promotion of a religious interpretation of alchemy supported by the study of numbers, a science which harked back to the creation of the Temple, and the use of geometry to define the quantity of perfection. The *Manifestos*, and the age of enlightenment they proposed to usher in, burst upon a Europe on the brink of profound change. The Enlightenment in seventeenth- and eighteenth-century France owes its origin largely to the perpetuation of hermetic thought. At the core of this belief, which encapsulated the religious philosophy of tolerance and natural harmony, lay Gnosticism – still viewed by the Church as heretical.

The revival of Pythagoreanism enhanced by Platonism, so obviously revered by Nicolas Poussin, can be seen as an extension of the ancient practice of preserving wisdom through the use of geometry, and in his most famous painting *Les Bergers d'Arcadie II* this was clearly demonstrated. English Freemasonry still contains a degree of initiation described as the 'Rose Arch', and it is in the light of this that the 'Constitution of Freemasons' published in 1723 can be more fully understood. The admission of a new brother is prefaced by the following declaration:[1]

> Adam our first parent, created after the image of God, the great Architect of the Universe, must have had the liberal sciences, particularly Geometry, written on his heart: for ever since the Fall, we find the Principles of it in the heart of his offspring.

The use of a geometry held sacred by the Pythagoreans had been of extreme importance to our research as it indicated the philosophical origins of those who had originally preserved the Secret. The confusion surrounding the revival of Rosicrucianism in the early seventeenth century and the publication of the *Manifestos* had, in our view, effectively shrouded the origins of the order of the Rose Cross and its true significance. Our research had cast new light on its real origins and its links with the Templars, showing that the Rose Cross related to a particular meridian and parallel.

The symbols of Rosicrucianism had constantly cropped up as we had sought the solution to the Parchments, providing a recurring link between the clerics of Rennes-le-Château: Saunière with the Rose and *Croix* over the entrance to his church and his rose-emblazoned chasuble; Abbé Gélis and his gravestone. During our research into the Rosicrucians we had come across a strange symbolic drawing that appeared to encapsulate a number of these recurring features (Figure 19.1). That the rose should have eight petals within eight petals and be prominent was no surprise, but the whole design was contained within a square with diagonals (these are actually the four nails of the crucifixion) and so may be seen as the pyramid plan. At the centre, where the capstone – or pyramidion – would be found, is the figure of Jesus, showing his hands. In the nineteenth century – probably under Masonic influences – it was popular to see in the missing capstone of

FIGURE 19.1 Rosicrucian symbolism – Jesus within the Rose within the Pyramid.

the Great Pyramid the 'stone which the builders refused', because this was to be 'at the head of the corner'. This latter description, which makes little sense when applied to normal buildings, fits perfectly the capstone of a pyramid. Now, these phrases, originally from Psalm 117, were taken up in the New Testament and applied to Jesus Christ, and a new symbolism becomes possible. Jesus becomes the capstone of the pyramid. Casting our minds back to the cipher square, and our visit to *La Croix*, we recall that this psalm was the one that provided the verse on the tablet. And now we may wonder again whether the 'N' of DNS *had* been changed to appear as an 'X' in order to endorse the pyramid–square symbolism.

The Church and the Secret of the Rose

Since it is highly unlikely that at the end of the nineteenth century the Roman Catholic Church had decided that Rosicrucianism formed an integral part of its doctrine, what can be deduced about the extra-curricular affiliations of the three priests of Rennes-le-Château and their contemporaries?

At this point it is worth looking again at one of the most significant conspirators of all – Julien Sacaze, a highly respected academic who compromised his integrity, and therefore his reputation, in order to incorporate the geometry. We have in Sacaze a man with a lot at stake (not least his impressive list of honorific titles) who gambled everything with the false recording of a Roman inscription. The falsification of data is normally associated with a desire for immediate acclaim, or wealth, or both. Examples where the beneficiary is invisible are – within a rare phenomenon – even rarer. The prize must have been great indeed. The cause was obviously one where self was a secondary consideration.

There can be no doubt that the cause was, and still is, the preservation of the Secret, and that its custodians have been Rosicrucians. This would appear to be the appropriate title for this group in the nineteenth century, and it may even have been so in more ancient times, as attested by the rose-covered crosses on Templar gravestones and sarcophagi preserved in the Cluny museum in Paris. When the prime motivation of these elusive organisations is seen to be the preservation and protection of a geographic location, this choice of badge – the equal-armed cross representing the intersection of lines of latitude and longitude at the Site – is appropriate. Confusion with the cross of the crucifixion would have been a bonus as the inherent heresy is concealed. We may also deduce that the colour adopted for the cross of the Templars derives from the cross being 'rosy' or rose-covered – the red rose being visualised – rather than the reverse hypothesis that the cross was intended to be pink. (This latter theory is occasionally proposed, and is derived from the modern French meaning of the word *rose*.) So perhaps it may be appropriate to use the term Rosicrucian for all the various groups of the past, even though they may have gone under a variety of different titles.

If these groups were Rosicrucian, this need not imply that they were always allied. We can see in the variety of devices used to record the location not only a need to spread the net wide, in order to minimise the risk of total loss, but also a struggle for control between factions of the same organisation. More sinister is the role of the Church. It cannot be denied that the involvement of the priesthood at parish-priest level is proven; and, if it is accepted that Saunière's bishop, Billard, has been clearly implicated, at episcopal level as well. But why stop there? For what other interpretation are we now able to put on the relationship between Nicolas Poussin and Cardinal Rospigliosi who, when elected Pope, regretted that Poussin had died before he had been adequately honoured, and honoured as only the Pope was able, with the papal benediction of the *Golden Rose*?

Can we doubt that the Secret is known within the Vatican – at only the highest levels – and perhaps not always by the Pope? Was it really the philosophy of that illuminated philosopher of the sixteenth century,

Giordano Bruno, that led to his ghastly death by burning? Or was it his strange geometric drawings that sealed his fate? And if, as would seem to be implied, a time is awaited when the Secret *is* to be revealed, when the true Resurrection is to occur, it would be essential for the right Pope to be in residence at that moment.

So what of the personalities that we can name in this affair? Curiously, the secular element has been quite successful in maintaining a low profile, whereas the priests have indulged in activities that drew attention to themselves. One would be justifiably surprised to hear that a representative from the Vatican had recently visited Rennes-le-Château, but indeed this has happened.[2] Of course, there will have been some innocuous reason for the visit, but one would have thought that the notoriety of the place would have ensured that it is strictly 'off limits' to the Roman Catholic hierarchy. Any attempt, however, to trace the trail further into the dark recesses of the 'Vatican cellars' is doomed to failure. The Bishop of Carcassonne fired warning shots across the bows of researchers and writers, when in the *Semaine religieuse* of June 1967, M.G. Boyer, Vicaire Général, responded to many of the oft-quoted aspects of the Saunière affair. Denigration of the clergy by implicating them in the Rennes 'affair' would, he said, elicit the appropriate legal response from the 'Association de Défense Sacerdotale'. The good-humoured tone of his statement is overshadowed by the dark warning of the powers of Rome.

Greater success may await an investigation of the secular Rosicrucians, for, despite their avoidance of the limelight, records of any formally instituted organisation in France have, by law, to be lodged with the French police. But, more interestingly, from one name other names are bound to follow. Gérard de Sède has made a major contribution along these lines with his works on esotericism in politics, and has revealed the 'family tree' of the 'Rosicrucian' group of secret societies, working backwards from Pierre Plantard. But a word of caution. Wherever secrets are involved, so are the lunatic fringe and the dubiously motivated. While some people are undoubtedly seeking the 'transcendental meaning of existence', others become mere camp followers, motivated by their own inadequacies and short-term goals.

Some of the personalities tracked down and included in this family tree were evil, some mad. So we had found ourselves asking the question: are Rosicrucians good or bad? Alternatively, are there good and bad Rosicrucians? Probably the latter, but then a bad one is probably beyond the pale and thus excluded from this classification anyway, since the rare published pronouncements of self-styled Rosicrucians emphasise the 'good of mankind' as one of their aims. What sort of company is kept by the elevated cadre? Perhaps we may find out by using Sacaze as a point of departure, for he was surely one of the select few to be entrusted with at least one part of the Secret. It is perhaps also worth noting that Julien Sacaze died unexpectedly at the age of forty-two.

Saunière's benefactors

The only conclusion, in the light of all the available evidence, is that there existed, at least until the beginning of the twentieth century, a nucleus conversant with ancient Rosicrucian knowledge. This knowledge had arisen out of exposure to the Gnostic gospels and been passed down via the Knights Templar. If Saunière had, as we believed, deciphered the Parchments himself, contact with Rosicrucians must somehow have been achieved. It is probable that this occurred in Paris in 1892. It is possible that, having learned so much from the Parchments, Saunière decided that further ancient secrets existed to be uncovered, and so gained funding on the grounds of research. But his precise involvement with this most secret of societies remains unclear. Was the allusion to Rosicrucianism, so blatantly displayed by the priest in his daily activities at Rennes-le-Château, a sign of membership of a Rosicrucian cell within the Catholic priesthood of the area, or was Saunière acknowledging the religious stance of benefactors, themselves avid for the Secret, who had changed the conditions of his life at Rennes by substantial donations?

If the area of Rennes-le-Château had attracted an exiled Jesus or, more indirectly, those who had concealed his remains, we could think of no other place so suited to the purpose. Rennes, remote from the axis of medieval European power in Paris and Rome, remains to the present day independent in spirit. It was the Languedoc that had suffered the terrible onslaught of the Albigensian Crusade in the thirteenth century, with the Dominican inquisition adding the finishing touches. The spirit of Cathar resistance had never died; and the indulgence of the nineteenth-century priests of Rennes – Saunière, Boudet and Gélis – in the secrets of Rosicrucian belief, and the dangers this posed to their station, cannot be underestimated. For a priest in the 1890s, tinkering with the Christian Gnosticism that lay at the heart of Rosicrucianism could be suicidal to his career, if not damaging to his health. The question remained: why had murder entered the scene?

After so much enquiry we remained convinced that Saunière had indeed found the Site and had understood the true nature of the 'treasure' concealed therein. His trip to Paris in 1892 had marked his transition from poor priest to monied *bon viveur*. Money, indeed, seemed no object. The spring of 1892 had seen the second of a series of artistic 'salons', headed by Joseph (or Joséphin) Péladan. Working under the title of the Rose Cross Veritas, this bizarre grouping perhaps typifies the more desperate attempts by many in the past to put some sense into the confusing history of Gnosticism and the Roman Catholic Church.

If the source of Saunière's wealth had been a Parisian benefactor, it may well have been a source other than Péladan and his cohorts. Saunière was astute enough to hedge his bets, and it seems unlikely that, having had the Parchments in his possession for five years before allegedly taking them to Paris, he did not understand the geometry they contained. If members of the church at St Sulpice were responsible for their decoding, what would they have done with the information?

Saunière was the man on the spot – he knew the area, having familiarised himself with the ground while still young and hungry. By 1905 he certainly knew that the Marie de Nègre gravestones held clues that were far too obvious, otherwise he would not have destroyed the inscription. If he knew this he probably understood the Parchments, and hence the Site and its Secret. Saunière received a steady income from an unknown source or sources throughout his life. In the course of this Gélis was murdered, not for money but for documentation. With no admission ever made by Saunière about his wealth, the truth of the matter will probably never be known, but it appears that after 1892 he received a vast payment against the promise of further information, from a benefactor whose appetite had been whetted by the discovery of the Parchments.

The size of the financial payments that Saunière received, and the constant allusion to the spiritual and Gnostic nature of the 'treasure', had led us almost reluctantly to the conclusion that the secret of Abbé Saunière was, as the message found in his personal documents stated, dangerous. It represented the ultimate heresy and challenged the power and authority of the most extensive and successful religious organisation in 'civilised' history: the Roman Catholic Church.

The words of the Gospel of Philip from the Nag Hammadi library reflect the heretical position of the Gnostic Christian:[3]

> Those who say they will die first and then rise are in error. If they do not receive the resurrection while they live, when they die they will receive nothing.

Our researches had revealed the significance of ancient Gnosticism throughout two thousand years of Western history, and the Catholic Church's triumph against such forces of self-determination and self-enlightenment. The doctrine of Resurrection had simultaneously tied the hands of the individual, for God had sacrificed his only son to expiate the sins of the world. Christian Gnosticism, which shared the same belief in the life of Jesus, had made the fundamental mistake of declaring his death in an overly human way. This difference of interpretation had effectively consigned the beliefs of the Gnostics to the marginalia of history.

Conversely, there can be no doubt that the Church has engendered many acts of charity and given support and meaning to the lives of countless millions. But at what cost? By distorting the message of the Messiah? By founding a Church on the alleged disappearance of a body? By holding the believer to moral ransom?

In The Apocalypse of Peter, another of the Nag Hammadi gospels, the words of Jesus provide a tragic and prophetic epitaph for his short life in Judea:[4]

They do business in my word.
And they will propagate harsh fate.

It hardly needs to be said that history has shown us he was right.

20
THE ULTIMATE
HIDING-PLACE

It is interesting to look back at a list we drew up, very early in our research, of the necessary features that the perfect site (*any* perfect site) would need to possess in order to ensure total security. When the 'treasure' of Rennes was still an abstract objective, when we did not have a clue what we were looking for, it gave us a clearer image of the sort of location likely to have been used. It was instrumental in our doubting of La Mort, when that had seemed a possibility.

Some requirements are obvious, others less so; some would not have occurred without knowledge of civil engineering or of the practicalities of heavy construction works. With the question of excavating the 'treasure' now being addressed, it is necessary to look at how it was deposited in the first place. The specifications for the ultimate place of concealment are as follows:

1. It must be readily concealed after construction and deposition of the 'treasure'.
2. It must be easily observable, to ensure that any attempt to re-open the entrance would not pass unnoticed. In fact, it would be necessary to guard the site carefully until vegetation had been re-established, or the scars of excavation otherwise erased. This could take a long time;

only an organisation with absolute autonomy would be able to ensure this.

3. With the 'treasure' successfully concealed, the site would have to be self-maintaining. There should be no possibility of the forces of nature – erosion, earth-boring creatures, decay, instability – uncovering the entrance. Nor must there be any chance of accidental exposure from human activity.

4. The ground should not be porous, or the rock fissured. A vertical hole in the ground can be ruled out completely because of the likelihood of water reaching the 'treasure'. A tunnel providing access to the chamber would need to slope upwards to be self-draining, or flooding could occur. Such a slope would, in any case, be a huge advantage as it would make the removal of spoil by wagon or sledge much easier.

5. There would need to be an adequate depth of solid rock above the roof of the tunnel and the chamber as a safeguard against collapse without the need for propping. So one is not looking for a gently sloping hill into which to bore. A vertical rockface would be perfect, but only if there were a way of blocking and concealing the entrance. For example, the closure to a tunnel entrance in a cliff-face in a river gorge would always be susceptible to high-water erosion, but an entrance closure above the maximum water-line would be impossible to disguise.

6. The site would have to be recognisable even after the passage of centuries. A large, natural, feature – unlikely to be removed or eroded – would be the best way of confirming the site.

This list might well have been written after the location of the Site had been determined, so well does it fit these requirements.

The rock, a mixture of types, is hard, not excessively fissured, but certainly amenable to pick and hammer. The mine tunnels of the area (some of Roman origin) that may be seen today are evidence of this.

The section through the Site shown in Figure 20.1 illustrates its

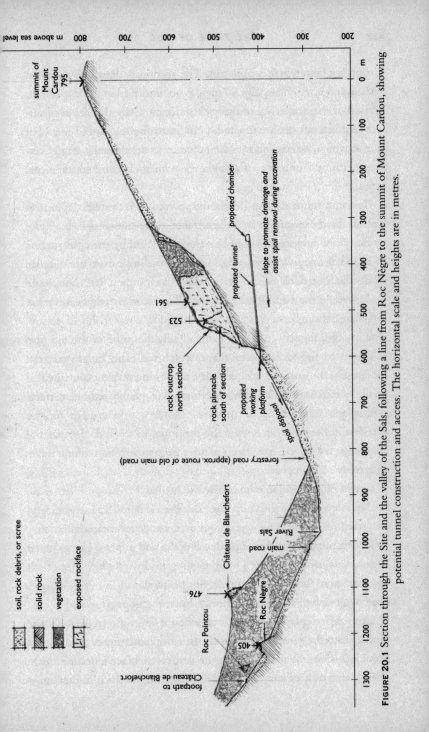

FIGURE 20.1 Section through the Site and the valley of the Sals, following a line from Roc Nègre to the summit of Mount Cardou, showing potential tunnel construction and access. The horizontal scale and heights are in metres.

Figure labels:
- soil, rock debris, or scree
- solid rock
- vegetation
- exposed rockface

- summit of Mount Cardou 795
- proposed chamber
- proposed tunnel
- slope to promote drainage and assist spoil removal during excavation
- 561
- 523
- rock outcrop north section
- rock pinnacle south section
- proposed working platform
- spoil disposal
- forestry road (approx. route of old main road)
- Château de Blanchefort
- River Sals
- main road
- Roc Pointou
- 476
- Roc Nègre
- 405
- footpath to Château de Blanchefort
- m above sea level
- 200 300 400 500 600 700 800
- 0 100 200 300 400 500 600 700 800 900 1000 1100 1200 1300

advantages better than words can. The section is drawn to the same vertical and horizontal scales, so there is no distortion in the slope of the ground or the verticality of the rock outcrops. Only the depth of surface deposits has been estimated, as indicated by the dotted line. The face at which we have shown the entrance to the tunnel is nearly vertical. This accounts for its popularity with rock-climbers in recent times.

Boring a tunnel at this height into a vertical face might appear to have its disadvantages. In fact, the advantages are substantial. Access for workers and equipment could be readily achieved by the construction of a modest roadway, zigzagging its way up the slope from the old road along the east bank of the River Sals – a few men with picks and spades would soon accomplish the task. The route for climbers is more direct and, though steep, it is easily managed by a reasonably fit person. The existing forestry road (following closely the route of the old road as shown on the 1750 Cassini map), which was easily bulldozed from the loose scree material, will not survive for long unless maintained, as further scree movement and water erosion will quickly remove all trace, with plants completing the process. This is a disadvantage for the foresters, if they wish to keep using this route to reach deeper parts of the forest, but would have been an advantage to anyone wishing traces of activity to disappear.

Getting the workforce up to the site is therefore no problem at all; the 'treasure' only slightly more so. But the elevation and existence of the scree are perfect for the removal of excavated material. It may simply be tipped over the edge, to roll down and disperse like so much natural detritus of erosion. The zigzagging road would have been built to one side of the tunnel entrance, not below it.

Having tipped excavated material down the slope, it would be difficult to raise replacement material when it was time to back-fill the cutting into the scree. However, the situation and gravity combine to provide a simple solution. Above the vertical rockface is another scree slope consisting of material eroded from the outcrops higher up –

THE ULTIMATE HIDING-PLACE 423

including the notable pointed rock that forms the centre of the 'W' – not shown on the map, but clear in the photograph (Plate 8). A team of men sent up on to this higher level would be able to excavate and tip fill over the edge, directly into the space at the mouth of the tunnel. Other methods might be adopted, but this would certainly be an option.

Once back-filled, the concealment would indeed be self-maintaining. The continuing processes of erosion would add to the mantle of debris, and the rapid establishment of vegetation would stabilise the loose material.

And all the while, nature would be erasing the marks of disturbance. The site could be left without a guard, but under constant surveillance from the garrison at the Château de Blanchefort. Today, only the memory of those ancient guardians remains, but the entrance to the tunnel is as safe from disturbance as it ever was. Buried under tons of rock in full view of the traffic on the road to Rennes-les-Bains, and under the feet of climbers, this is no job for the mindless treasure-hunters who have honeycombed the hill of Rennes-le-Château. Only an official excavation will ever prove the existence, or non-existence, of *this* treasure.

The Tomb of God

There can be no doubt that a secret location has been identified which logic and sheer weight of evidence has led us to believe is a place of concealment for an object of extraordinary value. More than three years of exhaustive research has enabled us to reach the conclusion that the 'treasure of Rennes' is not of intrinsic worth – it is not the legendary treasure of the Temple of Jerusalem, coins or ancient jewellery. Rather, the importance of the cache lies in what it represents. Human nature being what it is, it is unlikely that a treasure of monetary value would have survived exposure to succeeding generations of *cognoscenti*:

the temptation to dig it up would have been too hard to resist. Few things in the world are more valuable left buried – with the exception of objects of spiritual value, or objects that would completely undermine the fabric of society. We had remained sceptical to the last, but having accepted that the treasure related to the life of Christ we were forced to ask ourselves if bodily remains were the only candidate.

Could the treasure not consist of sacred texts, Gnostic in origin, which contain a version of the life and death of Jesus which differs radically from the Gospel accounts? Precedents existed. The Dead Sea Scrolls and the Nag Hammadi gospels are testament to both the existence of heretical knowledge which has otherwise slipped through the net and the fact that such valuable documents could survive for many centuries. It is also true that the knowledge they contained has proved disquieting for ecclesiastical authorities, raising questions which some members of the Church would undoubtedly have preferred left buried. Embarrassment maybe, but hardly a revolution. Moreover, it seems highly unlikely that the cryptic and extensive concealment we had battled through would have been dreamt up to bury words – however revealing – in a mountain. If the treasure were textual rather than corporeal, copies could easily be made and the originals concealed without going to the trouble of interring them under tons of rock.

The vast sums of money that had changed hands between the clergy in the Haut Razès area had appeared as baffling to us as it had to others during the early days of our investigation. For the Church to be involved on such an organised level indicated a connection with the heart of Catholic teaching. Catholic theology was founded on belief in the Resurrection of Christ, a belief which inherently curtailed the freedom of individuals to bring about their own salvation. The uncovering of a secret that completely refuted this central tenet would test even the staunchest Church members. We could think of no other scenario which would engender such secrecy, generate such finance and be associated with so many unexplained deaths.

Furthermore, the symbolism adopted appears to be so specific that, once appreciated in context, the meaning shrugs off any ambiguity. The logic of this symbolism begins with the blood of Christ, symbolised by, or *actually* being, the red wine of the Communion, or Mass. The source of the blood of Christ is the *body* of Christ. The source of the wine is the bunch of grapes. Therefore, the bunch of grapes may represent the body of Christ. The perfect form of a bunch of grapes would be one where the individual grapes are contained within the envelope of an equilateral triangle – a symbol already utilised as the perfect representation of three-in-one, the Trinity. Giordano Bruno had boldly, but foolishly, exposed this association by attaching tendrils to the triangle itself, a triangle tilted to acknowledge the geometric secret whereby the location of the body/triangle might be found.

The location, Lampos, the extraordinary formation of rock on the side of Mount Cardou, was easily identifiable to the initiate by the angle of the left-hand rock which rose at 75° for more than one hundred metres out of the side of the mountain. This location could be described as the secret shrine of Gnosticism, and the ancient Rose Line of France passed not to the west, or to the east, but directly through the mountain and the Site where the body, the mortal remains of the immortal son of God, lay in secret repose. Henri Boudet had given the name Lampos, or Lamb, to the Site, but what of the name of the mountain itself? The Languedoc, the region which contained the area of Rennes-le-Château, was named after the 'Langue D'Oc' for the regional word for 'yes'; the regions to the north were known as the 'Langue d'Oui'. Looking at Cardou, we thought of the anagram of 'Et in Arcadia ego sum' – in particular 'The Tomb of God', or perhaps 'The Tomb of God, Jesus'. To Gnostics, Jesus was a Divine Being, generally regarded as the human form temporarily inhabited by God; so *notionally*, the remains within the mountain would be those of a terrestrial manifestation of 'God'.

In French 'the body of God' would be 'le corps du bon Dieu' or 'le corps de Dieu'. Regional variations in pronunciation and phrasing within France are nowhere more pronounced than in the Languedoc, with roots in the Langue d'Oc, and with strong Catalan influences. There is a tendency to drop the *article* and the *preposition*, so one might expect to hear 'Corps Dieu'. But it is the sounds of words that are most markedly different, causing some difficulty to those unaccustomed: a softer sound and the rolling emphasis of word-ends. The *Languedocien* pronounces the 'o' as a soft, rounded 'a', and the clipped 'eu' becomes a more prolonged 'oo' – or 'ou' in French.

For a brief moment we placed ourselves in the shoes of the Templar initiate of Languedocian origin, standing in front of the secret location and thinking aloud of the nature of the secret in front of him, as he pronounces quietly to himself: 'CARDOU'.

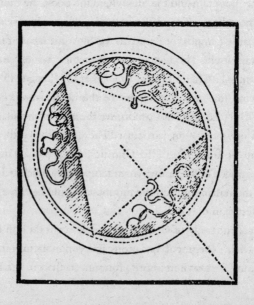

AFTERWORD

We had come to the conclusion that Mount Cardou is the last resting-place of the remains of Jesus Christ, God on earth; it is, in fact, the Tomb of God. Others, including some nineteenth-century priests, had arrived at the same conclusion. This 'fact' and concept of the Gnostic message, incorporating the opposing forces of light and dark, had over the course of two millennia endured the best efforts of the Roman Church to eliminate it from the Western mind. The hexagram of light and dark equilateral triangles and its relationship to the square had been employed over the centuries to indicate the position of a secret hidden on the side of Mount Cardou, but the concept of dualism also holds the key to the *nature* of the 'treasure' itself.

It was the nature of the Secret that had caused us to look in depth at the history of Christianity. We had embarked on this with no preconceived ideas, no intention of refuting the doctrine of Peter and Paul – or, for that matter, of placing Gnosticism on a pedestal. The suppression of Christian Gnosticism became apparent as a motive for the violent response of the Church to major and minor heresies. Having been brought up in the Christian faith, and ignorant – as will be the vast majority of Christians, whether mainstream or Nonconformist – of an alternative, underground stream of Christian tradition of great antiquity, the discovery had come to us as a surprise. When seen in the context of the Secret, the shock had been profound.

The Christian Church had severely narrowed its options for future change by promoting the concept of bodily resurrection and embodying it in the ritual of the Mass – the transubstantiation of the bread and wine into the body and blood of Jesus. The Church was to maintain its influence through this universal sacrament. The key to the success of the doctrine lay in the exploitation of human nature. The Catholic Church put the notion of guilt at the heart of its teachings, at the same time providing the means to alleviate that guilt. Confession, coupled with repentance, would – through the medium of the clergy – absolve the sinner. This could be guaranteed at any time, whatever the enormity of prior sins. One hardly needs to be versed in theology to understand why such a concept became popular.

In contrast, Gnosticism, which promotes the path of self-determination, as distinct from obedience to the written word and the priesthood, offers a radically different challenge to the individual. The discovery of the Nag Hammadi gospels supplied further confirmation that disagreement between the followers of Christ had existed from the earliest times, and was still rife in the third century. Followers of the Church of Rome were required to await the return of Jesus on the Day of Judgement in order to share in the experience of Christ and ascend into heaven. If Christ had not resurrected, there could be no return. Allusion in any form to the insignificance of the Resurrection, let alone to the existence on earth of Jesus' physical remains, struck at the very heart of the Pauline Church. The Apocalypse of Peter, one of the Nag Hammadi gospels, describes a visionary discussion between Peter and Jesus. Jesus warns against the future:[1]

Now then, listen to the things which they are telling you in a mystery and guard them. Do not tell them to the sons of this age. For they shall blaspheme you in these ages since they are ignorant of you, but they will praise you in knowledge . . . And they will cleave to the name of a dead man thinking that they will become pure. But they will become greatly defiled and they will fall into a name of error and into the hand of an evil, cunning man and a manifold dogma, and they will be ruled heretically . . . And there shall be others of those outside our number who name themselves bishop and also deacons, as if they have received their authority from God. They bend themselves under the judgement of the leaders. Those people are dry canals.

Whether this apocalyptic writing described the true feelings of Jesus some two centuries previously, or whether they reflect the frustration of a true Nazarene believer who awaited the spiritual return of Jesus the leader, we shall never know. If these words are those of Christ, the early Roman Church – the 'dry canal' of heresy – had great cause for alarm.

And well might the true followers of Jesus have cause for concern, for the message their Messiah had preached throughout the villages and towns of Judea and Samaria *was* to be lost, submerged by the Roman Church; and something of further and immense importance was also missing – his body. The concept of the Resurrection had removed his earthly remains from mortal existence.

The Nag Hammadi gospels were discovered in 1945. Twenty years later, less than ten percent had been translated and published in English; this, and the remainder, was finally published in one volume in 1978. In a manner which mirrors the translation of the Dead Sea Scrolls, the work has not proceeded unhindered nor has it been immune from the rivalry of academics. From the Vatican the silence remains profound.

There can be no doubt that the path to self-fulfilment promoted by the Gnostics in these scripts, written some sixteen hundred years ago, remains an elevated concept even in the modern world. The similarities with the meditative religions of the East are striking, leaving little doubt that this approach to spiritual development had roots deep in the ancient past. If Gnosticism could provide the answers to the enquiring philosophical mind, what had been the cause of its demise? The danger to the Church inherent in a philosophy that promotes the ability of individuals to achieve salvation through their own efforts is evident – it renders the church superfluous.

As the year 2000 approaches, Christianity is recognisably at a watershed, with the position of the Roman Church as precarious as at any time in the past. The religious scene that presents itself in the West today contains many parallels with that of first-century Judea, and that of the Palestine of the First Crusade. Inter-faith tolerance is at a stage typical of the millennial cycle. The moderate elements in the three main Jerusalem faiths – Christianity, Judaism and Islam – are overshadowed by the fanaticism which exists on their periphery.

The years leading up to the turn of the century hold anniversaries for both Christianity and Judaism. Nineteen ninety-six marks the beginning of celebrations to commemorate the completion of the third millennium since the founding of Jerusalem as the royal city of David and the capital city of Israel. In 1998 the Israeli nation celebrates the fiftieth anniversary of its independence: 1948 saw the re-establishment of Israeli sovereignty over the Western half of the city, and also of the existence of the nation after almost nineteen hundred years. The significance of the advent of the third millennium of the Christian era in the year 2001 is one that requires little explanation. There has seldom been a more auspicious time for the true resurrection of Jesus of Nazareth.

The discovery of what we believe, and what others in the past have believed, to be the remains of Christ presents a dilemma: should they remain where they have rested peacefully for at least nine hundred years? Having traced the path of Christianity over the last two thousand years, it is fairly obvious that proving the Resurrection did not happen would not be a revelation to vast numbers of people. That within those numbers there were a few – perhaps a *very* few – who also knew where the evidence was buried poses the question of why no one has brought such findings to the attention of the public before.

A report in the 31 March 1996 issue of the *Sunday Times*[2] that a collection of ossuaries now in a Jerusalem depository, all originally from the same tomb, had been found to bear the names 'Jesus, son of Joseph', 'Joseph', two 'Mary's, and 'Judah, son of Jesus' has fuelled the debate about the fate of Jesus. Israeli archaeologists who reviewed the find (made in 1980) have discounted the idea that the ossuaries are those of Jesus of Nazareth and his family. There are two previously excavated ossuaries bearing the name 'Jesus, son of Joseph', and many more are known on which the name 'Jesus' has been inscribed, in imprecation by early Christians to their leader. Jesus was a common name in the Jerusalem of Herod's time, even before the birth of Christ, and also it was common to name a child after a notable figure[3] – a practice evident in England today, following the christening of a royal baby.

However, we can at least consider how this discovery might fit into the picture that we have built up. The ossuaries from the tomb in question were empty when discovered, having been vandalised, according to the report, 'in antiquity'; and the tomb itself was destroyed as a result of construction work carried out shortly after its recent rediscovery. Therefore it is impossible to attach any date to the removal of the bones from the ossuaries. The ossuaries themselves, about fifty centimetres in length and thirty centimetres in depth and width, would have been cumbersome and conspicuous for someone wishing to remove them to a safer location, but the removal of just the bones would have required less exertion and attracted less attention. Human bones are not difficult for a person or persons to carry with them. The most prominent relic would have been the skull (the size of which, minus the jawbone, can be gauged from the Teniers painting of *St Antony and St Paul*). Now, the Knights Templar are on record as having carried out excavations in the city of Jerusalem, and we believe that they may have found such a tomb as this and removed certain remains from it.

If these remains were indeed the bones of Jesus of Nazareth, their significance to those who possessed them would have been colossal. If it was indeed the Knights Templar who located the remains, why did they not announce the fact, instead of transporting them and conceal-ing them elsewhere? The answer is more obvious to the historian than to the layman. To have declared, in the Middle Ages, that you were in possession, or had knowledge, of the remains of Jesus would lead to immediate execution for heresy. Family and friends would probably suffer a similar fate. And the ensuing centuries saw little softening in the Church's attitude to heretics. Although in the nineteenth century Saunière would not have been burnt at the stake had he declared his findings, he would have lost his post at Rennes and in any case his 'knowledge' was providing him with riches beyond his wildest dreams.

We are aware that the consequential issue of the reality of the Resurrection will be of greatest concern to committed Christians. Neither will the matter be without interest to those Christians who struggle daily with the conflict that exists between the conduct of a 'Christian' life and the mystic and 'other-worldly' aspects of faith. The pronouncements that appear from time to time from the hierarchy of the Church of England have sent clear messages to those Christians teetering on the verge of agnosticism. It does not require much insight to deduce that when great theological brains are applied to those aspects of faith that actually rely on just that – faith – the documentation is found to be lacking. It is not that the word of the Scriptures is unreliable *per se*, simply that the provenance of such is found to be wanting. But true faith is unassailable. Even if the authenticity of the Scriptures were shown beyond doubt to be *un*reliable, the believer will still see in them the true word of God. And this is how the argument becomes interminable.

Would the excavation of the Site settle the matter? Certainly it would reveal whether the evidence for the concealment had been correct. There is, however, a practical problem. The 'treasure' is buried under thousands of tons of rock deep within a hill which does not belong to us. It has been deposited via a tunnel carved into a sheer rockface, and natural erosion has completed the concealment. The removal of thousands of tons of rock from the face of Cardou would prove impossible to accomplish without the permission of the local authorities and, in view of the implications, perhaps the French government.

If the tunnel were to be opened and the 'treasure' revealed to be a body, this would vindicate our deductions to a large extent, but it would still not convince the hardened sceptic. Techniques such as DNA testing need a comparative sample to detect a person's ancestry. Carbon-14 dating might tell us that the remains are from the first century, but could not be any more specific than that. Perhaps the only correspondence that would lead to a substantial acceptance would be the matching of an embalmed corpse to the image on the Shroud of Turin – which may yet be proved to be of first-century date, the present carbon-14 dating having been shown to be tainted by the probability of subterfuge.[4]

The passage of time further increases the difficulty of proving that the body is that of Jesus of Nazareth. However, the great minds who have conspired to produce this most cryptic of concealments certainly believed that to be the case, and left extensive clues to indicate precisely that fact. At the end of three years of research we also believe the remains to be those of Jesus and therefore, in order to substantiate our findings (overriding moral considerations about digging up sacred remains), we believe that excavation is required.

Perhaps the Church will argue that it is not necessary to dig up the remains of a figure of such importance. No other religion would sanction the excavation of prophets and saints, so why should the Christian Church wish to dig up remains so revered – and which, according to its Gospels, should not exist? Many will argue that the temporary enlightenment that excavation would offer to the curious would be massively counterbalanced by the spiritual chaos and uncertainty that would be felt by Christians the world over. The only answer to this is that the true message of Jesus was lost with the Resurrection, that many millions of people who might otherwise call themselves Christians have a problem with this most fundamental tenet of the Christian faith and that, with the millennium approaching, the time has come for a reappraisal not just of the *life* of Jesus, but of the *death* of Jesus.

Richard Andrews
April 1996

ACKNOWLEDGEMENTS

The process of research and writing by two authors has left us with a number of people whom we both wish to thank together, and those to whom we individually owe a debt of gratitude.

David Mason gave us advice and assistance without which the story would not have been told.

Janet Madden gave precious time and much appreciated effort in the early stages of research. Richard Drake provided the practical assistance and support so essential to the successful conclusion of our trips abroad, including our induction into G.P.S. navigation. Gillian and David Holl have given generously of their time and advice. Sophie has withstood the absences of her father without complaint, and Andrew Schellenberger, whose inspiration led to the completion of the Arcadia anagram, likewise. Ruth and Richard Boulton in the U.K. and Ruth and Paul in Israel have given assistance and encouragement at all times.

We are greatly indebted to our agent, Vivienne Schuster, for her belief in the project, and to Diana Mackay and Ursula Bender for all their hard work. Philippa Harrison, Alan Samson and Andrew Gordon of Little, Brown have given us the support and direction crucial to the completion of our task. Sally Abbey, who gave absolute dedication to a work of great complexity, has produced wonders. Our thanks also go to our hard-working art-history researcher, and to John Woodruff, who has given us invaluable assistance during the final stages of editing.

Finally, wherever we have directed our enquiries we have encountered kindness, enthusiasm and patience, and in many instances people have gone out of their way to help without asking about the nature of our project. Indeed, in acknowledging their contribution we would like to make it clear that their assistance or advice in no way presupposes either knowledge of, or agreement with, the conclusions we ultimately reached. To all those unnamed, and to those we cannot mention, we extend our heartfelt thanks.

Picture credits

The authors and publishers have made every effort to contact copyright holders for material reproduced in the book, but in many cases copyright proved difficult to trace because the illustrations carried no accreditation. Should any person feel that material has been used without proper authority, he or she is invited to contact the publisher. Grateful acknowledgement is made to the following sources for permission to reproduce illustrations: Art Resource, New York; the Ashmolean Museum, Oxford; the Bibliothèque Nationale de France, including the *Arsenal* collection, Paris; the Bodleian Library, Oxford; the Bridgeman Art Library, London; the British Library, London; the collection of Her Majesty Queen Elizabeth II at Windsor; the Courtauld Institute, London; Graphische Sammlung der ETH, Zurich; the Institut Géographique National, Paris; the Koninklijke Bibliotheek, The Hague; the Musée du Louvre, Paris; the Musée de Rennes-le-Château; the Musée Saint-Raymond, Toulouse; the National Austrian Library, Vienna; the National Library of Russia, St Petersburg; the National Portrait Gallery, London; Photographie Giraudon, Paris; and the Service Photographique de la Réunion des Musées Nationaux, Paris.

Some illustrations have been reproduced and adapted from the following publications (see Bibliography for further details): *La Vraie Langue celtique* by Henri Boudet; *De triplici minimo et mensura* by Giordano Bruno; *The Cathedral Builders* by Jean Gimpel; *The Holy Place* by Henry Lincoln; *Admiral of the Ocean Sea* by Samuel Eliot Morison; *Composition et Nombre d'Or dans les oeuvres peintes de la Renaissance* by Charles Funck-Hellet; *On the Correct Building of Pinnacles* by Wenzel Roritzer; *Inscriptions antiques des Pyrénées* by Julien Sacaze; *L'Or de Rennes* by Gérard de Sède; and *Giordano Bruno and the Hermetic Tradition* by Frances Yates.

The book's original maps – of the area around Rennes-le-Château and of the provinces of the Holy Land at the time of Christ – were drawn by Alec Herzer. Other original diagrams, photographs and geometric illustrations are copyright © Pactolus 1996. All rights reserved.

CHRONOLOGY

THE ROMAN CHURCH AND THE SECRET	CENTURY AD	GNOSIS AND THE SECRET
	1st	
c. **33**: Jesus is crucified		Jesus survives the crucifixion
Paul spearheads the new 'Christianity'		Judaic elements of Jesus' fellowship resist the Hellenisation of their leader's message
Paul dies in Rome, having succeeded in his mission to promote Jesus as the 'resurrected Son of God'		**62**: James, brother of Jesus, is killed and his church dispersed
	2nd, 3rd	
Pauline Church continues to attack the Gnostics, condemning them as heretics and libertines		Original message of Jesus is carried into Jordan, Syria and Egypt by the survivors of the Church of James. Their stance on the physical resurrection of Jesus is confined to the doctrine of 'gnosis' – that resurrection is spiritual and achievable by all who seek the 'wisdom'
The Church consolidates the message of the New Testament: the death and Resurrection of Jesus of Nazareth, the one Christ		
The structure of the Roman Empire provides an ideal vehicle for the spread of the Christian message		The rose, ancient Persian symbol of rebirth and resurrection, enters the psyche of the Christian Gnostic
	4th	
312: Emperor Constantine adopts 'Christianity' as the official religion of the Empire. Pagans and Gnostics are regarded with increasing intolerance by the Church		Legend has Joseph of Arimathea travelling to southern France 'with the Grail'

THE ROMAN CHURCH AND THE SECRET	CENTURY AD	GNOSIS AND THE SECRET
	4th *(cont)*	
325: Council of Nicea declares Jesus to be True God of True God		Gnostic Christians preserve their belief in sacred texts. Under persecution from the Church of Rome, they hide a collection of these texts in a cave in the area of Nag Hammadi, Upper Egypt; grain receipts found in the bindings date their concealment to *c.* **350**
		Christian Gnosticism survives in the Middle East as the Pauline Christian doctrine expands into the Western Roman Empire
	5th	
Christianity prepares for the 'end of the world' by the year **500**; the Day of Judgement is awaited when the Son of Man will return at the right hand of his father to judge the living and the dead		Fall of Rome leaves the East isolated from the West
	6th–10th	
Roman Empire disintegrates; Christianity survives. The Visigoths and Merovingians adapt to the Roman Catholic faith. The Church becomes increasingly integrated into Western society. Pagan rites are replaced by the established ritual of the Mass, worship of saints, belief in miracles and the reward of an 'afterlife' in heaven. Any hint of gnostic thought is attacked as heretical as it questions the backbone of the Church's doctrine: the bodily Resurrection of Jesus. The concept of guilt, sin and the necessity of penance is further instilled into the Christian believer by the employment of confession within the liturgy		Arab geographers and scientists uphold the legacy of the ancients. Methods of accurate geographical survey are preserved

THE ROMAN CHURCH AND THE SECRET	CENTURY AD	GNOSIS AND THE SECRET
	11th	

1078: A group of 'heretics' is condemned by the Church and put to the stake in France. Church and State now form an axis of supreme power over the common man. Feudalism and the threat of damnation provide the means of controlling populace and raising taxes, essential for the prosecution of war. The Church becomes rich in land and property

1095: Pope Urban II urges the formation of a crusading army to retake Jerusalem from the hands of the Muslims, and secure the pilgrim routes. Thus begins the crusading era

1099: Jerusalem is taken, and Godfroi de Bouillon elected king

1100: On Godfroi's death, he is succeeded by his brother, who becomes King Baldwin I

12th

1118: Baldwin II, cousin of Baldwin I, succeeds to the throne of Jerusalem

c. **1120**: Formation of the Templar Order. The founder-members are granted quarters on the Temple Mount

1127: Templar founder-members return to France

Templars conduct excavations under the Temple Mount in Jerusalem

Templars immerse themselves in the mysteries of the Near East; they adopt the Atbash cipher

1119: Château de Blanchefort is given to the abbeys of St Giles and Alet. Alet-les-Bains is the nearest town of any size to Peyrolles, and the Matri Deum stone came from Alet Abbey, property of the Templar Order between **1132** and **1180**. It is

THE ROMAN CHURCH AND THE SECRET	CENTURY AD	GNOSIS AND THE SECRET
	12th *(cont)*	
1129: Hugues de Payens, first Templar Grand Master, speaks before the Council of Troyes, having first visited Scotland, England and Flanders. The papal convocation accept the Order, which is placed under the Latin Rule of poverty, chastity and obedience to their Grand Master and the Patriarch of Jerusalem, in that order		therefore possible that both Blanchefort and the abbey at Alet were in the hands of the Templar Order within the lifetime of its founder-members
Rise of Catharism in the Languedoc		**1130**: Grant of land to the Templars in the area of Rennes-le-Château and the mention of 'Peirois' (Peyrolles), which is sited at the centre of the hexagram in the Parchment geometry
		1133: Bernard de Blancafort witnesses at the Abbey of St Hilaire, 20 km north of Rennes-le-Château, a transaction in favour of his order, the Knights Templar
		1146: Templars adopt the 'Rose Cross' as their symbol
		The Grail legends arise
	13th	
Suppression of Catharism in the Languedoc by the Albigensian Crusade		Accounts of the Grail continue to appear. Although they are all specific about an endless search, they are less so about the exact nature of the elusive Grail. As Gnostic thought is heretical, the search is concealed within a Romance
Dominic spearheads the inquisition in his name to extirpate the last Cathar remnants. The area around Rennes-le-Château is included in the Dominican itinerary		
1257: Olivier de Termes bequeaths part of his property to the 'Commanderie de Peyriès'. The Voisins family acquires the *domaine* of Arques, once Termenois property		Templars are depicted on a map of Jerusalem which incorporates the earliest known example of the geometry present in the Parchments

THE ROMAN CHURCH AND THE SECRET	CENTURY AD	GNOSIS AND THE SECRET
	13th *(cont)*	
1296: Pope Celestine V dies at the hands of his successor, Boniface VIII		
	14th	
1307: Arrest of all French Templar knights by order of the king of France; some escape to Scotland while others take refuge in Lorraine, the future inheritance of René d'Anjou		The Grail romances decline with the demise of the Templar Order
1314: Jacques de Molay, last Templar Grand Master, is burned at the stake		
	15th, 16th	
Advent of printing and the Reformation create upheaval in the Roman Catholic Church; the Counter-Reformation is launched. As in Roman times, heresy is equated to disloyalty to the state		**1406**: The Duc de Berry purchases the *Lancelot* miniature, in which features of the geometry appear
1534: Society of Jesus formed to combat theological adversaries of the Roman Church; thereafter the Inquisition is pursued by arbitrary and violent means		**1457**: René d'Anjou compiles *Le Livre du cuer d'amour espris*, of which one plate, *La Fontaine de fortune*, contains the geometry
Europe enters a period of religious conflict of Catholic against Protestant		Late sixteenth century: anonymous painting of the coronation of Pope Celestine V contains the geometry
By the end of the sixteenth century, Gnosticism and the pursuit of ancient wisdom is embodied in the revival of the Fraternity of the Rose Cross		
1600: Giordano Bruno is burnt at the stake in Rome as a 'heretic'		

THE ROMAN CHURCH AND THE SECRET	CENTURY AD	GNOSIS AND THE SECRET
	17th	
1614: *Rosicrucian Manifestos* are published at Cassel. The central figure, Christian Rosencreutz, is connected with an unspecified order which uses a red cross and red roses as symbols		*c.* **1630**: Nicolas Poussin paints *Les Bergers d'Arcadie II*, which contains the geometry. The painting is reframed by Louis XIV, which invalidates the geometry
		c. **1650**: David Teniers the Younger paints *St Antony and St Paul*, which contains the geometry
	18th	
1717: Organised Freemasonry is established in London		**1781**: Death of Marie de Nègre. Her tombstones bear independent geometrical confirmation of the Site
Freemasons are declared enemies of the Church of Rome		
French Revolution causes social upheaval in France. Antoine Bigou leaves Rennes-le-Château for exile in Spain, having buried Marie de Nègre		
	19th, 20th	
Industrialisation and colonial ambition diminish the importance of the Church in French state affairs		**1886**: Saunière starts work in the church of St Mary Magdalene at Rennes-le-Château, and discovers parchments
1885: Bérenger Saunière is appointed parish priest of Rennes-le-Château		**1891**: Entry in Saunière's diary for 21 September reads 'Découverte d'une tombe . . . Secret'
In Paris, the Society of the Rose Cross Veritas is formed, and interest in the Templars and the Grail resurrected		**1892**: Saunière visits Paris, and also commences extensive restoration of his church
		1897: Antoine Gélis found murdered

THE ROMAN CHURCH AND THE SECRET	CENTURY AD	GNOSIS AND THE SECRET
	19th, 20th *(cont)*	
1909: Saunière is replaced as priest and subjected to trial for traffic in the sale of Masses, disobedience to his bishop, and exaggerated and unaccountable expenses		**1898**: Saunière purchases land and commences grand works at Rennes – construction of the Villa Bethania and the Tour Magdala
1995: A Vatican priest visits Rennes-le-Château		**1905**: Tesseyre draws the de Nègre stones at Rennes-le-Château
		Saunière defaces the de Nègre tombstones
		1915: Death of Boudet
		1917: Death of Saunière

APPENDICES

A

THE HIDDEN WORDS OF PARCHMENT 2

Intermingled with the text of Parchment 2 are some minute letters, so small as to be almost illegible at the size at which the illustrations are reproduced in this book. They spell out two words: REX MUNDI. This, meaning 'King of the World', was the epithet used by the Cathar heretics to refer to the creator of the physical universe.

Although they considered themselves to be good Christians, the Cathars regarded the Catholic Church as having betrayed the true doctrine of the Gospels. They believed in the existence of two powerful deities – one was God, the other Satan. (It would be more correct to say that these were opposing principles, rather than deities.) Catharism was not a formal, regulated religion, and the beliefs of those who have called themselves (or who have been called) 'Cathars' have varied greatly in detail and in degree of extremism. The good or *light* principle was God, the representative of things spiritual; the physical world was *dark*, corrupt, carnal – the creation of Rex Mundi. Catharism, or Albigensianism (after the town of Albi, where members of the sect concentrated) was an extreme development of Gnosticism, and had been a widespread heresy in south-western France until it was ruthlessly suppressed by the Albigensian Crusade. The atrocities committed against the Cathars in the name of God scarcely bear recounting.

The appearance of these words in Parchment 2 is problematical. It does not affect the outcome of our researches, but it does provide us with an indication of the beliefs of those most implicated in the mystery. The development and philosophy of Gnosticism are considered in Chapter 17.

B

THE COMPLETION OF HENRY LINCOLN'S DIAGRAM

Having accepted the early stages of the diagram constructed by Henry Lincoln on Parchment 1, but noting that the circle he drew does *not* pass through the cross on line 7 as he states, and should not be forced to do so, we have a diagram that looks like Figure 1.6. The small triangular device at the top has two short lines – 'loose ends' – pointing to the right, suggesting that the diagram has to be completed in some way. The two triangles ABC and ABD do not share an axis of symmetry, but it would take only a small adjustment to rectify this.

If a new line is drawn from B to pass through the end of the short line pointing upwards to the right and is terminated on the circle at E, we discover that the new line has also passed through the other short line, pointing to the right and slightly downwards, which had already been incorporated into the line AC (Figure B.1). This is unlikely to be a coincidence (Figure 1.7).

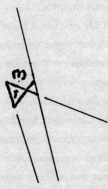

FIGURE B.1 The triangular device at the top of Parchment 1.

Joining A to E (Figure 1.7) completes a new triangle ABE, which is isosceles and, unlike the triangle ABC, has a common axis of symmetry with the smaller triangle ABD: the line that passes through the apices E and D of the two triangles. This centre-line is perpendicular to the base-line AB, which passes through the word SION, and is also tangential to the 'O' in SION. We now have a diagram that is comparable to that of the Dalle de Coume Sourde.

C

THE REMAINING LETTERS ON THE DALLE DE COUME SOURDE

Although not of great significance, the remaining letters on the Dalle de Coume Sourde should be explained. At the top of the stone there are two groups each of three letters: on the left, SAE, and on the right, SIS. These are not Latin words as they stand, but anyone familiar with Roman memorial inscriptions will know that it was common to use abbreviations, particularly when there could be no ambiguity. CAE for CAESAR is an obvious example.

Logically, there is only one word for which SAE can stand. There are just five roots in Latin that begin with these three letters, of which four are unlikely to be candidates: they are *saepe*, 'often'; *saepes*, 'hedge'; *saeta*, 'bristle'; and *saevus*, 'cruel'). The fifth is *saeculum*, meaning 'lifetime' or 'indefinitely long period'. To those who still recall the Latin services of the Roman Catholic Church, this word will be familiar from the phrase *in saecula saeculorum*, generally translated as 'for ever and ever'. Likewise, SIS can represent only one word, and that is *sistere*, which in this context most likely means 'to endure'. So one may deduce that the abbreviation stands for 'to endure for ever and ever'.

At the bottom of the stone, PS probably refers to the Prieuré de Sion – the Priory of Sion. PRAECUM seems to be a conjunction of *prae* and *cum*, 'before' and 'with'. One might speculate endlessly on this; doubtless someone knows the significance.

D

THE 'LOBINEAU DOCUMENT'

The following is an English translation of one of the *Dossiers secrets* composed by Henri Lobineau.[1] The translation attempts to be fairly idiomatic, but without departing too far from the strangely phrased and punctuated French original. The original text is also punctuated by small pictograms, here represented by '●'.

ONE DAY THE DESCENDANTS OF BENJAMIN LEFT THEIR COUNTRY, SOME REMAINED, TWO THOUSAND YEARS LATER GODFREY VI BECAME KING OF JERUSALEM AND FOUNDED THE ORDER OF SION – From this wonderful story which adorns history, in the same way that the architecture of a temple whose pinnacle is lost in the immensity of space and time, of which POUSSIN wished to declare the mystery in his two pictures, the 'Shepherds of Arcadia', there is without doubt the secret of the treasure before which the descendants, countryfolk and shepherds, of the proud Sicambrian Franks reflect on '*et in Arcadia ego*', the [hexagram appears here] and King '*Midas*'. Before 1200 BC, an important event is the arrival of the Hebrews in the Promised Land and their tardy installation in Caanan. In the Bible, Deuteronomy 33; it is said of BENJAMIN: This is the beloved one of the Eternal, he shall dwell in security by him, the Eternal shall shelter him always, and reside between his shoulders. ● It is moreover stated in Joshua 18 that the lot given as inheritance to the sons of BENJAMIN included among the fourteen towns and their villages: JEBUSI, these days JERUSALEM with its three points of a triangle: GOLGOTHA, SION and BETHANY. ● And finally it is written in Judges 20 and 21: 'Not one of us shall give his daughter as wife to a Benjamite – O Eternal, God of Israel, why has this occurred in Israel for one tribe to be missing today in Israel.' From the great enigma of Arcadia VERGIL who was in the secret of the gods, lifted the veil in the Pastorals X – 46/50: 'You far from your homeland (let me not believe such). Without me, you gaze upon the snow-clad Alps and the frosty Rhine. May you not be injured by frostbite! May the soles of your delicate feet not be cut by sharp ice!' [hexagram appears here] SIX DOORS or the seal of Destiny, here are the secrets of the parchments of the Reverend Saunière, priest of Rennes-le-Château, and which before him the great initiate POUSSIN knew when he realised his work to the order of the POPE, the inscription on the tomb is the same.

This passage is considered in *The Holy Blood and the Holy Grail*, in particular for the implication that the Tribe of Benjamin is the origin of the line leading to the Merovingians; but other aspects of the strange text are not mentioned, possibly because no particular sense was to be made of them. Two points are worth noting as they will later be seen to reveal 'Lobineau' as an initiate:

1. The Arcadian shepherds reflect not only on *et in Arcadia ego*, but also on the hexagram. Furthermore, the significance of the *two* paintings of the Arcadian Shepherds is known to Lobineau.
2. The hexagram, Saunière's parchments, Poussin's knowledge and the inscription on the tomb are said (in a rather confusing way) to be interrelated.

E

THE GOLDEN MEAN

An attempt to explain briefly the *significance* that has been placed on the Golden Mean in times past would be like attempting a one-page summary of a telephone directory. However, it is possible to indicate its derivation and properties, and also some of the contexts in which it appears. In passing, it must be said that, for reasons scarcely understood, it is to be found in nature, governing the proportions of organisms such as the spacing of buds on a stem, and the spirals of sea-shells. It has been used by architects and artists to generate harmonious proportions in buildings and works of art.

The concept is quite simple. If a point C divides a line AB (Figure E.1) such that the ratio of the whole length AB to the longer part AC – i.e. AB : AC – is equal to the ratio of the longer part AC to the smaller part CB – i.e. AC : CB, then the ratio AB : AC (or AC : CB) is known as the Golden Mean (other names are Golden Ratio, Golden Section and Golden Number). It is denoted by the symbol Φ, and has the numerical value 1.618 033 9 ..., the dots indicating that this is a non-recurring decimal: i.e. an infinite number of decimal places are required to enumerate Φ, which is to say that it may not be expressed precisely as a decimal number. It is often quoted as 1.618 for brevity, but this inaccurate value should be used in calculations only with caution.

A   C   B

FIGURE E.1 The Golden Mean: the ratio AB : AC equals the ratio AC : CB.

How is the point C located? By trial and error certainly, but how might this be done at a single attempt? One method is shown in Figure

E.2. This diagram also leads to the derivation of the precise mathematical expression for Φ. From Pythagoras' theorem, the length of the hypotenuse a is the square root of the sum of the squares of b and c:

$$a = \sqrt{b^2 + c^2} = \sqrt{1^2 + \tfrac{1}{2}^2} = \sqrt{1 + \tfrac{1}{4}}$$

Therefore

$$L = \tfrac{1}{2} + \sqrt{1 + \tfrac{1}{4}} = \tfrac{1}{2}(1 + \sqrt{4+1}) = \tfrac{1}{2}(1 + \sqrt{5})$$

The latter is the simplest mathematical expression for the precise value of Φ, and if entered into a computer, or pocket calculator, will give the precise value in decimals *to the limit of accuracy attainable* by that computer or calculator.

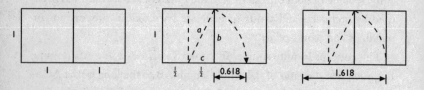

FIGURE E.2 A possible construction for Φ.

It may be shown that Φ is involved with the pentagonal geometry. Figure E.3 illustrates that each line of the pentagram, or regular five-pointed star, divides the one it crosses in the Golden Ratio, thus: $AB/AC = \Phi$. Figure E.4 illustrates the 'pentagonal' angles. Trigonometric functions of these angles also involve Φ, thus:

$$\sin 18° = 1/2\Phi, \quad \sec 36° = 2/\Phi, \quad \sin 54° = \Phi/2, \quad \sec 72° = 2\Phi$$

It can also be shown that Φ may have been the basis for the proportions of the Great Pyramid (as discussed briefly in the text). Calculating the value of Φ to (say) nine decimal places (possible on many pocket calculators) and using this value in the following, we have:

$$\Phi = 1.618\ 033\ 989 \quad \text{and} \quad 1/\Phi = 0.618\ 033\ 989$$

(which incidentally reveals one of the peculiarities of Φ, that $1/\Phi = \Phi - 1$) and the angle whose cosine is 0.618 033 989 is 51°.827 292 37, which in degrees, minutes and seconds is 51° 49' 38".

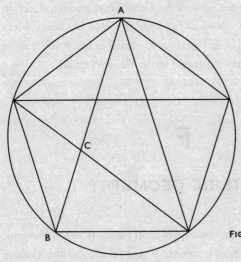

FIGURE E.3 The Golden Mean in pentagonal geometry.

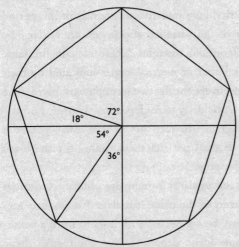

FIGURE E.4 The angles of pentagonal geometry.

The north face of the Pyramid has a measured angle of 51° 50′ 40″ ± 1′ 5″.[2] These two values may be regarded as equal to within the accuracies of measurement and tolerances of construction available in ancient Egypt, and so the angle of this face may well have been based on Φ. This was certainly the view of the Greek historian Herodotus, in the fifth century BC. The slope of the west face may be shown,[2] in a similar manner, to have been based on π, which is the mathematical proportion most popularly attributed to the Great Pyramid.

F

ESOTERIC GEOMETRY

When the geometric design underlying most paintings of the sixteenth century is investigated, it is invariably found to involve the Golden Mean (Appendix E) or pentagonal geometry – probably both, for, as shown in Appendix E, the latter is governed by the former. The most common type of geometric figure underlying paintings of this period is the polygram.[3] Many of the varieties of polygon are familiar by name, such as the pentagon and hexagon. These contain the same number of sides as the number of internal angles indicated by their names – five and six, respectively, for the two examples just given. The best-known polygram – particularly to readers of black magic novels – is the five-pointed pentagram. (In such novels it is usually called a pentacle or pentangle; we shall not use these names, for the black magic association is inappropriate.)

Only *regular* polygons and *regular* polygrams are of interest to us (as they have been to geometers of the past). It is clear that any five (say) points on a flat surface may be connected with lines to form a pentagram or pentagon of some form, departing from the regular shape according to the disposition of the points. These aberrations are of no interest to us (see Figure 6.1, on p. 149). A regular polygram or polygon is one in which the sides are of equal length, and the angles at the vertices, or 'points', are thus all equal. The vertices all lie on a particular circle called the circumscribing circle, and have a mathematical relationship to that circle. This is of particular significance in pentagonal geometry, and suggests why it was important to the Pythagoreans.

The recognition of a small element of pentagonal geometry in, for example, a painting often allows one to deduce the whole underlying geometric scheme. Just as one might suspect the geometry of an equilateral triangle from the presence of a 60° angle, so one might deduce that 'if it's 72°, it must be a pentagram'. (This use of geometry as a kind of esoteric language is discussed in the text.) An understanding of the mathematical basis for the construction of polygrams will be useful later.

All regular polygrams may be constructed by drawing a series of equal-length chords of a circle. An example will make this clear. Take a pair of compasses and draw any circle. Without changing the setting of the compasses, prick the compass-point into any point on the circle, and mark off another point on the circle. Move the compass-point to that mark, and repeat the process until the starting-point has been reached; if the construction has been done carefully there will be no gap between the first mark and the last. Join successive pairs of points with straight lines – the chords – to form a perfect (regular) hexagon. (We may legitimately use the word 'perfect' regardless of the competence of the particular draughtsman, since in principle the figure is mathematically correct. Had the drawing been done by computer-controlled robot to an inconceivably high precision, the statement would be no truer. This concept of *precision in principle regardless of accuracy* is most important. It ensures that if the intended principle has been recognised, small inaccuracies in presentation will not obscure the result. The relevance of this will become evident.)

With polygons such as the regular hexagon, the chords do not overlap one another. If, however, a figure is constructed by joining, not successive pairs of points marked off at equal intervals around a circle's circumference, but every other point, or every third point, etc., the result is a polygram. Such constructions require more than one circuit of drawing chords around the circle to complete them, and the chords do overlap. For a pentagram two circuits are required, whereas the pentagon is completed in one (Figure F.1).

The length of each chord that makes up the regular hexagon has a

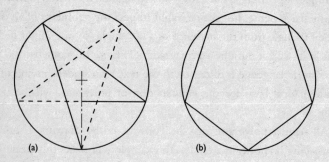

(a)   (b)

FIGURE F.1 Two circuits of chord-drawing (the second shown dashed) are required to complete a pentagram (a), but only one circuit for a regular pentagon (b).

very straightforward relationship to the circle: its length is equal to the circle's radius; expressed as an equation, $c = r$. It is possible to establish a general equation that relates c and r for any regular polygon or polygram. This equation may be expressed in forms which permit one to calculate either the length of a chord for a particular type of polygram, or the number of sides of the polygram from the values of the radius and chord.

Whole families of polygrams may be derived from a base number. Those based on five include the pentagon (five interior angles and five sides), pentagram (five points) and decagram (ten points). In terms of the equation mentioned above, the decagram has the most overt association of the Golden Mean, denoted by Φ, with pentagonal geometry, for the chord length is given by the radius of the circle multiplied by Φ: $c = \Phi r$. Pentagonal geometry was sacred to the Pythagoreans, and during the Renaissance it reigned supreme as the occult geometric basis for the composition of paintings; Figure F.2 illustrates the recurrence of the decagram.[4] Indeed, so universal was its use in Renaissance

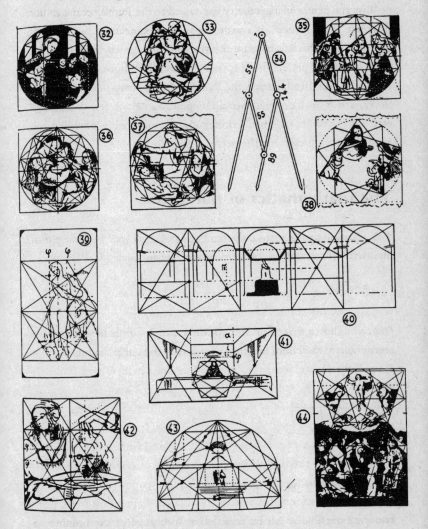

FIGURE F.2 Geometrical analyses of Renaissance paintings,
by Charles Funck-Hellet.

art that if one wished to incorporate an element in a painting in such a way that it would be recognisable solely to an elite coterie, an alternative device would be required. It is shown in Chapter 9 just how potent the combination of pentagonal geometry with other star polygons would prove to be.

Why the pentagonal geometry was sacred to the Pythagoreans, rather than just a 'nice secret', is a matter for much conjecture, but we may speculate that this was because the whole of this geometry is ruled by Φ. A symbol of perfection, it appears to have been honoured with the status of a god. In a later age, the Pythagorean veneration of number as the regulator of all existence would suggest to a certain few that geometry — the visible, tangible, manifestation of number — provided the ideal means of preserving the Secret.

The mathematics of polygons

The equation that governs polygrams and polygons may be arranged in different ways to suit the calculation to be performed:

$$c = 2r \sin\left(\frac{180}{n}\right) \quad \text{or} \quad n = \frac{180}{\sin^{-1}(c/2r)}$$

It may be shown that this is true for the example of the hexagon given above: where the chord length is the same as the circle's radius ($c = r = R$, say), then:

$$n = \frac{180}{\sin^{-1}(R/2R)}$$

$$= \frac{180}{\sin^{-1} 0.5}$$

$$= \frac{180}{30} = 6 \quad \text{(a hexagon)}$$

Here the variable n can be regarded as indicative of the number of 'chord-drawing' circuits of the circumscribing circle that have to be made to complete the figure in the process of construction with compasses described above. With the hexagon and other regular polygons the chords do not overlap each other, and the value of *n* given by the equation is the number of sides. However, the equation is also applicable to polygrams (whose chords do overlap), but the interpretation is less obvious. In this case the result is not an integer (whole number), and the number of 360° circuits of the circle required to complete the figure must be deduced. For a pentagram, $n = 2.5$, and two circuits are required to complete the figure, so the number of points is $2.5 \times 2 = 5$.

A figure particularly favoured by the great masters of sixteenth-century painting – especially as the geometric basis for circular works – was the decagram, the ten-pointed star. It requires three circuits of the circle to complete a true polygram of ten points. Imagine a circle divided into ten arcs by ten points spaced equally around its circumference. Now imagine drawing chords that join adjacent pairs of points in succession, round the circle and back to the starting-point. The result is a ten-sided polygon – a decagon. Now imagine a chord joining a point and the next-but-one point (that is, missing out the one in between), and so on around the circle. In only one circuit there will have been completed a five-sided polygon, a pentagon, and a further circuit will merely join the same points again, going over the lines of the first polygon. This is not what is required, either. Try again, this time with a chord that misses out two points. Now the starting-point will not be returned to until three circuits have been completed, and a star-shaped figure with points will have been formed.

This sequence may be summarised mathematically as follows:

$n = 10/1 = 10$ (a decagon)
$n = 10/2 = 5$ (a pentagon)
$n = 10/3 = 3.333\ldots$ (a decagram)

The value obtained for *n* is an indication of the number of circuits required to make ten points, i.e. 3.333 ... × 3 = 10. Using this value for *n* in the earlier equation gives:

$c/2r = \sin(180/n) = \sin(180/3.333...) = \sin 54°$ (exactly, a pentagonal angle)

or

$c/r = 2 \sin 54° = 1.618\ 033\ 989\ ... = \Phi$

Thus the relationship stated above has been demonstrated.

But there are many other possibilities for varieties of polygram and polygon. Most would be very difficult to deduce by trial and error in drawing, but using the equation makes it relatively easy. We may show that for various values of *n*, at least one regular polygon and a variety of related polygrams may be derived. For example, based on the number 7:

n = 7/1　(a regular heptagon, in one pass)
n = 7/2　(a heptagram in two passes)
n = 7/3　(a heptagram in three passes)

Inserting these, or other values for *n*, where *n* = 7/*x* and *x* is an integer, into the equation will give the length of chord required to produce the polygram for any radius of circle. The example of the 7-group has been chosen to show that the principle is applicable to numbers and figures that are of no particular relevance beyond their curiosity value. Such figures often have internal angles at their points which are not integer values in degrees. For example, in the seven-pointed heptagram formed in two passes these angles are 51°.428 571 43 ... . Internal angles which do have integer values are much more interesting, and it was these that exercised the minds of the ancient geometers. Thus, the pentagonal family has angles of 18°, 36°, 72°, 54°, 108°, ...

As discussed in the text, the figure we have described as a hexagram does not actually fall within our own definition of a polygram, which we regard as a discrete figure determined by one equation. In terms of the compasses-and-chords construction, our definition requires each new chord to start from the end of the previous one until the figure is completed. The hexagram consists of two such discrete figures – the equilateral triangles. Each is a polygon in its own right; in fact, the equilateral triangle with its three equal sides may be called a *trigon*. Reference is also made in the text to the ultimate completion of the relationship between the square and the equilateral triangle. This would have four triangles arranged around the sides of the square, the overall effect being of a twelve-pointed star – a dodecagram. But this is defective in the same way as the hexagram: it is not a true polygram. But is it possible to draw a true dodecagram? This question was to be answered by Bérenger Saunière and Nicolas Poussin, in a way that is particularly satisfying.

G

TILTING THE Φ PYRAMID

We have seen that there appeared to be two justifications for rotating the square. Tilting the Pyramid triangle by 15° along with the square (the plan view of the Pyramid) brought its apex on to the horizontal line previously occupied by the top side of the square. From a drawing it is impossible to know whether this is a precise result, or a close approximation. But this may be determined mathematically as follows.

The geometry is illustrated in Figure G.1. Here,

$$z = x \tan \alpha$$

and

$$\tan \theta = \frac{x + z}{x} = \frac{x + x \tan \alpha}{x} = 1 + \tan \alpha$$

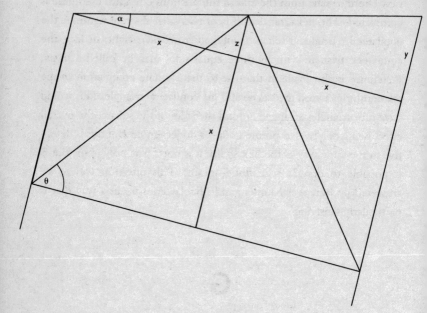

FIGURE G.1 The 15° tilt and the geometry of the Great Pyramid.

If α = 15°, then θ = 51°.738, remarkably close to the Pyramid angle of 51°.83. So we may deduce that, prior to the availability of trigonometry (as used above), the result may well have been considered precise. It may even have been what suggested the 15° rotation in the first place.

H

THE DODECAGRAM

Appendix F illustrates the use of the equation that governs polygons, and how it may be used to predict the form of a polygon for particular values of the generating chord and radius of the circumscribing circle. The process involves determining how many chord-drawing circuits of the circle are necessary to complete the figure, and may be used for any family of polygons.

The dodecagram belongs to the 12-family. The other members of the family are found by dividing 12 by the number of circuits, N.

$N = 1$: $12 \div 1 = 12$; in one circuit, obviously a dodecagon.

$N = 2$: $12 \div 2 = 6$; after only one circuit a hexagon is formed, so the second circuit will just be a repeat.

$N = 3$: $12 \div 3 = 4$; after only one circuit a square is formed, so the second and third circuits will be repeats.

$N = 4$: $12 \div 4 = 3$; after only one circuit a trigon (equilateral triangle) is formed, so the next three will be repeats.

$N = 5$: $12 \div 5 = 2.4$; as the answer is not an integer, all five circuits will be required to complete the figure, and the result will be a true dodecagram. This is the figure indicated by the third staff in Poussin's *Les Bergers d'Arcadie II*.

This sequence demonstrates that the effect of five circuits is unique, an association between the sacred pentagonal and hexagonal geometries that would have been irresistible. As stated in the text, superimposing the dodecagram on to the four triangles of the pseudo-dodecagram reveals that the chord of the former cuts off a segment of circle subdivided into five arcs by the points of the latter (Figure 9.6, on p. 198). And going back to the polygram formula (Appendix F), the next step would have been to calculate $180° \div 2.4$, which is $75°$! The dodecagram must have been looked upon as having immense significance.

I

THE DOUBLE-SIDED PARCHMENT

There are ways other than those described in the text in which the geometric relationship between the two sides of the Parchment receives further confirmation. In the final arrangement, where the 7½° lines are parallel, the top left-hand corner of the triangle is equidistant from the upper side and left side of the large square. Consider Plate 14 (which is printed 'square on' in order to maximise use of the page; rotating the book 15° clockwise restores the more familiar orientation). As we have shown, the 'Teniers transformation' from tilted triangle to square produces a square, shown in black in the Plate, of size equal to the inner, canted square; so if this transformation is performed and the square rotated clockwise, we find that the top right-hand corner of the square (now shown in red) is also equidistant from the upper and right sides of the large square.

The role of large square, which might have been thought superfluous as it is not the one associated with the triangle, is now apparent: it is there to signal the rotation of the inner square. This is the Masonic secret contained in Roritzer's diagrams; without it, the small square would be simply a square. When in Chapter 4 we (apparently rather arbitrarily) introduced Plato's theorem and its medieval applications, we said that it was not enough to know of it, one also had to know how to use it. Its significance is now clear.

Another feature to which attention should be drawn is the intersection of the 7½° line of Side 2 ('Parchment 2') with the most southerly of the 'fan' lines from Antugnac. This is located on the lower side of the large square when the correct alignment has been achieved.

This is by no means an exhaustive analysis of the geometric correlations that exist, or that may be perceived, but it covers those considered most significant and justifiable. The clear association of the Tour Magdala, the churches at Antugnac and Peyrolles, and the cross at *La Croix* with the double-sided Parchment geometry suggests that the nineteenth-century structures were erected as part of a definitive scheme, the ultimate clarification of the 'map'. The siting of *La Croix* relative to Peyrolles church, to give a 45° bearing, and the siting of the Tour Magdala relative to Antugnac church, also to give a 45° bearing, must be seen as the logical basis for a triangulation, the completion of which would have brought the survey up to the standard of the 'modern' État-Major map – a suitable replacement (or companion) for the 'château geometry'. One might wonder whether there is evidence of any intention to establish further permanent beacons. There is none, but an anecdote (related in Lincoln's *The Holy Place*) has it that in 1917 Saunière signed a contract for the construction of another tower. This one, much grander, was to have been sixty metres high!

J

SAUNIÈRE'S BOOKPLATE: THE CONSTRUCTION SEQUENCE

The object is to construct three polygons circumscribed by three circles of the same diameter and spaced by one quarter of that diameter. This aim is not merely a whim, but is inspired by the knowledge that the corners, sides and centre of the equilateral triangle of the hexagram, and the squares of Plato's theorem when circumscribed by the same circle, are related by the 'quarter-diameter' of that circle. This concept is also apparent in the drawing by Leonardo da Vinci (Figure 4.10, on p. 96) in which he derives a tilted equilateral triangle.

The eight steps

1. Draw the large circle, and within it the two equilateral triangles of the hexagram (Figure J.1). The horizontal lines of the hexagram divide the circle's diameter at points midway between the centre and the circumference (this is geometrically precise, not a fortuitous result).

FIGURE J.1

2. The outer of the two small circles on the bookplate – half the diameter of the large circle – may now be drawn, but for clarity, and as it has no influence on the rest of the construction, it is not shown again until Step 7.

3. The point that will be the centre of the cross is marked with a dot (Figure J.2).

4. The circle to circumscribe the pentagram is drawn, to have the same diameter as the hexagram and the pentagram drawn within it, starting with the sides that meet at the dot marking the centre of the cross.

FIGURE J.2

5. A circle tangential to the sides of the small pentagon at the centre of the pentagram is the inner of the two small circles below the cross (Figure J.3).

6. A similar procedure is followed for the dodecagram and its circle, except that instead of the internal circle being drawn as in Step 5, the ends of the cross are eventually drawn in (Figure 11.2).

7. When the lower side of the square has been drawn so as to pass through the points of the pentagram, and the upper side

FIGURE J.3

determined in a similar manner with respect to the dodecagram, the largest circle may be drawn within these sides, leaving a small margin; this being slightly different at top and bottom, as observed in the original (Figure J.4).

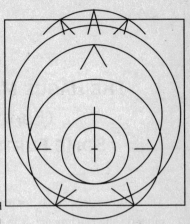

8. Assuming that these constructions have been made in light pencil, the features intended to be visible and the other details – the cross and the inscriptions – may be drawn over in black ink. The letters of the inscriptions will be arranged to reflect the geometry. Unwanted pencil lines may then be erased.

FIGURE J.4

The geometric basis for the bookplate shows clearly that Bérenger Saunière, if he was the draughtsman, was privy to the same esoteric geometry as practised by Bruno and Poussin. Leonardo's role is harder to fathom, and requires further research. His paintings and drawings give nothing away; his purported Grand Mastership of the Priory of Sion leads one to expect more than a tentative – and finally inaccurate – groping through the geometry. One might imagine that he had been set the task of deducing the particular application of the geometry behind the preservation of the Secret. His last employer, Francis I, brought him to France where, by all accounts, he was a virtual prisoner; the king was vigorously anti-heretic. Was Leonardo, who survived only one year after his move to France, actually ignorant of the Secret, or merely feigning ignorance while putting on a show of diligent research into something he was fully aware of? Our present view, based on the meagre evidence of one quick sketch and the glaring absence of the geometry in Leonardo's *surviving* paintings, is that he was not *au fait* with the details, but may have been provided with some basic material on which to work – perhaps by Francis. We reserve the right to revise that view.

K

THE HAGUE MAP OF JERUSALEM (FIGURE 13.5): SOME FURTHER COMMENTS

The Château de Serres is not represented on this map; neither is it indicated on the Parchments. It may be that even the earliest, unrecorded construction on this site post-dates the map. Blanchefort is not marked; this clearly would have been difficult – or, rather, impossible – as at this scale it would be less than the span of the cross of the calvary from the Site, and no building is ever marked there.

The identification with Peyrolles of a church depicted on the map is unreliable. It is not exactly on its spot, as the Château d'Arques is. It may have been beyond the scope of the mapmaker to make suitable adjustments to the locations of the famous buildings of Jerusalem, even though there is considerable disagreement between this map and the others we have studied; for example, the Latin Church is in a different place. However, one would not expect Peyrolles to have been used to define the bearing from the north-west since it does not lie on a notable bearing from the Site; its remarkable relationship to the triangle and square of the Parchment geometry does not place it in a similarly notable position with respect to the Site. The most logical position for the other point is the top-left corner of the square, which is on a 30° bearing from the Site, but as this is rather far away it may have been another point on this line. (With a geometric map such as this, only certain strategic points need be marked; features would be fleshed out in the mind of the user.) There is a monument at la Courbatière exactly on this line, which may have been erected in later recognition of the line, but is too far from the Site for sighting to be carried out. There may once have been a marker at the corner of the square.

There is, however, a line which does not figure in the triangle–square geometry, and which has been carefully marked nevertheless. The 72° line shown passing through the Calvary of Golgotha may be drawn on the 1:25,000 map, and examined for potential marker-points. To within a little more than half a degree, this line passes through a *calvaire* just west of Peyrolles church. We had visited this, and found a sad little stump – no nineteenth-century *calvaire*, but the remains of a stone cross of some antiquity.

Careful examination of the map and the superimposed geometry reveals details that differ in small degree from the later versions. For example, the expected difficulty with the two 1½° rotations is incomprehensible here; little wonder that successive custodians of the Secret struggled to resolve this problem.

L

THE MATRI DEUM ALTAR:
DETAILED ANALYSIS

The analysis of the letters and other features is presented here. The Figure numbers refer to those in the text, on pages 301–13.

The right-hand leg of the 'M' of MATRI is at 75° + 1½° to the horizontal, the latter increment being determined by the border moulding. The tops of the letters of MATRI DEVM define the top of the 'square' (before its 15° rotation); the left side of the 'square' is a vertical from the top-right apex of the 'M'. This vertical coincides with the inner vertical line of the border (Figure 15.3).

The 'M' crossing the border marks the right-hand line of the inner pair of moulding lines as the 'old' meridian. This line extended passes through a 'chip' just below the cornice. A line drawn through point A at 45° − 1½° to the horizontal forms the right side of the triangle, which is completed by the top side drawn at 15° + 1½° to the horizontal passing through the corner of the cornice at B (Figure 15.4). The left side passes through the top-left corner of the 'N' of CN★, and the right side touches the end of the leg of the smaller 'M' (the final letter), as it does with the 'M' of TEM-PLI.

The uprights of letters in MATRI DEVM are at 1½° to the vertical (Figure 15.5), indicating that the triangle should be rotated through this angle. When this is done, the right side is then at 45° to the horizontal, and when extended it gives the size of the square. The square, when rotated through 15°, has its left side passing down the line of the 'M' which also joins the top-left corner of the square (Figure 15.5). The complementary triangle that completes the hexagram (both triangles shown as dashed lines in Figure 15.6) is confirmed by the inscription in two ways:

1. The right side passes along the right-hand leg of the 'M' of DEVM, this being at 75° + 1½° (the last two 'M's of the inscription are also at this angle).
2. The right leg of the 'V' of DEVM, when extended, passes through the apex of the second triangle.

With the hexagram rotated through 1½° (shown as solid lines in Figure 15.7), the new location of the apex of the second triangle is confirmed by the leg of the 'M' adjacent to the 'V': the left side extended is tangential to the outer circle of the patera. The 'old' meridian is confirmed; this line, extended upwards, also passes through this apex (as indicated elsewhere, for example in *La Fontaine de fortune*). The centre of the right-hand side of the first triangle now falls on the right-hand line of the outer pair of moulded border-lines; before correction, it fell on the left-hand line of this pair – the present Zero Meridian. The moulding lines indicate the old and new meridians, an important feature which aids correct solution – and casts doubt on the age of the stone.

The inner triangle of the Coume Sourde diagram may be superimposed on the Matri Deum diagram (Figure 15.8). The 'old' meridian and the 7½° line, indicated on the Parchment by the 'm over I' symbol, intersect the upper side of this triangle at points which divide it into quarters. Extended, this passes through Antugnac church and the top-right corner of the first equilateral triangle, and drawn thus it is found to be tangential to a circle of the patera. The Coume Sourde triangle is also recognised by the border running around the main inscription, for the triangle's lower corner falls on a horizontal line of the border, while its upper side passes through a corner of the border.

The 7½° line drawn through the mid-point of the upper side, as on Parchment 1, is also confirmed: it is tangential to the corner of the cornice and to the bottom-right corner of the border. This correspondence is revealing. The inferred geographical layout of the châteaux at Arques, Blanchefort and Serres and the church at Peyrolles suggested to us that their locations must have been established by survey. The distance from Peyrolles to Blanchefort defined the radius of the circle tangential to the sides of the hexagram. The origin of the Coume Sourde diagram appeared to have been revealed: the Peyrolles–Blanchefort line is possibly the left side of the inner triangle, and the internal angles of this triangle are 36°, 108° and 36°. That these are pentagonal angles must be seen as highly reassuring. But there was a problem. This layout puts Peyrolles church on the left side of the inner Coume Sourde triangle, and in Parchment 1 this is not precisely so. But the Matri Deum stone shows quite clearly that the centre of the hexagram (when 'corrected') – i.e. Peyrolles church – does fall on this line; also the internal angles may be measured with some accuracy, and are confirmed as 36°, 108° and 36°. Whoever redrew the Parchments had neglected to ensure the accuracy required to maintain these features, and perhaps was not aware of them. (See the text for the connection between the patera and the canted squares of Plato's theorem.)

There are correlations between the patera and the drawing of the front of the stone: the patera is on the side of the stone. A line drawn from the centre of the patera to the upper-right corner of the 'M' of DEVM touches a corner in the border and the bottom of the 'V' of DEVM; it is also tangential to the small arc representing a remnant of the carved scroll at the top right of the stone. This line is at 30° to the horizontal. We drew in Plato's squares in this orientation to elaborate the point; this was clearly the correct action, as shown by the relationship of the squares (Figure 15.11).

The right side of the first triangle had been tangential to the base of the wine-jug before the 1½° correction; afterwards, it was tangential to the curved body of the jug (Figures 15.6 and 15.7).

The differences between the Sacaze drawing and the stone itself

The photographs and the corresponding drawings are illustrated side by side to aid comparison (Figures 15.2a and 15.2b). The real stone differs in the following respects, starting from the top:

1. The uprights of the letters 'T', 'R', 'I', 'D' and 'E' of MATRI DEVM do not lean uniformly backwards. The slopes of the 'M's are different to the drawing – in particular, the last is much closer to the vertical. The second apex of the first 'M' is not vertically above the inner edge of the moulded 'frame' around the main inscription.

2. Damage to the cornice is not as drawn. The right-hand limit to the damaged area is not the near-vertical line of the drawing, but a jagged line running off to the bottom-right corner, and it does not correspond to the right-hand edge of the moulding below. There is no sign of the small mark below the cornice which in the drawing corresponds to the moulding line representing the 'old' meridian.

3. The moulded 'frame' has raised components of unequal width; the

drawing could have indicated this better, but with poorer definition of the meridional lines. The overall proportions of the frame are different, the original having a greater height, so clearly this was how the border was made to correspond to the Coume Sourde triangle.

4. The layout of the main inscription is more competently planned (this is discussed in general terms in the text) and reveals a serious effort to achieve a harmonious, workmanlike effect. Unlike the 'M' that crosses the border in the drawing, the 'M' on the stone is parallel to the moulding, and far less obvious.

5. CN ⋆ POMP is tightly framed and neatly executed. But the diagonal of the 'N' is at a different angle and, when extended, does not pass through the centre of an 'O'.

6. Other letters are located such that the other geometric correspondences do not occur. The 75° line from the 'M' of MATRI does not pass through the apex of the 'N' of CN⋆, nor the 'I' of TEMPLI, and so on.

7. The patera on the stone is a succession of equi-spaced circles; the wine-jug is a different shape. Their modification in the drawing and the purpose of the modification are described in the text.

The text describes how the derivation of a succession of squares – each twice the area of that preceding, in accordance with Plato's theorem – is a process that may be repeated *ad infinitum*; and that Sacaze had arranged for the patera squares to be in this proportion to the large square of the main diagram.

The mathematical means of testing this may be pursued as follows: The $2:1$ ratio of areas of the squares means that the lengths of their sides will be in the ratio $\sqrt{2}:1$. In other words, the next larger square will have a side measuring $L \times \sqrt{2}$; where L is the length of side of the preceding square. So if one were to start with a square of unit side ($L = 1$), after (say) three duplications of area the resulting square would have a side of length $1 \times \sqrt{2} \times \sqrt{2} \times \sqrt{2}$. The approximate ratio of the size of the large diagram square to that of the larger of the patera squares may be obtained by scaling from the drawing. Doing this as carefully as possible gives a ratio $L_1 : L_2 = 5.67$. Dividing this number successively by $\sqrt{2}$ gives the following sequence of numbers (all to three decimal places): 5.670, 4.009, 2.835, 2.005, 1.417, 1.002. It is clear that this last number should be exactly 1, from which we can work back to find the original ratio as 5.656, for this is $1 \times \sqrt{2}$ *five times*, and the large square is five times the area of the larger of the patera squares. Five again! (The difference between 5.67 and 5.656 is within the difference in accuracy that would result from measuring from the 'inside' of a line rather than the 'outside'.) The resulting drawing is shown in Figure 15.11.

NOTES

INTRODUCTION

1 Guilleme de Catel, *Mémoires de l'histoire du Languedoc*, Vol. 1, p. 51.

2 G. P. Baker (*Twelve Centuries of Rome*, p. 533) relates the events thus: 'The story was afterwards told, how they diverted the stream, buried him in the River Busentinus with all his [Alaric's] treasures, released the stream again, and hid for ever the golden grave of the man who had sacked Rome. It was at any rate certain that they buried him somewhere: though his treasures most likely found their way into the hands of his kinsmen and friends.'

3 The Visigoths gained their initial foothold in the area of Rennes-le-Château via the port of Narbonne. For extensive historical evidence, see Dom Cl. Devic and Dom J. Vaissette, *Histoire général du Languedoc*, Vol. 1; for archaeological evidence, see Ernest Roschach and Auguste Molinier, *Histoire graphique de l'ancienne province de Languedoc*. See also Ian Wood, *The Merovingian Kingdoms*.

4 *Whiston's Josephus*, p. 594. (See under Josephus in the Bibliography.)

5 Herod Antipas was banished by the Emperor Caligula to the town of Lugdunum. Fritz Otto Busch (*The Five Herods*, p. 135) identifies Lugdunum with the modern Lyons, though H.W. Hoehner (*Herod Antipas*, p. 262) disputes this, identifying the place of exile as St Bernard de Comminges, once the Roman town of Lugdunum Convenarum. (In *Jesus the Man*, p. 160, Barbara Thiering suggests that Herod was exiled to south-west France.) There is no surviving evidence for Pilate's place of exile, indeed his very existence was confirmed only by the twentieth-century discovery of a memorial stone in Israel. However, tradition gives his place of exile as Viènne (on the Rhône) in Gaul.

6 Baigent, Leigh and Lincoln, *The Holy Blood and the Holy Grail*.

7 The details of the formation of the Templars – original membership, numbers and date – are disputed. The twelfth-century historian William of Tyre gave 1118 for the year of foundation; Malcolm Barber, in his *The New Knighthood* (p. 9), gives 1120.

8 René Descadeillas, *Mythologie du trésor de Rennes* (p. 17, note 6): 'Concerning this point we can rely uniquely on witnesses. Several of them were still alive in 1958. They were unanimous in confirming the occasion' (our translation).

9 Much controversy has surrounded this macabre discovery. In *Mythologie du trésor de Rennes* (p. 57), Descadeillas recounts the presence of a group of Spanish Maquis who sheltered in the gardens in the winter of 1944/45. Gérard de Sède (*Rennes-le-Château*, p. 83) contests this, saying that the Languedoc was liberated in August 1944 and that during the German occupation the nearest Maquis were to be found seventy-five kilometres from Rennes-le-Château. How long human flesh can survive underground depends on soil type, temperature and aerobic conditions. In 1956, less than forty years separated Saunière from the three bodies; under the right conditions, such human remains can be preserved for much longer than that.

1 THE PARCHMENTS

1 Lincoln, *The Holy Place*, p. 24.

2 Because of the Parchments' nature and size (the actual size is unknown, but can be assumed to be limited by their reputed hiding-place) there is an inevitable lack of accuracy in the alignments, and in studying them one has to decide what qualifies as an acceptable degree of misalignment and what does not. This particular circle falls into the latter category.

3 Lincoln, *The Holy Place*, p. 27.

2 THE CIPHER CODE

1 These details (source unknown) were communicated in a letter from de Sède to Henry Lincoln (*The Holy Place*, pp. 42, 43).

2 Baigent *et al.*, *The Messianic Legacy*, p. 298.

3 THE GUARDIAN SPIRIT

1 Gérard de Sède, *L'Or de Rennes*, p. 67.
2 Frances Yates, *Giordano Bruno and the Hermetic Tradition*, p. 133.
3 On the *Sang Réal* ('Royal Blood') or Holy Grail, see W. Jennings, *The Rosicrucians*, p. 369.
4 For more details, see Joan du Plat Taylor, *Marine Archaeology*, p. 24.

4 ANCIENT SIGNS AND SECRETS

1 Jean Gimpel, *The Cathedral Builders*, p. 84.
2 Thirteenth century, Bibliothèque Nationale, Paris.
3 D.M. would normally be expected to stand for DE MANIUM, meaning 'for the spirits (of the dead)'. But in this case one would expect the remaining part of the inscription also to be in Latin; clearly it is not, for the letter 'U' is included as well as the 'V'. The latter performs two phonetic functions in Latin: as a consonant pronounced (depending on what one was taught) as *w* or *v*, or as a vowel pronounced as a *u*. Memorial inscriptions in the antique manner never mix the two forms of Roman capitals. No one has satisfactorily analysed this inscription, but perhaps a solution will be forthcoming as a result of the present work.
4 Frances Yates, *Giordano Bruno and the Hermetic Tradition*, p. 313.
5 In *Giordano Bruno and the Hermetic Tradition* (p. 324), Yates describes Bruno's endplate as 'three curious things rather like worms, outside the triangle' – which she believes are intended to represent 'links with demons'. She also mentions (p. 323) Bruno's high opinion of Cecco d'Ascoli, who was burned by the Inquisition in 1327. In *De monade*, Bruno gives Cecco the title 'Ciccus Asculanus – born in the time of light' – a possible reference to a fellow-Gnostic.
6 There is some circumstantial evidence to support this assertion (Baigent *et al.*, *The Holy Blood and the Holy Grail*, p. 97).

5 THE PRIEST AND THE PAINTINGS

1 Richard Khaitzine, *Les Faiseurs d'Or de Rennes-le-Château*, p. 124.
2 Funck-Hellet, *Composition et Nombre d'Or dans les oeuvres peintes de la Renaissance*.
3 An artist wishing to convey the concept of death being ever-present

would incorporate a *memento mori*. This would most often be the skull, but sometimes it would a tomb, and when a tomb was used it would normally be ogee-sided – that is, having sides with an S-shaped cross-section.

4 Oskar Bätschmann, *Nicolas Poussin: Dialectics of Painting*, pp. 54–56.

5 Baigent *et al.*, *The Holy Blood and the Holy Grail*, p. 193.

6 For recent discussion on this topic, see G. Hancock, *The Sign and the Seal*.

7 Baigent *et al.*, *The Messianic Legacy*, p. 210.

8 E. Panofsky, *Meaning in the Visual Arts*, pp. 340–367.

9 Wright, *French Painters of the Seventeenth Century*.

10 Lincoln, *The Holy Place*, p. 51.

6 'X MARKS THE SPOT'

1 Wood's rather individual ideas are set out in his book *Genisis* [sic].

2 Readers will have to trust that the lines drawn on the maps are genuine, or obtain the map and try for themselves: formerly on two sheets, the I.G.N. 'TOP25' sheet 2347 OT, 'Quillan – Alet-les-Bains' now includes all the features referred to in this book.

3 Lagarde, 'Historique du problème du Méridien origine en France'.

8 THREE ERRANT PRIESTS

1 Gérard de Sède, *Rennes-le-Château*, p. 81 (our translation). This was said to Noël Corbu. According to Corbu, Denarnaud repeatedly promised to give him information concerning the secret of Saunière which would make him not only rich but powerful as well. However, a stroke left Denarnaud incapacitated, and she died on 29 January 1953, aged eighty-five, never having revealed her secret.

2 Pierre Plantard's preface to the 1978 reprint of Boudet, *La Vraie Langue celtique*, p. 17.

3 Boudet, *La Vraie Langue celtique*, p. 231.

4 In *Rennes-le-Château* (pp. 46–47), Gérard de Sède gives a reckoning of the contemporary (1988) value of Saunière's wealth. He values ten gold francs at 350 francs. The sum of 659,413 gold francs, given by documentation alone (i.e. excluding other monies), he therefore estimates at 23,079,455 francs.

9 THE POUSSIN ENIGMA

1 This is the view expressed in the R.M.N. catalogue of the Poussin exhibition, which illustrates the Anson portrait. (See under Réunion des Musées Nationaux in the Bibliography.)
2 This was the opinion of Christies when they provided this information in October 1995.
3 Sewell, 'The Blunt truth about Poussin?'.
4 *Ibid*.
5 Beresford, *A Dance to the Music of Time*, pp. 34–36.

10 THROUGH THE PARCHMENTS AND BEYOND

1 Baigent *et al*., *The Messianic Legacy*, p. 216.
2 *Ibid*., p. 215.

11 FRESH CLUES AND FURTHER CONFIRMATION

1 There is still further confirmation. Upward extensions of the lines forming the apex of the figure are marked by the 'U' and 'R' of UNUS and TRIA in the outer inscription. Also, the two lower points of the pentagram fall on the edge of the enclosing 'square' of the paper label. This is no coincidence, as will be shown later.
2 In other words, if the straight-edge were to be placed at the centre of the small circles, is there an indication of a radius around the centre of the cross? There is no circle, evidently, but the arms of the cross could fulfil that role. Checking this, one finds an angle to the vertical of close on 15°, but this angle depends on just where the straight-edge is placed. One may set an adjustable set-square to 15° and see what figure will result. Actually, we know that it will be a dodecagram with angles of 30° at its points; we have seen this before. The completed figure receives extensive confirmation from various letters in the inscriptions of the large and small rings. The sides of the polygram combine to form at the centre an 'envelope' in the form of a putative circle circumscribing the top and arms of the cross. A particularly dark patch of shading is visible on the bookplate where the top of the cross has been adjusted to the required height (Figure 11.2). Once again, two of the points fall on the edge of the square, and this has

been contrived by appropriately adjusting the gap between the square and the circle, which is not the same width as the gap at the bottom.

3 See Claire Corbu and Antoine Captier, *L'Héritage de l'Abbé Saunière*, p. 80. This is one of several works which reproduce Saunière's surviving correspondence.

4 This is an accusation which seems, unlike many of the legends surrounding Saunière, to have foundation in fact. De Sède (*Rennes-le-Château*, p. 35) confirms the finding of the tombstone by Saunière and his attempt to remove all record of the epitaph by defacing the stone, and mentions that the epitaph was published in the *Bulletin de la Société des Études Scientifiques de l'Aude*.

5 Lincoln (quoting Gérard de Sède), *The Holy Place*, p. 44.

6 Readers familiar with the solution to the cipher will wonder why we reject the possibility that the de Nègre inscription was the key. Actually we do not. Careful examination of the manner in which the grave inscription is involved in the cipher will show that this might still be the case.

7 See, for example, Bruno de Monts, 'Le Mystère de Rennes-le-Château (suite)'; Lincoln (quoting de Sède), *The Holy Place*, p. 44; Pierre Plantard's preface to Boudet, *La Vraie Langue celtique*.

8 'Jean Delaude' (i.e. *de l'Aude*, 'of the Aude' – clearly an alias), *Le Cercle d'Ulysse* – one of the so-called Priory Documents.

9 L.A. Brown, *The Story of Maps*, p. 60.

10 The six-petalled flower that every child draws using compasses divides the original circle into six sectors – and thus into 60° divisions. These may be halved and halved again using only the compasses, and if the circle is sufficiently large, great accuracy is possible.

11 For the development of the wind rose, and the twelve-point version, see L.A. Brown, *The Story of Maps*, pp. 123–126.

12 THE GRAVE ON THE ROSE LINE

1 Other examples of central lines dividing grave inscriptions may be seen in the same graveyard, but these have more obviously decorative terminations such as the fleur-de-lis.

2 Plantard's preface to Boudet, *La Vraie Langue celtique*, p. 30.

3 The Priory Document *Le Cercle d'Ulysse* by 'Jean Delaude', in referring to the Poussin tomb, states that 'In reality the tomb is not at

Arques, but situated on the Zero Meridian between Peyrolles and Serres. [Yet again!] This tomb, mentioned in a work of the eighteenth century by Abbé Delmas, had on its north face a vertical stone which carried this motto: "ET IN ARCADIA EGO", and it was transported in 1789 to the cemetery of Rennes-le-Château' (our translation). The statement about the siting of the tomb is so at odds with the Poussin depiction and with the known location of the site (still showing the base-slab as all that remains of the demolished tomb) that it is clearly nonsense. In such cases, one should be on guard for hidden meanings. The opening sentence of this quoted passage reads in the original text, 'En realité, le tombeau n'est pas à Arques, mais situé sur le méridien zéro entre Peyrolles et Serres.' There is no reference here to the Poussin tomb – it is the reader who infers that association from the statements that precede and follow. It is surely telling us that *the* tomb (i.e. the Site) is on the Rose Line. Whatever the origin of the de Nègre recumbent stone or its original location, the quality of the survey information it provides is indisputable.

4 L.A. Brown, *The Story of Maps*, Chap. 8.

5 Plantard's preface to Boudet, *La Vraie Langue celtique*, pp. 33–34.

6 L. Perey, *Charles de Lorraine et la cour de Bruxelles.*

7 Another interesting deduction may also be made: that the much-disputed recumbent stone of the de Nègre grave may very well have existed in much the form of the published drawing. Why? Because it is more likely that Boudet used the line with an arrowhead at each end for the grave of his mother and sister, having first seen it on the de Nègre stone, than vice versa. But perhaps the stone had never been intended for the grave (it certainly is not appropriate) and had been placed closer to Arques – possibly even at the 'Poussin tomb', quite close to the line indicated by the bearing of N 120° E from the keep of the Château d'Arques, and relatively safe from disturbance on this 'island' rock.

8 Building the church in Espéraza at the same latitude as the Site would have been a singular aim for the period, but it would have been readily achievable by making meridional observations of the Sun; this was the method '… long used by Arabs in "camel navigation" of the desert … [but] unknown to Columbus' (Morison, p. 184). The Templars may well have acquired this knowledge during their sojourn in the Holy Land. Columbus may not have known of this technique,

but navigators of his day were not noted for their competence in celestial navigation (*Ibid.*, pp. 186–187). If navigators did not know of these techniques, philosophers, mathematicians and astronomers certainly did.

The task is in fact far simpler than it might first appear, for the aim is not to calculate the latitude of one place in relation to another – as one would in navigation – but to determine the same latitude at another longitude. Repeated observation of the Sun's altitude at midday, and successive adjustments of one's position on the ground further north or south, would lead in just a few days to a tolerably precise result. Contemporary instruments – the astrolabe, quadrant and cross-staff – would have enabled such observations to be made.

Thus we may note that two simple techniques would permit the marking of the two components of the 'Rose Cross': the Meridian and the Latitude. Perhaps more surprising than the possibility of this having been established is the apparent lack of permanent features to record the position. The meridional line carefully established on the floor of St Sulpice in Paris may have more to do with the esoteric Rose Line than with its stated purpose of calculating the date of Easter. Curiously, the survival of the church's fine balustrading at the entrance to the choir from the wave of iconoclastic destruction in the days of the Revolution is attributed (in the visitor's guide available at the church) to respect for the preservation of the Meridian. This seems unlikely: quite enough remains of the brass line set into the marble floor to preserve the Meridian, even after destruction of the balustrading. It is at least possible that the Revolutionary forces were actually respecting the Rose Line. They did, however, tarry long enough to obliterate with hammer-blows the inscriptions to the king and his ministers, leaving ugly scars on the elegant gnomon that carries the vertical extension of the meridional line.

9 The west corner of the Château de Serres is very close to being on the meridian that passes through the Site. In fact, a line drawn through these two points deviates from true (I.G.N. grid) north by approximately 2°. It is possible that the château was sited using compass bearings from rock S.H. 547 on Cardou, which also happens to be on the Site–Serres line. It is possible that the error could be within the accuracy achievable with contemporary instruments. Sighting Polaris from the base of S.H. 547 and transferring this line accurately to the

ground at a convenient spot would depend for its accuracy on the precision of the trunnion of the sighting-tube, or of the sights of the theodolite. In the fifteenth century Polaris was some 3° off the north celestial pole, and if it were sighted at any time when not lying due south or due north of the pole, and no correction were made for the angular error, a discrepancy of 2° would be understandable. If the Château de Serres were in fact intended to lie on the Rose Line, this would represent a greater justification for its existence than that of a mere survey station.

13 THE KNIGHTS TEMPLAR AND THE PLACE OF THE SKULL

1 The most complete collection of Templar land transactions in France, published in 1913, is the *Cartulaire général de l'Ordre du Temple* compiled by Albon. This work presents the Latin texts in chronological order and by area. The Bodleian library holds an original copy.

2 Malcolm Barber, *The New Knighthood*, p. 12.

3 Baigent *et al.*, *The Holy Blood and the Holy Grail*, p. 409 (note 12). These authors also discuss the chronology of the Grand Masters of the Temple (pp. 97–100), and describe Bertrand de Blanchefort as the fourth Grand Master (p. 63). We prefer to adhere to the view that he was the sixth Grand Master, as stated in Barber's *The New Knighthood*, p. xxi.

4 Barber, *The New Knighthood*, p. 256.

5 In their *Histoire générale du Languedoc*, Devic and Vaissette mention that this transaction is recorded in the Papal Bull of 19 June 1119 (Vol. V, p. 1980).

6 British Library, Royal Ms 6, fo. 108v.

7 Ezekiel 5:5. (This and other extracts from the Bible are taken either from *The Book of Common Prayer* (including the Psalms of David), 1753, Thomas Baskett, London, or from *The English Version of the Polyglot Bible*, 1854, Samuel Bagster, London.)

8 India Office Library, the British Library.

9 British Library, Additional Ms 32343, fo. 15v.

10 Dated by the Royal Library at The Hague.

11 Such non-representational decoration is often to be found as the background in paintings of this period, but is normally more decorative and uniform in its coverage than it is here.

12 Baigent and Leigh, *The Temple and the Lodge*; see also Andrew Sinclair, *The Sword and the Grail.*

13 Begg and Begg, *In Search of the Holy Grail and the Precious Book*, p. 23.

14 In *The Rosicrucians* (pp. 260–261), W. Jennings explains the Persian 'crucified rose', and goes into some detail about the use of the red rose on *calvaires.*

14 ET IN ARCADIA EGO

1 Baigent *et al.*, *The Holy Blood and the Holy Grail*, p. 267; see also W. Jennings, *The Rosicrucians*, p. 369.

15 ONE ERRANT ACADEMIC

1 Pierre Plantard bought several parcels of land not far from the Site – as the land registries reveal – but they are on the wrong side of the valley, near Roc Nègre and Blanchefort. So in spite of his apparent knowledge of meridians and the Rose Line, did he slip up?

2 Lagarde, 'Historique du problème du Méridien origine en France'.

3 See, for example, Baigent *et al.*, *The Holy Blood and the Holy Grail* and *The Messianic Legacy*; Gérard de Sède, *L'Occultisme dans la politique.*

4 The original inscription reads: 'C'est encore une singularité fort grande que ne soit que sous le seul Méridien de Paris et par un plan moyen entre l'Equateur et l'Axe de la Terre que notre Globe puisse nous donner des spectacles aussi différents que ceux de ces deux planis-phères et que ce Méridien déjà distingué par les travaux de MM. de l'Académie royale des Sciences soit le seul de tous qui les divise chaqu'un en deux parties égales et qui puisse y être tracé à la fois comme Méridien et comme Diamètre par une même ligne droite lorsque tous les autres n'y forment que des courbes toujours variées, sans pouvoir prendre n'y donner une pareille situation. Cette propriété est une sorte de prééminence qui doit à l'avenir le faire regarder comme le premier Méridien, son titre n'est point dans notre imagina-tion, il est pour ansi dire dans la nature ...' (Julien, *Nouvelle Mappemonde dediée au progrès de nos connaissances*, 1753; Bibliothèque Nationale, Paris, Ge DD 2987 (104)). This passage is enigmatic, and its meaning is not easily discernible from a straightforward English trans-lation. It is Julien's apparently muddled justification of the Meridian's

geographic or cartographic significance that leads one to suspect that there was another reason for stressing its importance.

5 L.A. Brown, *The Story of Maps*, p. 214.

16 THE SECRET AND ITS GUARDIANS

1 René d'Anjou, *Le Livre du coeur d'amour épris du Roi René*.

2 Bibliothèque Nationale, Paris.

3 Bibliothèque Nationale, Paris, Ms fr. 2360, fo. 14r.

4 Otto Pächt, 'René d'Anjou – Studien II', pp. 88–91.

5 *Ibid*.

6 *Ibid*. Artists working for René d'Anjou followed his explicit instructions (there is difficulty in distinguishing work by his own hand from that of his studio). It is surprising to find that René worked from small model figures in composing his pictures, as (later) did Poussin.

7 *Ibid*.

8 Conversation with Frances Yates, quoted by Baigent *et al.* in *The Holy Blood and the Holy Grail*, p. 94.

9 J. Harthan, *Books of Hours*, p. 86.

10 We are not contradicting ourselves about the establishment of a meridional line extending to Paris and beyond. We refer here to the establishment of a local meridian, marked by features distant from the Site, but within reasonable surveying distance. René d'Anjou was announcing his sacerdotalism. So, perhaps, was de Gaulle!

11 J. Huizinga, *The Waning of the Middle Ages*, p. 137.

12 British Library, Egerton Ms 1070.

13 Huizinga, *The Waning of the Middle Ages*, p. 136.

14 From the introduction by L.R. Lind to *The Pastorals of Vergil*, p. 4. (See under Virgil in the Bibliography.)

15 Quoted from essay on Eclogue IV in *The Pastoral Poems*, pp. 102–103. (See under Virgil in the Bibliography.)

16 Bernstock, 'Guercino's "Et in Arcadia Ego" and "Apollo Flaying Marsyas" '.

17 Denis Mahon, *Il Guercino*, Vol. 1.

18 Blunt, *Poussin*, p. 177.

19 B. Walker, in his *Gnosticism: Its History and Influence*, quoting 'the British scholar Arthur Darby Nock' and 'the German authority Adolf Harnack'.

20 Blunt, *Poussin*, p. 178.

21 *Ibid.*

22 While he was still Cardinal Rospigliosi, Pope Clement IX had lamented that Poussin had not survived long enough to be honoured adequately. The honour that had to await the cardinal's elevation to the papal office would be the benediction of the Golden Rose, in the gift of the Pope only. Had Poussin survived to see Rospigliosi become Pope, would the benediction of the Golden Rose have taken place publicly, or behind closed doors? We shall never know, but we may guess.

23 Nicolas Poussin, *Correspondance*, p. 415 (quoted by Bätschmann, *Nicolas Poussin: Dialectics of Painting*, p. 49).

24 Bätschmann, *Nicolas Poussin: Dialectics of Painting*, p. 49.

25 National Galleries of London and Cardiff.

26 London, National Gallery.

27 Washington, National Gallery of Art.

28 The passage from this letter in which this statement appears is worth quoting at slightly greater length, for it shows that Fouquet may have had more than a hint of Poussin's motives. Fouquet says that he and Poussin 'discussed certain things of which I shall be able to inform you fully in a short while, which will give you, through M. Poussin, benefits . . . which kings would have great trouble extracting from him, and which after him perhaps no one in the world will rediscover in the centuries to come; and moreover, this will be without great expense and could even be turned to profit, and that these things are so hard to discover that nothing on earth can have a greater value nor be their equal . . .' (Lépinois, *Lettres de Louis Fouquet*, p. 269; our translation).

29 Bellori, *Le vite de pittori scultori et architetti moderni*.

30 A.K. Wheelock Jr, *Van Dyck Paintings*.

31 C. Brown, *Van Dyck*.

32 R. Heisler, 'Rosicrucianism: The first flowering in Britain'.

33 Heisler, *Ibid.*

17 THE BONES OF THE PROPHET

1 Tacitus, *The Histories*, quoted in Edmund Wilson, *Israel and The Dead Sea Scrolls*, pp. 308–309.

2 Tacitus, *The Histories*, quoted in Edmund Wilson, *Israel and The Dead Sea Scrolls*, p. 309.

3 Vermes, *The Dead Sea Scrolls*, p. 69.

4 *Ibid.*, p. 69 (1.11–12; 4 Q. 174).

5 *Ibid.*, p. 53 (Fig. 2, 2.1, 11–12; 4 Q. 521).

6 John 19:41.

7 Acts 21:20–22.

8 Herodotus, Book IV (Melpomene), p. 14. (See also Gerd Lüdemann, *The Resurrection of Jesus*, p. 119.)

9 Thiering, *Jesus the Man*, Chap. 9.

10 See the various translations of Josephus. *Whiston's Josephus* (p. 379) gives a full account of the development of the Josephan text; see also John Dominic Crossan, *The Historical Jesus*, p. 373.

11 Crossan (*Ibid.*) presents this passage as showing the anomalies present in 'Christianised' Josephan texts.

12 Hoehner, *Herod Antipas*, p. 262; Busch, *The Five Herods*, p. 135.

13 As also described by Andrew Sinclair in *The Sword and the Grail*.

14 The references to spices can be found in the New Testament. John 19:39 gives the weight as one hundred pounds (this was the Roman pound, of 12 ounces), equivalent to about 30 kg.

15 The Pesher method gets its name from the Hebrew word *pishro* ('its interpretation is'). Robert Eisenman and Michael Wise, in *The Dead Sea Scrolls Uncovered* (pp. 76–77), describe the use of this method at Qumran. The incorporation of a double or hidden meaning within a standard text enabled the preservation of a prophetic or revelatory text to be secretly perpetuated. The manner in which the secret geometry of Rennes-le-Château has been preserved down the centuries in the Parchments, in paintings, on a tombstone and on a faked drawing of a Roman votive stone indicates that those who sought to preserve the Secret of the Site at Mount Cardou knew of this ancient form of codification.

16 Thiering, *Jesus the Man*, p. 160.

17 Thiering, *Jesus of the Apocalypse*, p. 38.

18 Ian Wood, *The Merovingian Kingdoms*, p. 35.

19 See Pope John Paul II, *Crossing the Threshold of Hope* (p. 90). John Paul is scathing about Gnosticism, labelling it an attitude of spirit which distorts the word of God and replaces it with mere human words.

20 All extracts from the Nag Hammadi Gospels are taken from James Robinson, *The Nag Hammadi Library in English*.

18 IN THE NAME OF JESUS

1 Norbert Brox, *A History of the Early Church*, p. 157.
2 Baigent and Leigh, *The Temple and the Lodge,* p. 72.
3 Baigent *et al.*, *The Messianic Legacy*, plates 31 and 32.
4 'The Splitting of the Elm' reputedly occurred at a meeting at Gisors in France between Henry II of England and Philippe II of France during which Richard, son of Henry, became involved in an armed fracas over who should benefit from the shade of an elm tree. Although there is no proof of Templar engagement in this affair, Richard (the Lionheart, later King Richard I of England) did favour the Order, and at the battle of Arsuf (1191) in Palestine his trust in the Templars was justified when they played a major role in the defeat of Saladin's forces.

19 THE ROSE CROSS: ITS REBIRTH AND BENEFACTORS

1 Frances Yates, *The Rosicrucian Enlightenment*, p. 213.
2 Reported to a BBC researcher in May 1995.
3 *The Nag Hammadi Library in English*, p. 153.
4 *The Nag Hammadi Library in English*, p. 376. These words can be read as a Gnostic attack on the established Roman Church, its bishops and their message.

AFTERWORD

1 *The Nag Hammadi Library in English*, p. 376.
2 Joan Bakewell, 'The Truth That Dare Not Speak Its Name', *Sunday Times*, News Review section, 31 March 1996.
3 Everett Ferguson, in *Backgrounds of Early Christianity* (pp. 554–555), says of the various ossuaries from this region and period that 'Most of the names on the ossuaries were common enough Jewish names that their identity with any New Testament figure is problematic. Even the name Jesu itself (the Greek for the Hebrew Joshua) was quite common.'
4 Holger Kersten and Elmar Gruber, *The Jesus Conspiracy*, part 4.

APPENDICES

1 (APPENDIX D) Henri Lobineau, 1967, *Dossiers secrets*, Paris, planche no. 1, 400–600.

2 (APPENDIX E) W.M. Flinders Petrie, 1883, *The Pyramids and Temples of Gizeh*, London. This is still unsurpassed as an authority on certain aspects of the proportions of the Great Pyramid. See also L.C. Stecchini's Appendix to *Secrets of the Great Pyramid* by P. Tompkins.

3 (APPENDIX F) Mathematicians now refer to these objects as 'star polygons', even though specific varieties are known as, for example, the pentagram (five-pointed star) and the decagram (ten-pointed star). We choose to call them 'polygrams' to avoid any possible confusion with the familiar (regular) polygons.

4 (APPENDIX F) C. Funck-Hellet, *Composition et Nombre d'Or dans les oeuvres peintes de la Renaissance*.

BIBLIOGRAPHY

Albon, M. d' (editor), 1913, *Cartulaire général de l'Ordre de Temple*, Paris. [Bodleian Library reference 127324195.]

Arnaudies, Fernand, 1986, *Les Templiers en Roussillon*, Belisane, Nice.

Arnold, Paul, 1995, *Histoire des Rose-Croix et les origines de la Franc-Maçonnerie*, Mercure de France.

Ashdown, C.H., 1988, *History of Arms and Armour*, Wordsworth Editions. [1st edn 1909.]

Baigent, Michael and Leigh, Richard, 1989, *The Temple and the Lodge*, Jonathan Cape, London.

Baigent, Michael and Leigh, Richard, 1991, *The Dead Sea Scrolls Deception*, Jonathan Cape, London.

Baigent, Michael, Leigh, Richard and Lincoln, Henry, 1982, *The Holy Blood and the Holy Grail*, Jonathan Cape, London.

Baigent, Michael, Leigh, Richard and Lincoln, Henry, 1986, *The Messianic Legacy*, Jonathan Cape, London.

Baker, G.P., 1934, *Twelve Centuries of Rome*, G. Bell & Sons, London.

Barber, Malcolm, 1978, *The Trial of the Templars*, Cambridge University Press.

Barber, Malcolm, 1994, *The New Knighthood: A History of the Order of the Temple*, Cambridge University Press.

Barnes, S.J. and Wheelock, A.K. Jr, 1994, *Van Dyck 350*, National Gallery of Art, Washington, D.C.

Barrère, A., 1889, *Argot and Slang*, Chiswick Press, London.

Bass, George F., 1972, *A History of Seafaring, Based on Underwater Archaeology*, Thames & Hudson, London.

Bätschmann, Oskar, 1990, *Nicolas Poussin: Dialectics of Painting*, Reaktion, London. [Original German edition published by Schweizerisches Institut für Kunstwissenschaft, Zurich, 1982.]

Begg, I. and Begg, D., 1995, *In Search of the Holy Grail and the Precious Book*, Thorsons, London.

Bellori, Giovanni Pietro, 1672, *Le vite de scultori et architetti moderni*, Rome.

Belperron, Pierre, 1943, *La Croisade contre les Albigeois et l'Union du Languedoc à la France*, Librairie Plon, Paris.

Beresford, R., 1995, *A Dance to the Music of Time*, The Trustees of the Wallace Collection, London.

Bernstock, J.E., 1988, 'Guercino's "Et in Arcadia ego" and "Apollo Flaying Marsyas" ', Cornell University.

Betz, Otto and Riesner, Rainer, 1994, *Jesus, Qumran and the Vatican*, S.C.M. Press, London. [Original German edition published by Brunnen-Verlag, 1993.]

Blum, Jean, 1994, *Rennes-le-Château: Wisigoths, Cathares, Templiers*, Éditions du Rocher.

Blunt, A., 1995, *Poussin*, Pallas Athene, London.

Boudet, Henri, 1886, *La Vraie Langue celtique et le cromleck de Rennes-les-Bains*, François Pomiès, Carcassonne. [Reprint: Pierre Belfond, Paris, 1978.]

Boumendil, Cl., Tappa, G. and Corbu-Captier, A., 1994, *L'Incroyable Destin de l'Abbé Saunière*, Belisane, Nice.

Brandon, S.G.F., 1968, *The Trial of Jesus of Nazareth*, Batsford, London.

Braudel, Fernand, 1966, *La Méditerranée et le monde Méditerranéen à l'époque de Phillipe II*, Librarie Armand Colin, Paris.

Brauer, George C. Jr, 1970, *Judea Weeping*, Thomas Y. Crowell, New York.

Brown, C., 1982, *Van Dyck*, Phaidon, Oxford.

Brown, L.A., 1949, *The Story of Maps*, Little, Brown, Boston, Mass. [Reprint: Dover, New York, 1979.]

Brownrigg, Ronald, 1971, *Who's Who in the New Testament*, Weidenfeld & Nicolson, London.

Brox, Norbert, 1994, *A History of the Early Church*, S.C.M. Press, London. [Translated from *Kirchengeschichte des Altertums*, 4th edn, Patmos-Verlag, Dusseldorf.]

Brumbaugh, R.S., 1954, *Plato's Mathematical Imagination*, Indiana University Press, Bloomington.

Bruno, Giordano, 1591, *De triplici minimo et mensura*, Frankfurt.

Busch, Fritz Otto, 1958, *The Five Herods*, Hale, London.

Cassini de Thury, César-François, 1744, *Nouvelle carte qui comprend les principaux triangles de France*, 1:2,600,000. [Facsimile: T. Seifert, Verlag W. Uhl, l973.]

Cassini de Thury, César-François, 1744–89, *Carte de France, levée par ordre du Roy*. [178 Sheets in 2 vols, 1:86,400, Languedoc sheet compiled by the Académie Royal des Sciences, Montpellier.]

Catel, G. de, 1623, *Histoire des Comtes de Toulouse*, 2 vols, Toulouse.

Catel, G. de, 1633, *Mémoires de l'histoire du Languedoc*, Toulouse.

Champion, P., 1925, *Le Roi René écrivain*, Imprimerie de Monaco.

Clayton, Martin, 1995, *Poussin – Works on Paper*, Merrell Holberton, London.

Corbu, Claire and Captier, Antoine, 1985, *L'Héritage de l'Abbé Saunière*, Belisane, Nice.

Cotter, C.H., 1966, *The Astronomical and Mathematical Foundations of Geography*, Hollis & Carter, London.

Crossan, John Dominic, 1991, *The Historical Jesus: The Life of a Mediterranean Jewish Peasant*, Harper, San Francisco.

Crossan, John Dominic, 1995, *Who Killed Jesus? Exposing the Roots of Anti-Semitism in the Gospel Story of the Death of Jesus*, Harper, San Francisco.

Daillez, Laurent, 1972, *Les Templiers, ces inconnus*, Librairie Académique Perrin, Paris.

de Monts, Bruno, 'Le Mystère de Rennes-le-Château (suite)', *L'Indépendant*, 8 September 1978.

Descadeillas, René, 1991, *Mythologie du trésor de Rennes*, Éditions Collot.

de Sède, Gérard, 1967, *L'Or de Rennes*, Juillard, Paris. [Published in paperback as *Le Trésor maudit*, Éditions J'ai lu, Paris.]

de Sède, Gérard, 1988, *Rennes-le-Château*, Robert Laffont, Paris.

de Sède, Gérard and de Sède, Sophie, 1994, *L'Occultisme dans la politique*, Robert Laffont, Paris.

Devic, Cl. and Vaissette, J., 1872, *Histoire générale du Languedoc*, 15 vols, Édouard Privat, Toulouse.

Dix, Gregory and Chadwick, Henry, 1968, *The Treatise on the Apostolic Tradition of Saint Hippolytus of Rome*, The Alban Press, London.

Eisenman, Robert and Wise, Michael, 1992, *The Dead Sea Scrolls Uncovered*, Element Books, Shaftesbury.

Evergates, Theodore, 1993, *Feudal Society in Medieval France*, University of Pennsylvania Press, Philadelphia.

Fabre, Albert, 1885, *Histoire d'Arques*, Carcassonne. [Reprint: Phillipe Schrauben, Brussels, no date given.]

Fanthorpe, Lionel and Fanthorpe, Patricia, 1991, *Rennes-le-Château: Its Mysteries and Secrets*, Bellevue Books, Ashford, Kent.

Ferguson, Everett, 1987, *Backgrounds of Early Christianity*, William Eerdmans, Grand Rapids, Mich.

Ferguson, G., 1954, *Signs and Symbols in Christian Art*, Oxford University Press.

Filoramo, Giovanni, 1990, *A History of Gnosticism*, translated by Anthony Alcock, Basil Blackwell, Oxford.

Frugoni, Arsenio, 1954, *Celestiana*, Istituto Storico Italiano per il Medio Evo, Rome. [Reprint: Stabilimento Tipografico Pliniana, Perugia, 1991.]

Funck-Hellet, C., 1950, *Composition et Nombre d'Or dans les oeuvres peintes de la Renaissance*, Vincent Freuls, Paris.

Gies, Frances, 1984, *The Knight in History*, Harper & Row, New York.

Gimpel, J., 1983, *The Cathedral Builders*, Michael Russel, Salisbury. [Original French edition published by Éditions du Seuil, 1980.]

Goodwin, Malcolm, 1994, *The Holy Grail*, Bloomsbury, London.

Hakluyt, Richard, 1972, *Voyages and Discoveries*, edited and abridged by Jack Beeching, Penguin, Harmondsworth, 1972.

Hancock, G., 1992, *The Sign and the Seal*, Heinemann, London.

Harley, J.B., 1975, *Ordnance Survey Maps: A Descriptive Manual*, Ordnance Survey, Southampton.

Harthan, J., 1977, *Books of Hours*, Thames & Hudson, London.

Harvey, P.D.A., 1991, *Medieval Maps*, The British Library, London.

Heisler, R., 1989, 'Rosicrucianism: The first flowering in Britain', in *The Hermetic Journal*, No. 43.

Herodotus, 1848, *The Histories*, translated by Henry Cary, published by Henry G. Bohn, London.

Heydenryk, H., 1963, *The Art and History of Frames*, Vane, London; Heinemann, New York.

Hoehner, H.W., 1972, *Herod Antipas*, Cambridge University Press.

Honnecourt, Villard de, 13th century, Notebooks, Bibliothèque Nationale, Paris.

Huizinga, J., 1982, *The Waning of the Middle Ages*, translated by F. Hopman, Penguin, London. [Original Dutch edition published in 1924.]

Jaquot, F., 1882, *Défense des Templiers*, Féchoz et Letouzey, Paris. [Reprint: C. Lacour, Nimes, 1992.]

Jarnac, Pierre, 1988, *Les Archives du trésor de Rennes-le-Château*, Belisane, Nice.

Jennings, H., 1870, *The Rose Cross and the Age of Reason*, Chatto & Windus, London.

Jennings, H., 1879, *The Rosicrucians*, Chatto & Windus, London.

John Paul II, His Holiness, 1994, *Crossing the Threshold of Hope*, translated by J. McPhee and M. McPhee, Jonathan Cape, London.

Josephus, Flavius, 1981, *The Jewish War*, translated by G.A. Williamson, revised by Mary Smallwood, Penguin, London.

Josephus, Flavius, 1890, *Whiston's Josephus*, W.P. Nimmo, Hay & Mitchell, Edinburgh. [Reprint of Josephus's *Antiquities of the Jews*, *The Wars of the Jews* and other writings, translated by William Whiston, 1st edn 1806.]

Keller, Werner, 1965, *The Bible as History*, Hodder & Stoughton, London.

Kersten, Holger and Gruber, Elmar, 1994, *The Jesus Conspiracy*, Element Books, Shaftesbury. [Translated by the author from the German original published by Albert Langen/Georg Muller Verlag, Munich, 1992.]

Khaitzine, Richard, 1994, *Les Faiseurs d'or de Rennes-le-Château*, A J, Paris.

Kiess, George, 1990, *Des Templiers en Haut-Razès*, Imprimerie Tinena, Quillan.

Klinge, Margret, 1991, *David Teniers de Jonge*, Snoeck Ducaju & Zoon. [Catalogue.]

Knight, Steven, 1984, *The Brotherhood: The Secret World of Freemasons*, Granada, London.

Lagarde, Lucie, 1979, 'Historique du problème du Méridien Origine en France', in *Revue d'Histoire des Sciences et de Leurs Applications*, Vol. 32, no. 4, pp. 289–304.

Lambert, Malcolm, 1992, *Medieval Heresy*, Blackwell, Oxford.

Lane Fox, R., 1986, *Pagans and Christians*, Viking, London.

Lanman, J.T., 1989, *Glimpses of History from Old Maps*, Map Collector Publications, Tring.

Larousse, Pierre, 1866–90, *Grand Dictionnaire universel du XIXe siècle*, Paris.

Lasserre, Joseph Théodore, 1887, *Recherches historiques sur la ville d'Alet et son ancien diocèse*, Carcassonne. [Reprint: Philippe Schrauben, Brussels, no date given.]

Lecoy de la Marche, A., 1875, *Le Roi René*, 2 vols, Librarie de Firmin-Didot, Paris.

Le Goff, Jacques, 1988, *Medieval Civilization*, Blackwell, Oxford.

Léonard, E.G., 1930, *Introduction au Cartulaire Manuscrit du Temple 1150–1317*, Édouard Champion, Paris.

Le Roy Ladurie, Emmanuel, 1975, *Montaillou: Village occitan de 1294 à 1324*, Éditions Gallimard, Paris.

Lévy, Paul, 1960, *Les Noms des Israélites en France*, Presses Universitaires de France, Paris.

Lincoln, Henry, 1991, *The Holy Place*, Jonathan Cape, London.

Lizerand, Georges, 1923, *Le Dossier de l'affaire des Templiers*, Librarie Ancienne Honoré Champion, Paris.

Lüdemann, Gerd, 1994, *The Resurrection of Jesus*, translated by John Bowden, S.C.M. Press, London. [Original German edition published by Vandenhoeck u. Ruprecht, Göttingen, 1994.]

Lunel, Armand, 1975, *Juifs du Languedoc, de la Provence et des États Français du Pape*, Éditions Albin Michel, Paris.

Mack, Burton L., 1993, *The Lost Gospel: The Book of Q and Christian Origins*, HarperCollins, New York.

Mahon, Denis, 1968–1969, *Il Guercino: Nostra biennale d'arte antica*, 2 vols, Bologna.

Morison, S.E., 1942, *Admiral of the Ocean Sea: A Life of Christopher Columbus*, Little, Brown, Boston, Mass.

Nebenzahl, Kenneth, 1986, *Maps of the Holy Land*, Abeville Press, New York.

Nock, A.D., 1964, *Early Christianity and its Hellenistic Background*, Harper, New York.

Pächt, Otto, 1977, 'René d'Anjou – Studien II', in *Jahrbuch der Kunsthistorischen Sammlungen in Wien*, Band 73 (XXXVII), Verlag Anton Schroll, Vienna.

Palmi, Enrico and Bonvicini, Eugenio, 1988, *Templari e Rosacroce*, Atanor, Rome.

Panofsky, E., 1955, *Meaning in the Visual Arts*, Penguin, Harmondsworth.

Panofsky, E., 1970, *'Et in Arcadia ego': Poussin and the Elegiac Tradition in his Meaning of the Visual Arts*, Penguin, Harmondsworth. [1st edn 1936.]

Perey, L., 1903, *Charles de Lorraine et la cour de Bruxelles*, C. Lévy, Paris.

Pines, Shlomo, 1966, 'The Jewish Christians of the early centuries of Christianity according to a new source', *Proceedings of the Israel Academy of Sciences and Humanities*, Vol. 2, No. 13, pp. 1–74.

Popham, A.E., 1946, *The Drawings of Leonardo da Vinci*, Jonathan Cape, London.

Procacci, Giuliano, 1970, *History of the Italian People*, Wiedenfeld & Nicolson, London. [First published in France: Arthème Fayard, 1968.]

René d'Anjou, n.d., *Le Livre du cuer d'amours espris*, Nationalbibliothek, Vienna, Cod. 2597.

René d'Anjou, 1923, *Regnault et Jeanneton*, edited and published by E. de Boccard, Paris.

René d'Anjou, 1949, *Le Livre du coeur d'amour épris du Roi René*, commentary by André Chamson, Éditions Verve, Paris.

Réunion des Musées Nationaux, 1994, Poussin Exhibition Catalogue, Paris.

Reznikov, Raimonde, 1993, *Cathares et Templiers*, Éditions Loubatières, Portet-sur-Garonne.

Rivière, Jacques, 1983, *Le Fabuleux Trésor de Rennes-le-Château*, Belisane, Nice.

Robinson, James (general editor), 1988, *The Nag Hammadi Library in English*, E.J. Brill, Copenhagen. [Translated by members of the Coptic Library Project, Institute for Antiquity and Christianity, Claremont, Calif. A facsimile edition of the Nag Hammadi Codices has been published under the auspices of the Egyptian Government's Department of Antiquities and U.N.E.S.C.O., with Robinson as editor-in-chief (12 vols, Leiden, 1972–84).]

Roritzer, W., 1486, *On the Correct Building of Pinnacles*, Regensburg.

Roschach, Ernest and Molinier, Auguste, 1905, *Histoire graphique de l'ancienne province de Languedoc*, Édouard Privat, Toulouse.

Rosenberg, P., 1994, *Nicolas Poussin, 1594–1665*, Réunion des Musées Nationaux, Paris.

Rouge, Jean, 1977, *Navi e navigazione nell'antichità*, Vallechi Editore, Florence. [Original French edition published by Presses Universitaires de France, Paris, 1975.]

Runciman, Steven, 1990, *A History of the Crusades*, 3 vols, Penguin, London. [1st edn: Cambridge University Press, 1952.]

Sacaze, Julien, 1892, *Inscriptions antiques des Pyrénées*, Édouard Privat, Toulouse.

Saunière, Bérenger, 1984, *Mon Enseignement à Antugnac 1890*, Belisane, Nice.

Schonfield, Hugh, 1984, *The Essene Odyssey*, Element Books, Shaftesbury.

Sewell, Brian, 'The Blunt truth about Poussin?', London *Evening Standard*, 2 February 1995.

Sinclair, Andrew, 1993, *The Sword and the Grail*, Century, London.

Smital, O. and Winkler, E., 1927, *Réne of Anjou, King of Naples and Sicily*, 3 vols, Nationalbibliothek, Vienna, M 2597.

Soggin, J. Alberto, 1978, *I manoscritti del mar morto*, Newton Compton, Rome.

Spong, John Shelby, 1992, *Born of a Woman*, HarperCollins, New York.

Spong, John Shelby, 1994, *Resurrection: Myth or Reality?* HarperCollins, New York.

Stecchini, L.C., 1973, 'Notes on the relation of ancient measures to the Great Pyramid', Appendix to Tomkins, *Secrets of the Great Pyramid* (q.v.).

Stoyanov, Yuri, 1994, *The Hidden Tradition in Europe*, Penguin, London.

Suetonius, Gaius, 1979, *The Twelve Caesars*, translated by Robert Graves, Penguin, London.

Sussmann, Ayala and Peled, Ruth, 1993, *Scrolls from the Dead Sea*, Library of Congress, Washington, D.C., in association with the Israel Antiques Authority.

Tacitus, Cornelius, 1966, *The Histories*, translated by W.J. Brodribb and A. Church, edited and abridged by Hugh Lloyd-Jones; Sadler & Brown, Chalfont St Giles.

Taylor, Joan du Plat (editor), 1965, *Marine Archaeology*, Hutchinson, London. [Published for C.M.A.S, the World Underwater Federation.]

Thiering, Barbara, 1992, *Jesus the Man*, Doubleday, New York and London.

Thiering, Barbara, 1996, *Jesus of the Apocalypse*, Doubleday, New York and London.

Thuillier, J., 1995, *Poussin Before Rome, 1594–1624*, translated by C. Allen, Richard L. Feigen & Co.

Tisseyre, E., 1905, 'Excursion du 25 juin, 1905, à Rennes-le-Château', in *Bulletin de la Société d'Études Scientifiques de l'Aude*.

Tompkins, P., 1973, *Secrets of the Great Pyramid*, Allen Lane, London.

Tompkins, P., 1986, *The Magic of Obelisks*, Harper & Row, New York.

Tuchman, Barbara, 1957, *Bible and Sword*, Redman, New York.

Tuchman, Barbara, 1978, *A Distant Mirror*, Alfred Knopf, New York.

Unterkirchner, F., 1975, *King René's Book of Love*, G. Brazillier, New York.

Verdi, R., 1995, *Nicolas Poussin 1594–1665*, Exhibition Catalogue, Royal Academy of Arts, London.

Vermes, Geza, 1977, *The Dead Sea Scrolls – Qumran in Perspective*, William Collins, London 1977. [Revised edn: S.C.M. Press, London, 1994.]

Virgil, 1949, *The Pastoral Poems*, translated by E.V. Rieu, Penguin, Harmondsworth.

Virgil, 1960, *The Pastorals of Vergil*, translated by G. Johnson, University of Kansas Press, Lawrence.

Von Eschenbach, Wolfram, 1980, *Parzival*, translated by A.T. Hatto, Penguin, London.

Walker, B., 1983, *Gnosticism: Its History and Influence*, Crucible, Leighton Buzzard.

Wheelock, A.K. Jr, 1991, *Van Dyck Paintings*, National Gallery of Art, Washington, D.C.

Wilson, Edmund, 1978, *Israel and the Dead Sea Scrolls*, Farrar Straus Giroux, New York. [1st edn 1954.]

Wilson, Ian, 1978, *The Shroud of Turin*, Doubleday, New York.

Wood, David, 1985, *Genisis*, Baton Press, Tunbridge Wells.

Wood, Ian, 1994, *The Merovingian Kingdoms, 450–751*, Longman, London.

Wright, C., 1985, *French Painters of the Seventeenth Century*, Orbis, London.

Wright, C., 1985, *Poussin Paintings: A Catalogue Raisonné*, Harlequin Books, London.

Yates, Frances A., 1972, *The Rosicrucian Enlightenment*, Routledge & Kegan Paul, London.

Yates, Frances A., 1964, *Giordano Bruno and the Hermetic Tradition*, Routledge & Kegan Paul, London.

INDEX

Page numbers in *italic* refer to the illustrations

Ashmolean Museum, Oxford, 8, 119, 132, 297

Asmodeus, *182*, 184

Association de Défense Sacerdotale, 414

astrolabes, 244, *244*, 482

Atbash cipher, 399, 400

Aude, River, 50, 51, 57, 64, 65, 70, 71, 251

Augustus, Emperor, 82

Aven, 153

Avignon, 331, 337

Axat, 11, 176, 178, 259, 260

Bacchus, 342

Baigent, Michael, *The Messianic Legacy*, 214–15, 218

Baldwin II, King of Jerusalem, 7, 396

Baphomet, 348, 399

Baptism (Poussin), 348

Barberini, Cardinal Antonio, 340–1

Barbieri, Giovanni Francesco *see* Guercino

Barnabus, 372

Barrère, Albert, *Argot and Slang*, 49

Bätschmann, Oskar, 344

Beaucéan, Nicolas, 258

Beaumarchais, Pierre de, 49

Beauséjour, Bishop of Carcassonne, 176, 179

Beaux Arts, 190

Bellori, Giovanni Pietro, 351

Benjamin, tribe of, 449–50

Beresford, Richard, 207

Les Bergers d'Arcadie I (Poussin), 212, 341; alterations, 203; differences from second version, 104–5, 106–7; geometric analysis, 140–6, *141*, *143–5*, 151, 158, 198, 205; and the Lobineau documents, 449–50; in *Portrait of Lady Anson*, 203, *204*

Les Bergers d'Arcadie II (Poussin), 140, 339, 410; alterations to mountains, 113–15, *114*, 200, 207, 210; brushstrokes, 207–8; dark spot, 208–9; date, 349; differences from first version, 104–5, 106–7; engraving, 113, 200–1; female figure of Wisdom, 348, 353; frame, 202; geometric analysis, 110–12, *111–12*, 191–8, *192–4*, *196–9*, 205–6, 209–10; hidden part, 190–1, 200–3, 208, 209, 210; inscription, 105–7; and the Lobineau documents, 449–50; and Mount Cardou, 163; and the 'Poussin tomb', 8, 117–18; and the Priory Documents, 93; restoration, ix–x, 190–1; Saunière acquires copy, 61, 86, 100, 110, 118; in the Shugborough bas-relief, 86–8, *87*, 107, 205, 354

Bernard, St, 7

Bernstock, Judith, 340

Berry, Duc de, 328

Bethany, 18

Bethlehem, 277

Bible, 67, 179, 407; *see also* Old Testament; New Testament

Bibliothèque Nationale, Paris, 16, 115, 175, 328, 385

Bigou, Abbé Antoine, 15, 211, 259

Billard, Bishop of Carcassonne, 99, 170, 176, 179, 231, 413

'Blanca Fort', Arnaldus de, 264

'Blanca Fort', Bernardi de, 264

'Blanca Fort', Raimundus de, 264

Blanche de Castille, 214, 215

Blanchefort, Bertrand de, 264, 483

Blanchefort, Château de, 165, 262–3; château geometry, 241–3, *243*, 246, 249, 250, 252; and the Jerusalem map, 468; and the Marie de Nègre gravestones, 237, *238*; as protection